Shojo Beat

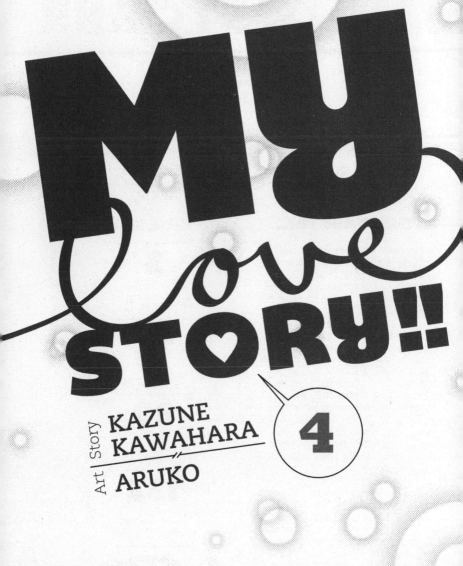

My Love Story!!

Story KAZUNE KAWAHARA

Art ARUKO

4

STORY Thus Far...

Takeo Goda, a first-year high school student, is a hot-blooded guy who is 6'6" tall and weighs 265 pounds. Boys look up to him, but the girls he falls in love with all end up liking his handsome best friend, Sunakawa!

When Takeo and Yamato go out to have a picnic in the mountains, they get lost! Takeo tries his best to protect Yamato, and Yamato is thrilled that it's their first night alone together...♡ Also, they get excited seeing each other in their swimsuits when they go to the beach! Later in town, Takeo saves a girl whom he used to have a crush on. When Yamato finds out about his old crush, she starts to feel insecure...

Yamato says that she wants to go to the same college as Takeo, so he begins to study very hard! Takeo takes the mock entrance exam for the college Yamato wants to go to, but he gets rejected. What Takeo didn't know is that the school is actually a women's college!

Chapter 12
3

Chapter 13
47

Chapter 14
89

Chapter 15
133

Bonus Chapter
177

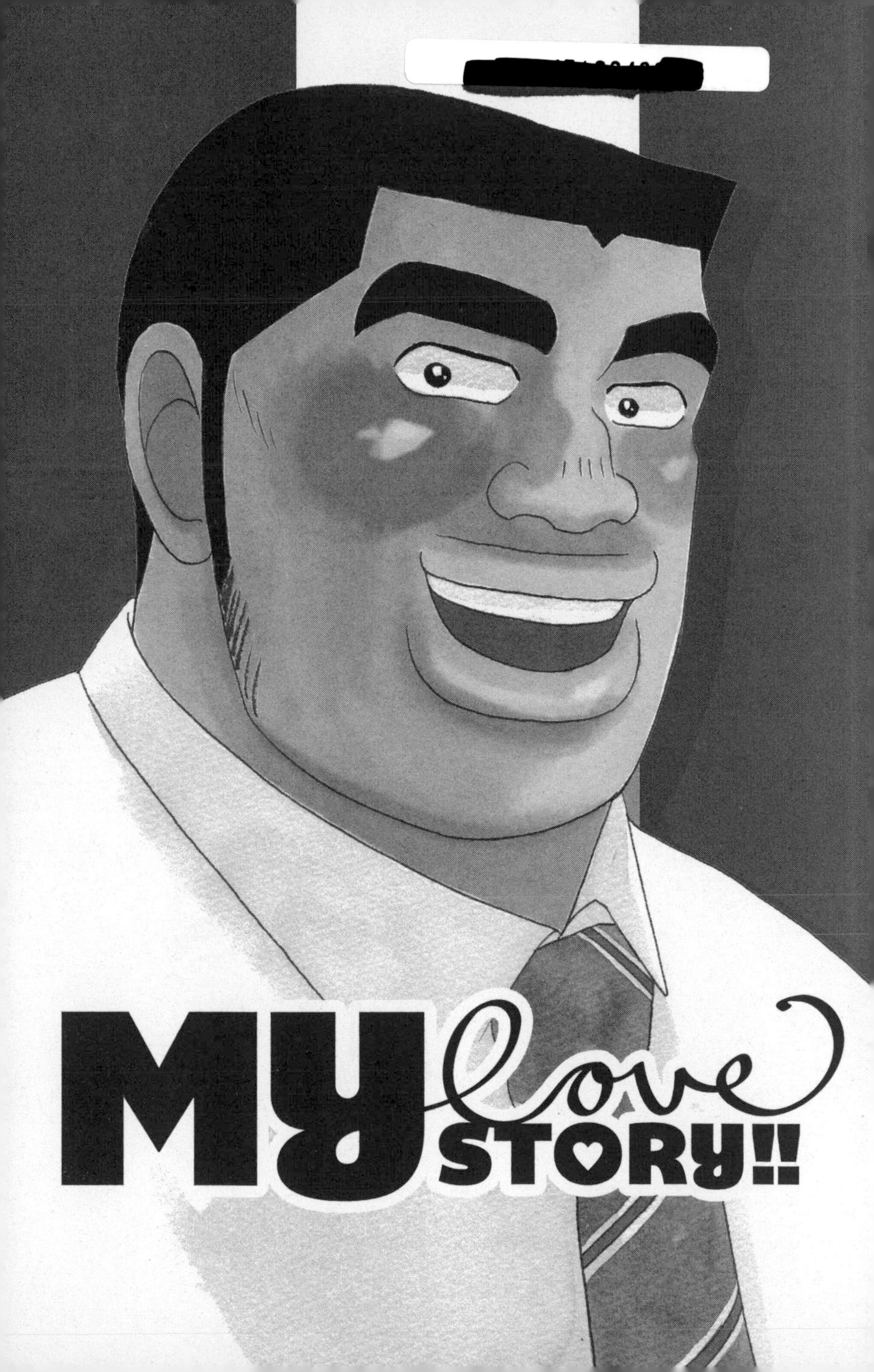
[redacted]
MY love STORY!!

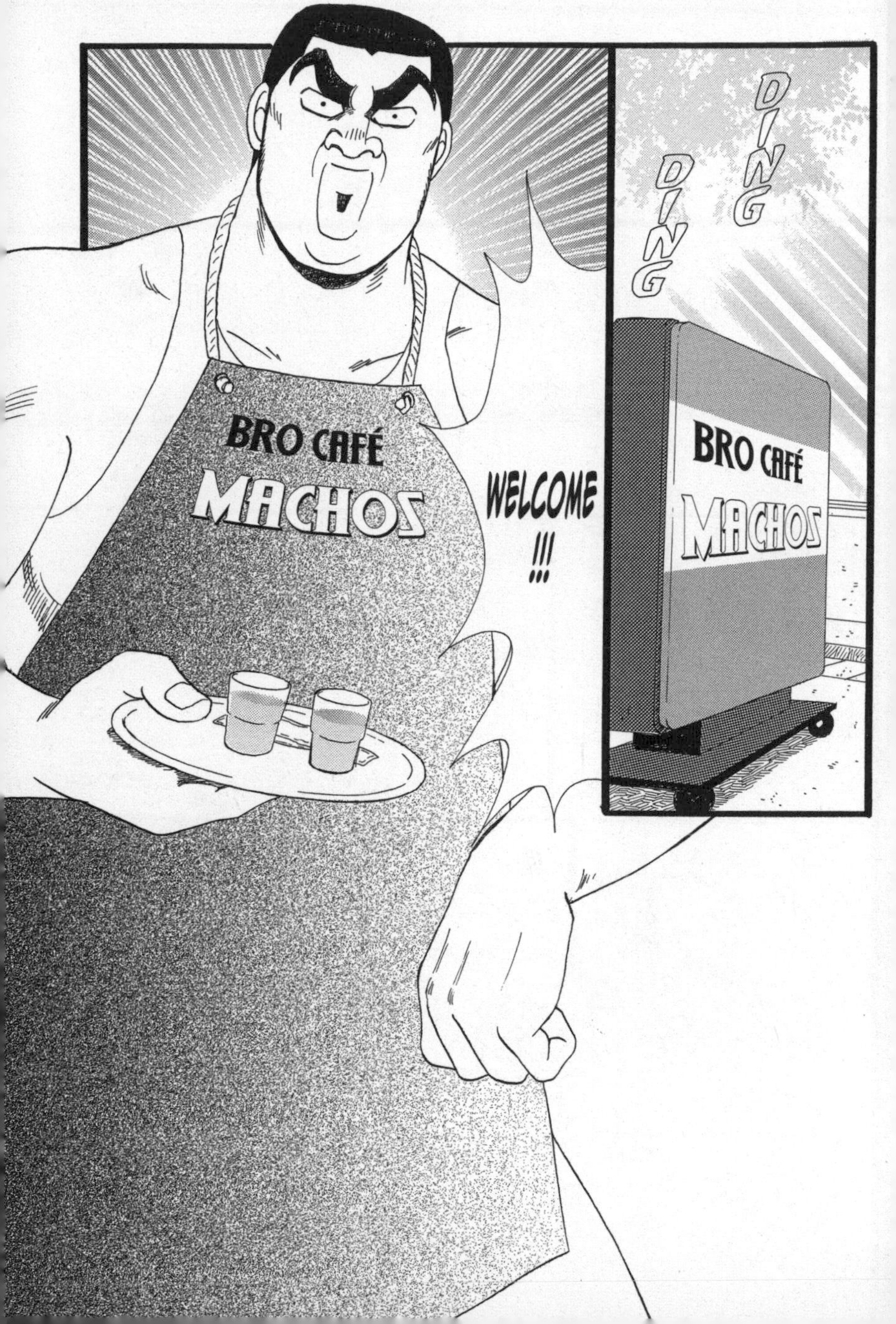
DING
DING
BRO CAFÉ
MACHOS
BRO CAFÉ
MACHOS
WELCOME!!!

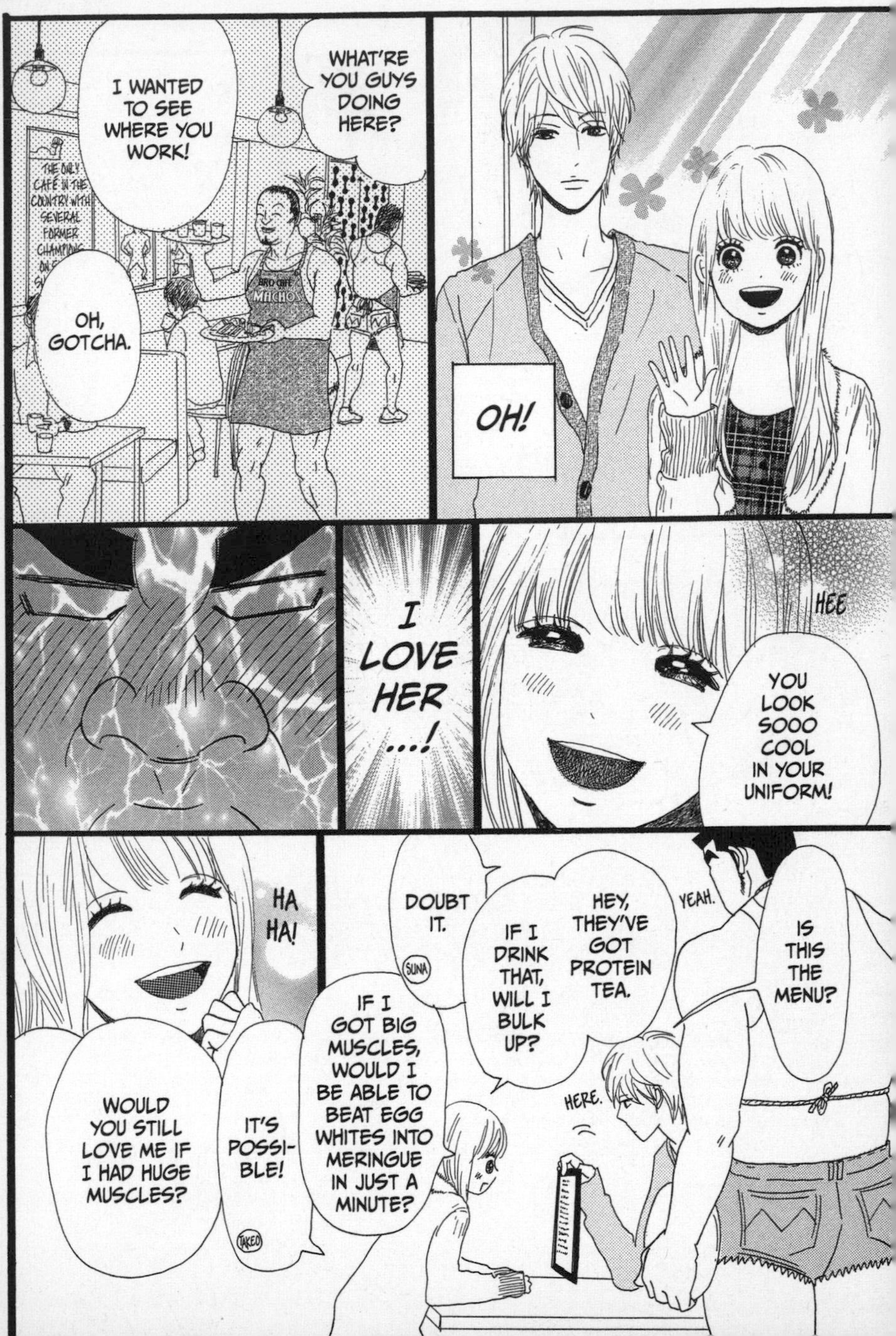
OH!
WHAT'RE YOU GUYS DOING HERE?
I WANTED TO SEE WHERE YOU WORK!
THE ONLY CAFE IN THE COUNTRY WITH SEVERAL FORMER CHAMPIONS
BRO CAFE MACHOS
OH, GOTCHA.
HEE
YOU LOOK SOOO COOL IN YOUR UNIFORM!
I LOVE HER ...!
IS THIS THE MENU?
YEAH.
HEY, THEY'VE GOT PROTEIN TEA.
IF I DRINK THAT, WILL I BULK UP?
DOUBT IT.
SUNA
HERE.
IF I GOT BIG MUSCLES, WOULD I BE ABLE TO BEAT EGG WHITES INTO MERINGUE IN JUST A MINUTE?
IT'S POSSI-BLE!
TAKEO
HA HA!
WOULD YOU STILL LOVE ME IF I HAD HUGE MUSCLES?

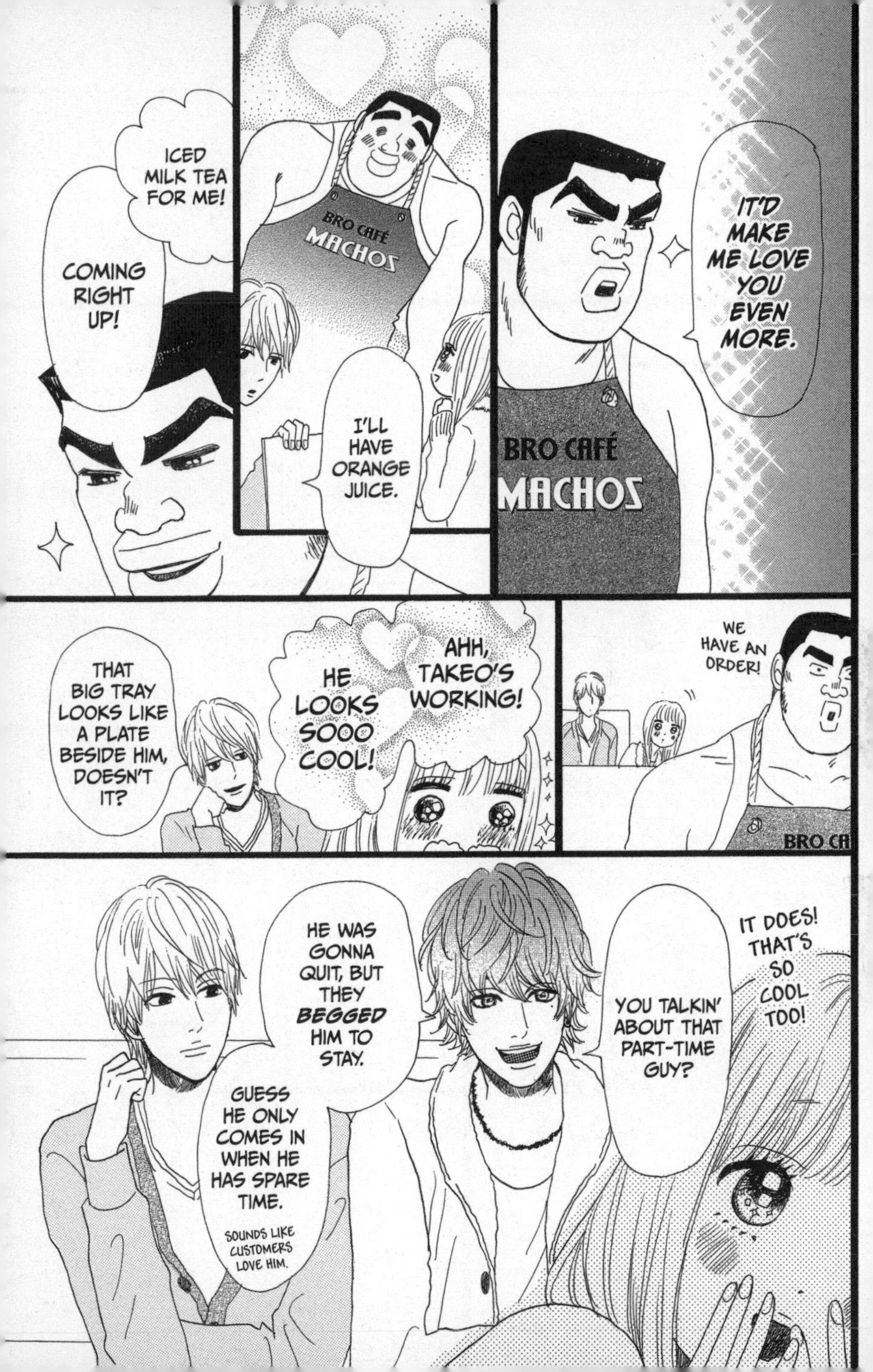
IT'D MAKE ME LOVE YOU EVEN MORE.
BRO CAFÉ MACHOS
BRO CAFÉ MACHOS
I'LL HAVE ORANGE JUICE.
ICED MILK TEA FOR ME!
COMING RIGHT UP!
WE HAVE AN ORDER!
BRO CA
AHH, TAKEO'S WORKING!
HE LOOKS SOOO COOL!
THAT BIG TRAY LOOKS LIKE A PLATE BESIDE HIM, DOESN'T IT?
IT DOES! THAT'S SO COOL TOO!
YOU TALKIN' ABOUT THAT PART-TIME GUY?
HE WAS GONNA QUIT, BUT THEY *BEGGED* HIM TO STAY.
GUESS HE ONLY COMES IN WHEN HE HAS SPARE TIME.
SOUNDS LIKE CUSTOMERS LOVE HIM.

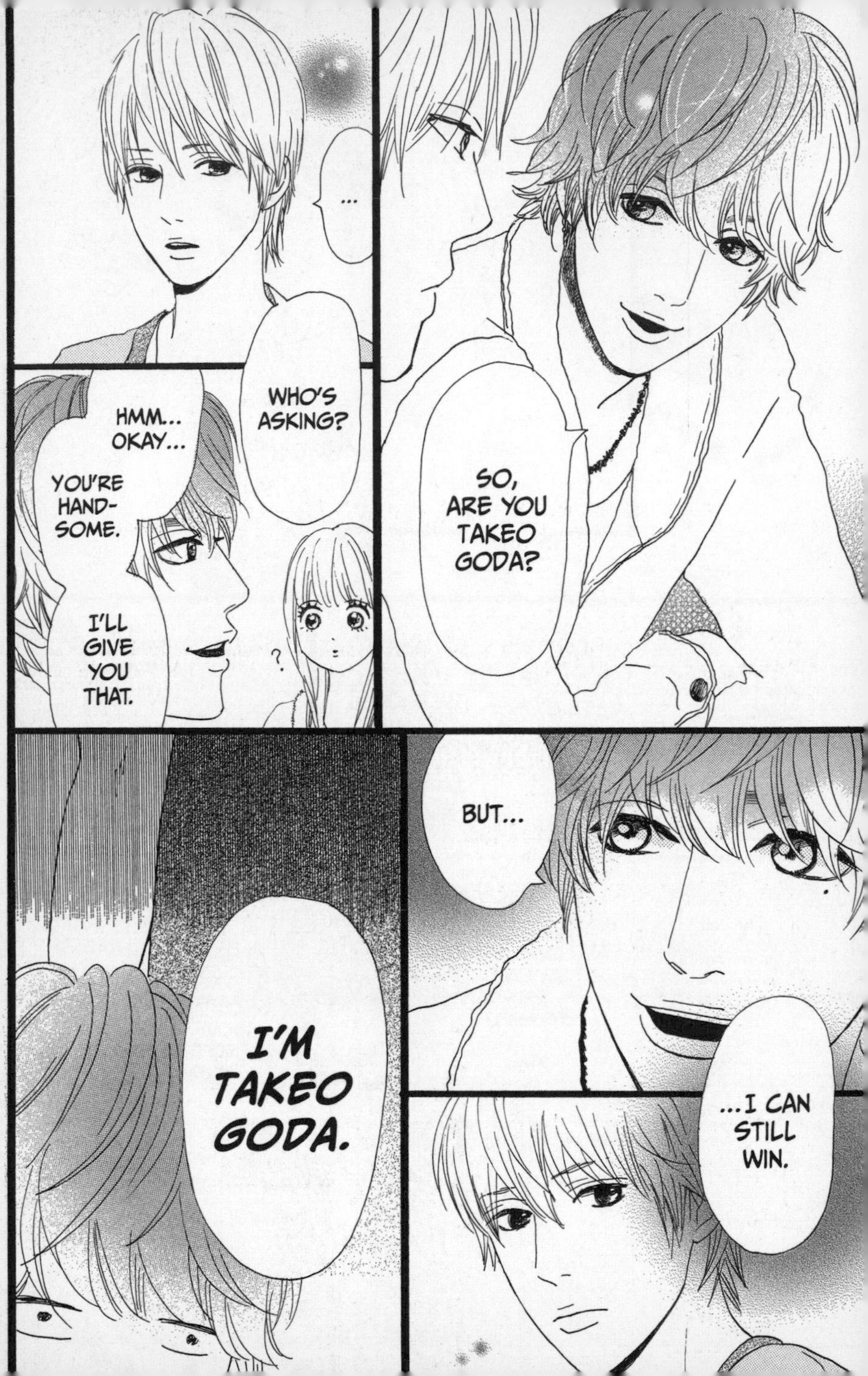
SO, ARE YOU TAKEO GODA?
...
WHO'S ASKING?
HMM... OKAY...
YOU'RE HAND-SOME.
I'LL GIVE YOU THAT.
?
BUT...
...I CAN STILL WIN.
I'M TAKEO GODA.

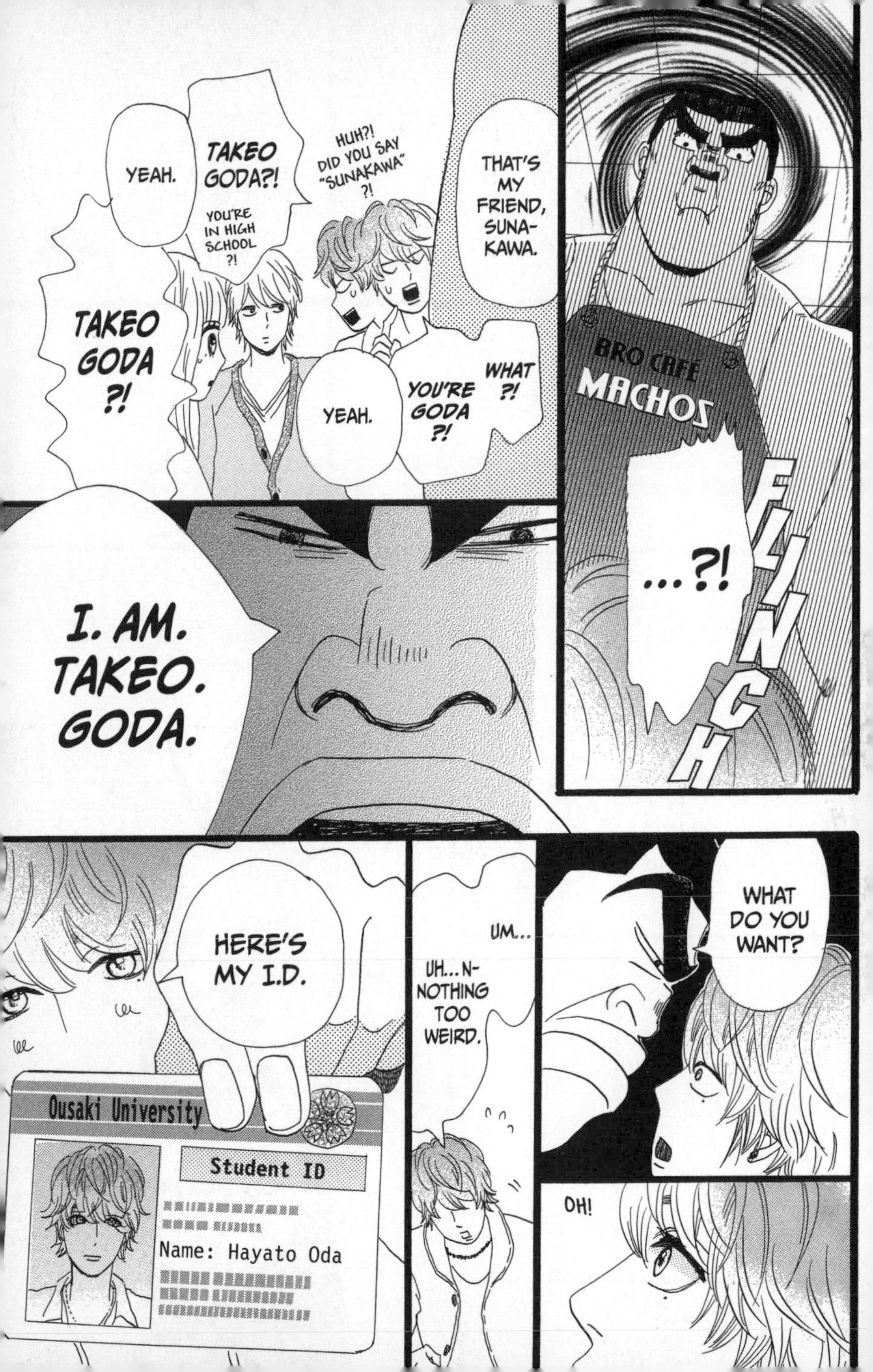
...?!
FLINCH
THAT'S MY FRIEND, SUNAKAWA.
HUH?! DID YOU SAY "SUNAKAWA" ?!
WHAT ?!
YOU'RE GODA ?!
YEAH.
TAKEO GODA?!
YOU'RE IN HIGH SCHOOL ?!
YEAH.
TAKEO GODA ?!
I. AM. TAKEO. GODA.
WHAT DO YOU WANT?
OH!
UM...
UH... N-NOTHING TOO WEIRD.
HERE'S MY I.D.
Ousaki University
Student ID
Name: Hayato Oda

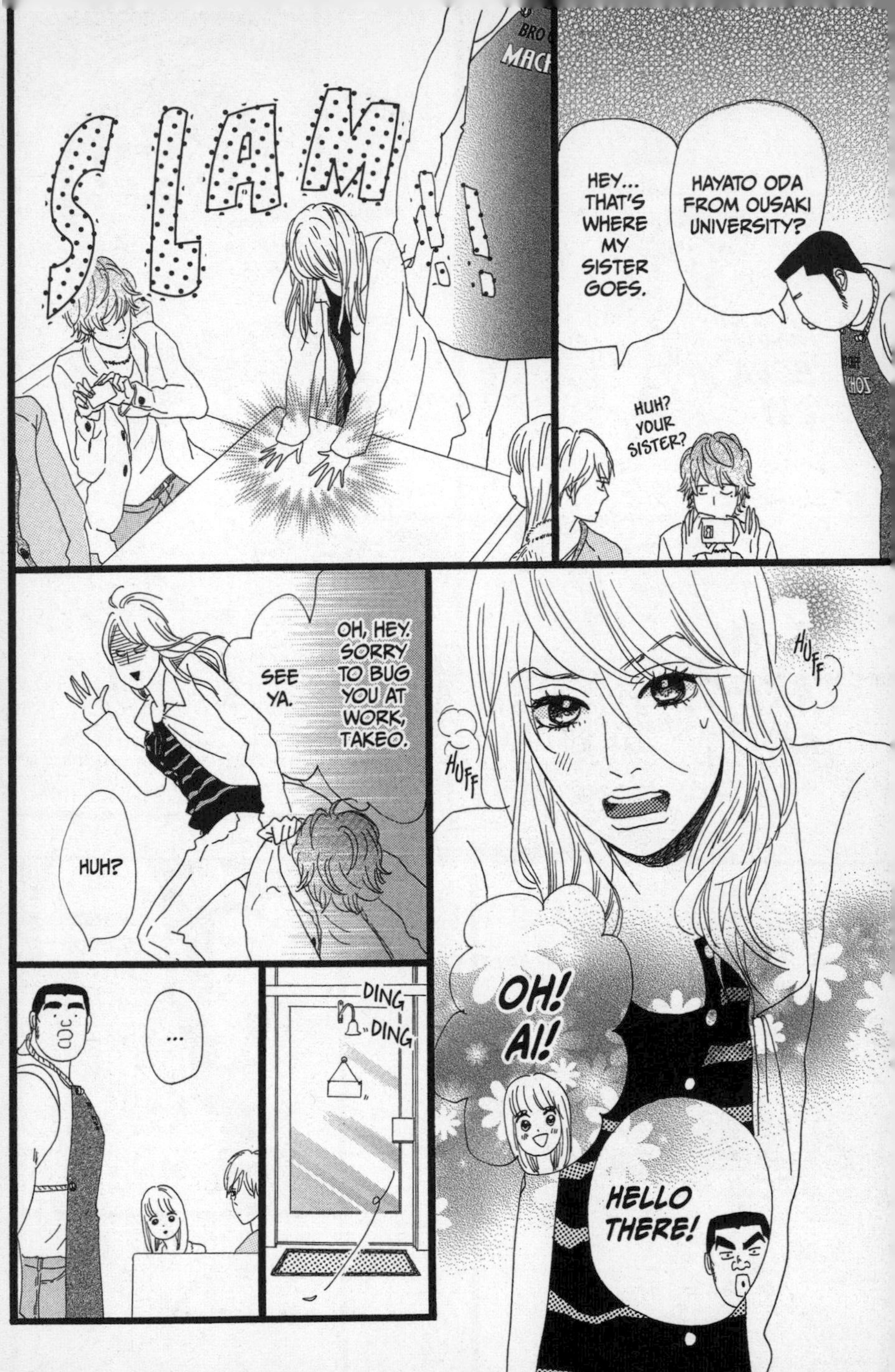

HAYATO ODA FROM OUSAKI UNIVERSITY?
HEY... THAT'S WHERE MY SISTER GOES.
HUH? YOUR SISTER?
SLAM!!
HUFF
HUFF
OH! AI!
HELLO THERE!
OH, HEY. SORRY TO BUG YOU AT WORK, TAKEO.
SEE YA.
HUH?
DING DING
...

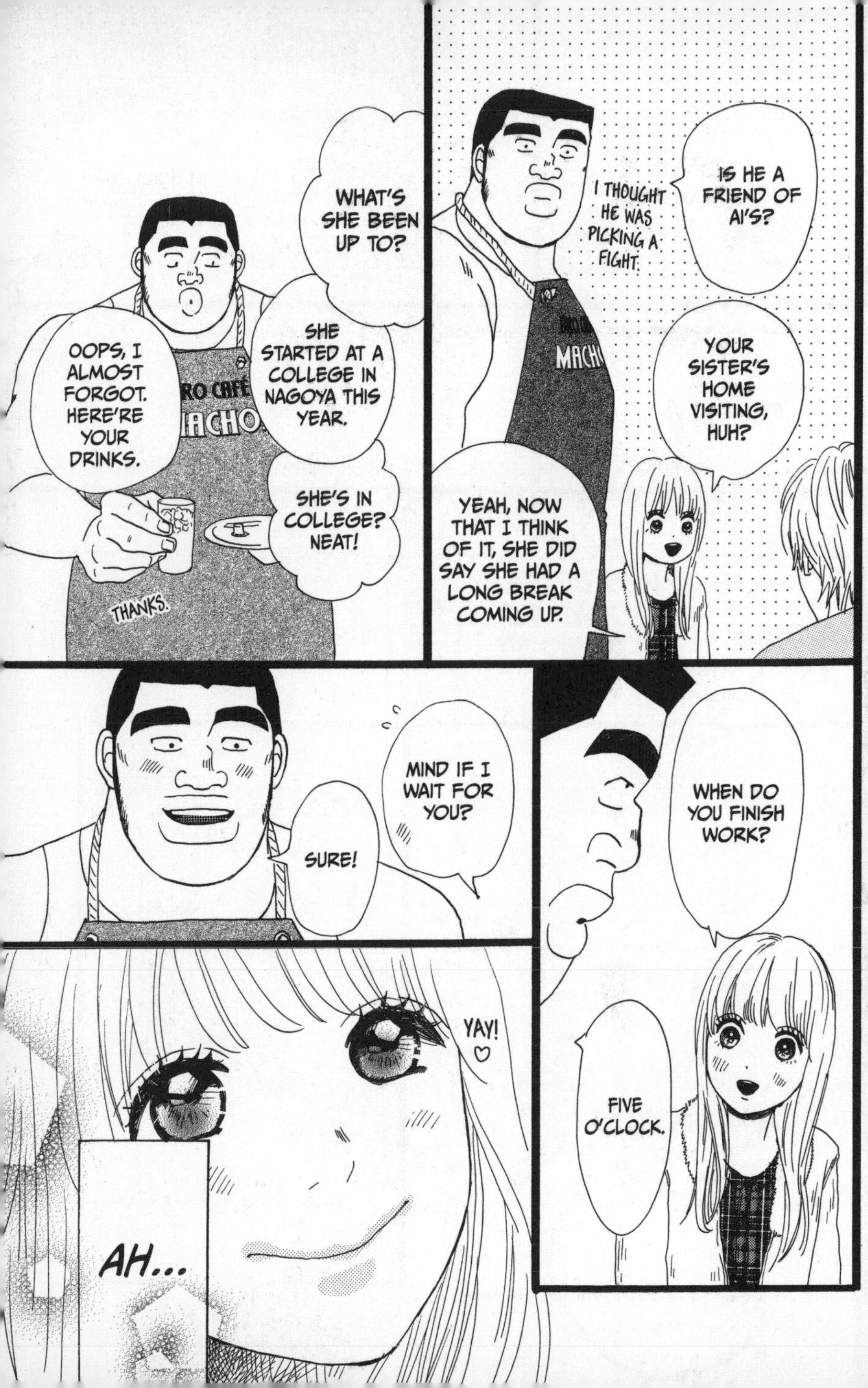
IS HE A FRIEND OF AI'S?
I THOUGHT HE WAS PICKING A FIGHT.
YOUR SISTER'S HOME VISITING, HUH?
YEAH, NOW THAT I THINK OF IT, SHE DID SAY SHE HAD A LONG BREAK COMING UP.
WHAT'S SHE BEEN UP TO?
SHE STARTED AT A COLLEGE IN NAGOYA THIS YEAR.
SHE'S IN COLLEGE? NEAT!
OOPS, I ALMOST FORGOT. HERE'RE YOUR DRINKS.
THANKS.
WHEN DO YOU FINISH WORK?
FIVE O'CLOCK.
MIND IF I WAIT FOR YOU?
SURE!
YAY! ♡
AH...

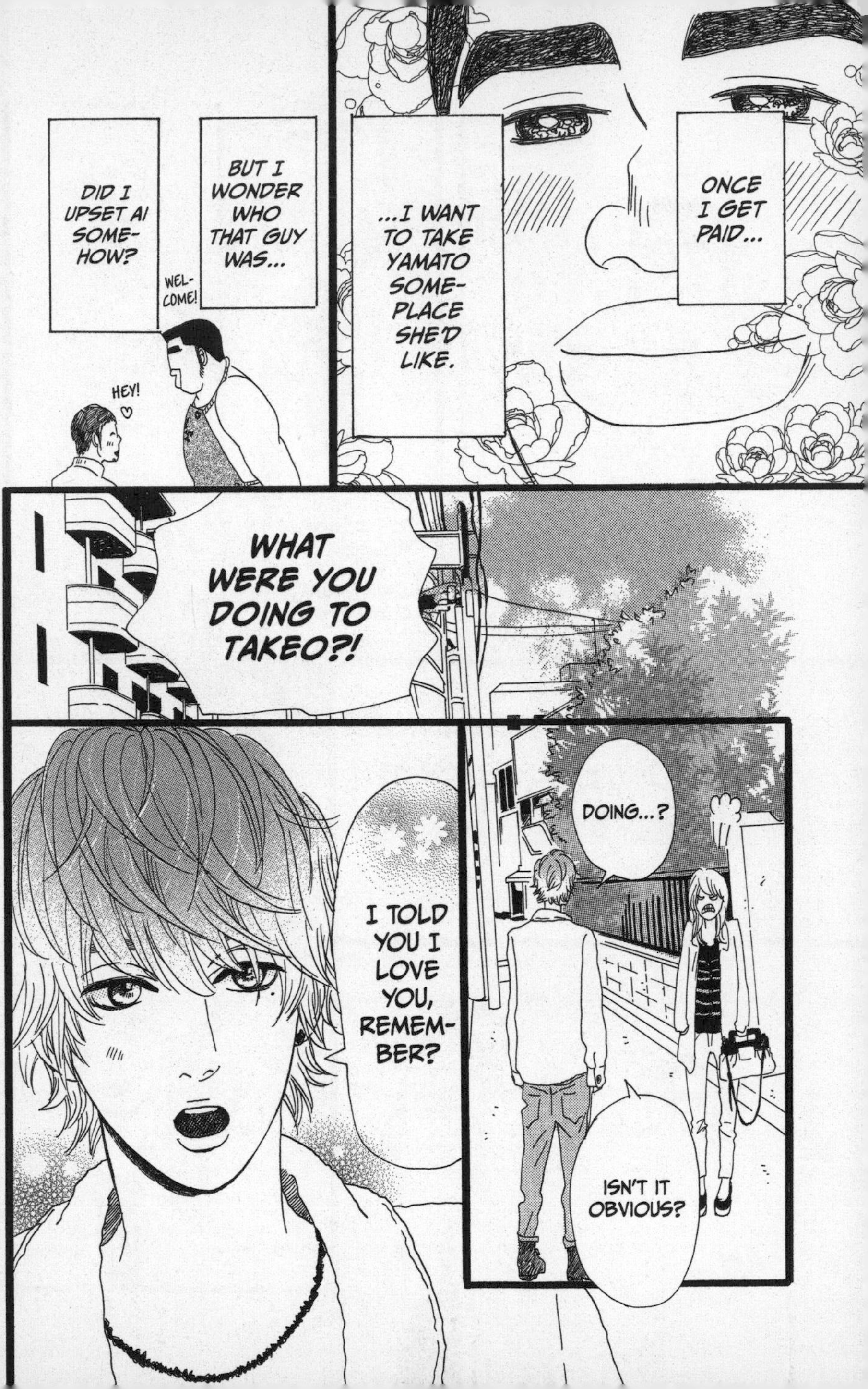
ONCE I GET PAID...
...I WANT TO TAKE YAMATO SOME-PLACE SHE'D LIKE.
BUT I WONDER WHO THAT GUY WAS...
DID I UPSET AI SOME-HOW?
WEL-COME!
HEY!
WHAT WERE YOU DOING TO TAKEO?!
DOING...?
ISN'T IT OBVIOUS?
I TOLD YOU I LOVE YOU, REMEM-BER?

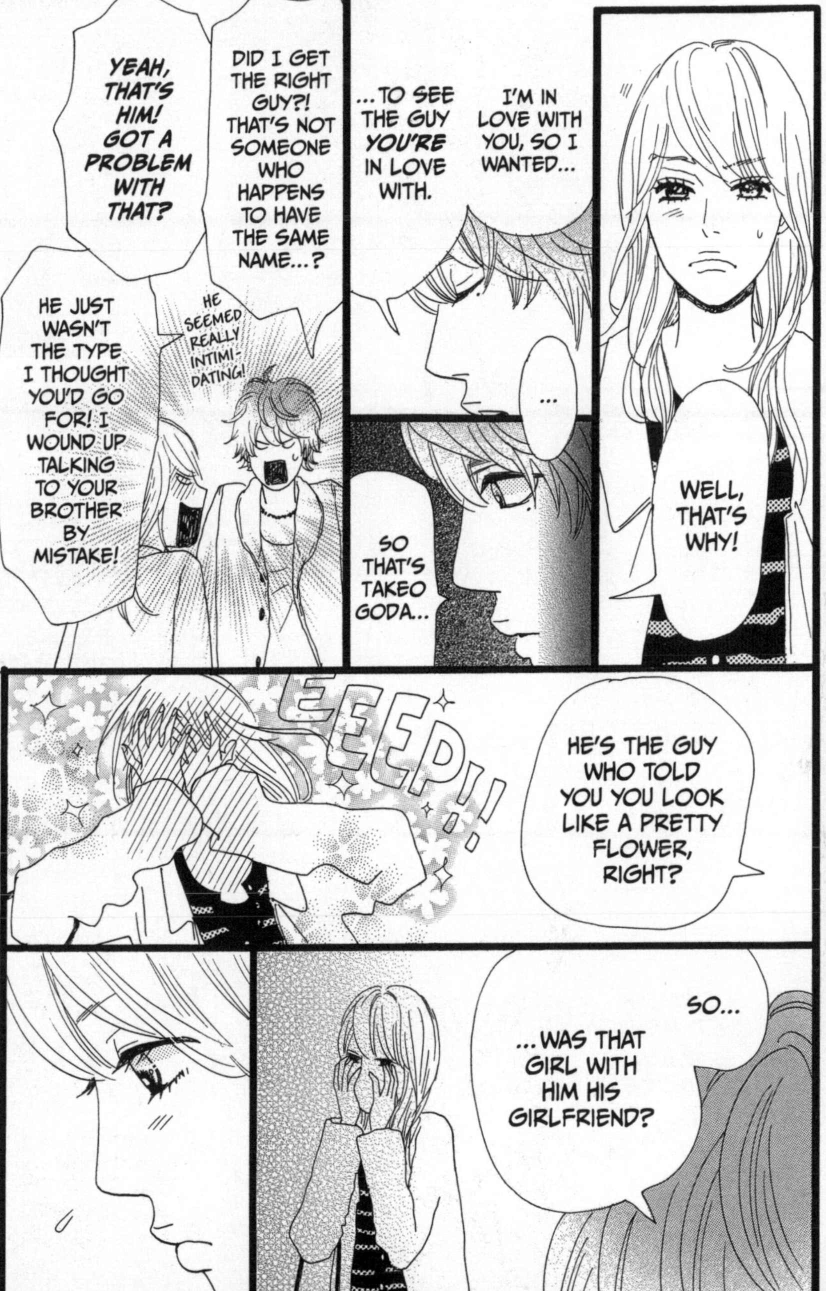
WELL, THAT'S WHY!
I'M IN LOVE WITH YOU, SO I WANTED...
...TO SEE THE GUY *YOU'RE* IN LOVE WITH.
...
SO THAT'S TAKEO GODA...
DID I GET THE RIGHT GUY?! THAT'S NOT SOMEONE WHO HAPPENS TO HAVE THE SAME NAME...?
YEAH, THAT'S HIM! GOT A PROBLEM WITH THAT?
HE SEEMED REALLY INTIMI-DATING!
HE JUST WASN'T THE TYPE I THOUGHT YOU'D GO FOR! I WOUND UP TALKING TO YOUR BROTHER BY MISTAKE!
HE'S THE GUY WHO TOLD YOU YOU LOOK LIKE A PRETTY FLOWER, RIGHT?
EEEEP!!
SO...
...WAS THAT GIRL WITH HIM HIS GIRLFRIEND?

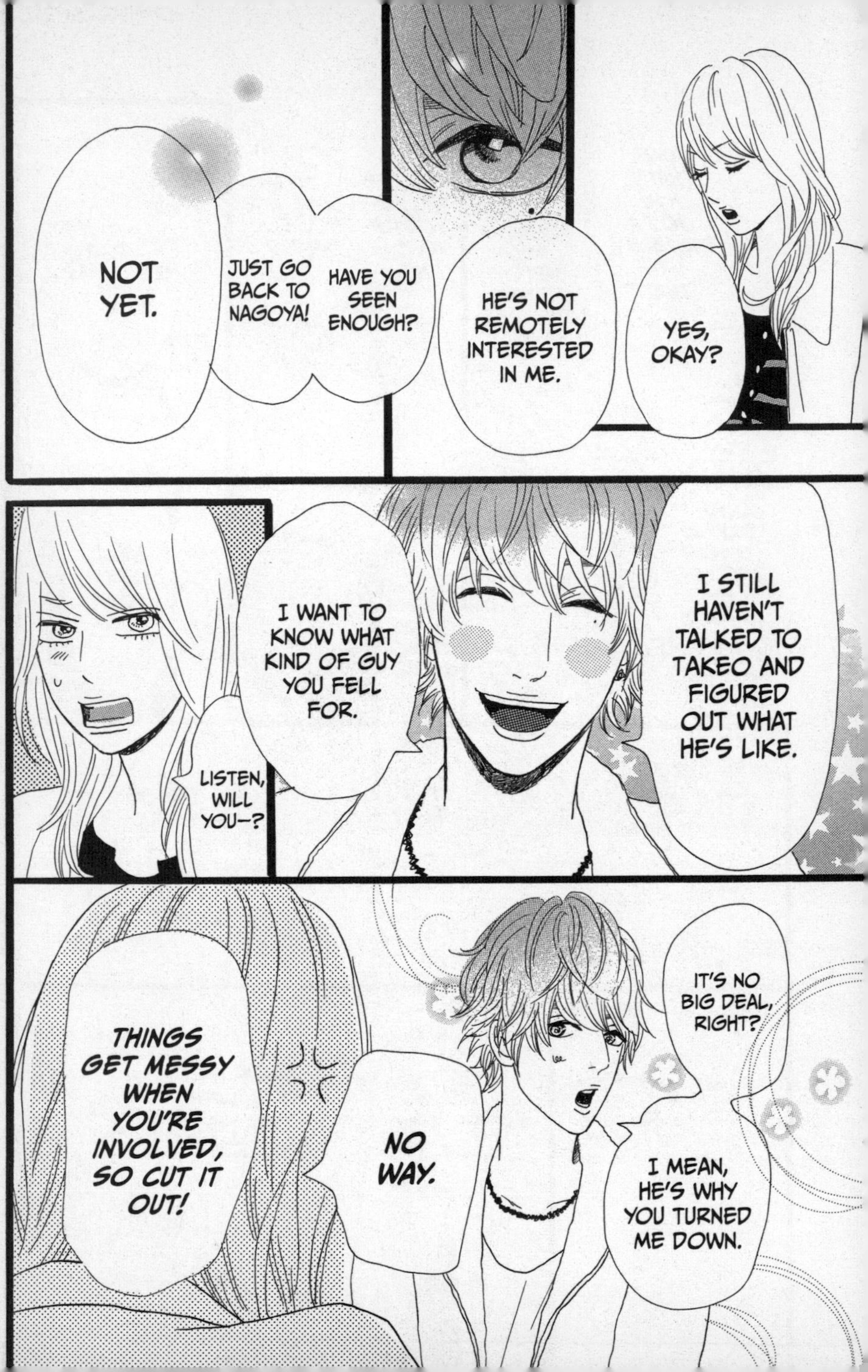
YES, OKAY?
HE'S NOT REMOTELY INTERESTED IN ME.
HAVE YOU SEEN ENOUGH?
JUST GO BACK TO NAGOYA!
NOT YET.
I STILL HAVEN'T TALKED TO TAKEO AND FIGURED OUT WHAT HE'S LIKE.
I WANT TO KNOW WHAT KIND OF GUY YOU FELL FOR.
LISTEN, WILL YOU—?
IT'S NO BIG DEAL, RIGHT?
I MEAN, HE'S WHY YOU TURNED ME DOWN.
NO WAY.
THINGS GET MESSY WHEN YOU'RE INVOLVED, SO CUT IT OUT!

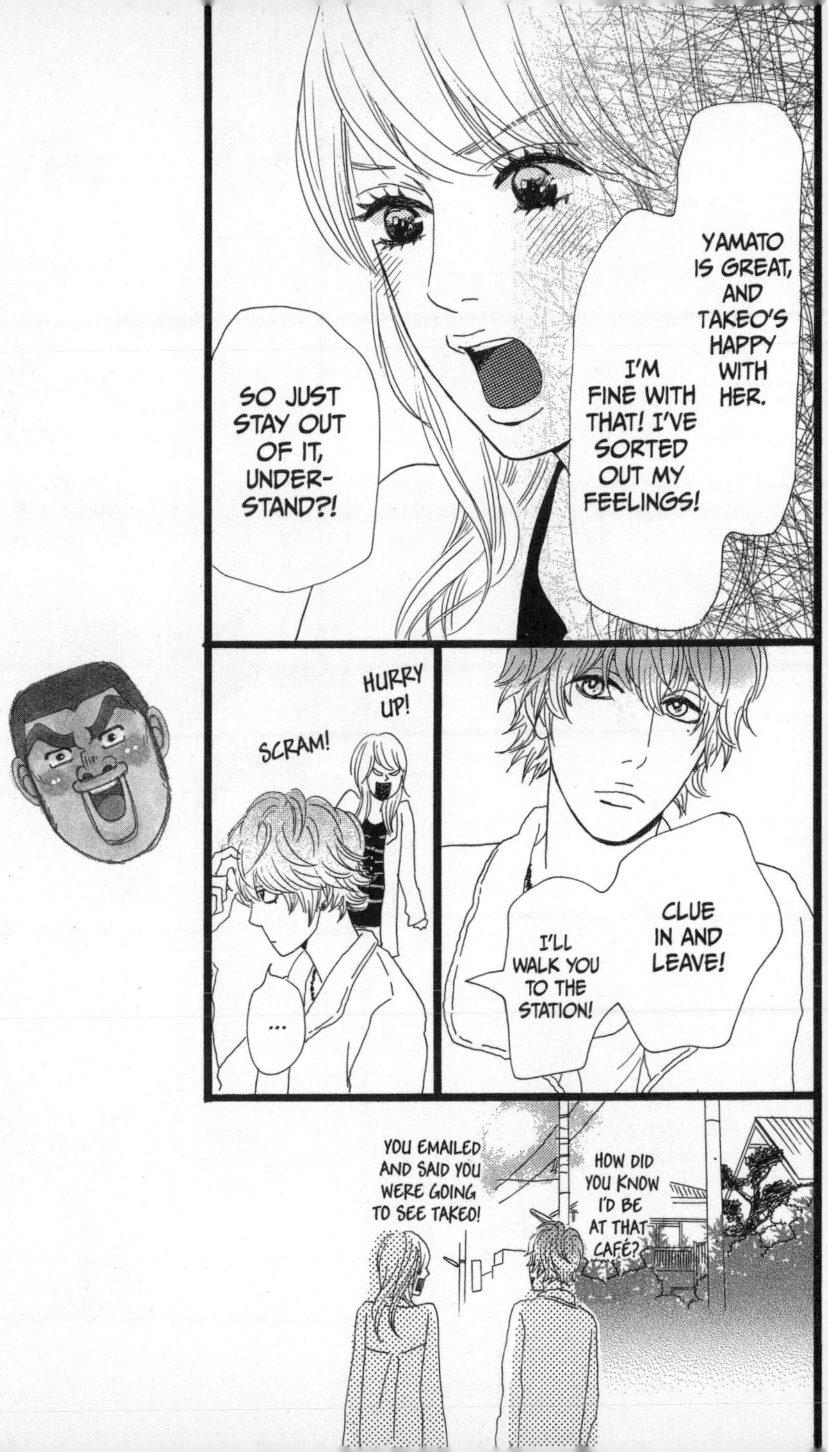
YAMATO IS GREAT, AND TAKEO'S HAPPY WITH HER.
I'M FINE WITH THAT! I'VE SORTED OUT MY FEELINGS!
SO JUST STAY OUT OF IT, UNDER-STAND?!
CLUE IN AND LEAVE!
I'LL WALK YOU TO THE STATION!
HURRY UP!
SCRAM!
...
HOW DID YOU KNOW I'D BE AT THAT CAFÉ?
YOU EMAILED AND SAID YOU WERE GOING TO SEE TAKEO!

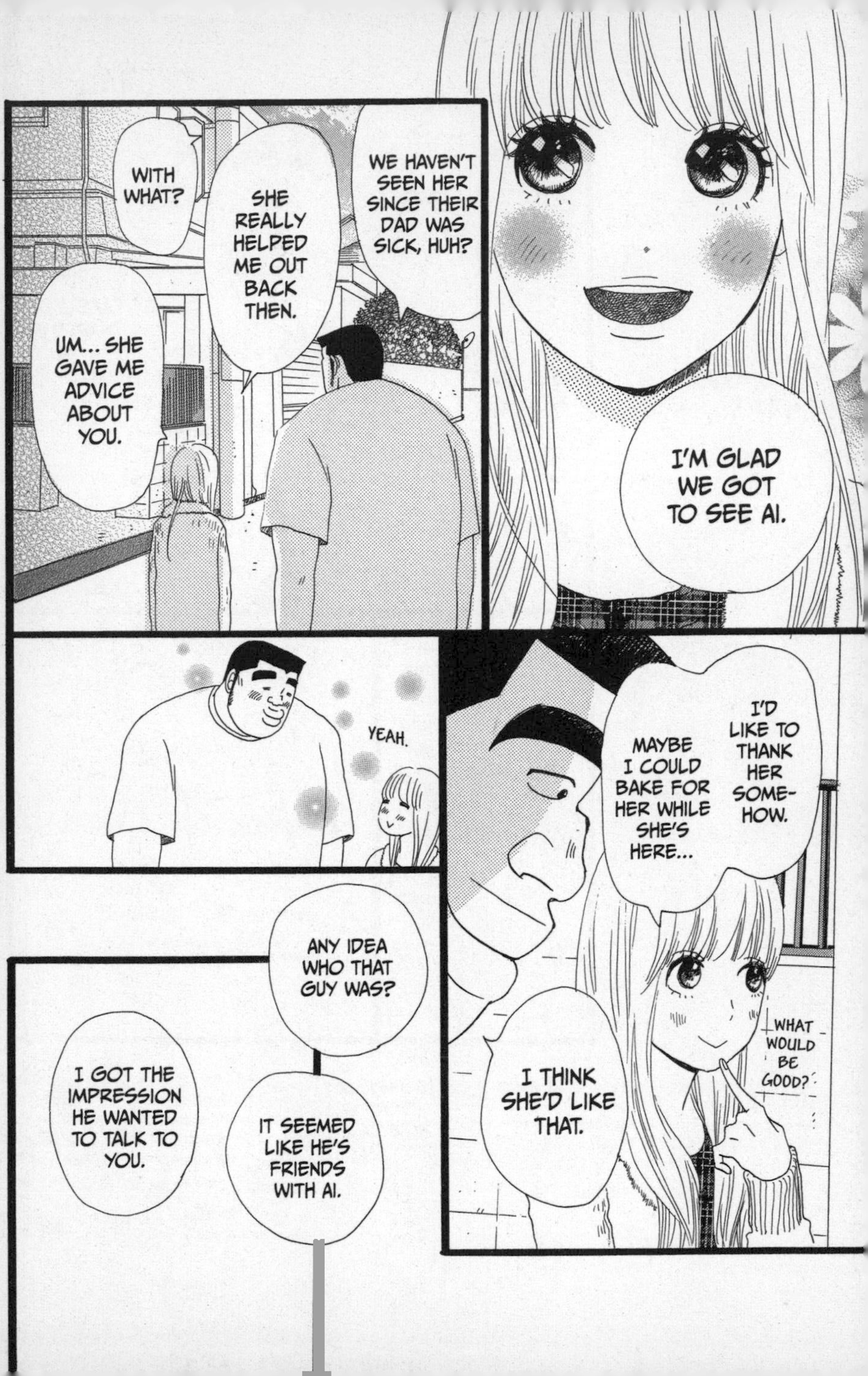
I'M GLAD WE GOT TO SEE AI.
WE HAVEN'T SEEN HER SINCE THEIR DAD WAS SICK, HUH?
SHE REALLY HELPED ME OUT BACK THEN.
WITH WHAT?
UM... SHE GAVE ME ADVICE ABOUT YOU.
I'D LIKE TO THANK HER SOME-HOW.
MAYBE I COULD BAKE FOR HER WHILE SHE'S HERE...
WHAT WOULD BE GOOD?
I THINK SHE'D LIKE THAT.
YEAH.
ANY IDEA WHO THAT GUY WAS?
IT SEEMED LIKE HE'S FRIENDS WITH AI.
I GOT THE IMPRESSION HE WANTED TO TALK TO YOU.

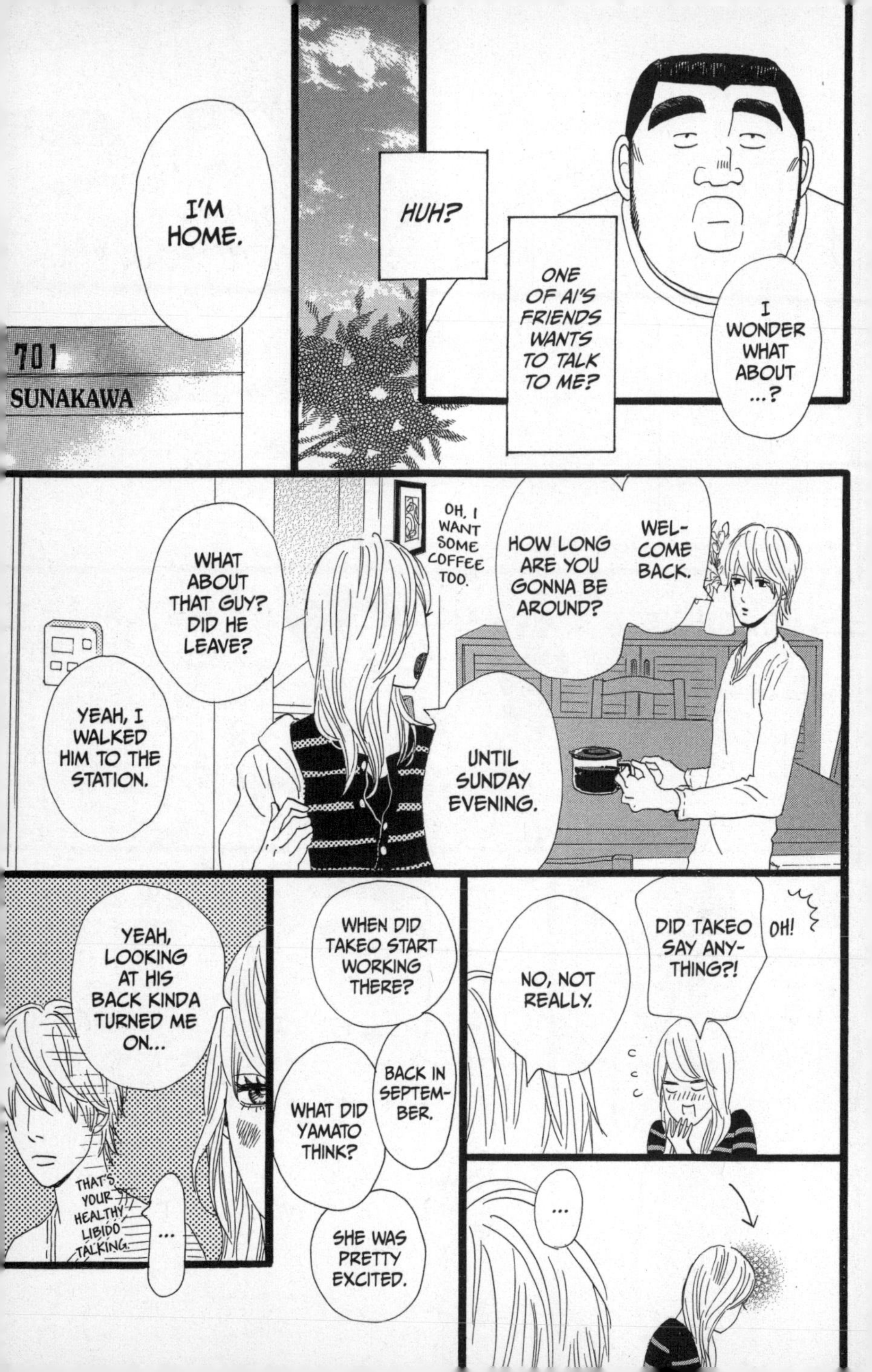

ONE OF AI'S FRIENDS WANTS TO TALK TO ME?
I WONDER WHAT ABOUT ...?
HUH?
701
SUNAKAWA
I'M HOME.
WEL-COME BACK.
HOW LONG ARE YOU GONNA BE AROUND?
UNTIL SUNDAY EVENING.
OH, I WANT SOME COFFEE TOO.
WHAT ABOUT THAT GUY? DID HE LEAVE?
YEAH, I WALKED HIM TO THE STATION.
OH!
DID TAKEO SAY ANY-THING?!
NO, NOT REALLY.
...
WHEN DID TAKEO START WORKING THERE?
BACK IN SEPTEM-BER.
WHAT DID YAMATO THINK?
SHE WAS PRETTY EXCITED.
YEAH, LOOKING AT HIS BACK KINDA TURNED ME ON...
THAT'S YOUR HEALTHY LIBIDO TALKING.
...

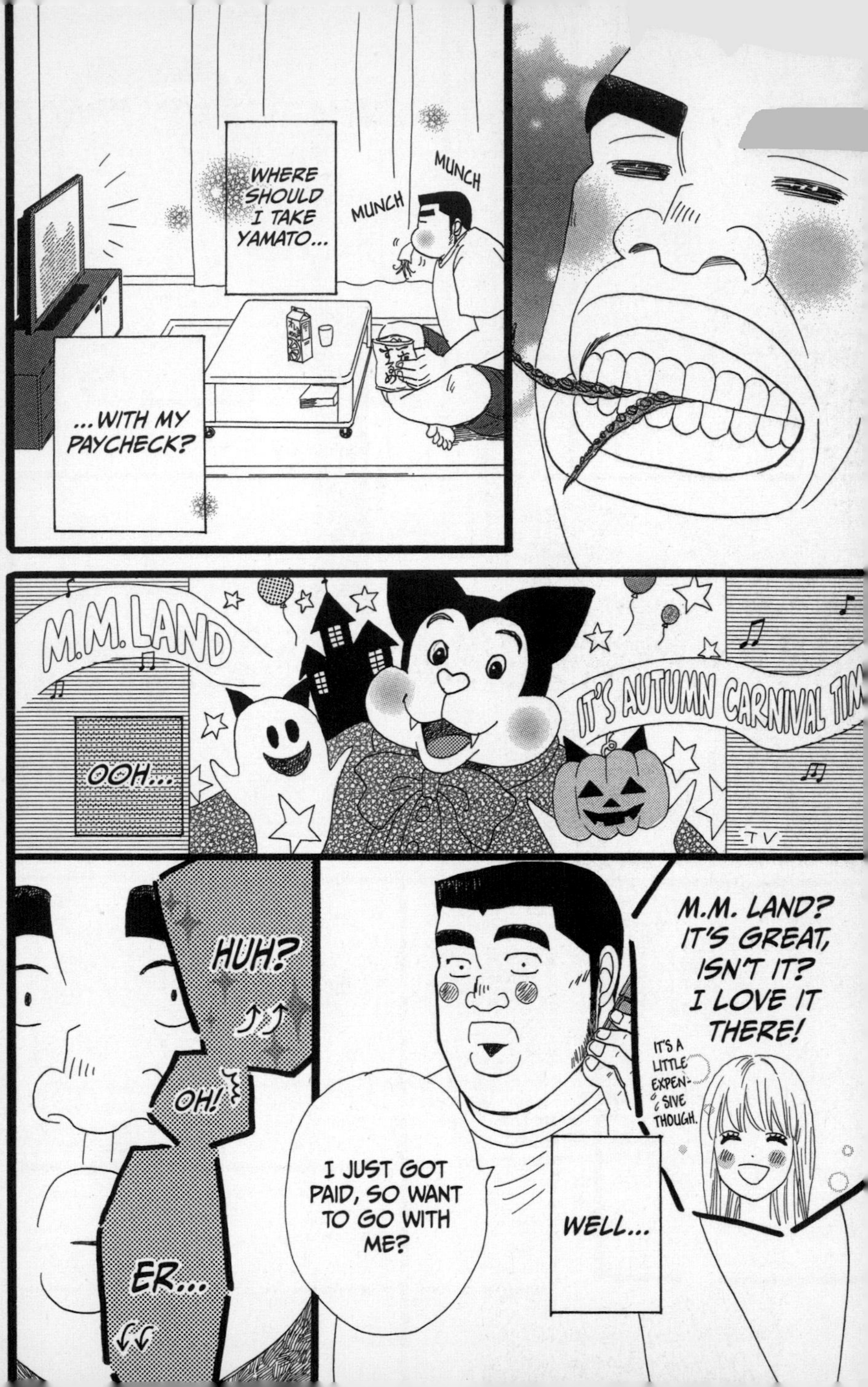
MUNCH
WHERE SHOULD I TAKE YAMATO...
MUNCH
...WITH MY PAYCHECK?
IT'S AUTUMN CARNIVAL TIM
M.M. LAND
TV
OOH...
M.M. LAND? IT'S GREAT, ISN'T IT? I LOVE IT THERE!
IT'S A LITTLE EXPEN-SIVE THOUGH.
WELL...
I JUST GOT PAID, SO WANT TO GO WITH ME?
HUH?
OH!
ER...

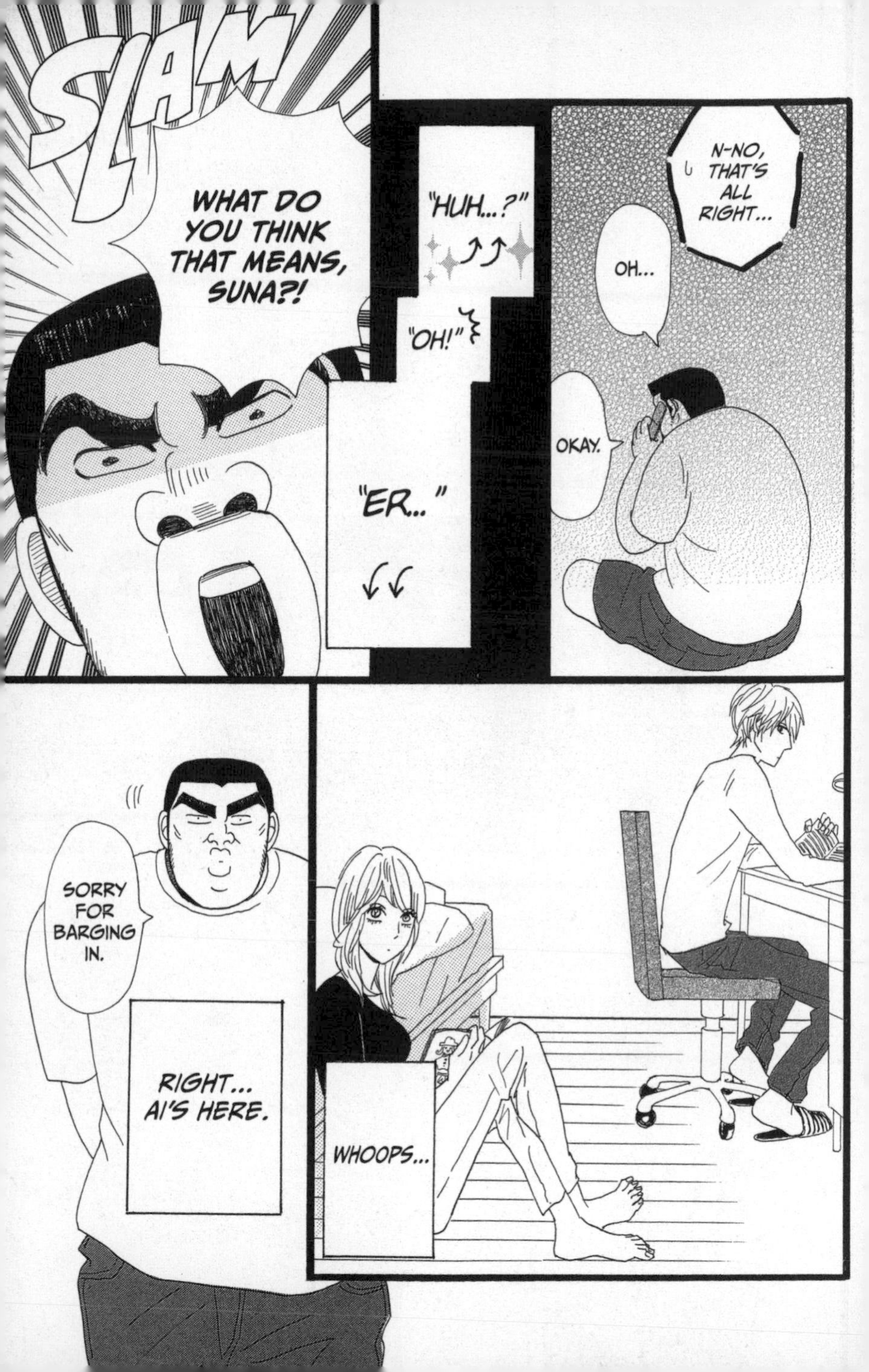
N-NO, THAT'S ALL RIGHT...
OH...
OKAY.
"HUH...?"
"OH!"
"ER..."
SLAM
WHAT DO YOU THINK THAT MEANS, SUNA?!
WHOOPS...
SORRY FOR BARGING IN.
RIGHT... AI'S HERE.

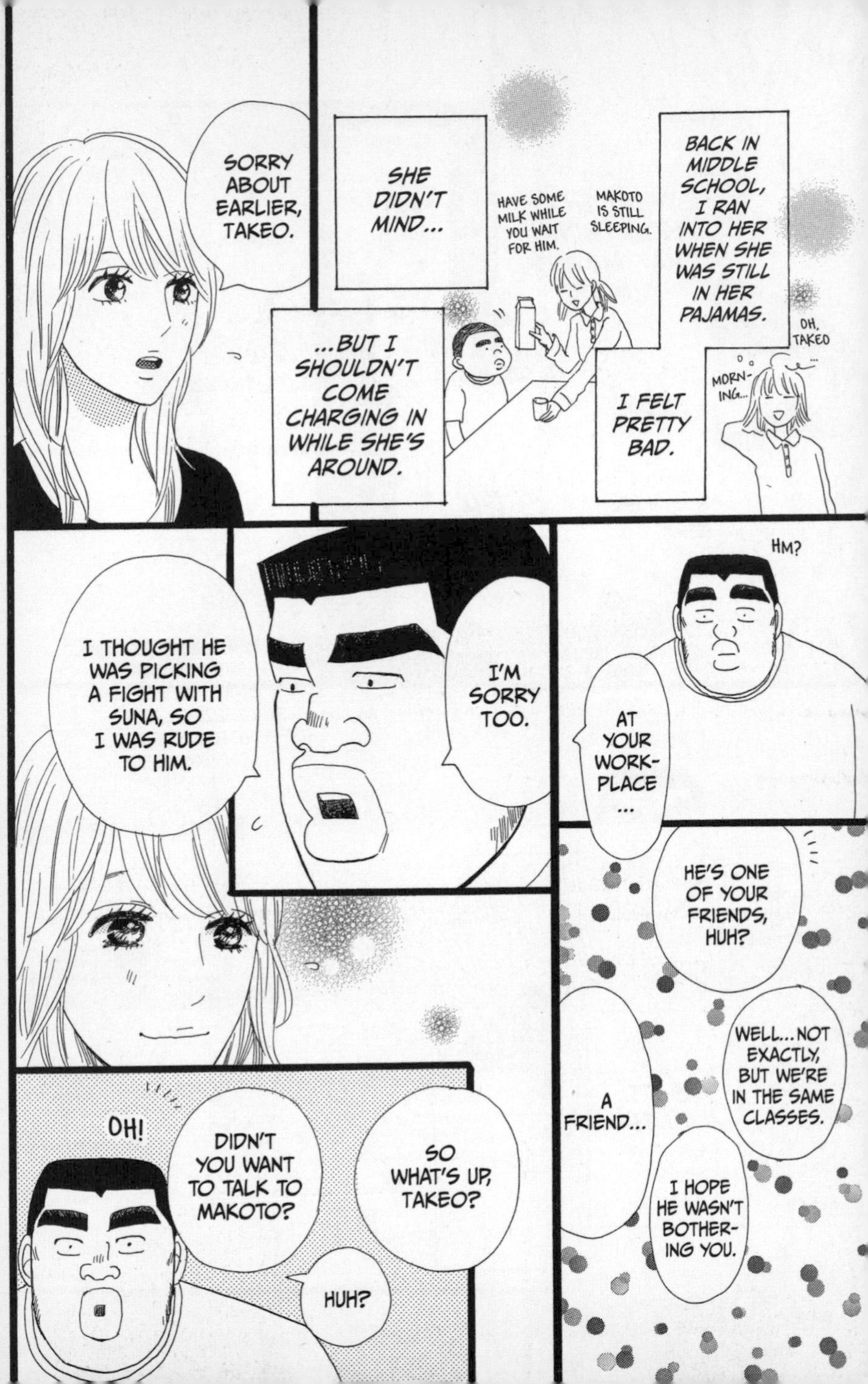
BACK IN MIDDLE SCHOOL, I RAN INTO HER WHEN SHE WAS STILL IN HER PAJAMAS.
OH, TAKEO...
MORNING...
I FELT PRETTY BAD.
MAKOTO IS STILL SLEEPING.
HAVE SOME MILK WHILE YOU WAIT FOR HIM.
SHE DIDN'T MIND...
...BUT I SHOULDN'T COME CHARGING IN WHILE SHE'S AROUND.
SORRY ABOUT EARLIER, TAKEO.
HM?
AT YOUR WORKPLACE...
I'M SORRY TOO.
I THOUGHT HE WAS PICKING A FIGHT WITH SUNA, SO I WAS RUDE TO HIM.
HE'S ONE OF YOUR FRIENDS, HUH?
WELL...NOT EXACTLY, BUT WE'RE IN THE SAME CLASSES.
A FRIEND...
I HOPE HE WASN'T BOTHERING YOU.
SO WHAT'S UP, TAKEO?
DIDN'T YOU WANT TO TALK TO MAKOTO?
OH!
HUH?

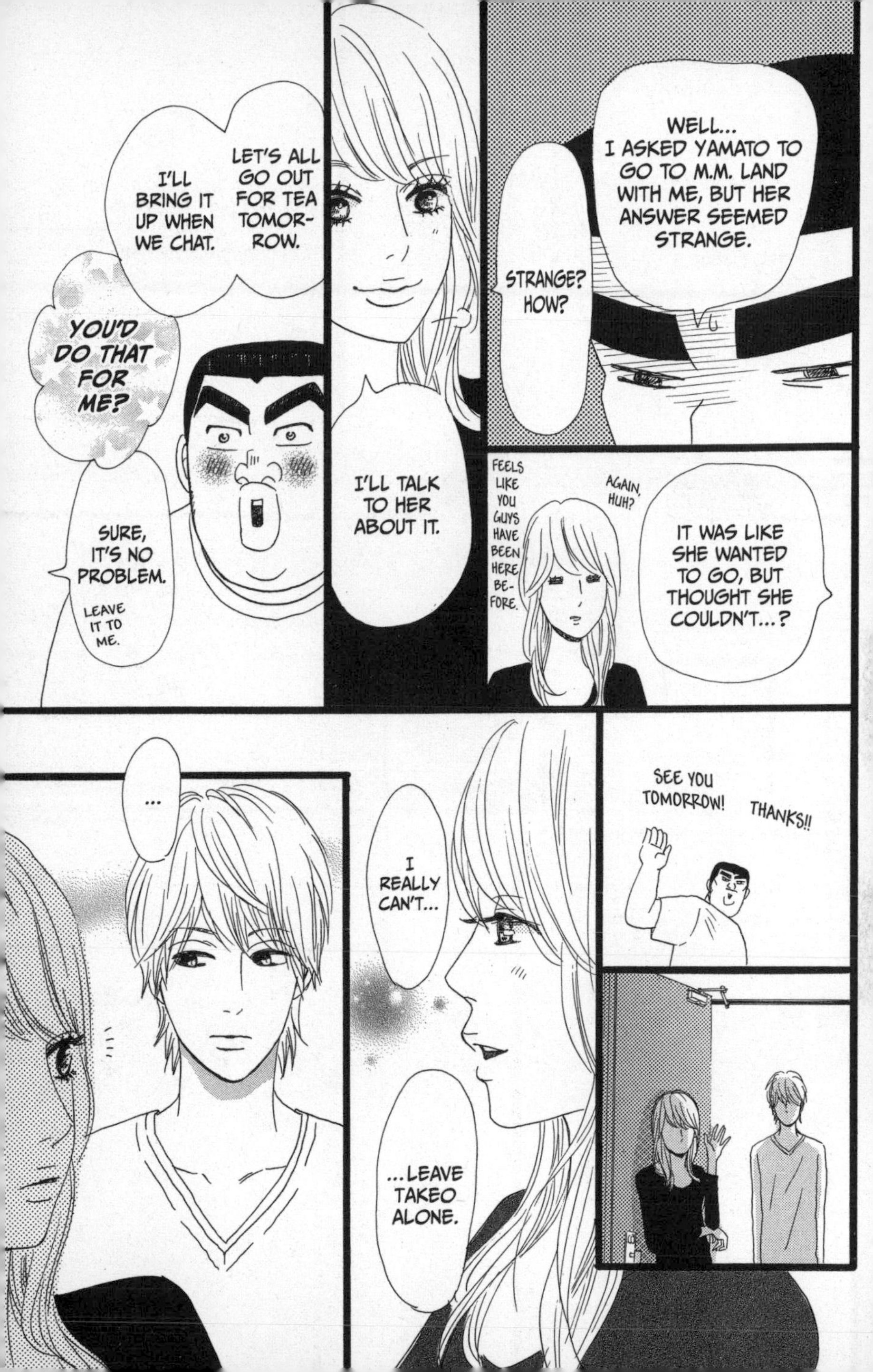
WELL... I ASKED YAMATO TO GO TO M.M. LAND WITH ME, BUT HER ANSWER SEEMED STRANGE.
STRANGE? HOW?
IT WAS LIKE SHE WANTED TO GO, BUT THOUGHT SHE COULDN'T...?
AGAIN, HUH?
FEELS LIKE YOU GUYS HAVE BEEN HERE BEFORE.
I'LL TALK TO HER ABOUT IT.
LET'S ALL GO OUT FOR TEA TOMORROW.
I'LL BRING IT UP WHEN WE CHAT.
YOU'D DO THAT FOR ME?
SURE, IT'S NO PROBLEM.
LEAVE IT TO ME.
SEE YOU TOMORROW!
THANKS!!
I REALLY CAN'T...
...LEAVE TAKEO ALONE.
...

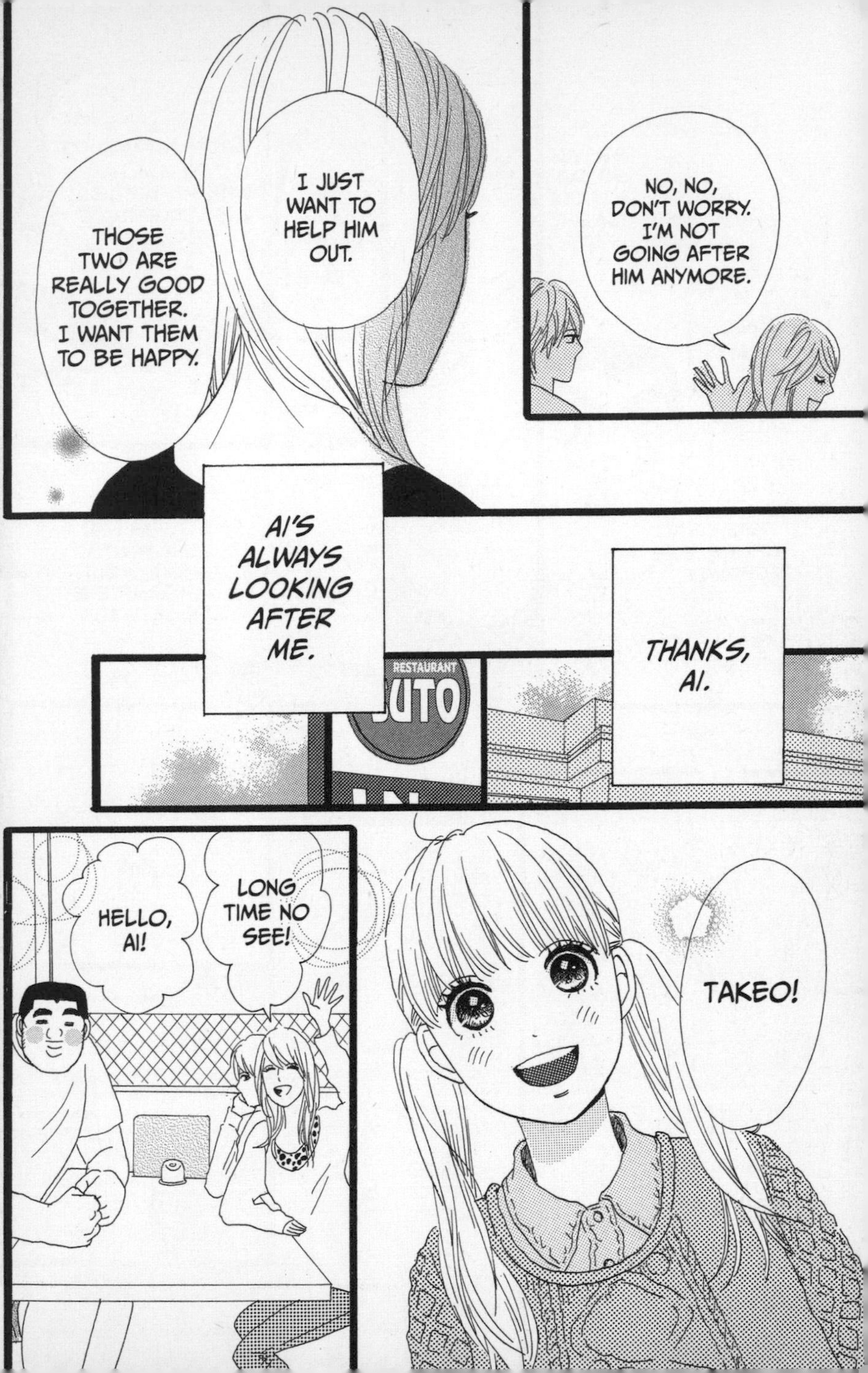
NO, NO, DON'T WORRY. I'M NOT GOING AFTER HIM ANYMORE.
I JUST WANT TO HELP HIM OUT.
THOSE TWO ARE REALLY GOOD TOGETHER. I WANT THEM TO BE HAPPY.
AI'S ALWAYS LOOKING AFTER ME.
RESTAURANT
THANKS, AI.
TAKEO!
LONG TIME NO SEE!
HELLO, AI!

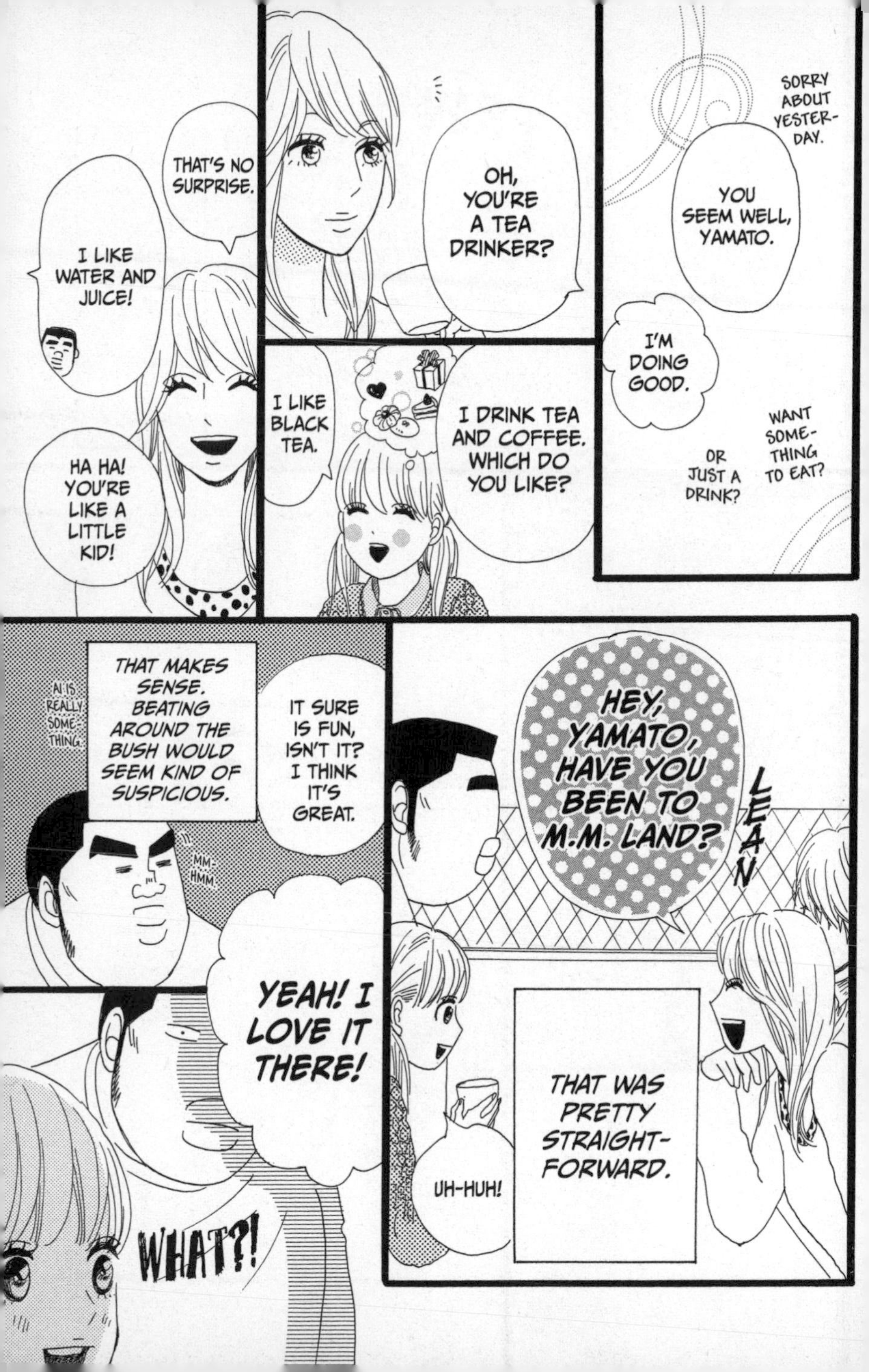
SORRY ABOUT YESTER-DAY.
YOU SEEM WELL, YAMATO.
I'M DOING GOOD.
WANT SOME-THING TO EAT?
OR JUST A DRINK?
OH, YOU'RE A TEA DRINKER?
I DRINK TEA AND COFFEE. WHICH DO YOU LIKE?
I LIKE BLACK TEA.
THAT'S NO SURPRISE.
I LIKE WATER AND JUICE!
HA HA! YOU'RE LIKE A LITTLE KID!
HEY, YAMATO, HAVE YOU BEEN TO M.M. LAND?
LEAN
UH-HUH!
THAT WAS PRETTY STRAIGHT-FORWARD.
IT SURE IS FUN, ISN'T IT? I THINK IT'S GREAT.
THAT MAKES SENSE. BEATING AROUND THE BUSH WOULD SEEM KIND OF SUSPICIOUS.
AI IS REALLY SOME-THING.
MM-HMM.
YEAH! I LOVE IT THERE!
WHAT?!

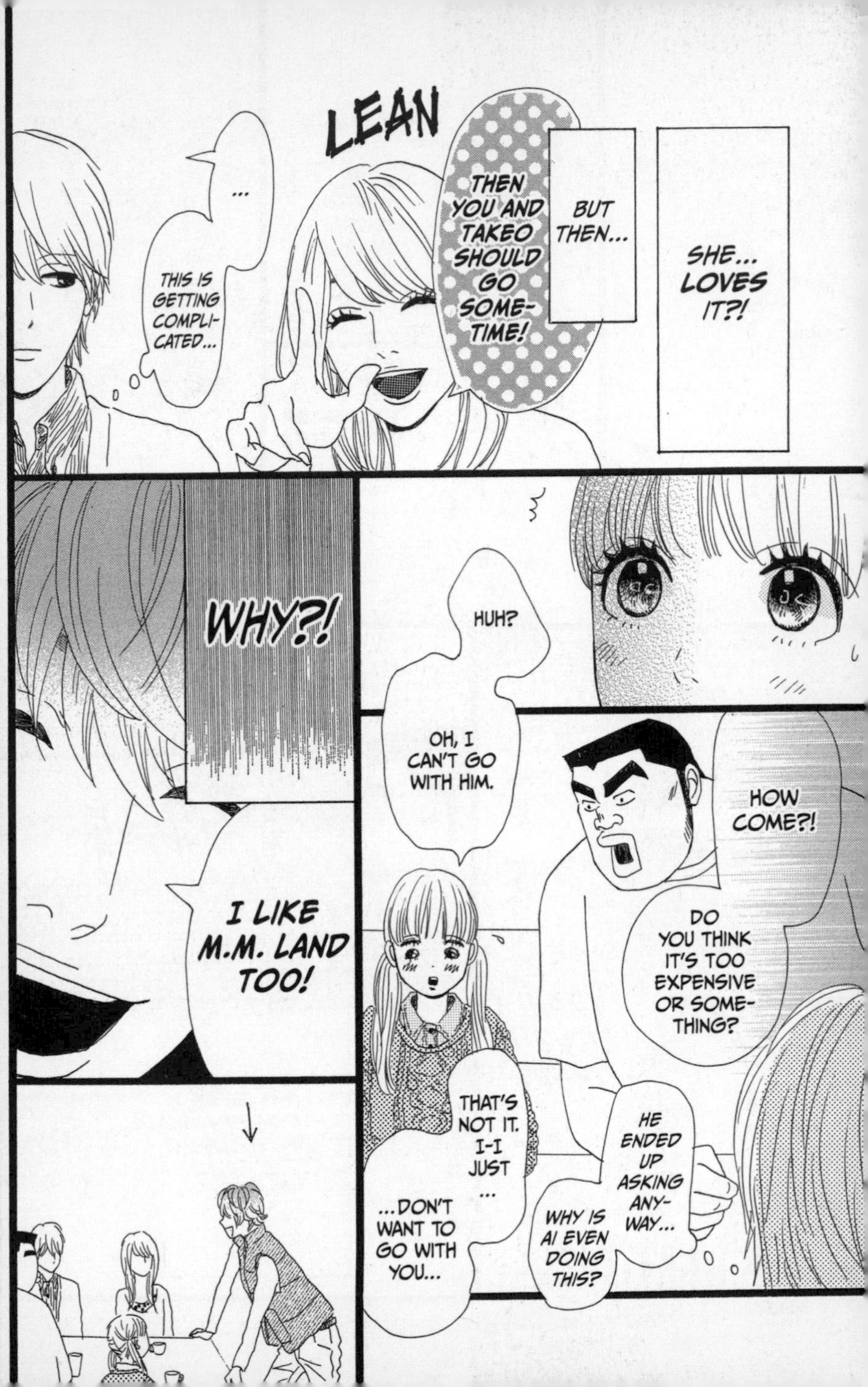
SHE... LOVES IT?!
BUT THEN...
THEN YOU AND TAKEO SHOULD GO SOME-TIME!
LEAN
...
THIS IS GETTING COMPLI-CATED...
HUH?
HOW COME?!
OH, I CAN'T GO WITH HIM.
DO YOU THINK IT'S TOO EXPENSIVE OR SOME-THING?
THAT'S NOT IT. I-I JUST ...
HE ENDED UP ASKING ANY-WAY...
WHY IS AI EVEN DOING THIS?
...DON'T WANT TO GO WITH YOU...
WHY?!
I LIKE M.M. LAND TOO!

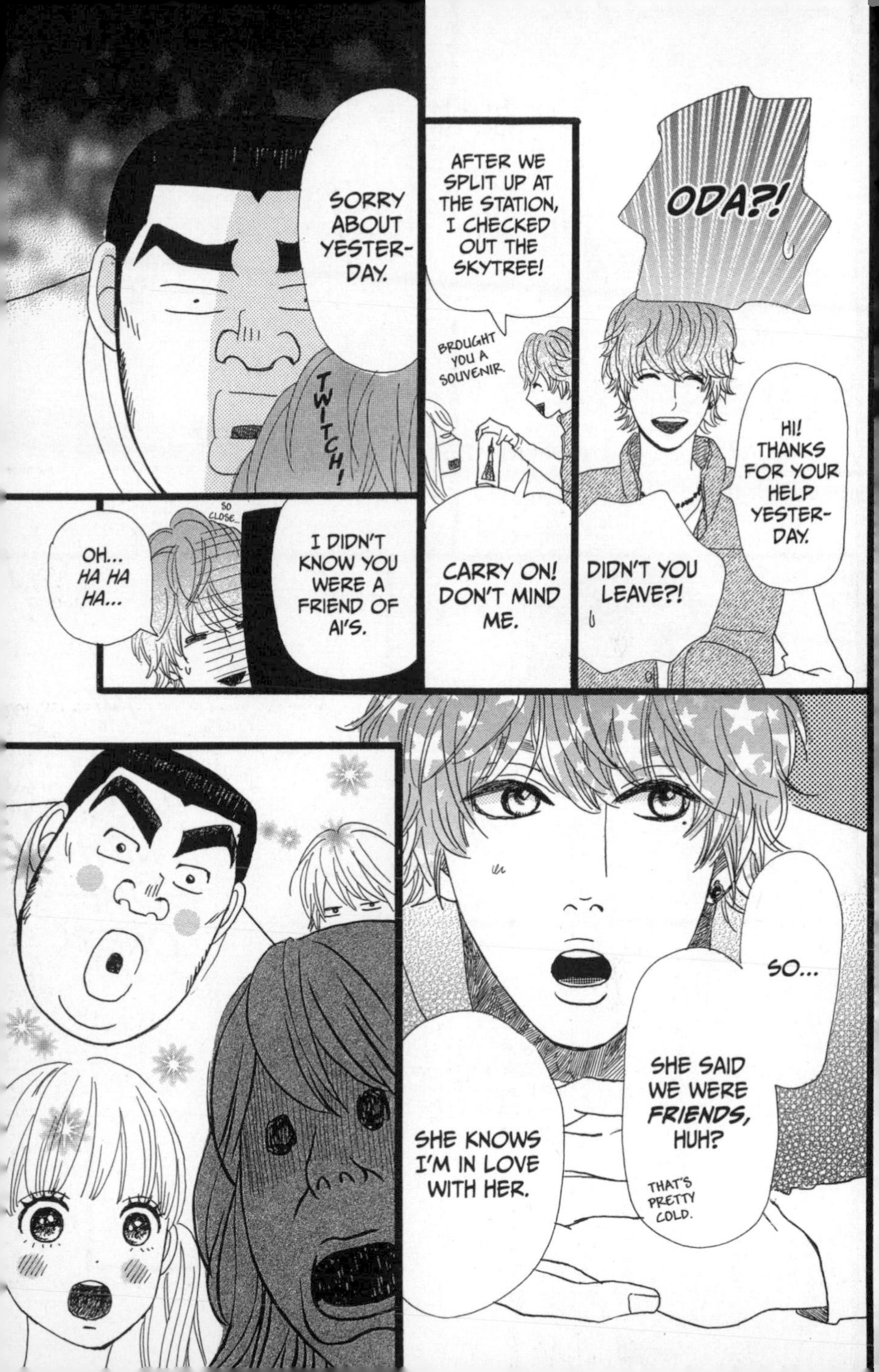
ODA?!
HI! THANKS FOR YOUR HELP YESTER-DAY.
DIDN'T YOU LEAVE?!
AFTER WE SPLIT UP AT THE STATION, I CHECKED OUT THE SKYTREE!
BROUGHT YOU A SOUVENIR.
CARRY ON! DON'T MIND ME.
SORRY ABOUT YESTER-DAY.
TWITCH!
I DIDN'T KNOW YOU WERE A FRIEND OF AI'S.
SO CLOSE...
OH... HA HA HA...
SO...
SHE SAID WE WERE FRIENDS, HUH?
THAT'S PRETTY COLD.
SHE KNOWS I'M IN LOVE WITH HER.

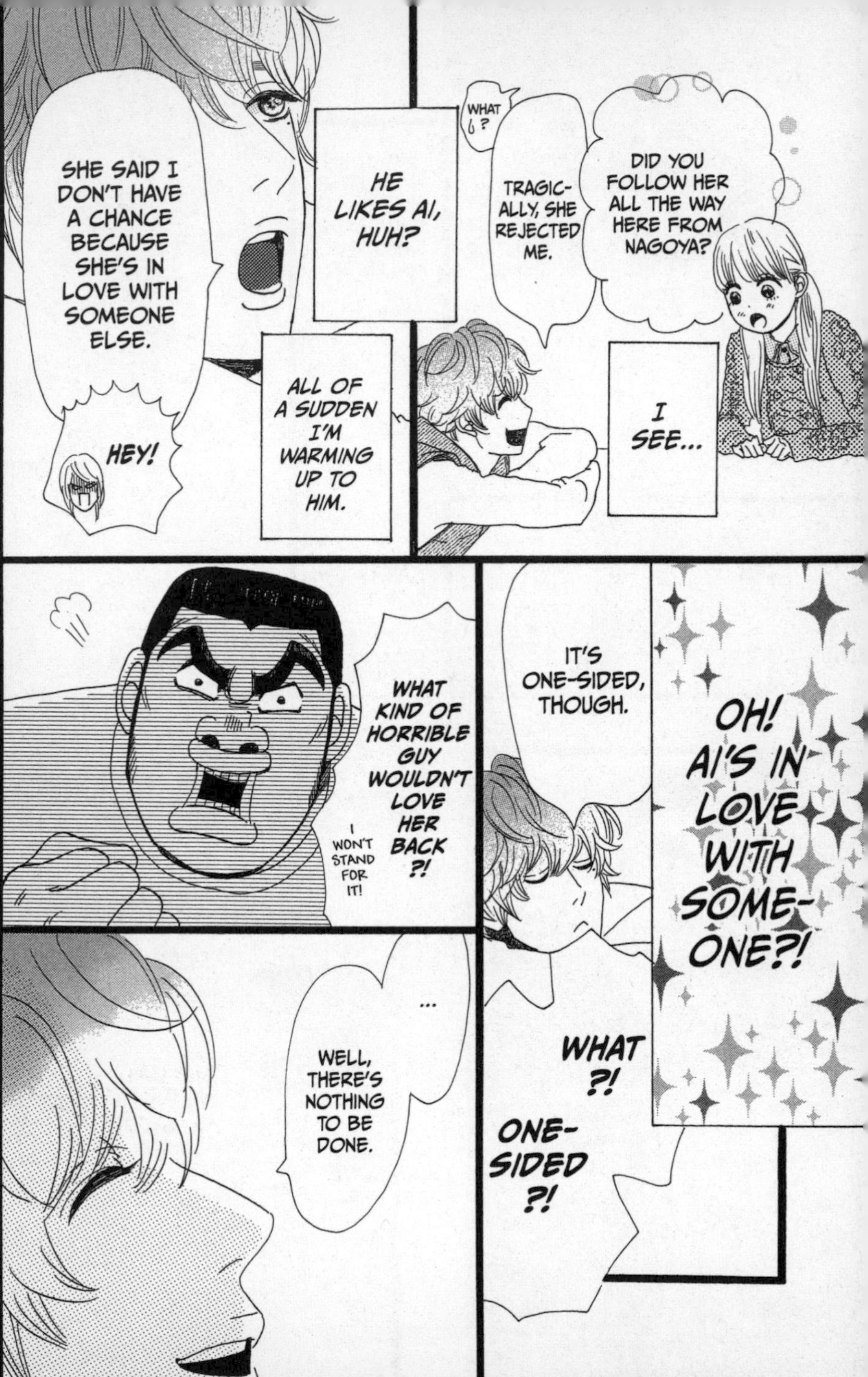
DID YOU FOLLOW HER ALL THE WAY HERE FROM NAGOYA?
WHAT ♪?
TRAGIC-ALLY, SHE REJECTED ME.
I SEE...
SHE SAID I DON'T HAVE A CHANCE BECAUSE SHE'S IN LOVE WITH SOMEONE ELSE.
HE LIKES AI, HUH?
HEY!
ALL OF A SUDDEN I'M WARMING UP TO HIM.
OH! AI'S IN LOVE WITH SOME-ONE?!
IT'S ONE-SIDED, THOUGH.
WHAT ?!
ONE-SIDED ?!
WHAT KIND OF HORRIBLE GUY WOULDN'T LOVE HER BACK ?!
I WON'T STAND FOR IT!
...
WELL, THERE'S NOTHING TO BE DONE.

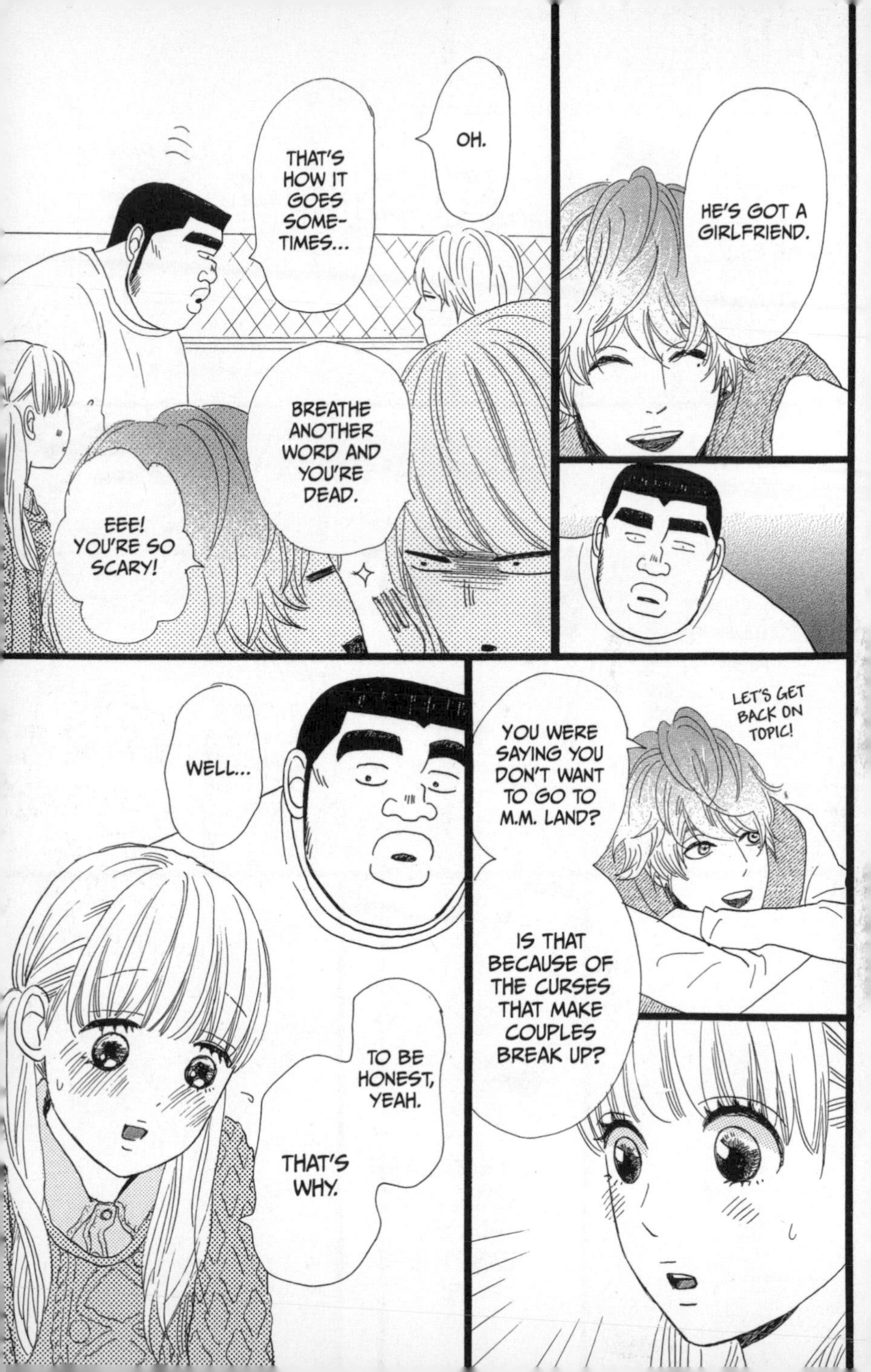
HE'S GOT A GIRLFRIEND.
OH.
THAT'S HOW IT GOES SOME-TIMES...
BREATHE ANOTHER WORD AND YOU'RE DEAD.
EEE! YOU'RE SO SCARY!
LET'S GET BACK ON TOPIC!
YOU WERE SAYING YOU DON'T WANT TO GO TO M.M. LAND?
IS THAT BECAUSE OF THE CURSES THAT MAKE COUPLES BREAK UP?
WELL...
TO BE HONEST, YEAH.
THAT'S WHY.

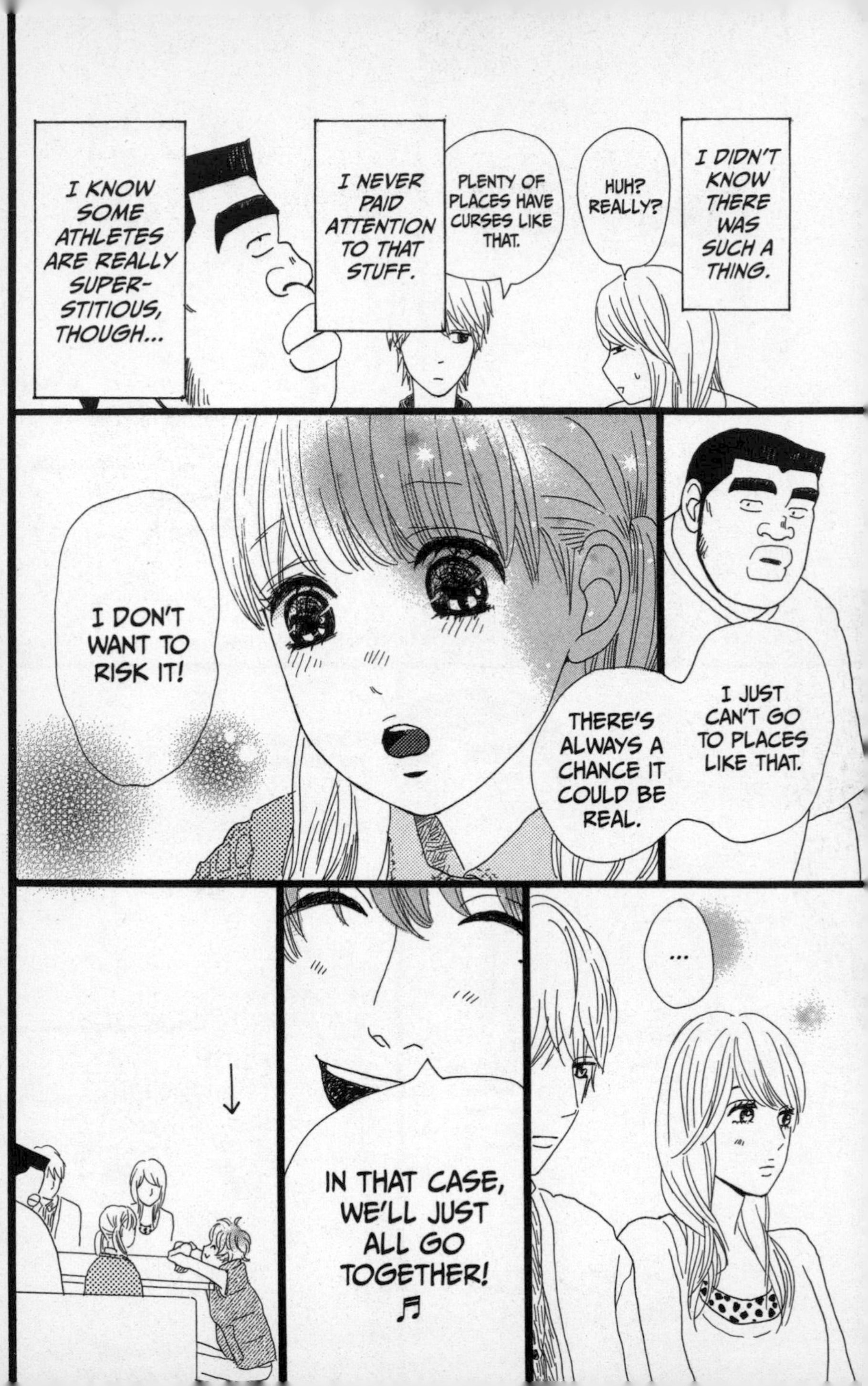
I DIDN'T KNOW THERE WAS SUCH A THING.
HUH? REALLY?
PLENTY OF PLACES HAVE CURSES LIKE THAT.
I NEVER PAID ATTENTION TO THAT STUFF.
I KNOW SOME ATHLETES ARE REALLY SUPER-STITIOUS, THOUGH...
I JUST CAN'T GO TO PLACES LIKE THAT.
THERE'S ALWAYS A CHANCE IT COULD BE REAL.
I DON'T WANT TO RISK IT!
...
IN THAT CASE, WE'LL JUST ALL GO TOGETHER! ♬

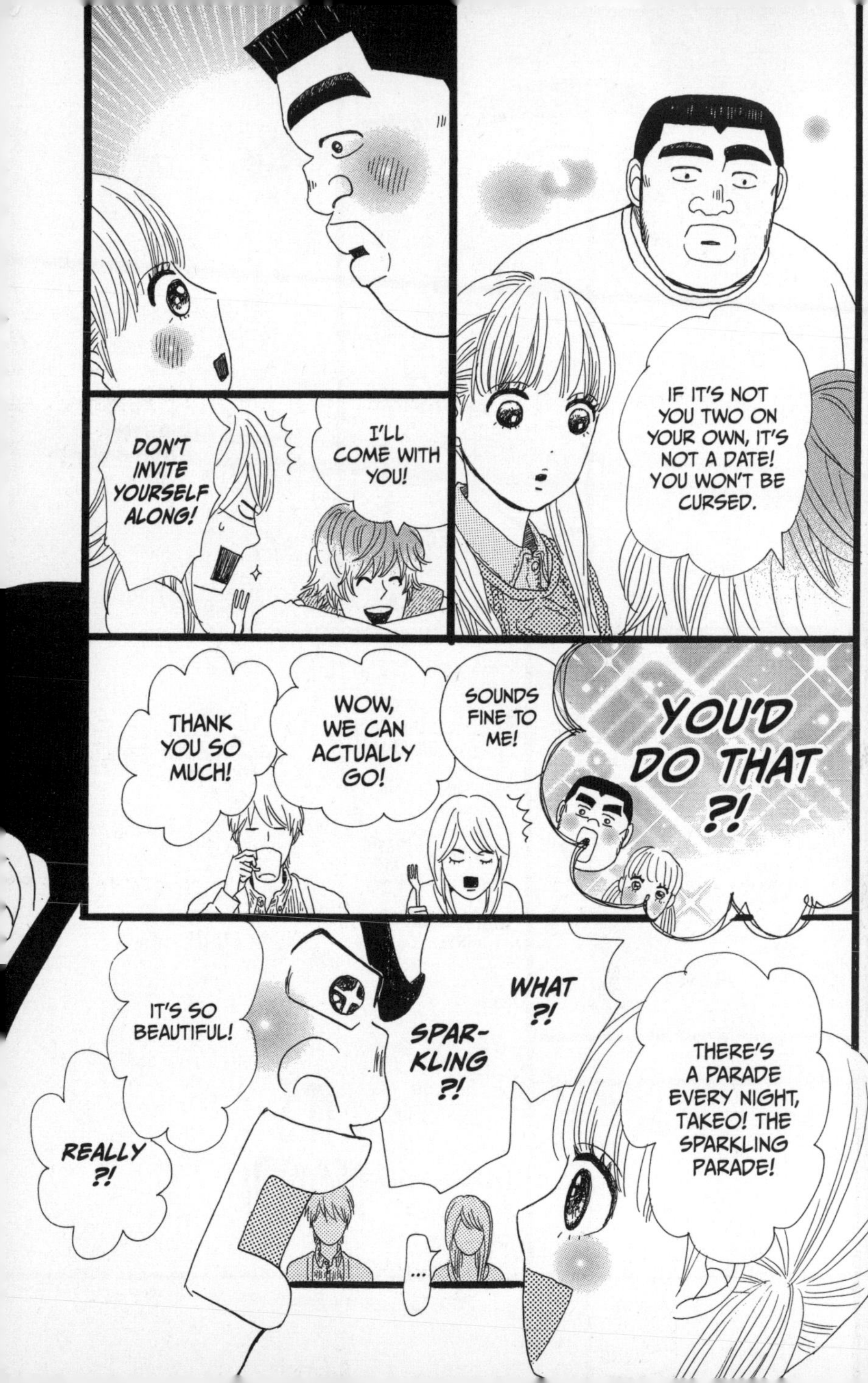
IF IT'S NOT YOU TWO ON YOUR OWN, IT'S NOT A DATE! YOU WON'T BE CURSED.
I'LL COME WITH YOU!
DON'T INVITE YOURSELF ALONG!
YOU'D DO THAT ?!
SOUNDS FINE TO ME!
WOW, WE CAN ACTUALLY GO!
THANK YOU SO MUCH!
THERE'S A PARADE EVERY NIGHT, TAKEO! THE SPARKLING PARADE!
WHAT ?!
SPAR-KLING ?!
IT'S SO BEAUTIFUL!
REALLY ?!
...

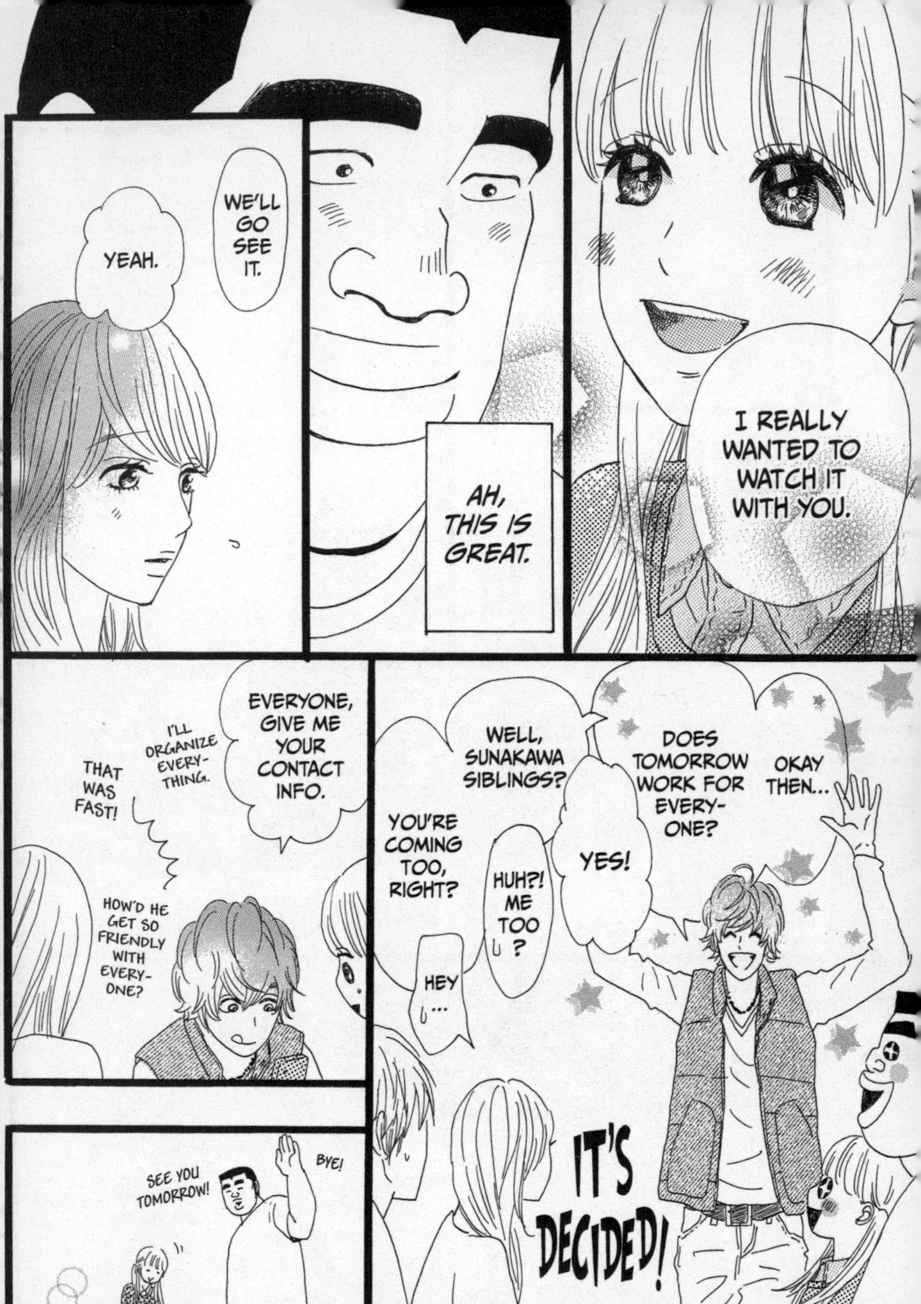
I REALLY WANTED TO WATCH IT WITH YOU.
AH, THIS IS GREAT.
WE'LL GO SEE IT.
YEAH.
OKAY THEN...
DOES TOMORROW WORK FOR EVERY-ONE?
YES!
WELL, SUNAKAWA SIBLINGS?
YOU'RE COMING TOO, RIGHT?
HUH?! ME TOO?
HEY...
IT'S DECIDED!
EVERYONE, GIVE ME YOUR CONTACT INFO.
I'LL ORGANIZE EVERY-THING.
THAT WAS FAST!
HOW'D HE GET SO FRIENDLY WITH EVERY-ONE?
BYE!
SEE YOU TOMORROW!

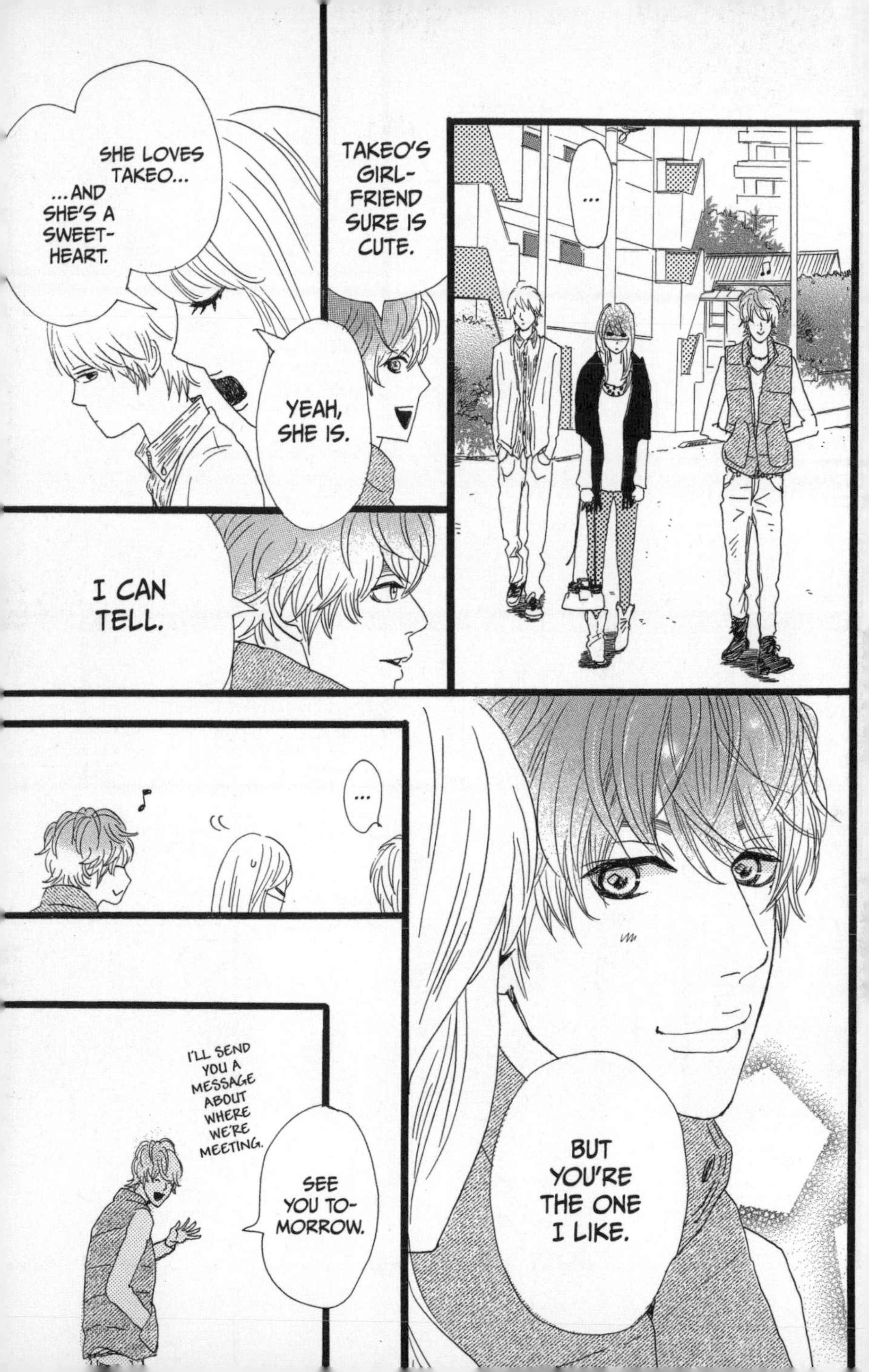
...
TAKEO'S GIRLFRIEND SURE IS CUTE.
YEAH, SHE IS.
SHE LOVES TAKEO...
...AND SHE'S A SWEETHEART.
I CAN TELL.
BUT YOU'RE THE ONE I LIKE.
...
I'LL SEND YOU A MESSAGE ABOUT WHERE WE'RE MEETING.
SEE YOU TOMORROW.

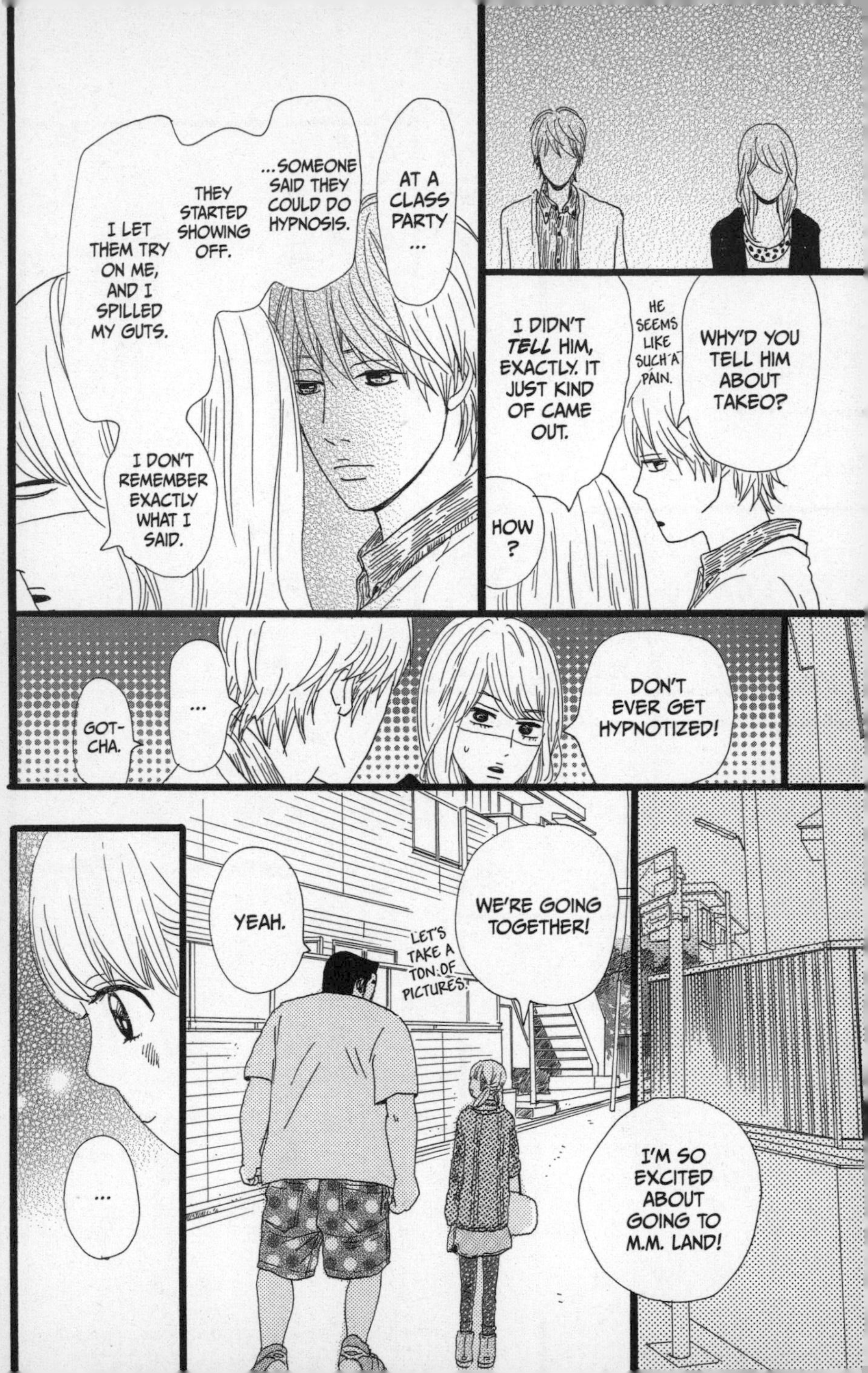
WHY'D YOU TELL HIM ABOUT TAKEO?
HE SEEMS LIKE SUCH A PAIN.
I DIDN'T *TELL* HIM, EXACTLY. IT JUST KIND OF CAME OUT.
HOW?
AT A CLASS PARTY ...
...SOMEONE SAID THEY COULD DO HYPNOSIS.
THEY STARTED SHOWING OFF.
I LET THEM TRY ON ME, AND I SPILLED MY GUTS.
I DON'T REMEMBER EXACTLY WHAT I SAID.
DON'T EVER GET HYPNOTIZED!
...
GOT-CHA.
I'M SO EXCITED ABOUT GOING TO M.M. LAND!
WE'RE GOING TOGETHER!
LET'S TAKE A TON OF PICTURES!
YEAH.
...

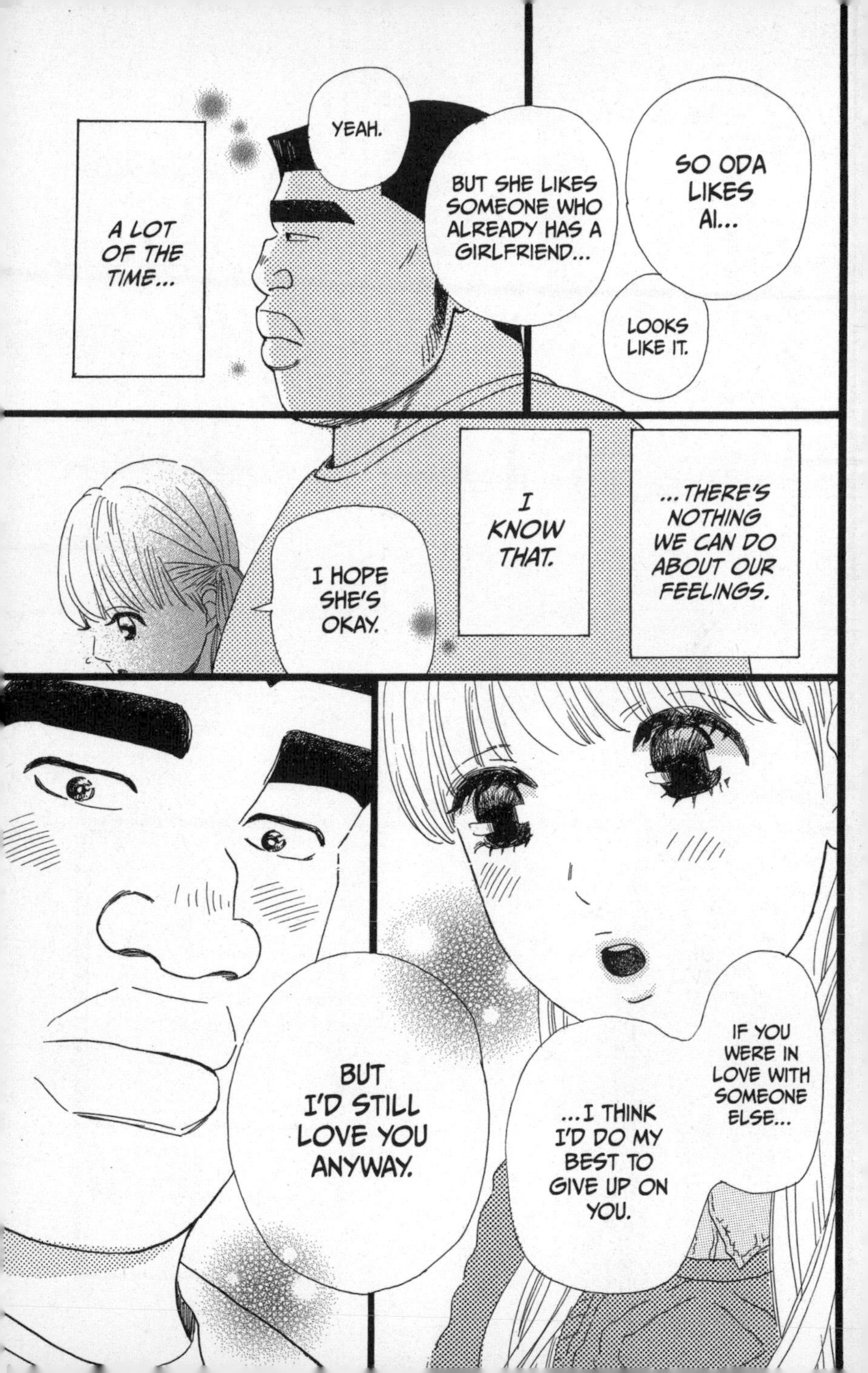
SO ODA LIKES AI...
LOOKS LIKE IT.
BUT SHE LIKES SOMEONE WHO ALREADY HAS A GIRLFRIEND...
YEAH.
A LOT OF THE TIME...
...THERE'S NOTHING WE CAN DO ABOUT OUR FEELINGS.
I KNOW THAT.
I HOPE SHE'S OKAY.
IF YOU WERE IN LOVE WITH SOMEONE ELSE...
...I THINK I'D DO MY BEST TO GIVE UP ON YOU.
BUT I'D STILL LOVE YOU ANYWAY.

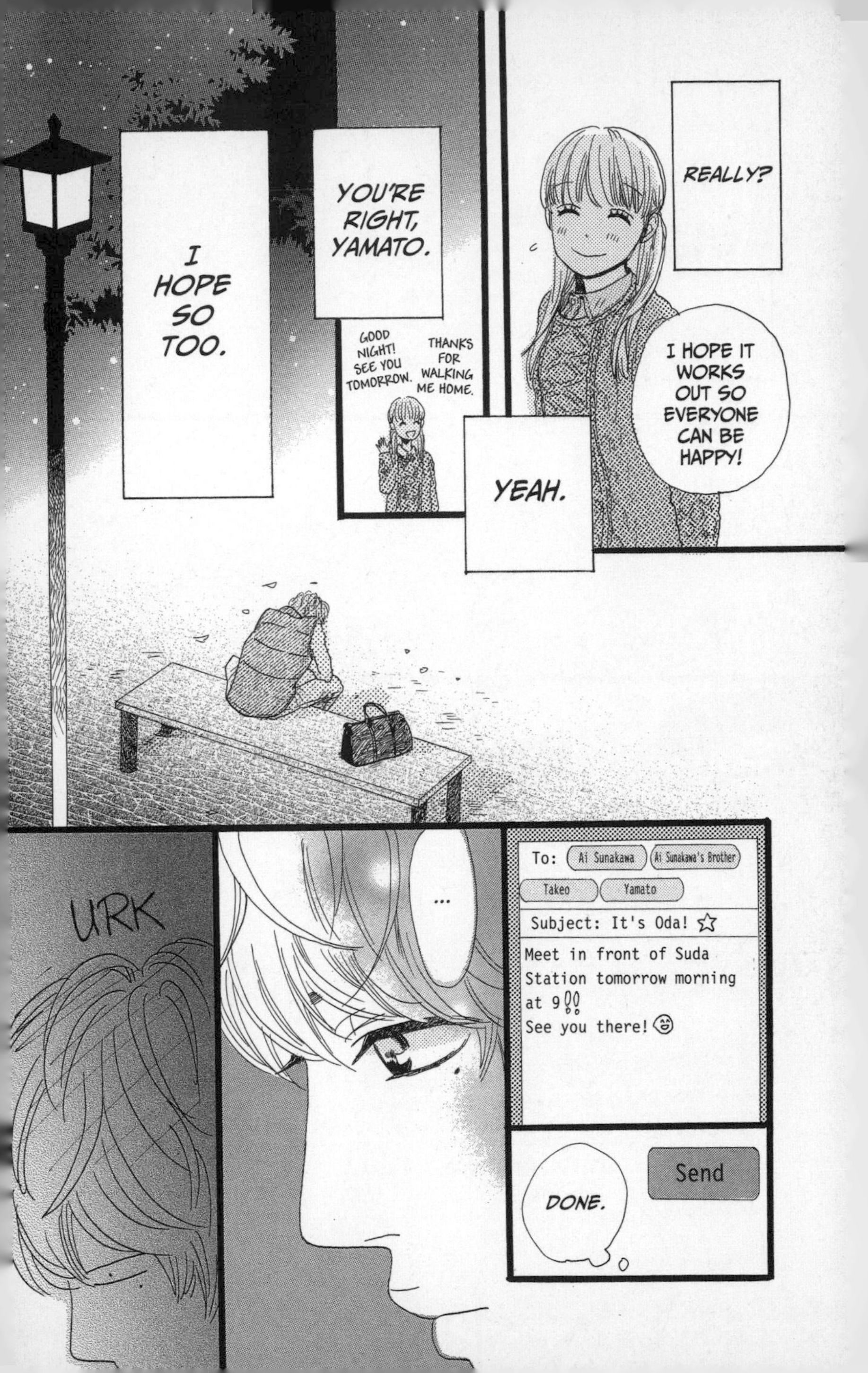
REALLY?
I HOPE IT WORKS OUT SO EVERYONE CAN BE HAPPY!
YEAH.
YOU'RE RIGHT, YAMATO.
THANKS FOR WALKING ME HOME.
GOOD NIGHT! SEE YOU TOMORROW.
I HOPE SO TOO.
To: Ai Sunakawa Ai Sunakawa's Brother Takeo Yamato
Subject: It's Oda! ☆
Meet in front of Suda Station tomorrow morning at 9!!
See you there!
Send
DONE.
...
URK

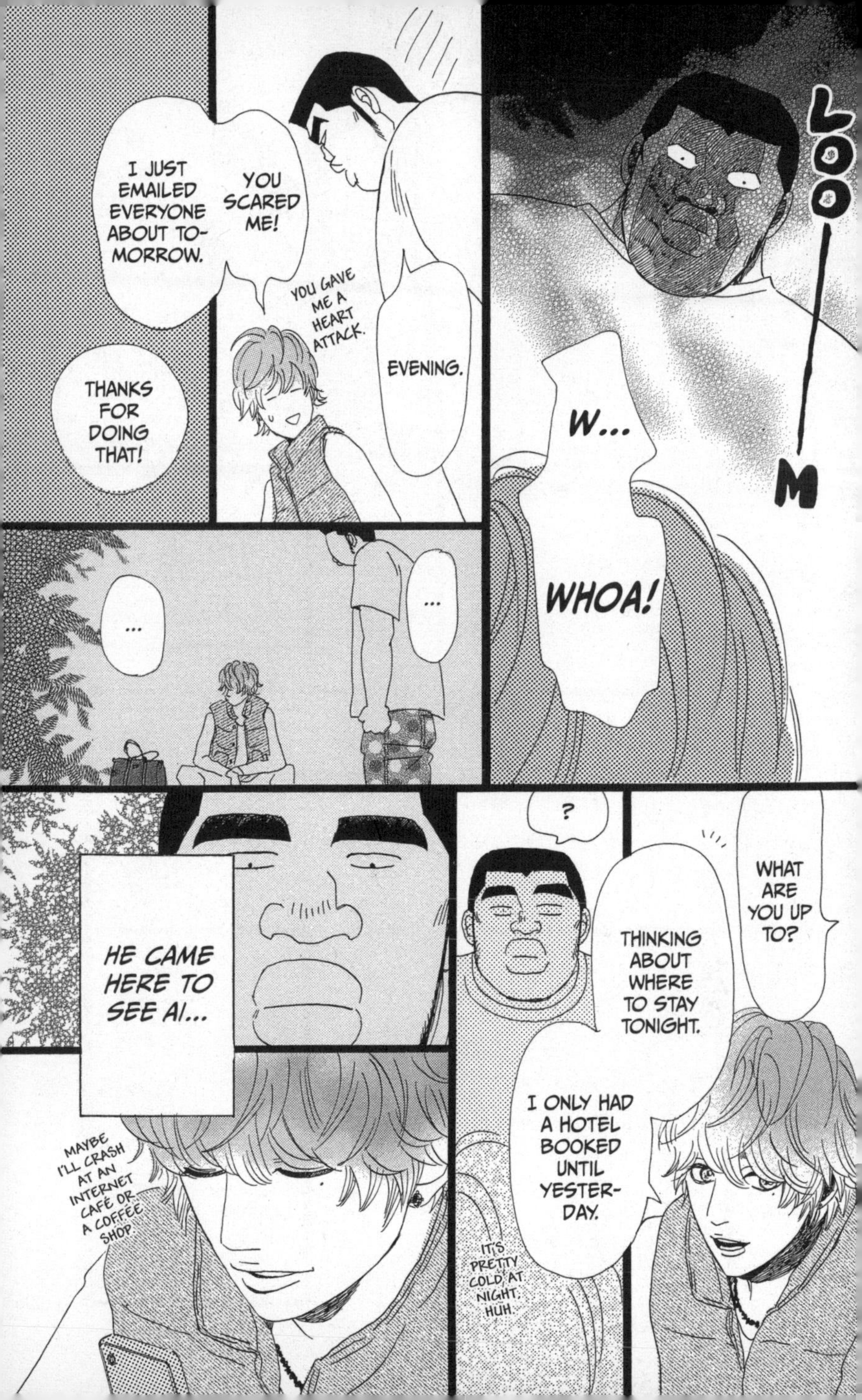
LOOOM
W...
WHOA!
EVENING.
YOU SCARED ME!
YOU GAVE ME A HEART ATTACK.
I JUST EMAILED EVERYONE ABOUT TO-MORROW.
THANKS FOR DOING THAT!
...
...
WHAT ARE YOU UP TO?
?
THINKING ABOUT WHERE TO STAY TONIGHT.
I ONLY HAD A HOTEL BOOKED UNTIL YESTER-DAY.
IT'S PRETTY COLD AT NIGHT, HUH.
HE CAME HERE TO SEE AI...
MAYBE I'LL CRASH AT AN INTERNET CAFÉ OR A COFFEE SHOP.

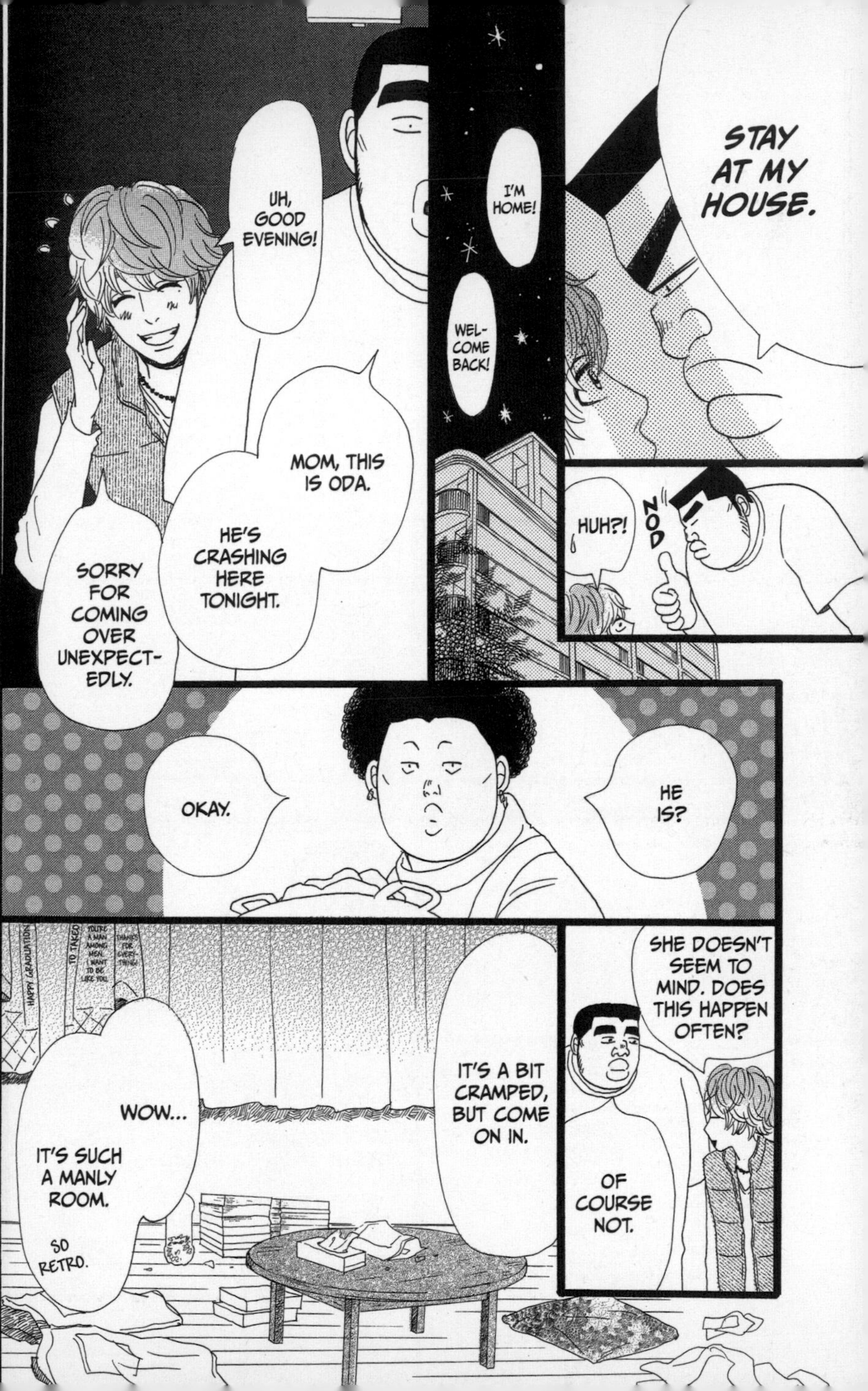
STAY AT MY HOUSE.
HUH?!
NOD
I'M HOME!
WEL-COME BACK!
MOM, THIS IS ODA.
HE'S CRASHING HERE TONIGHT.
UH, GOOD EVENING!
SORRY FOR COMING OVER UNEXPECT-EDLY.
HE IS?
OKAY.
SHE DOESN'T SEEM TO MIND. DOES THIS HAPPEN OFTEN?
OF COURSE NOT.
IT'S A BIT CRAMPED, BUT COME ON IN.
THANKS FOR EVERY-THING!
YOU'RE A MAN AMONG MEN. I WANT TO BE LIKE YOU.
TO TAKEO
HAPPY GRADUATION
WOW...
IT'S SUCH A MANLY ROOM.
SO RETRO.

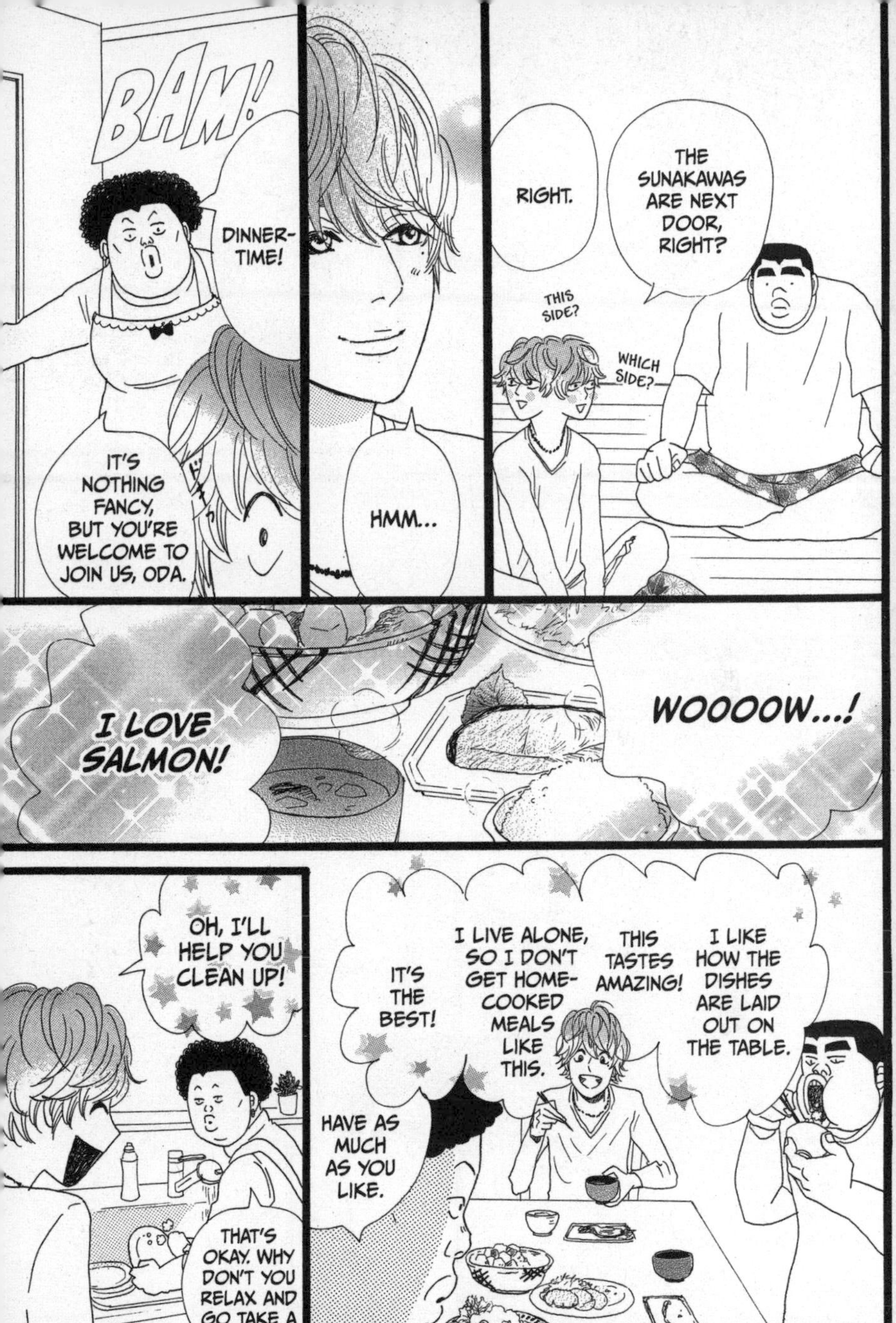
THE SUNAKAWAS ARE NEXT DOOR, RIGHT?
RIGHT.
WHICH SIDE?
THIS SIDE?
HMM...
BAM!
DINNER-TIME!
IT'S NOTHING FANCY, BUT YOU'RE WELCOME TO JOIN US, ODA.
WOOOOW...!
I LOVE SALMON!
I LIKE HOW THE DISHES ARE LAID OUT ON THE TABLE.
THIS TASTES AMAZING!
I LIVE ALONE, SO I DON'T GET HOME-COOKED MEALS LIKE THIS.
IT'S THE BEST!
HAVE AS MUCH AS YOU LIKE.
OH, I'LL HELP YOU CLEAN UP!
THAT'S OKAY. WHY DON'T YOU RELAX AND GO TAKE A BATH?

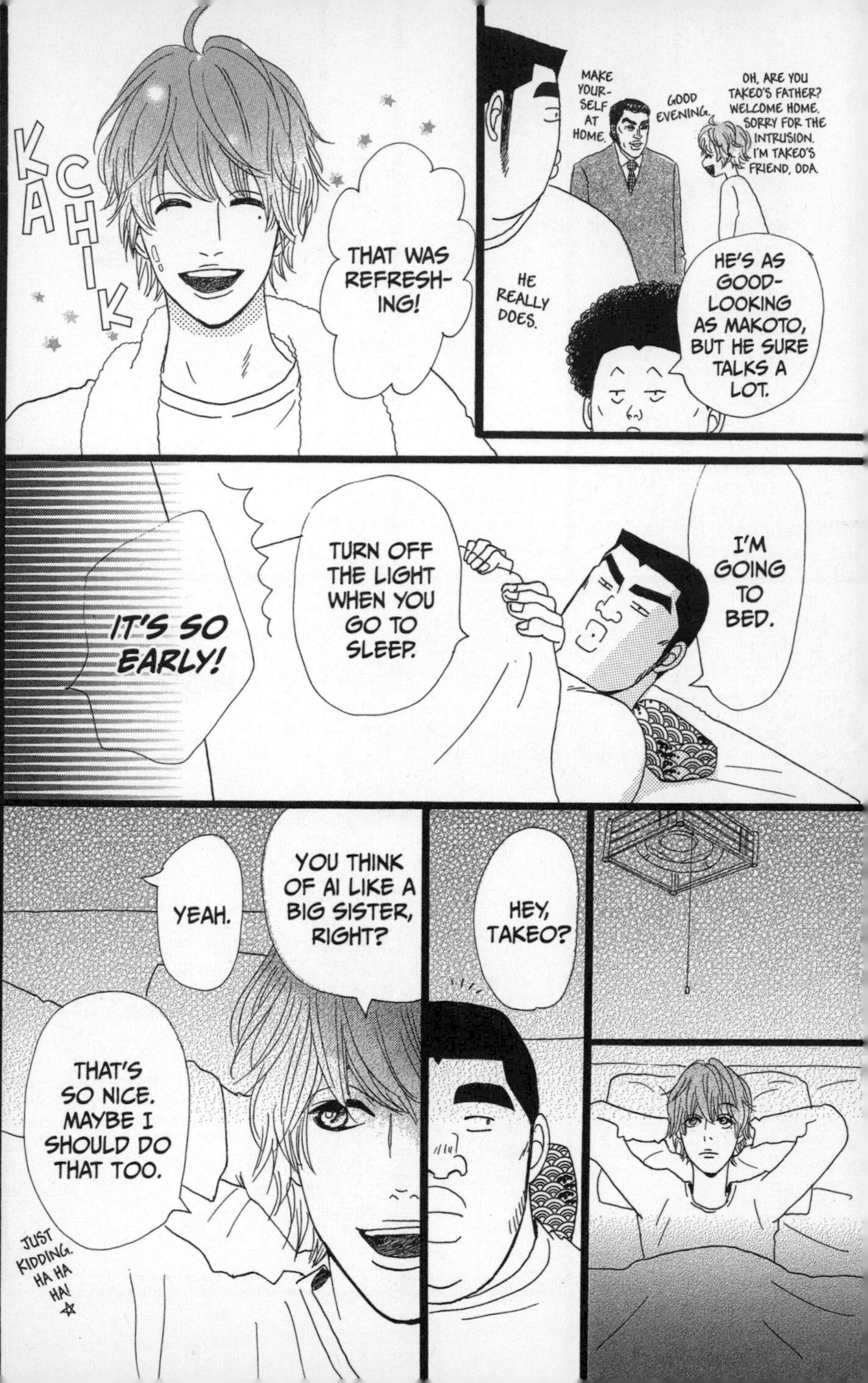
OH, ARE YOU TAKEO'S FATHER? WELCOME HOME. SORRY FOR THE INTRUSION. I'M TAKEO'S FRIEND, ODA.
GOOD EVENING.
MAKE YOURSELF AT HOME.
HE'S AS GOOD-LOOKING AS MAKOTO, BUT HE SURE TALKS A LOT.
HE REALLY DOES.
THAT WAS REFRESHING!
KACHIK
I'M GOING TO BED.
TURN OFF THE LIGHT WHEN YOU GO TO SLEEP.
IT'S SO EARLY!
HEY, TAKEO?
YOU THINK OF AI LIKE A BIG SISTER, RIGHT?
YEAH.
THAT'S SO NICE. MAYBE I SHOULD DO THAT TOO.
JUST KIDDING. HA HA HA!

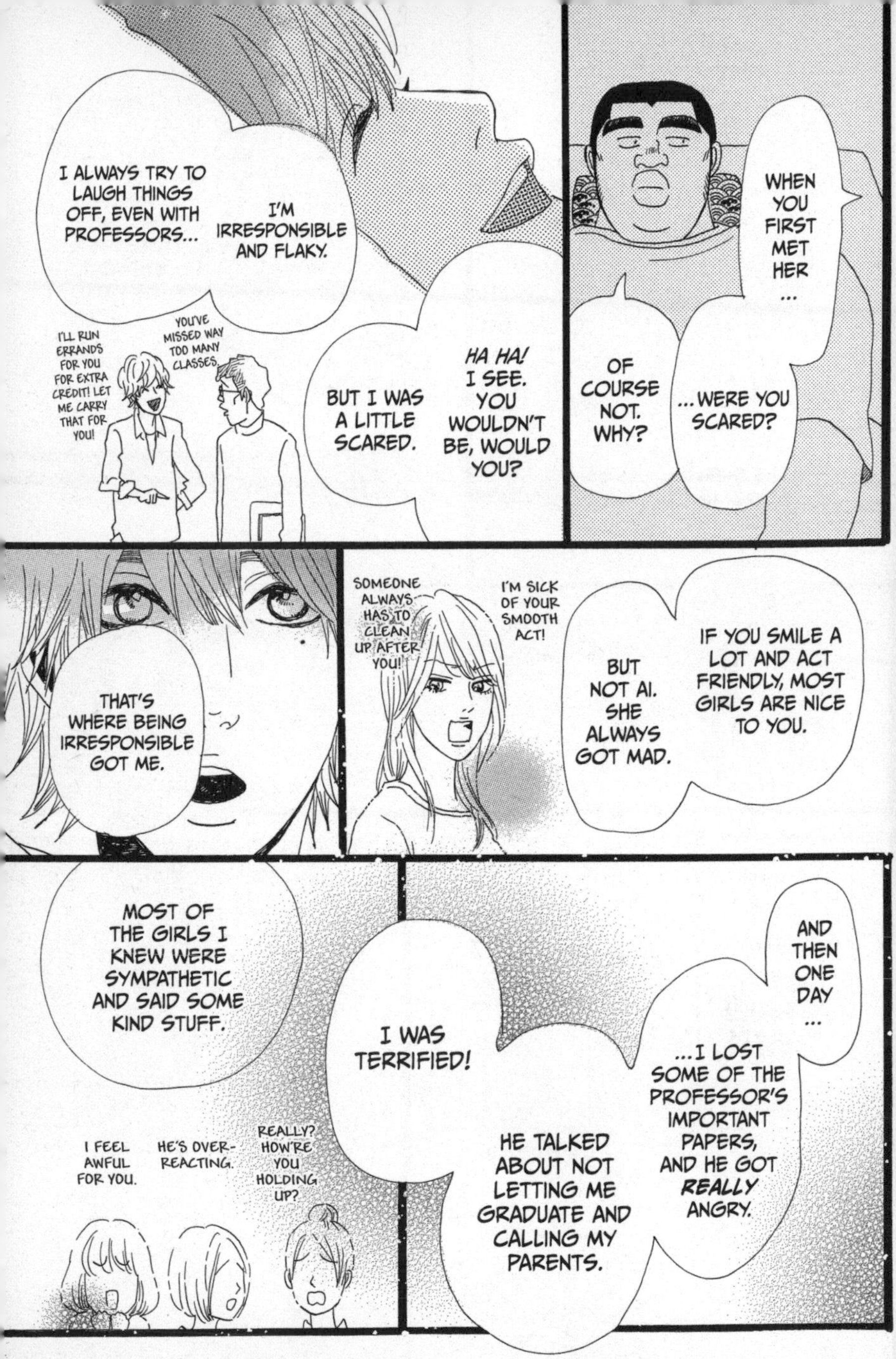
WHEN YOU FIRST MET HER ...
...WERE YOU SCARED?
OF COURSE NOT. WHY?
HA HA! I SEE. YOU WOULDN'T BE, WOULD YOU?
BUT I WAS A LITTLE SCARED.
I'M IRRESPONSIBLE AND FLAKY.
I ALWAYS TRY TO LAUGH THINGS OFF, EVEN WITH PROFESSORS...
YOU'VE MISSED WAY TOO MANY CLASSES.
I'LL RUN ERRANDS FOR YOU FOR EXTRA CREDIT! LET ME CARRY THAT FOR YOU!
IF YOU SMILE A LOT AND ACT FRIENDLY, MOST GIRLS ARE NICE TO YOU.
BUT NOT AI. SHE ALWAYS GOT MAD.
I'M SICK OF YOUR SMOOTH ACT!
SOMEONE ALWAYS HAS TO CLEAN UP AFTER YOU!
THAT'S WHERE BEING IRRESPONSIBLE GOT ME.
AND THEN ONE DAY ...
...I LOST SOME OF THE PROFESSOR'S IMPORTANT PAPERS, AND HE GOT ***REALLY*** ANGRY.
HE TALKED ABOUT NOT LETTING ME GRADUATE AND CALLING MY PARENTS.
I WAS TERRIFIED!
MOST OF THE GIRLS I KNEW WERE SYMPATHETIC AND SAID SOME KIND STUFF.
REALLY? HOW'RE YOU HOLDING UP?
HE'S OVER-REACTING.
I FEEL AWFUL FOR YOU.

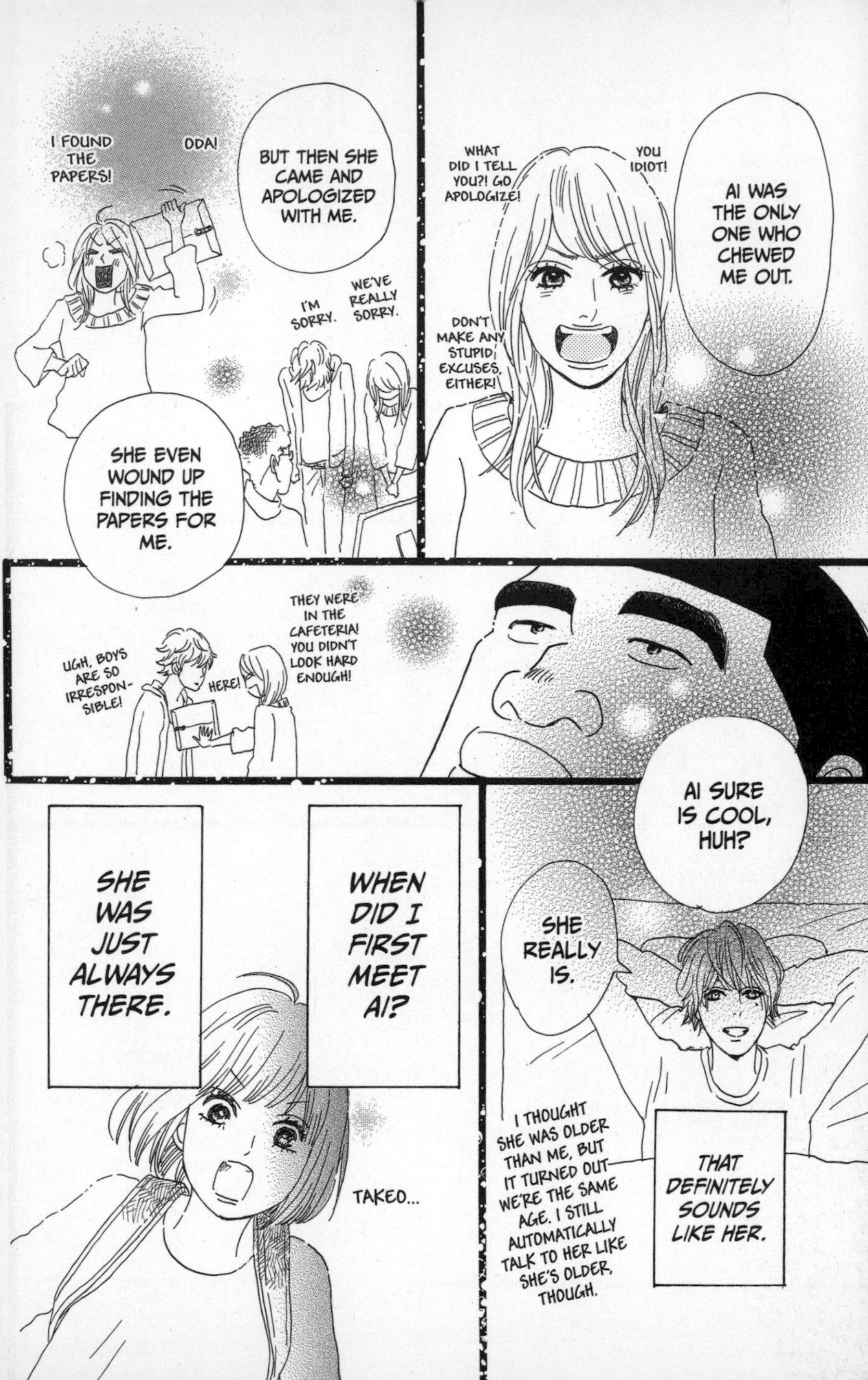
AI WAS THE ONLY ONE WHO CHEWED ME OUT.
YOU IDIOT!
WHAT DID I TELL YOU?! GO APOLOGIZE!
DON'T MAKE ANY STUPID EXCUSES, EITHER!
BUT THEN SHE CAME AND APOLOGIZED WITH ME.
ODA!
I FOUND THE PAPERS!
WE'VE REALLY SORRY.
I'M SORRY.
SHE EVEN WOUND UP FINDING THE PAPERS FOR ME.
AI SURE IS COOL, HUH?
THEY WERE IN THE CAFETERIA! YOU DIDN'T LOOK HARD ENOUGH!
HERE!
UGH, BOYS ARE SO IRRESPONSIBLE!
SHE REALLY IS.
THAT DEFINITELY SOUNDS LIKE HER.
I THOUGHT SHE WAS OLDER THAN ME, BUT IT TURNED OUT WE'RE THE SAME AGE. I STILL AUTOMATICALLY TALK TO HER LIKE SHE'S OLDER, THOUGH.
WHEN DID I FIRST MEET AI?
SHE WAS JUST ALWAYS THERE.
TAKEO...

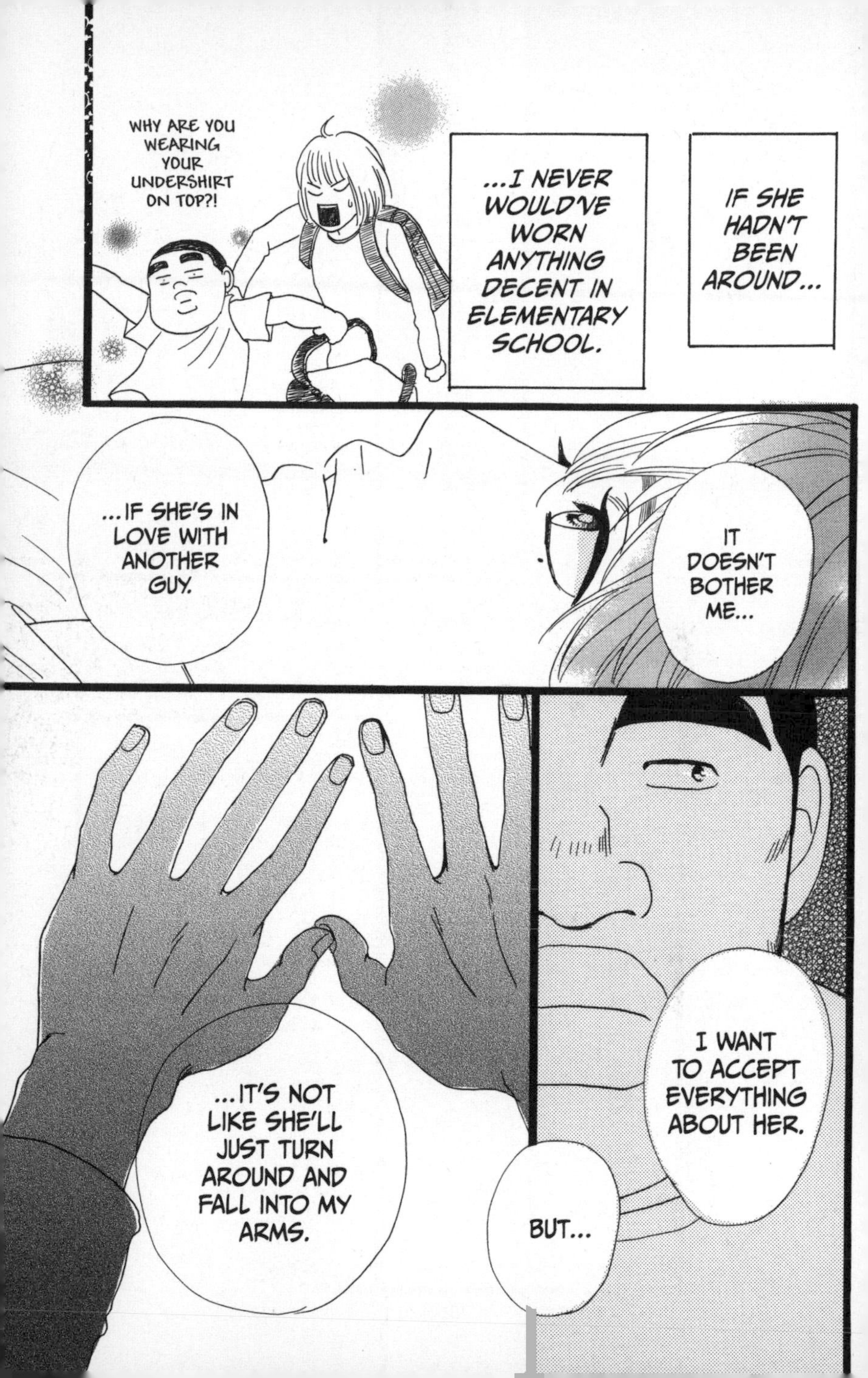
IF SHE HADN'T BEEN AROUND...
...I NEVER WOULD'VE WORN ANYTHING DECENT IN ELEMENTARY SCHOOL.
WHY ARE YOU WEARING YOUR UNDERSHIRT ON TOP?!
IT DOESN'T BOTHER ME...
...IF SHE'S IN LOVE WITH ANOTHER GUY.
I WANT TO ACCEPT EVERYTHING ABOUT HER.
BUT...
...IT'S NOT LIKE SHE'LL JUST TURN AROUND AND FALL INTO MY ARMS.

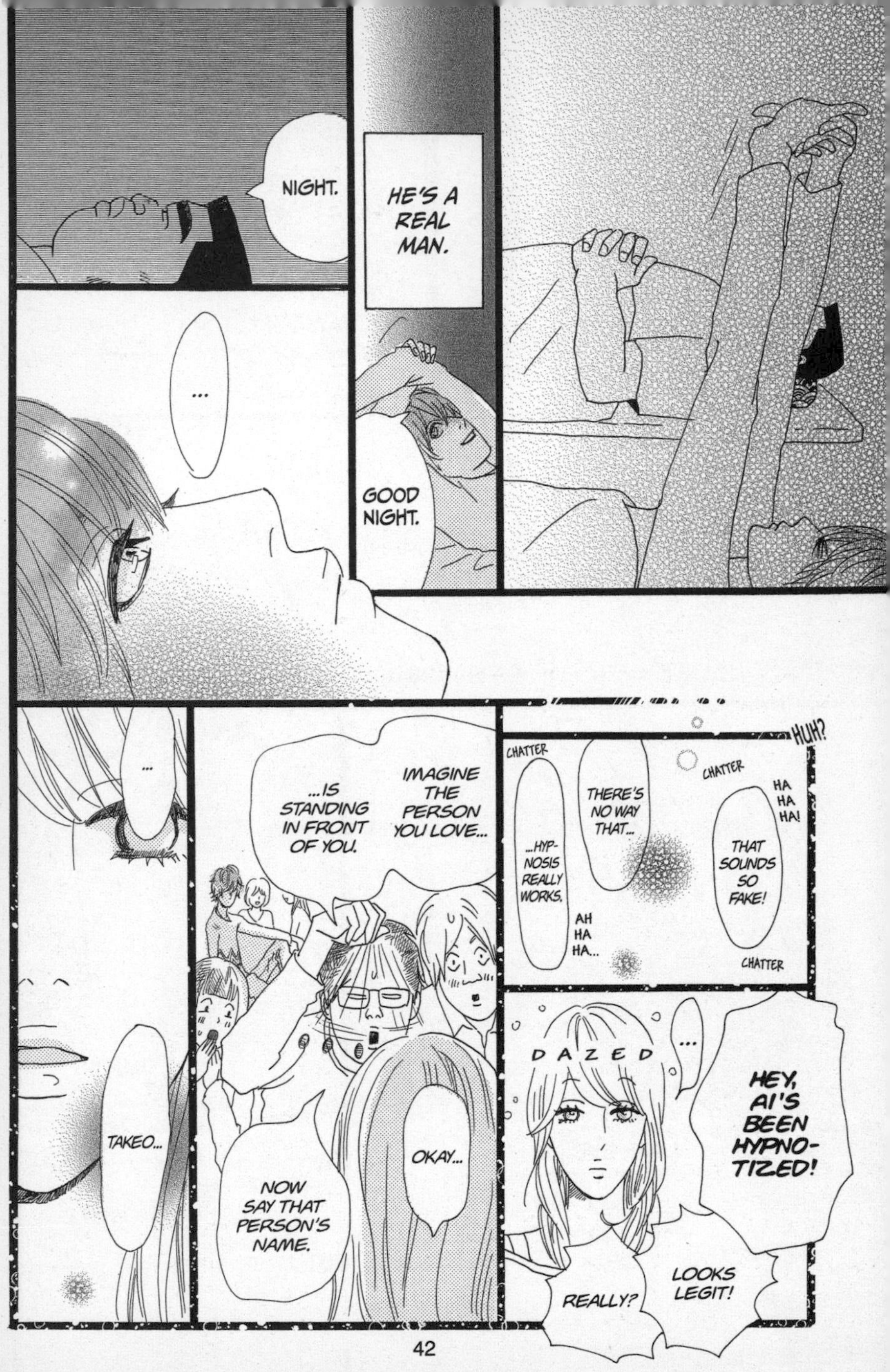
HE'S A REAL MAN.
GOOD NIGHT.
NIGHT.
...
HUH?
CHATTER
HA HA HA!
THAT SOUNDS SO FAKE!
THERE'S NO WAY THAT...
CHATTER
...HYPNOSIS REALLY WORKS.
AH HA HA...
CHATTER
HEY, AI'S BEEN HYPNOTIZED!
...
DAZED
LOOKS LEGIT!
REALLY?
IMAGINE THE PERSON YOU LOVE...
...IS STANDING IN FRONT OF YOU.
OKAY...
NOW SAY THAT PERSON'S NAME.
...
TAKEO...

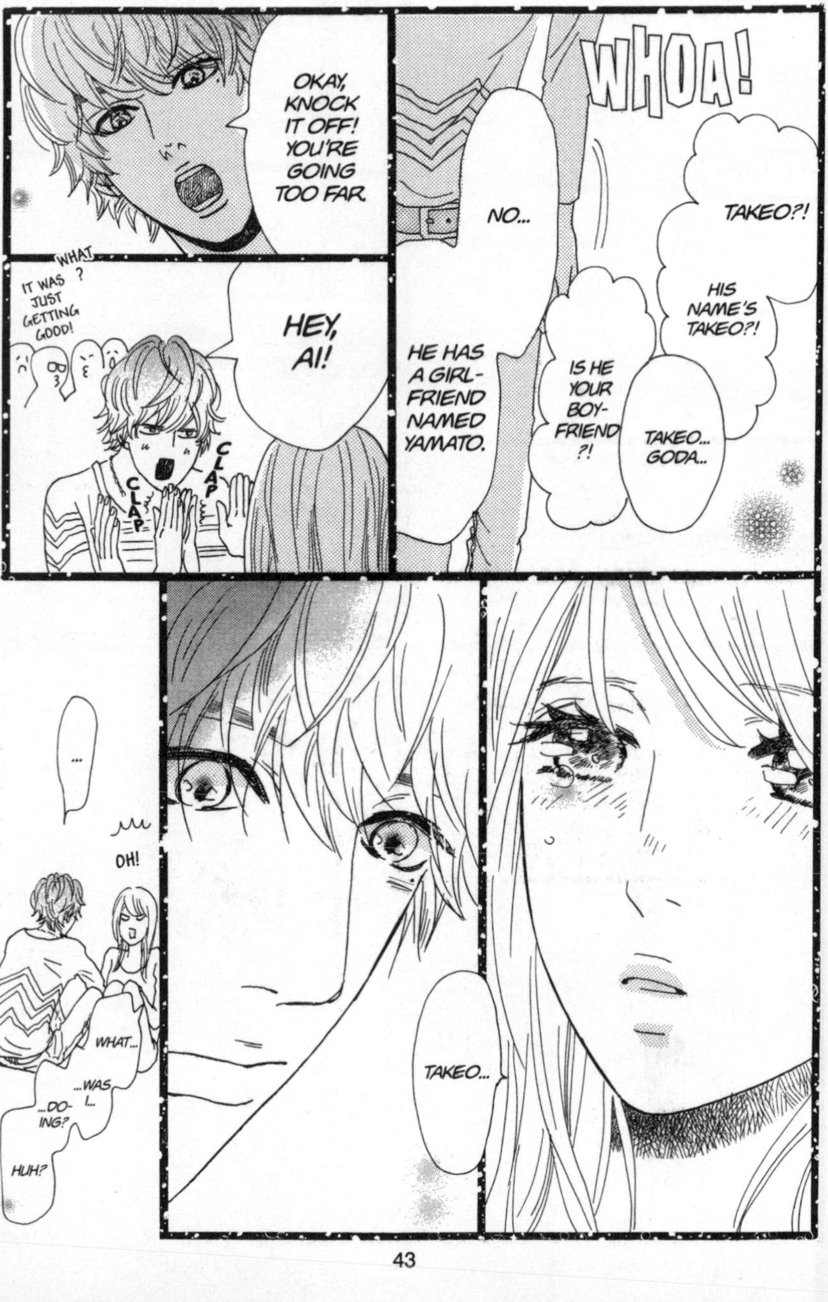
WHOA!
TAKEO?!
HIS NAME'S TAKEO?!
NO...
TAKEO... GODA...
IS HE YOUR BOYFRIEND?!
HE HAS A GIRLFRIEND NAMED YAMATO.
OKAY, KNOCK IT OFF! YOU'RE GOING TOO FAR.
HEY, AI!
CLAP CLAP
WHAT?
IT WAS JUST GETTING GOOD!
TAKEO...
...
OH!
WHAT...
...WAS I...
...DOING?
HUH?

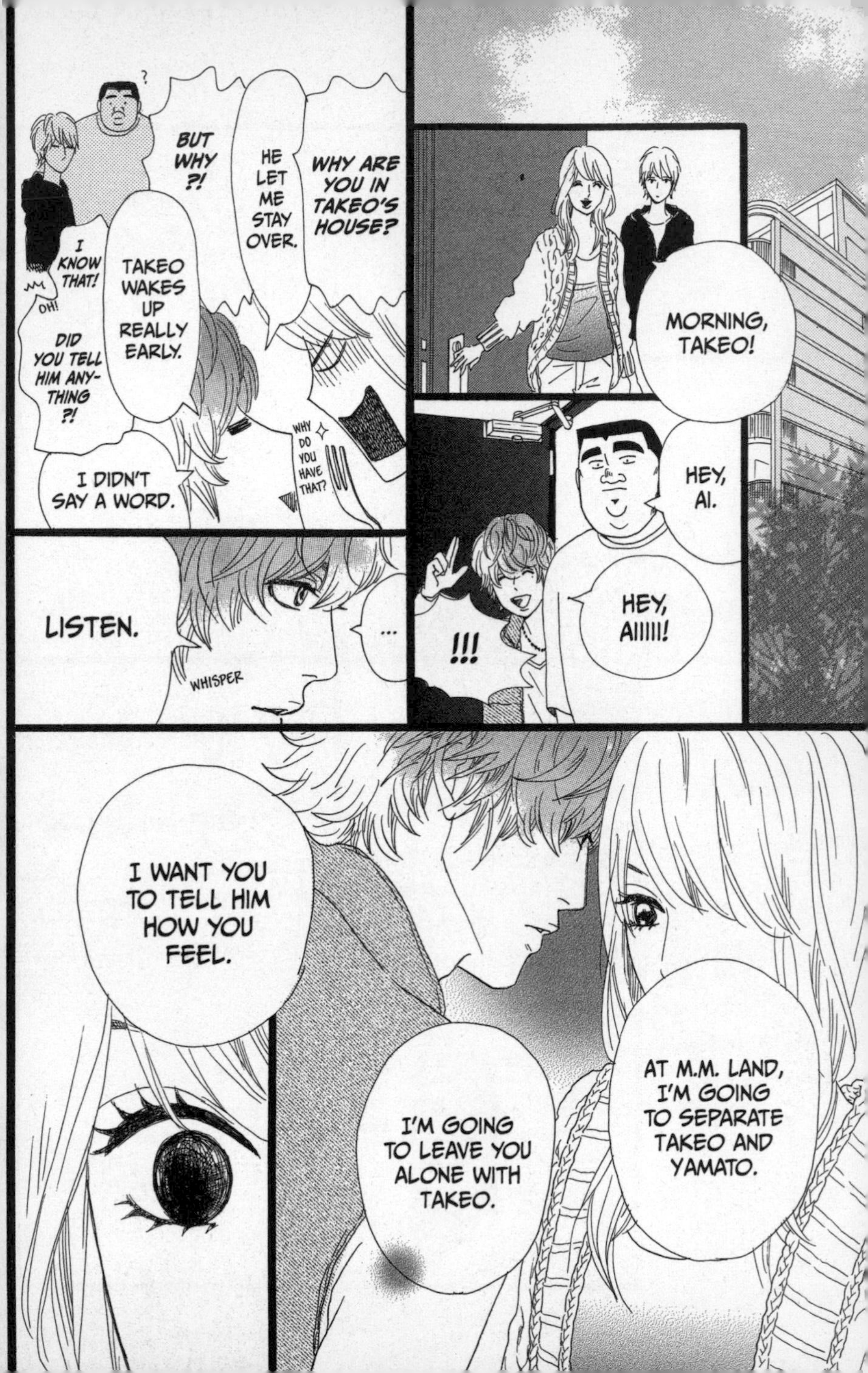
MORNING, TAKEO!
HEY, AI.
HEY, AIIIII!
!!!
WHY ARE YOU IN TAKEO'S HOUSE?
HE LET ME STAY OVER.
BUT WHY ?!
TAKEO WAKES UP REALLY EARLY.
I KNOW THAT!
OH!
DID YOU TELL HIM ANYTHING ?!
WHY DO YOU HAVE THAT?
I DIDN'T SAY A WORD.
...
LISTEN.
WHISPER
AT M.M. LAND, I'M GOING TO SEPARATE TAKEO AND YAMATO.
I'M GOING TO LEAVE YOU ALONE WITH TAKEO.
I WANT YOU TO TELL HIM HOW YOU FEEL.

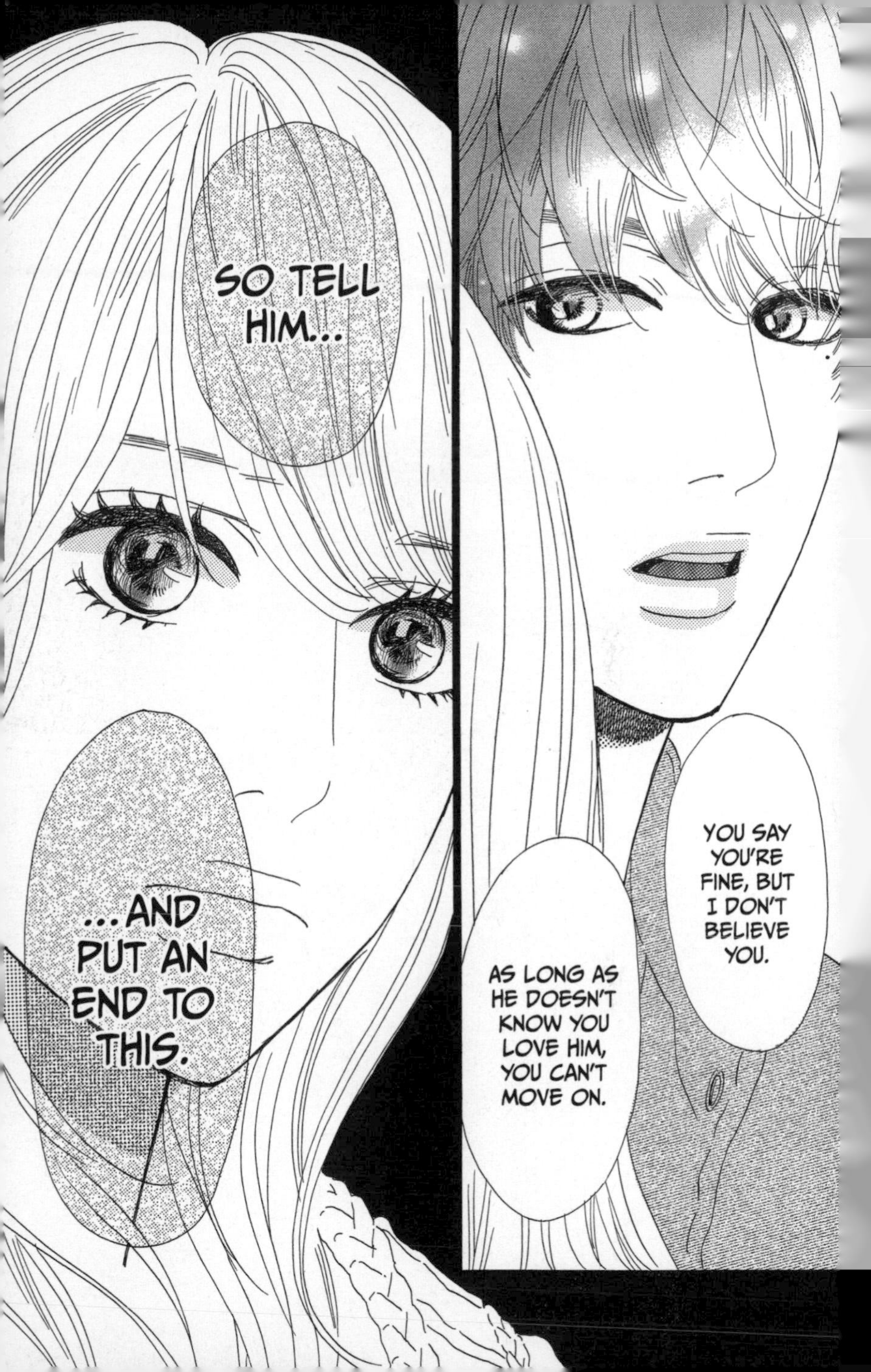
YOU SAY YOU'RE FINE, BUT I DON'T BELIEVE YOU.
AS LONG AS HE DOESN'T KNOW YOU LOVE HIM, YOU CAN'T MOVE ON.
SO TELL HIM...
...AND PUT AN END TO THIS.

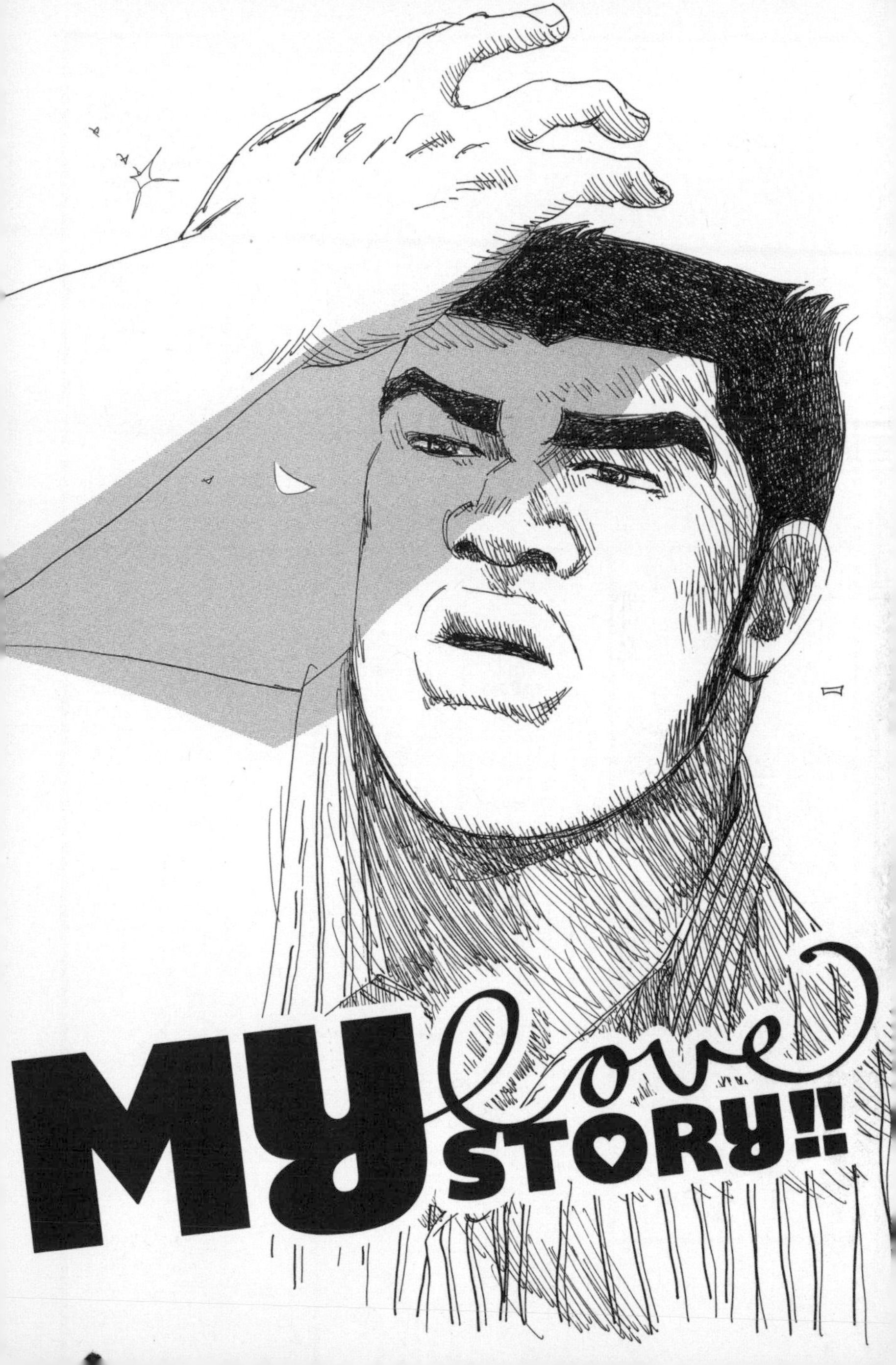
MY love STORY!!

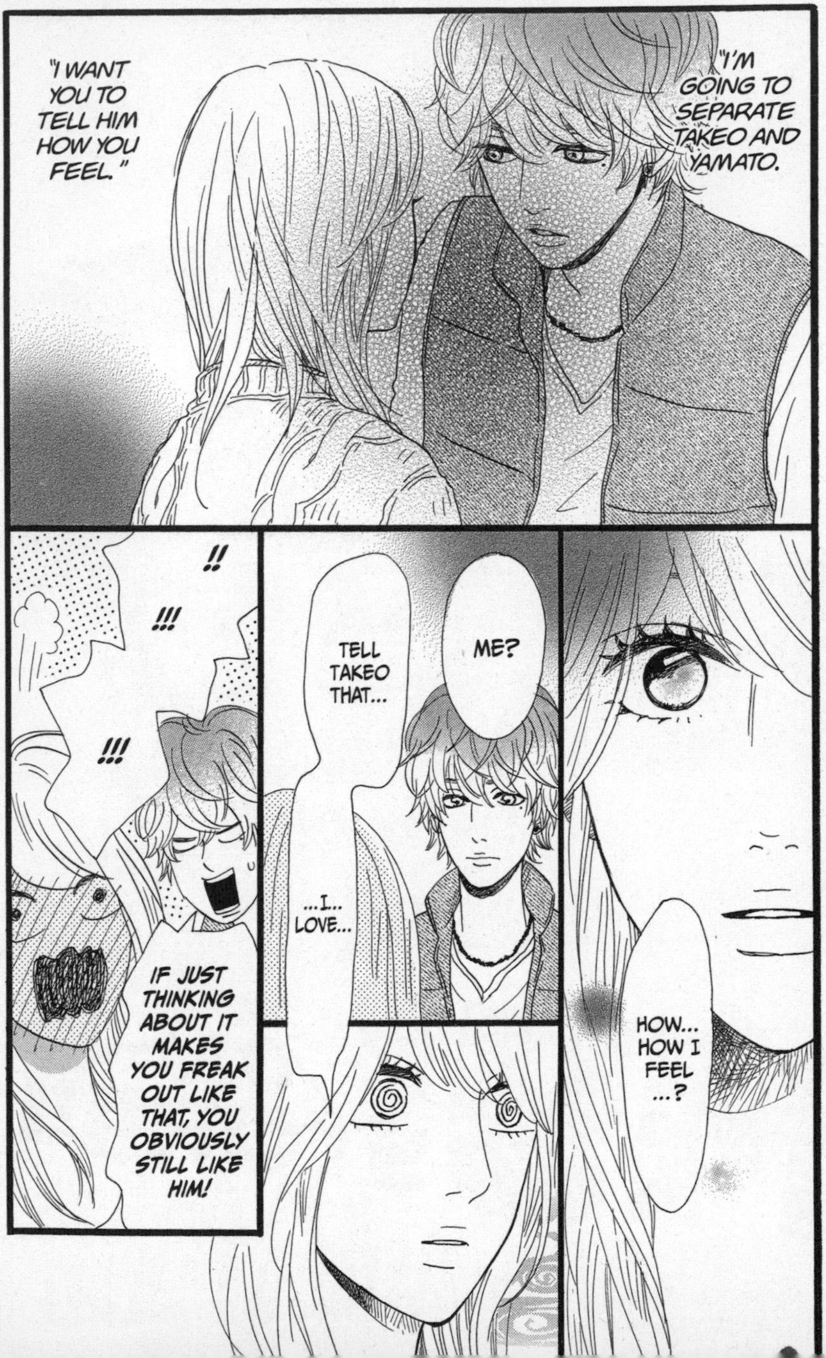
"I'M GOING TO SEPARATE TAKEO AND YAMATO.
"I WANT YOU TO TELL HIM HOW YOU FEEL."
HOW... HOW I FEEL ...?
ME?
TELL TAKEO THAT...
...I... LOVE...
!!
!!!
!!!
IF JUST THINKING ABOUT IT MAKES YOU FREAK OUT LIKE THAT, YOU OBVIOUSLY STILL LIKE HIM!

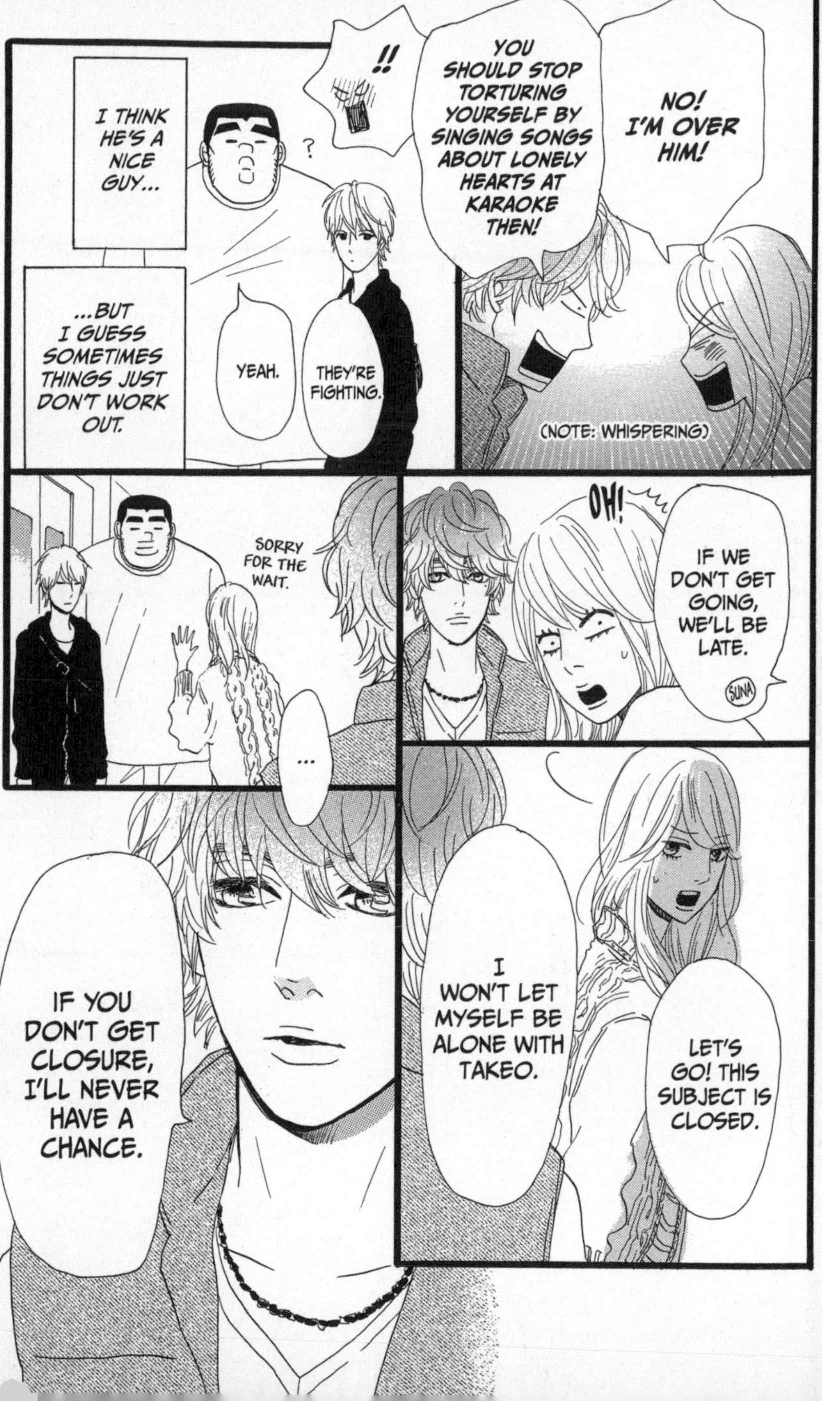
NO! I'M OVER HIM!
YOU SHOULD STOP TORTURING YOURSELF BY SINGING SONGS ABOUT LONELY HEARTS AT KARAOKE THEN!
(NOTE: WHISPERING)
!!
THEY'RE FIGHTING.
YEAH.
I THINK HE'S A NICE GUY...
...BUT I GUESS SOMETIMES THINGS JUST DON'T WORK OUT.
OH!
IF WE DON'T GET GOING, WE'LL BE LATE.
SUNA
SORRY FOR THE WAIT.
...
LET'S GO! THIS SUBJECT IS CLOSED.
I WON'T LET MYSELF BE ALONE WITH TAKEO.
IF YOU DON'T GET CLOSURE, I'LL NEVER HAVE A CHANCE.

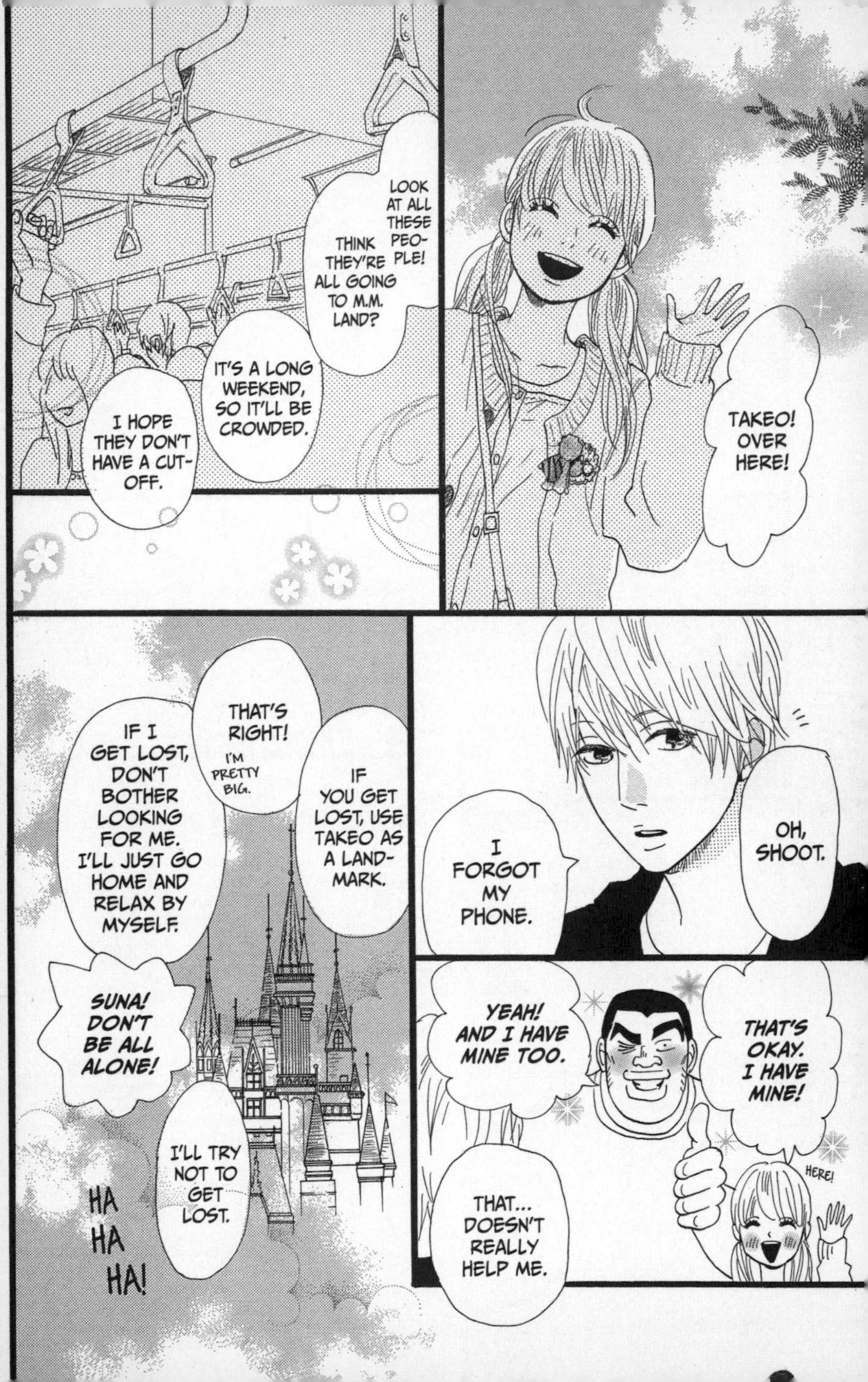
TAKEO! OVER HERE!
LOOK AT ALL THESE PEOPLE!
THINK THEY'RE ALL GOING TO M.M. LAND?
IT'S A LONG WEEKEND, SO IT'LL BE CROWDED.
I HOPE THEY DON'T HAVE A CUT-OFF.
OH, SHOOT.
I FORGOT MY PHONE.
THAT'S OKAY. I HAVE MINE!
HERE!
YEAH! AND I HAVE MINE TOO.
THAT... DOESN'T REALLY HELP ME.
IF YOU GET LOST, USE TAKEO AS A LANDMARK.
THAT'S RIGHT!
I'M PRETTY BIG.
IF I GET LOST, DON'T BOTHER LOOKING FOR ME. I'LL JUST GO HOME AND RELAX BY MYSELF.
SUNA! DON'T BE ALL ALONE!
I'LL TRY NOT TO GET LOST.
HA HA HA!

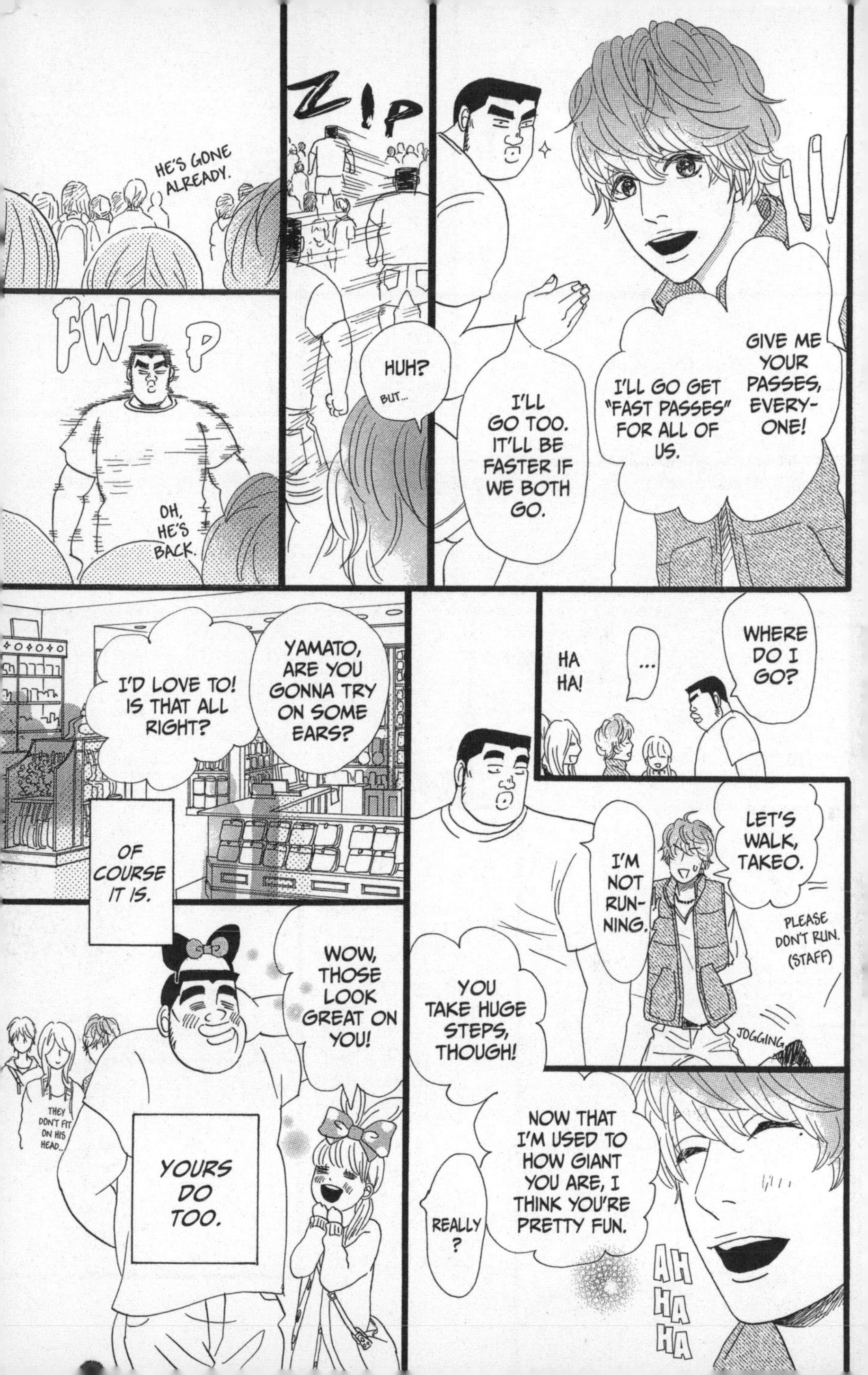
GIVE ME YOUR PASSES, EVERY-ONE!
I'LL GO GET "FAST PASSES" FOR ALL OF US.
I'LL GO TOO. IT'LL BE FASTER IF WE BOTH GO.
ZIP
HUH?
BUT...
HE'S GONE ALREADY.
FWIP
OH, HE'S BACK.
WHERE DO I GO?
...
HA HA!
LET'S WALK, TAKEO.
I'M NOT RUN-NING.
PLEASE DON'T RUN. (STAFF)
JOGGING
YOU TAKE HUGE STEPS, THOUGH!
NOW THAT I'M USED TO HOW GIANT YOU ARE, I THINK YOU'RE PRETTY FUN.
AH HA HA
REALLY?
YAMATO, ARE YOU GONNA TRY ON SOME EARS?
I'D LOVE TO! IS THAT ALL RIGHT?
OF COURSE IT IS.
WOW, THOSE LOOK GREAT ON YOU!
YOURS DO TOO.
THEY DON'T FIT ON HIS HEAD...

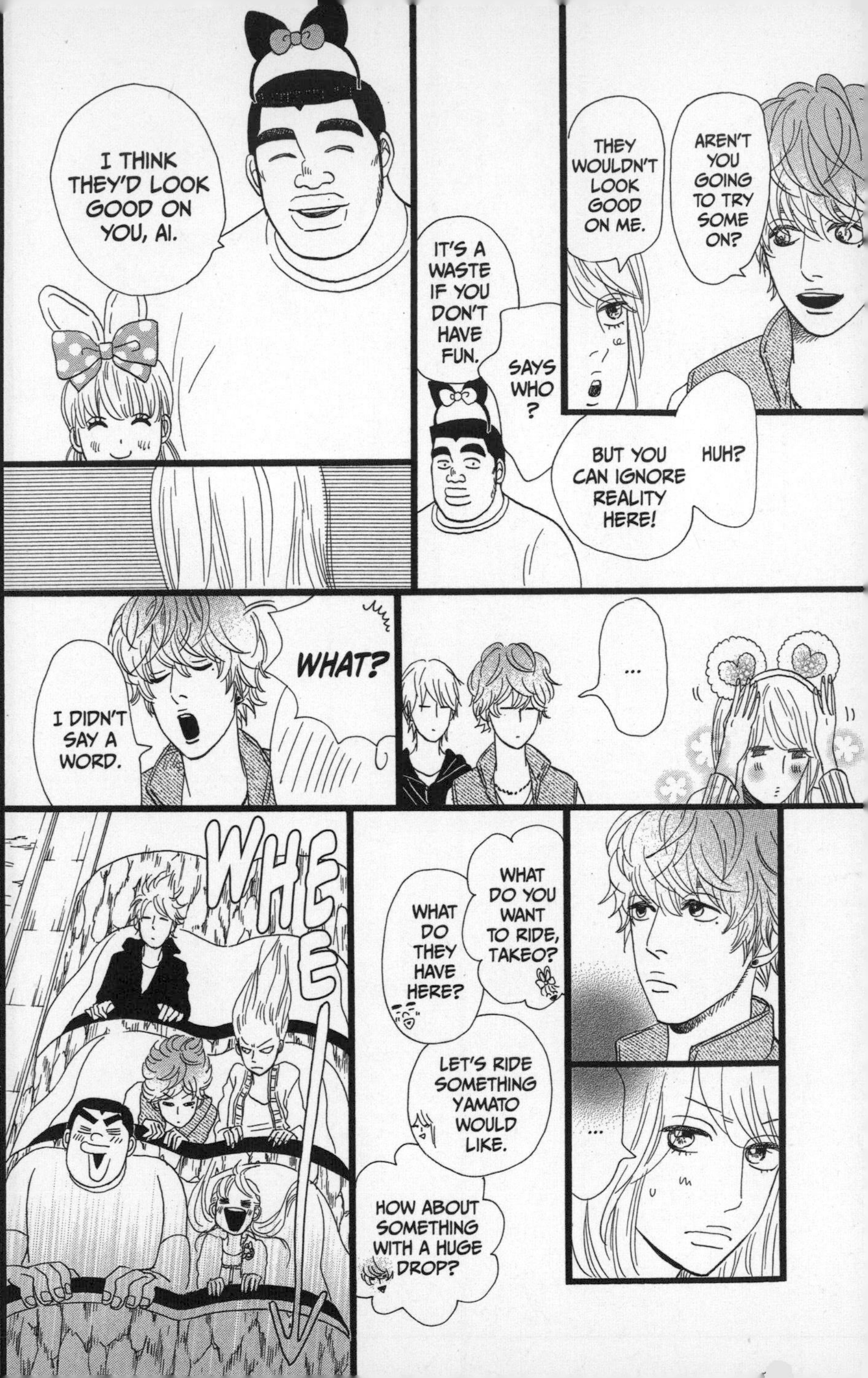
AREN'T YOU GOING TO TRY SOME ON?
THEY WOULDN'T LOOK GOOD ON ME.
IT'S A WASTE IF YOU DON'T HAVE FUN.
SAYS WHO?
BUT YOU CAN IGNORE REALITY HERE!
HUH?
I THINK THEY'D LOOK GOOD ON YOU, AI.
...
WHAT?
I DIDN'T SAY A WORD.
...
WHAT DO YOU WANT TO RIDE, TAKEO?
WHAT DO THEY HAVE HERE?
LET'S RIDE SOMETHING YAMATO WOULD LIKE.
HOW ABOUT SOMETHING WITH A HUGE DROP?
WHEE

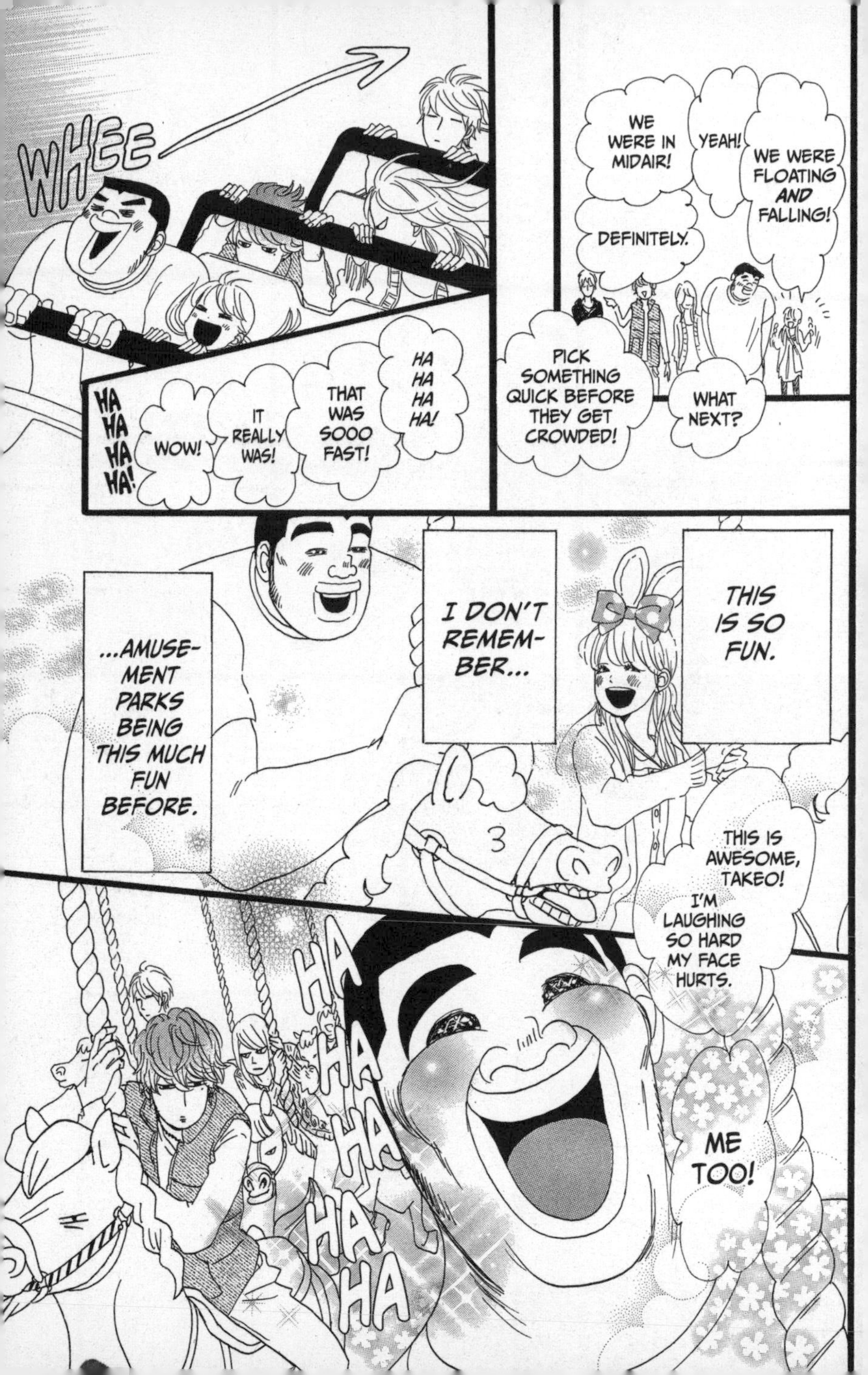
WE WERE FLOATING AND FALLING!
YEAH!
WE WERE IN MIDAIR!
DEFINITELY.
WHAT NEXT?
PICK SOMETHING QUICK BEFORE THEY GET CROWDED!
WHEE
HA HA HA HA!
THAT WAS SOOO FAST!
IT REALLY WAS!
WOW!
HA HA HA HA!
THIS IS SO FUN.
I DON'T REMEMBER...
...AMUSEMENT PARKS BEING THIS MUCH FUN BEFORE.
THIS IS AWESOME, TAKEO!
I'M LAUGHING SO HARD MY FACE HURTS.
ME TOO!
HA HA HA HA HA

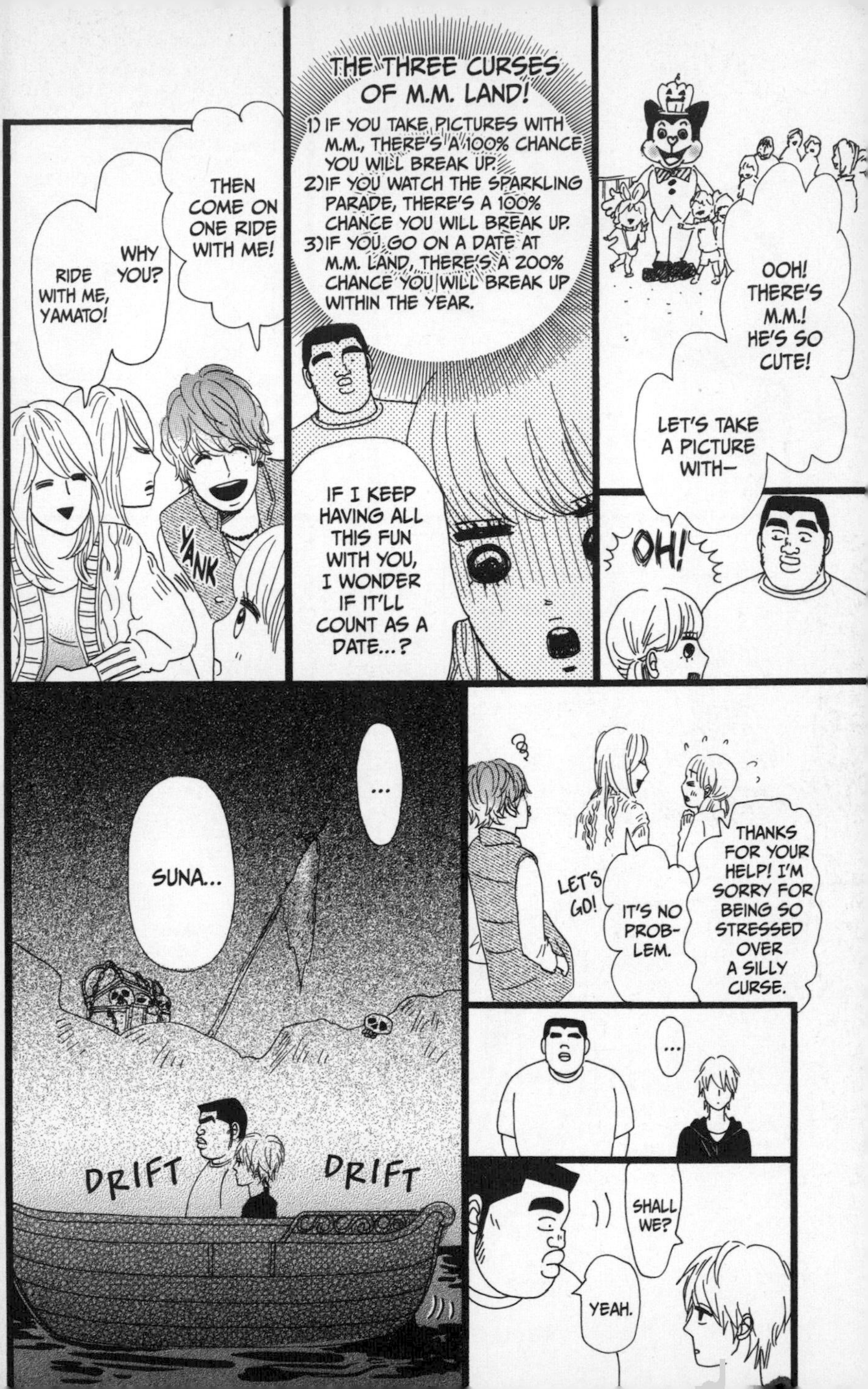
OOH! THERE'S M.M.! HE'S SO CUTE!
LET'S TAKE A PICTURE WITH—
OH!
THE THREE CURSES OF M.M. LAND!
1) IF YOU TAKE PICTURES WITH M.M., THERE'S A 100% CHANCE YOU WILL BREAK UP.
2) IF YOU WATCH THE SPARKLING PARADE, THERE'S A 100% CHANCE YOU WILL BREAK UP.
3) IF YOU GO ON A DATE AT M.M. LAND, THERE'S A 200% CHANCE YOU WILL BREAK UP WITHIN THE YEAR.
IF I KEEP HAVING ALL THIS FUN WITH YOU, I WONDER IF IT'LL COUNT AS A DATE...?
THEN COME ON ONE RIDE WITH ME!
WHY YOU?
RIDE WITH ME, YAMATO!
YANK
THANKS FOR YOUR HELP! I'M SORRY FOR BEING SO STRESSED OVER A SILLY CURSE.
IT'S NO PROBLEM.
LET'S GO!
...
SHALL WE?
YEAH.
...
SUNA...
DRIFT
DRIFT

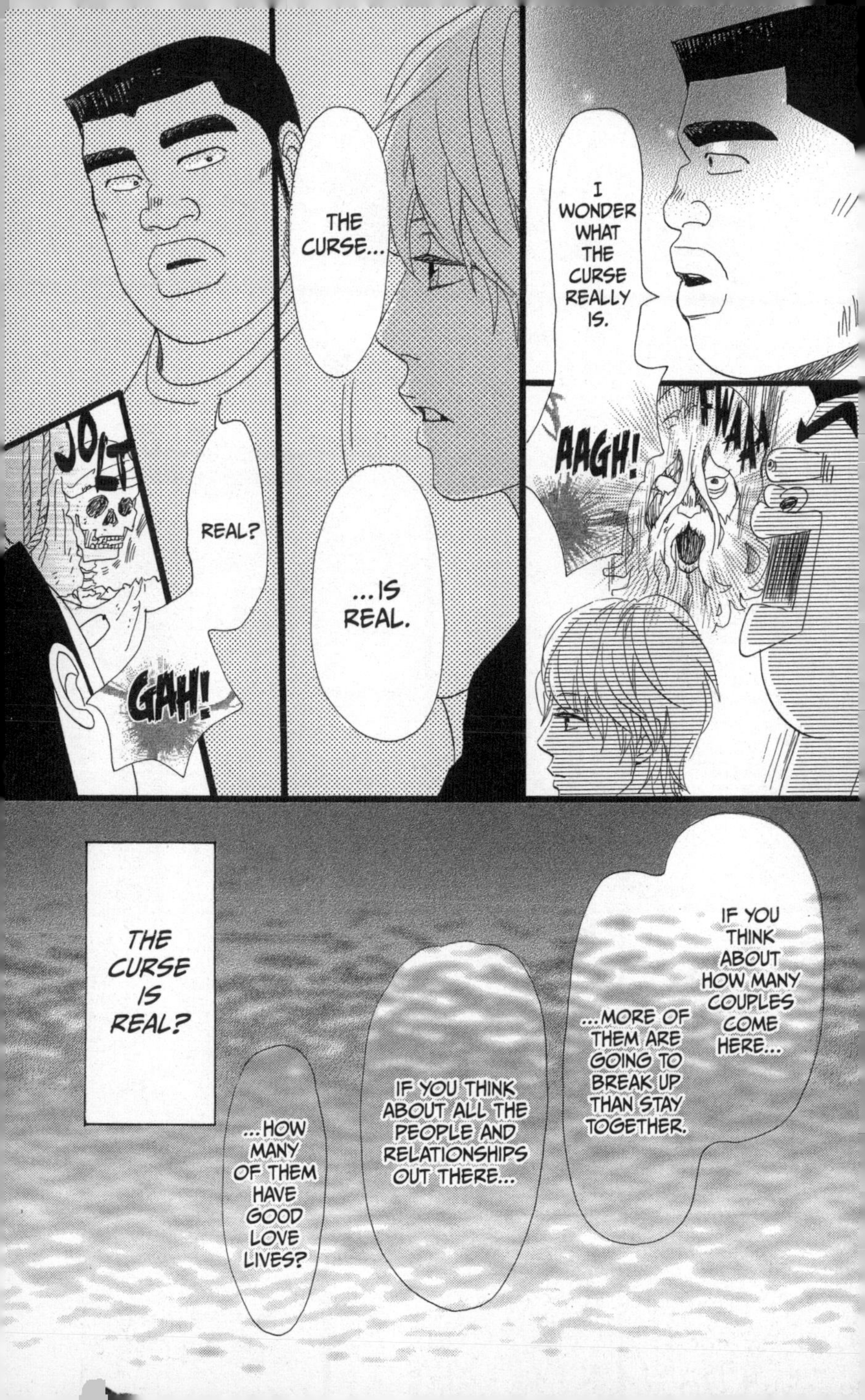
I WONDER WHAT THE CURSE REALLY IS.
FWAAA
AAGH!
THE CURSE...
...IS REAL.
REAL?
JOLT
GAH!
IF YOU THINK ABOUT HOW MANY COUPLES COME HERE...
...MORE OF THEM ARE GOING TO BREAK UP THAN STAY TOGETHER.
IF YOU THINK ABOUT ALL THE PEOPLE AND RELATIONSHIPS OUT THERE...
...HOW MANY OF THEM HAVE GOOD LOVE LIVES?
THE CURSE IS REAL?

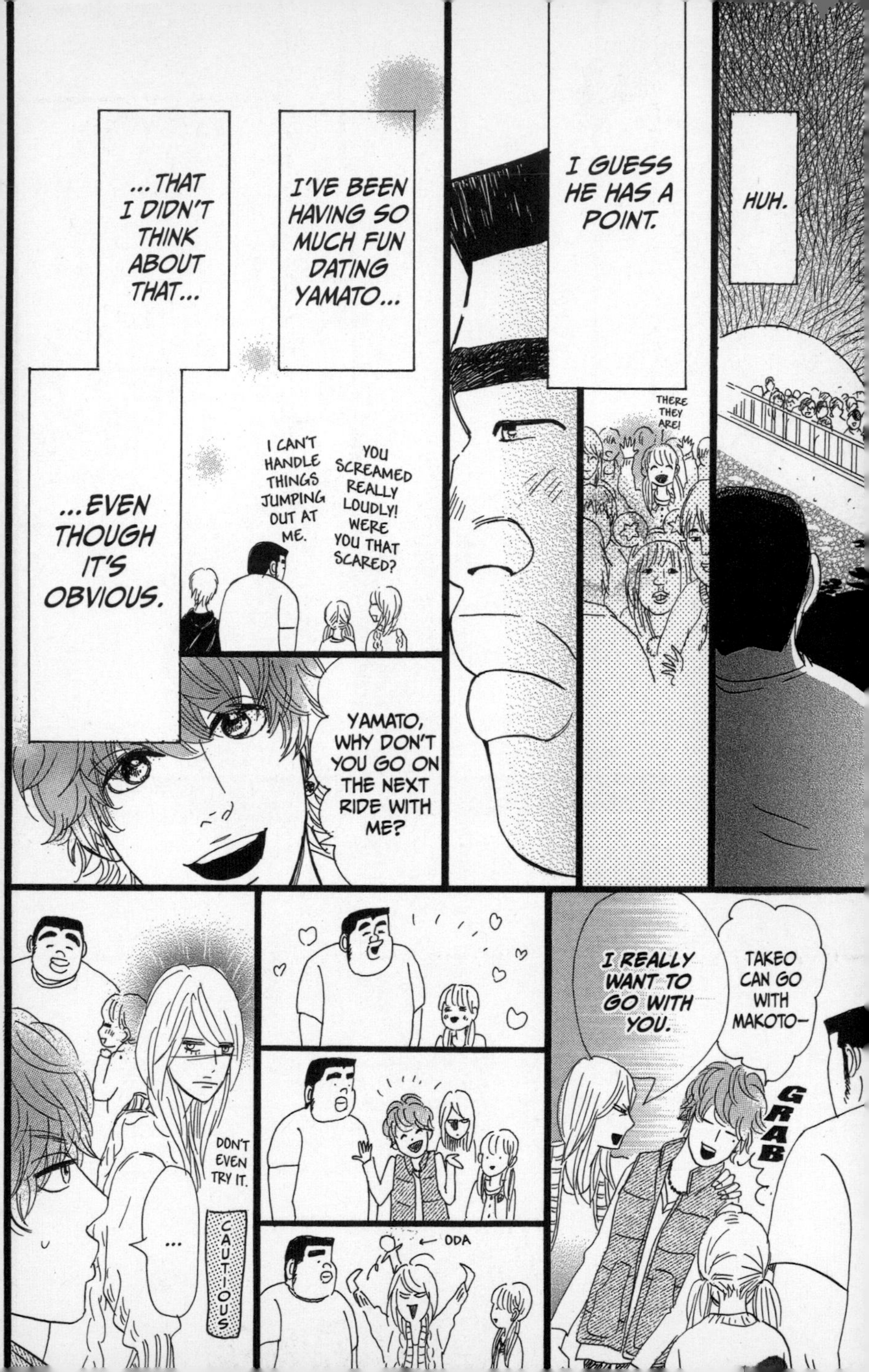
HUH.
I GUESS HE HAS A POINT.
THERE THEY ARE!
I'VE BEEN HAVING SO MUCH FUN DATING YAMATO...
...THAT I DIDN'T THINK ABOUT THAT...
...EVEN THOUGH IT'S OBVIOUS.
YOU SCREAMED REALLY LOUDLY! WERE YOU THAT SCARED?
I CAN'T HANDLE THINGS JUMPING OUT AT ME.
YAMATO, WHY DON'T YOU GO ON THE NEXT RIDE WITH ME?
TAKEO CAN GO WITH MAKOTO—
I REALLY WANT TO GO WITH YOU.
GRAB
← ODA
DON'T EVEN TRY IT.
...
CAUTIOUS

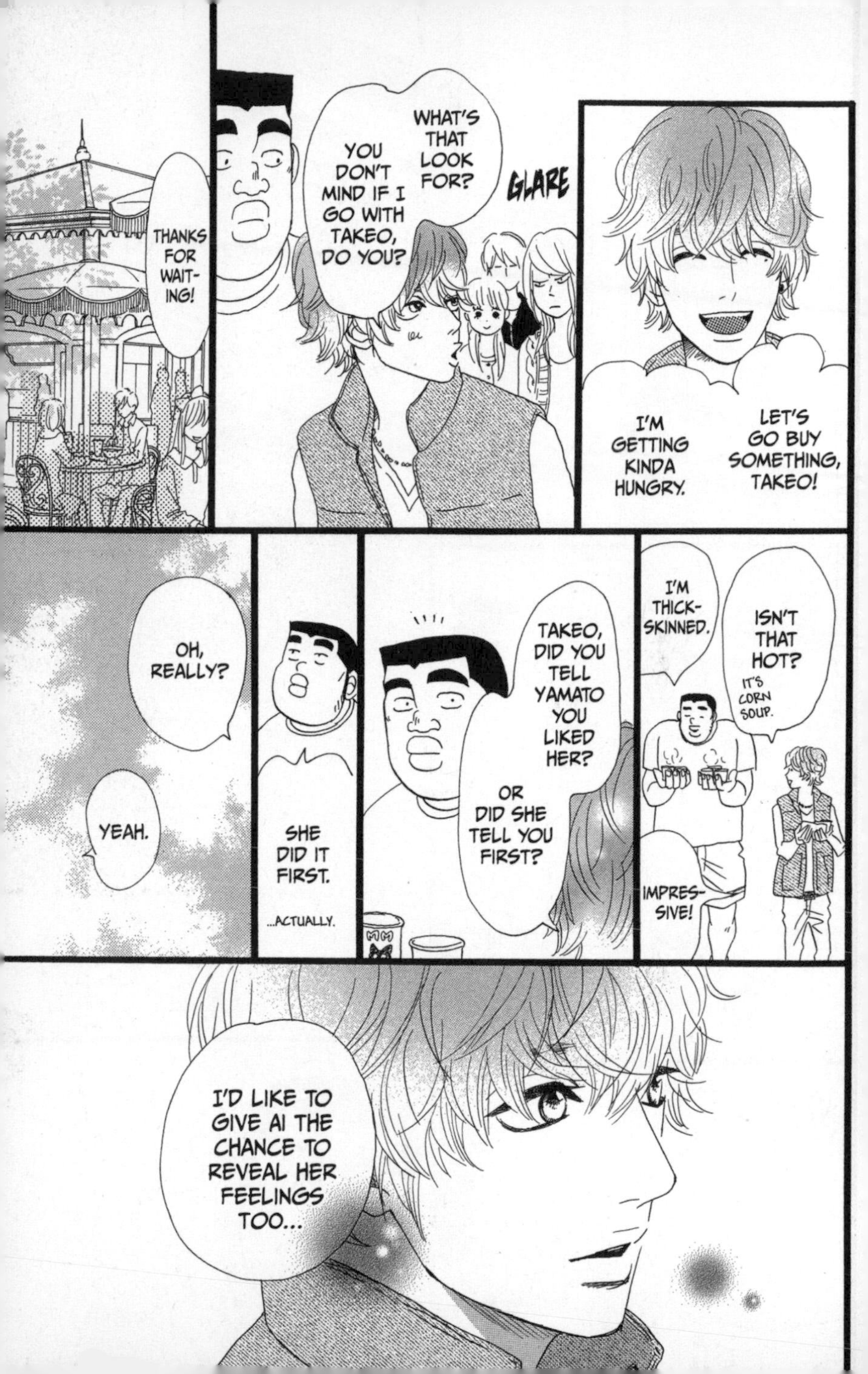
LET'S GO BUY SOMETHING, TAKEO!
I'M GETTING KINDA HUNGRY.
GLARE
WHAT'S THAT LOOK FOR?
YOU DON'T MIND IF I GO WITH TAKEO, DO YOU?
THANKS FOR WAIT-ING!
ISN'T THAT HOT?
IT'S CORN SOUP.
I'M THICK-SKINNED.
IMPRES-SIVE!
TAKEO, DID YOU TELL YAMATO YOU LIKED HER?
OR DID SHE TELL YOU FIRST?
SHE DID IT FIRST.
...ACTUALLY.
OH, REALLY?
YEAH.
I'D LIKE TO GIVE AI THE CHANCE TO REVEAL HER FEELINGS TOO...

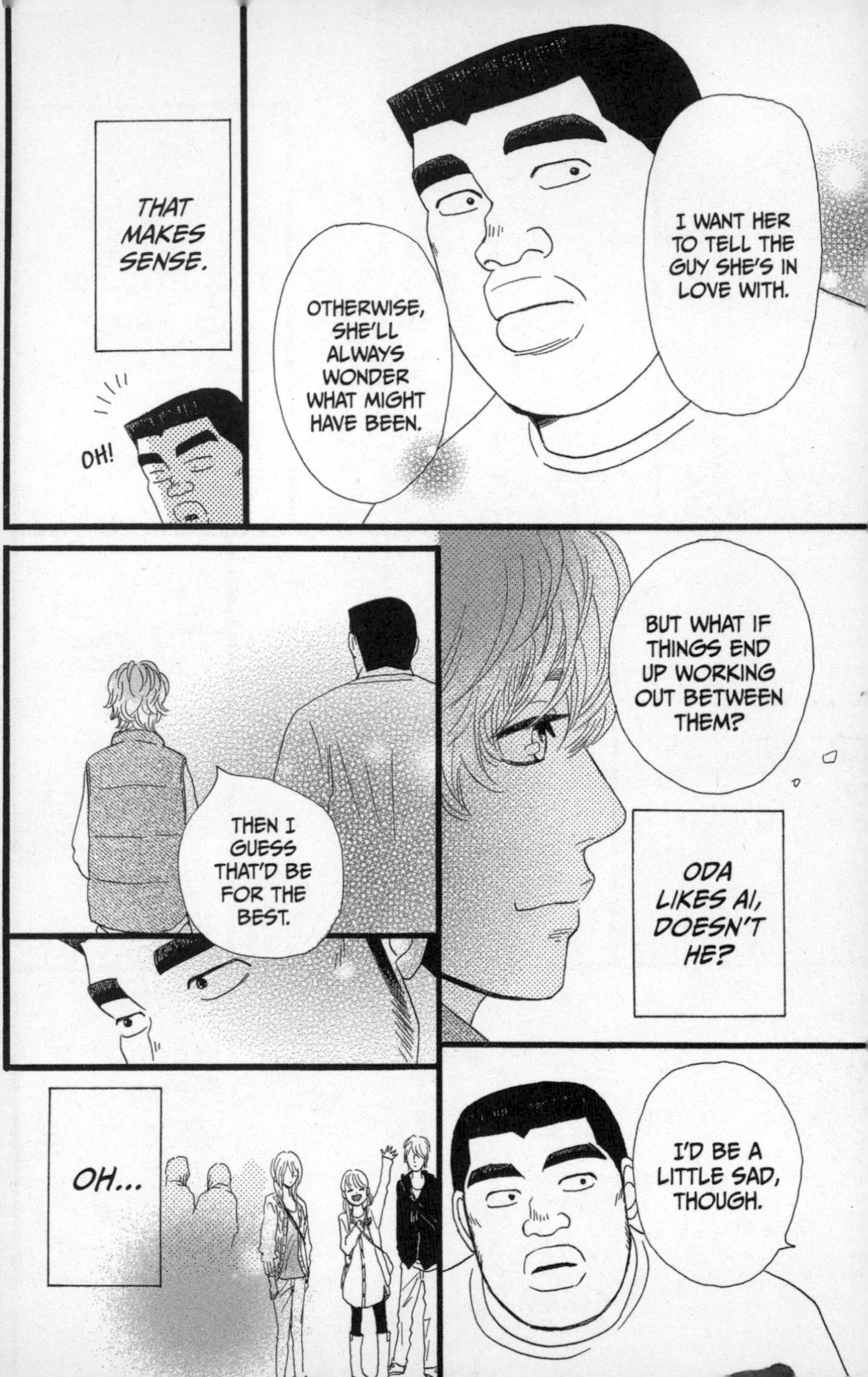
I WANT HER TO TELL THE GUY SHE'S IN LOVE WITH.
OTHERWISE, SHE'LL ALWAYS WONDER WHAT MIGHT HAVE BEEN.
THAT MAKES SENSE.
OH!
BUT WHAT IF THINGS END UP WORKING OUT BETWEEN THEM?
ODA LIKES AI, DOESN'T HE?
THEN I GUESS THAT'D BE FOR THE BEST.
I'D BE A LITTLE SAD, THOUGH.
OH...

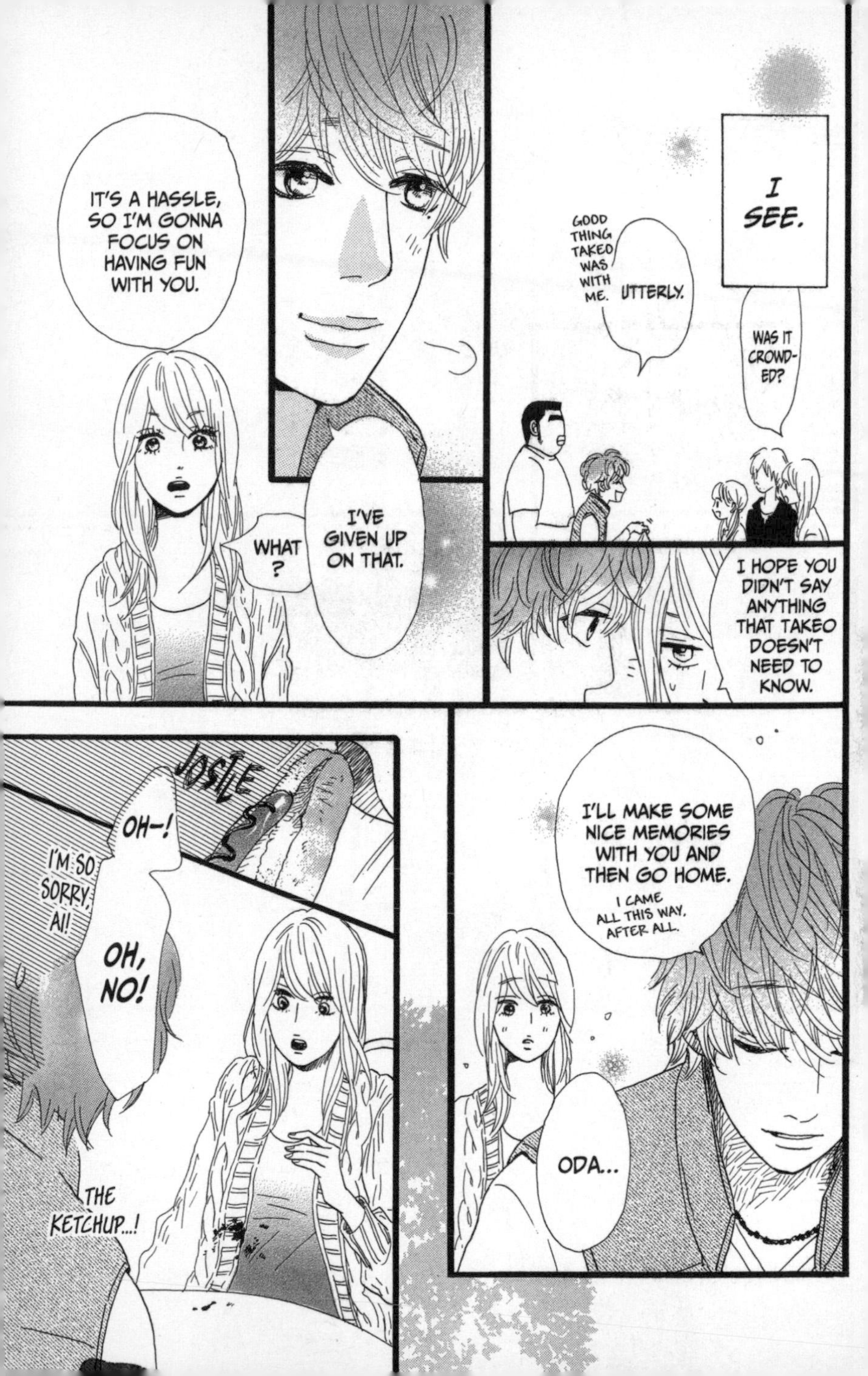
I SEE.
WAS IT CROWDED?
UTTERLY.
GOOD THING TAKEO WAS WITH ME.
I HOPE YOU DIDN'T SAY ANYTHING THAT TAKEO DOESN'T NEED TO KNOW.
I'VE GIVEN UP ON THAT.
IT'S A HASSLE, SO I'M GONNA FOCUS ON HAVING FUN WITH YOU.
WHAT?
I'LL MAKE SOME NICE MEMORIES WITH YOU AND THEN GO HOME.
I CAME ALL THIS WAY, AFTER ALL.
ODA...
JOSILE
OH-!
I'M SO SORRY, AI!
OH, NO!
THE KETCHUP...!

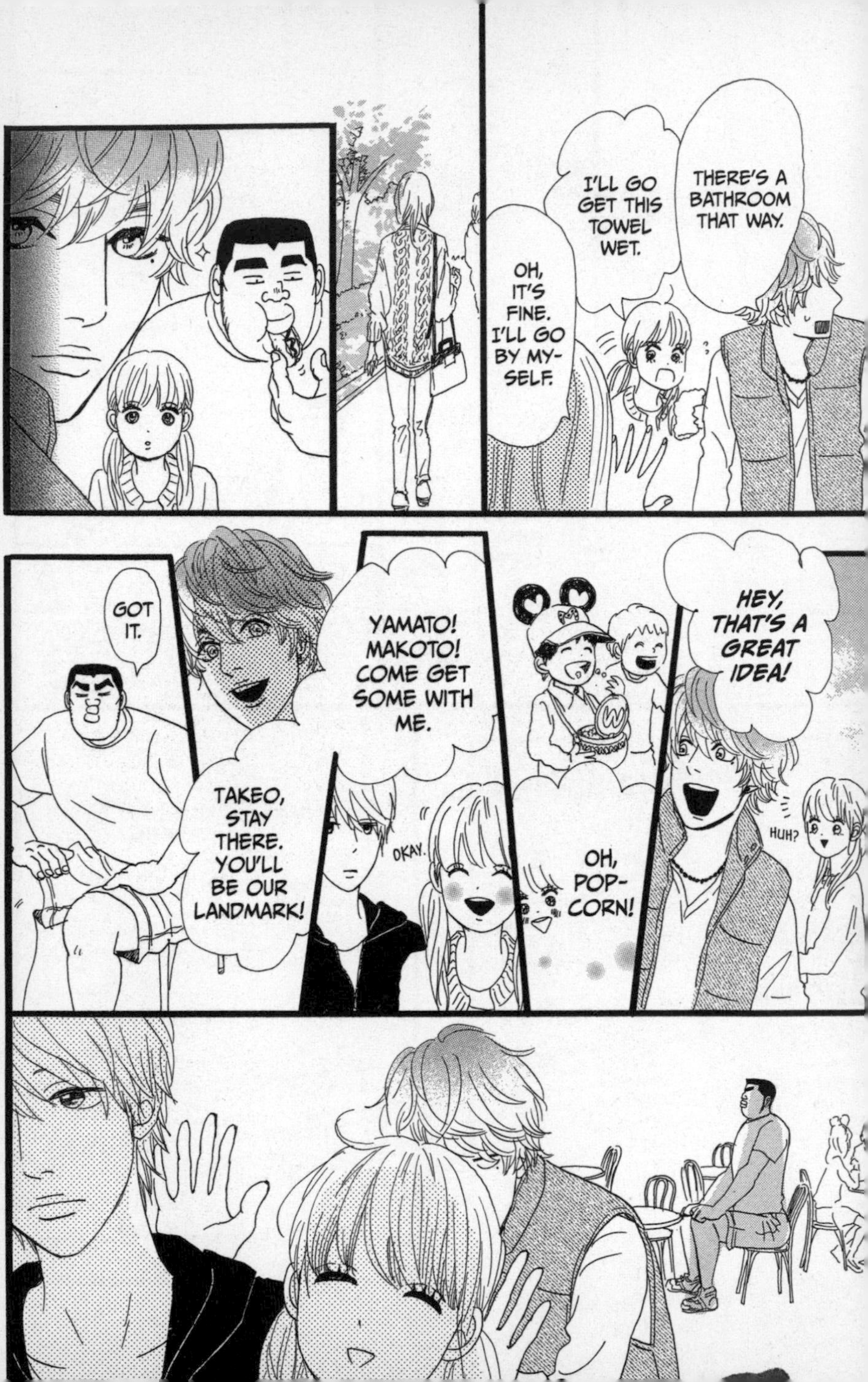
THERE'S A BATHROOM THAT WAY.
I'LL GO GET THIS TOWEL WET.
OH, IT'S FINE. I'LL GO BY MY-SELF.
HEY, THAT'S A GREAT IDEA!
HUH?
OH, POP-CORN!
YAMATO! MAKOTO! COME GET SOME WITH ME.
OKAY.
TAKEO, STAY THERE. YOU'LL BE OUR LANDMARK!
GOT IT.

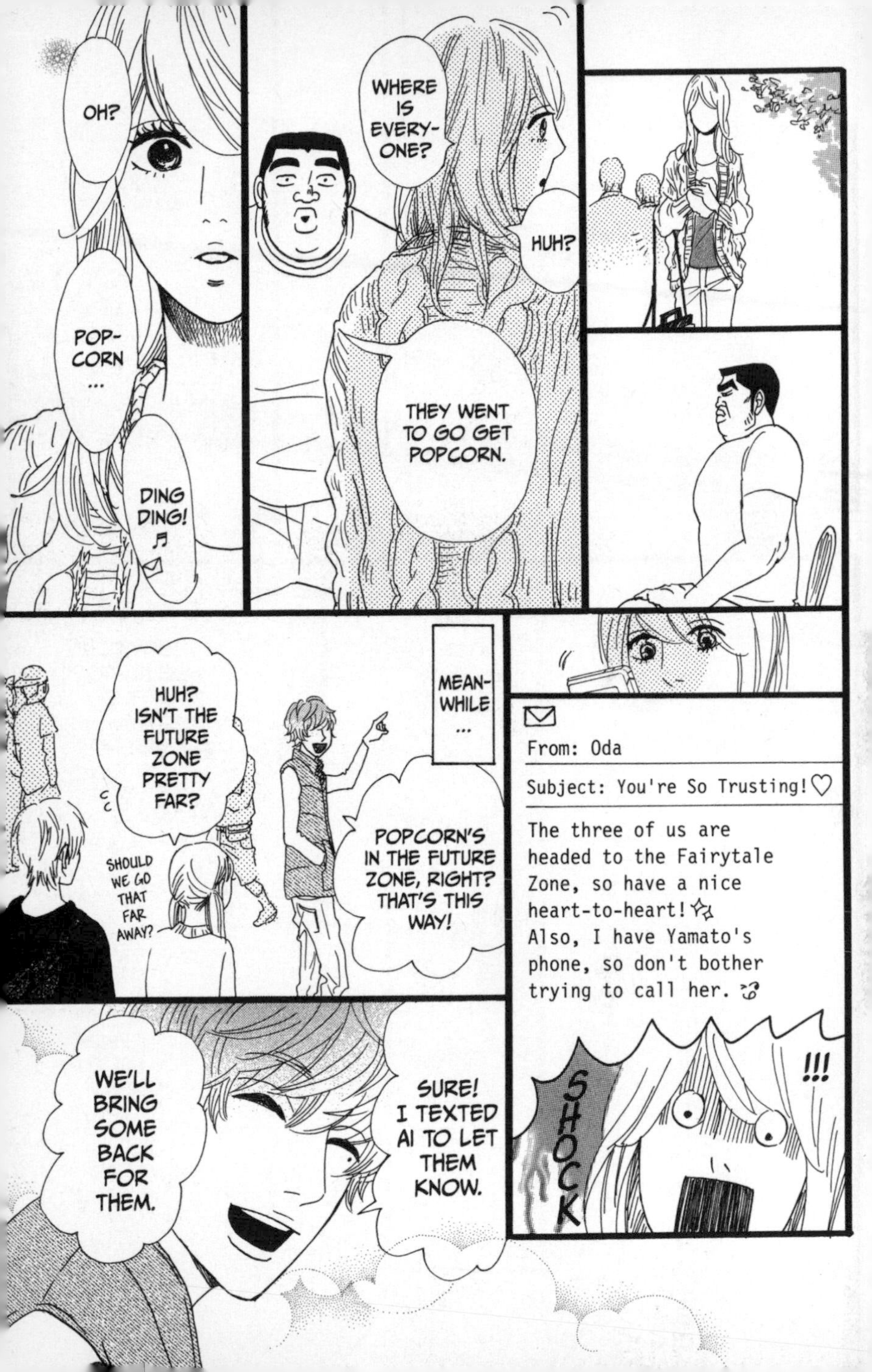
WHERE IS EVERYONE?
HUH?
THEY WENT TO GO GET POPCORN.
OH?
POP-CORN...
DING DING! ♫
From: Oda
Subject: You're So Trusting! ♡
The three of us are headed to the Fairytale Zone, so have a nice heart-to-heart! Also, I have Yamato's phone, so don't bother trying to call her.
!!!
SHOCK
MEAN-WHILE...
POPCORN'S IN THE FUTURE ZONE, RIGHT? THAT'S THIS WAY!
HUH? ISN'T THE FUTURE ZONE PRETTY FAR?
SHOULD WE GO THAT FAR AWAY?
SURE! I TEXTED AI TO LET THEM KNOW.
WE'LL BRING SOME BACK FOR THEM.

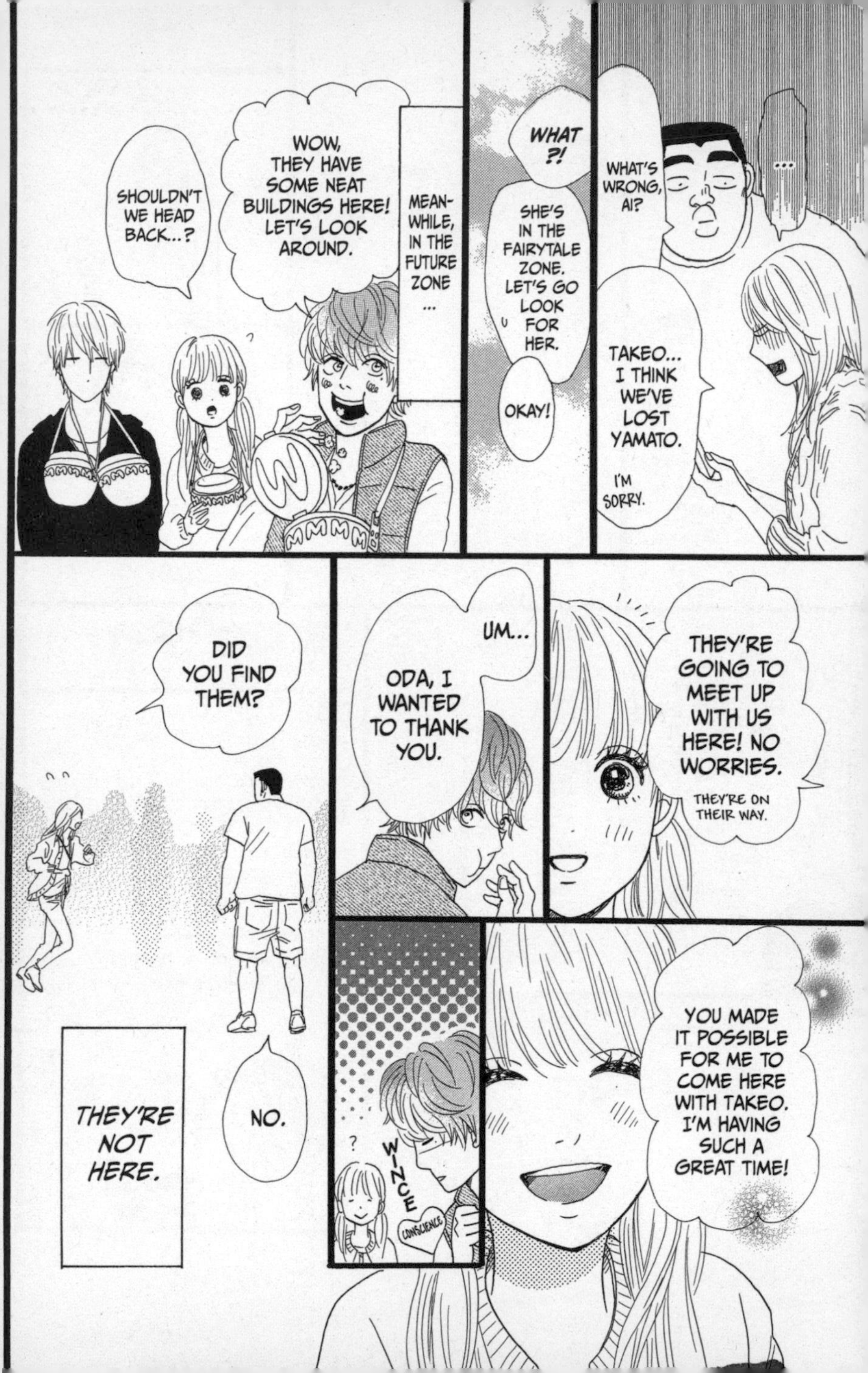
...
WHAT'S WRONG, AI?
TAKEO... I THINK WE'VE LOST YAMATO.
I'M SORRY.
WHAT?!
SHE'S IN THE FAIRYTALE ZONE. LET'S GO LOOK FOR HER.
OKAY!
MEAN-WHILE, IN THE FUTURE ZONE ...
WOW, THEY HAVE SOME NEAT BUILDINGS HERE! LET'S LOOK AROUND.
SHOULDN'T WE HEAD BACK...?
THEY'RE GOING TO MEET UP WITH US HERE! NO WORRIES.
THEY'RE ON THEIR WAY.
UM...
ODA, I WANTED TO THANK YOU.
YOU MADE IT POSSIBLE FOR ME TO COME HERE WITH TAKEO. I'M HAVING SUCH A GREAT TIME!
WINCE
CONSCIENCE
?
DID YOU FIND THEM?
NO.
THEY'RE NOT HERE.

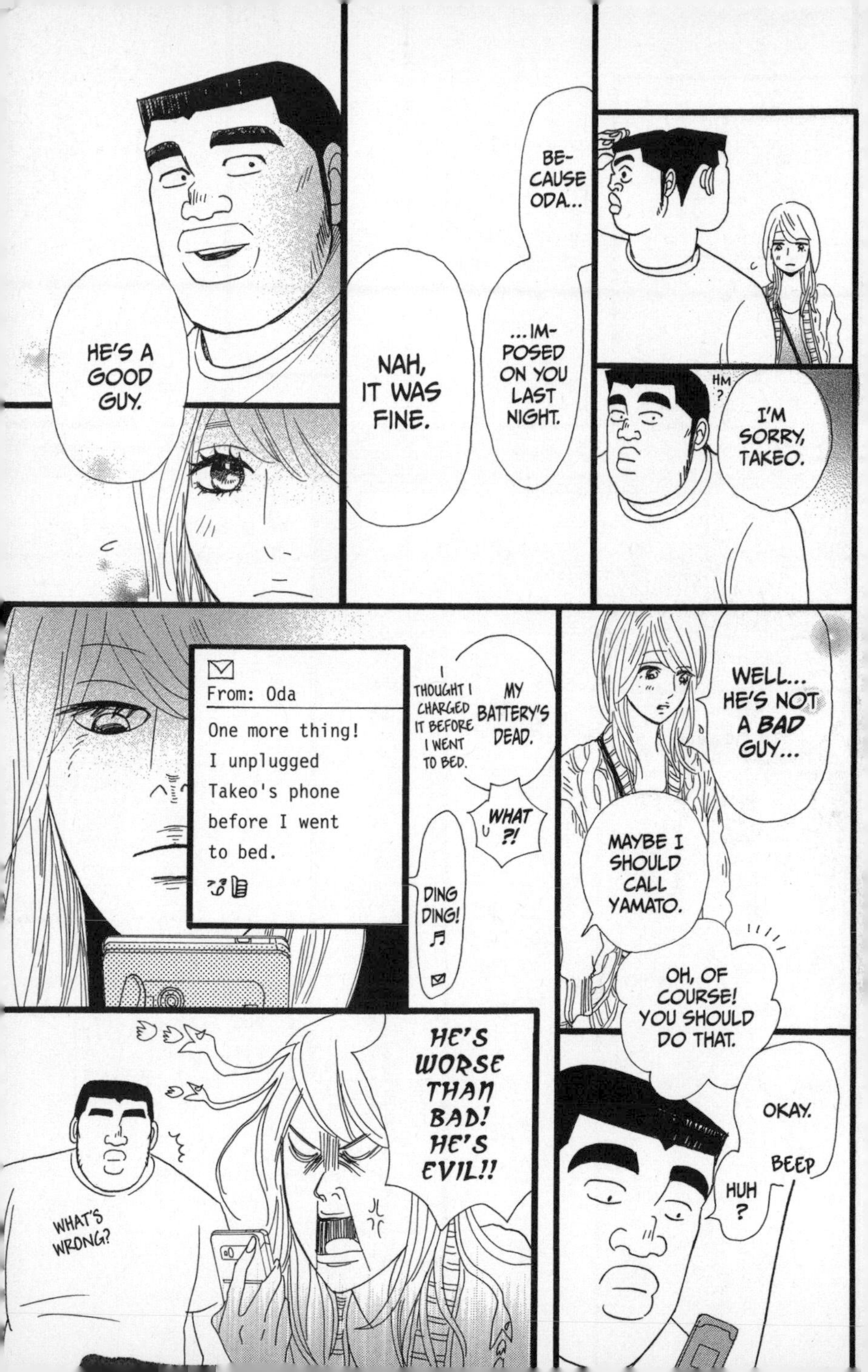
HM?
I'M SORRY, TAKEO.
BE-CAUSE ODA...
...IM-POSED ON YOU LAST NIGHT.
NAH, IT WAS FINE.
HE'S A GOOD GUY.
WELL... HE'S NOT A BAD GUY...
MAYBE I SHOULD CALL YAMATO.
OH, OF COURSE! YOU SHOULD DO THAT.
OKAY.
BEEP
HUH?
MY BATTERY'S DEAD.
I THOUGHT I CHARGED IT BEFORE I WENT TO BED.
WHAT?!
DING DING!
From: Oda
One more thing! I unplugged Takeo's phone before I went to bed.
HE'S WORSE THAN BAD! HE'S EVIL!!
WHAT'S WRONG?

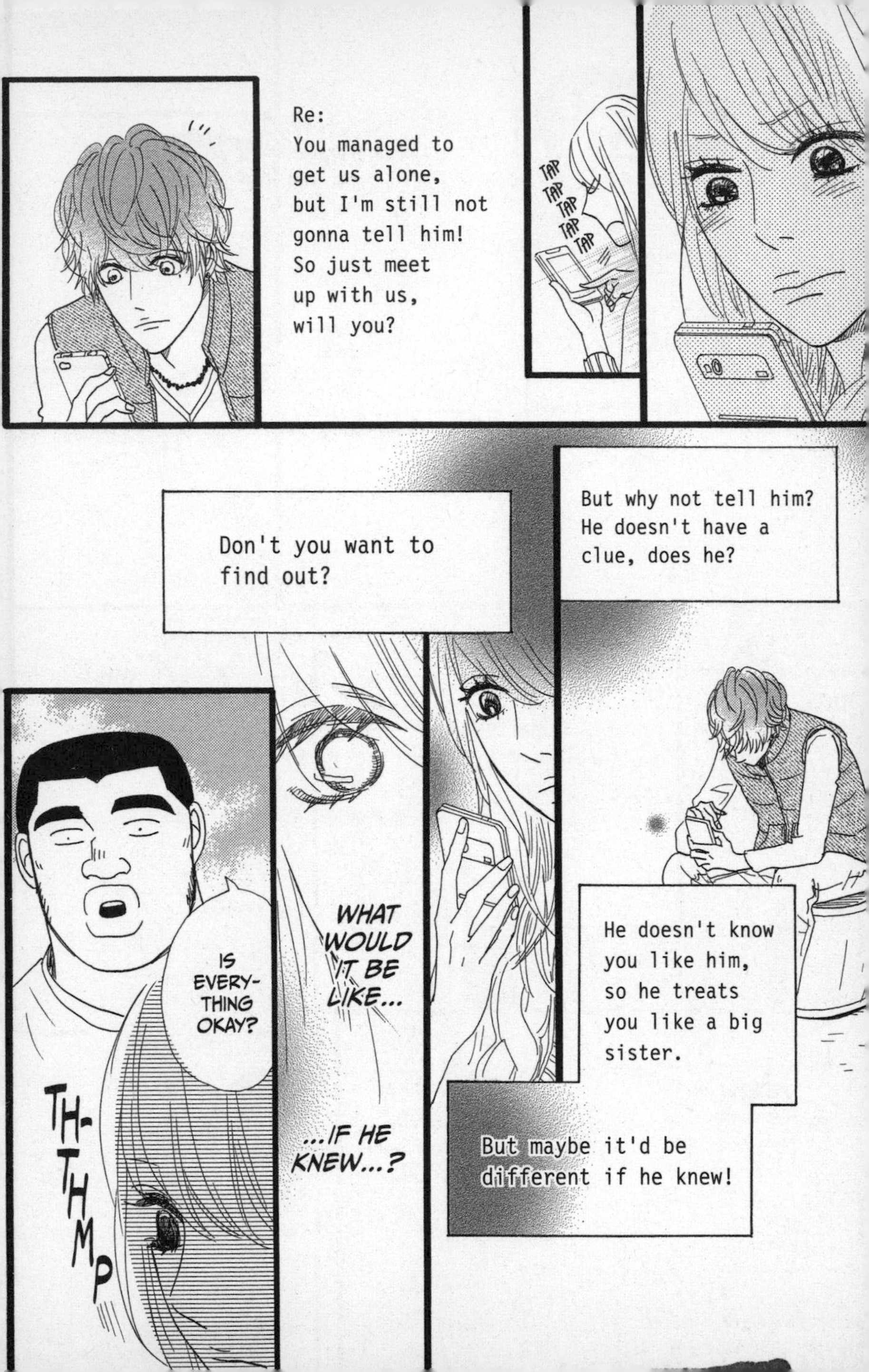
TAP TAP TAP TAP TAP
Re:
You managed to get us alone, but I'm still not gonna tell him! So just meet up with us, will you?
But why not tell him? He doesn't have a clue, does he?
He doesn't know you like him, so he treats you like a big sister.
But maybe it'd be different if he knew!
Don't you want to find out?
WHAT WOULD IT BE LIKE...
...IF HE KNEW...?
IS EVERY-THING OKAY?
TH-THMP

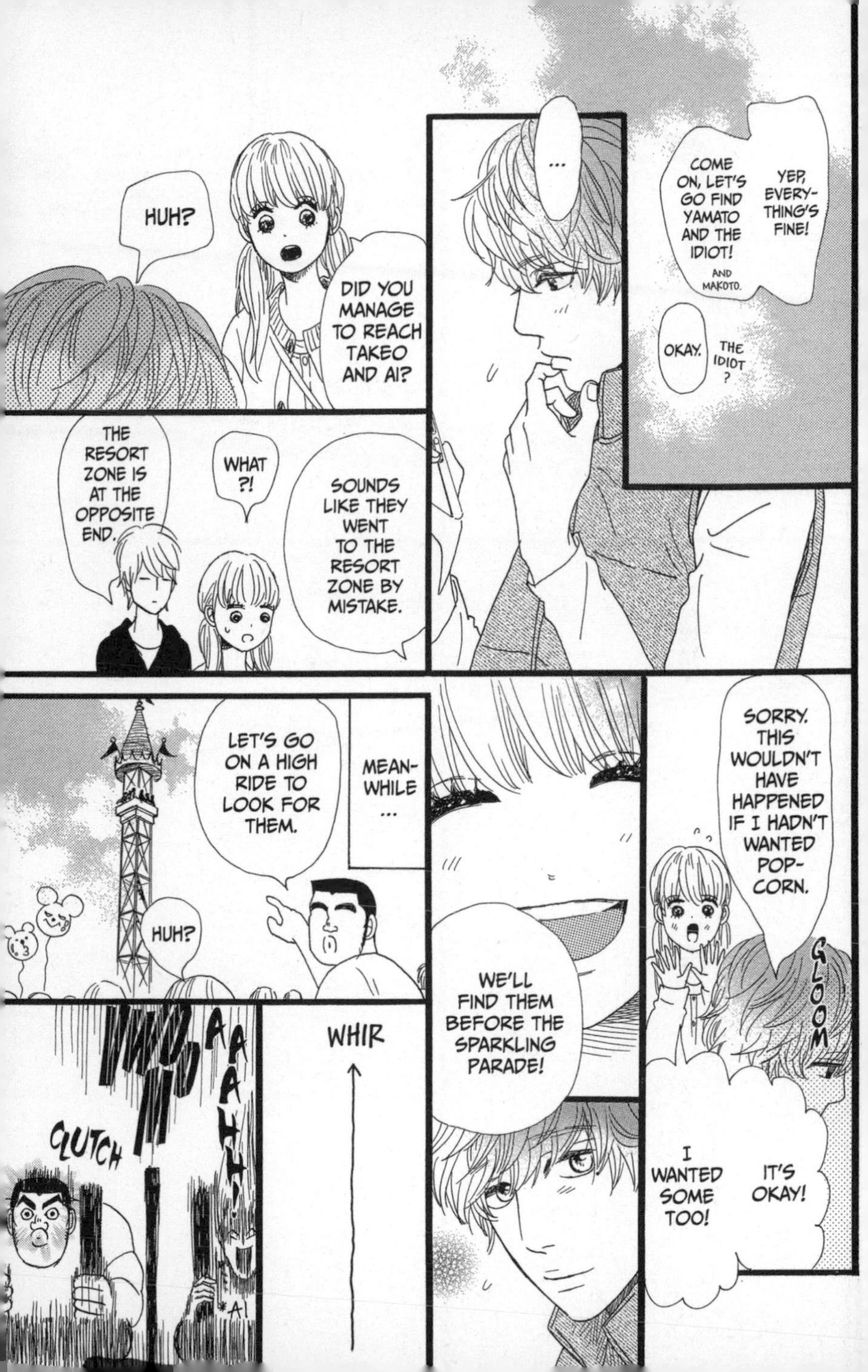
YEP, EVERYTHING'S FINE!
COME ON, LET'S GO FIND YAMATO AND THE IDIOT!
AND MAKOTO.
THE IDIOT?
OKAY.
...
DID YOU MANAGE TO REACH TAKEO AND AI?
HUH?
SOUNDS LIKE THEY WENT TO THE RESORT ZONE BY MISTAKE.
WHAT?!
THE RESORT ZONE IS AT THE OPPOSITE END.
SORRY. THIS WOULDN'T HAVE HAPPENED IF I HADN'T WANTED POPCORN.
GLOOM
IT'S OKAY!
I WANTED SOME TOO!
WE'LL FIND THEM BEFORE THE SPARKLING PARADE!
MEANWHILE...
LET'S GO ON A HIGH RIDE TO LOOK FOR THEM.
HUH?
WHIR
AAAHH!
CLUTCH
*AI

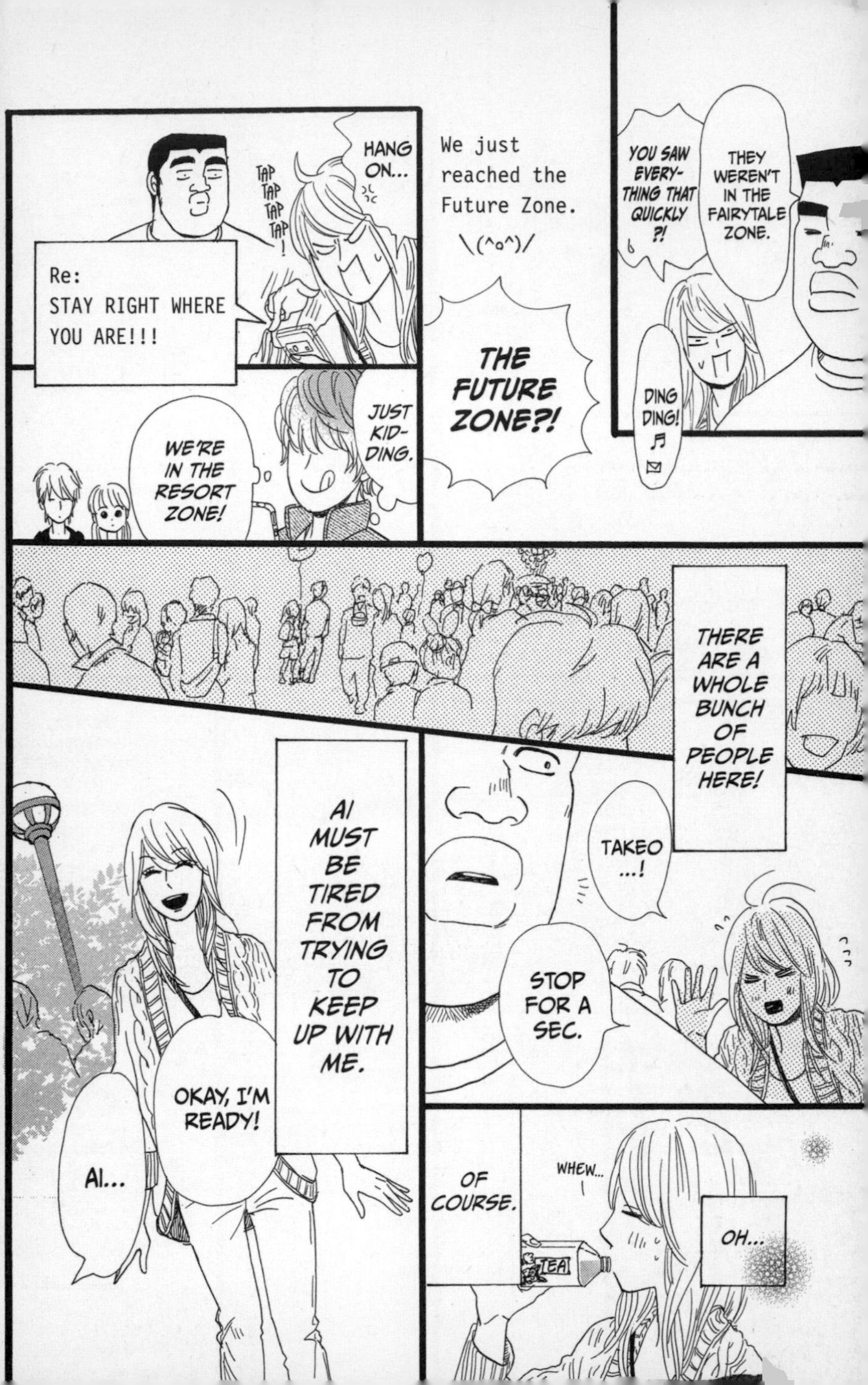
THEY WEREN'T IN THE FAIRYTALE ZONE.
YOU SAW EVERY-THING THAT QUICKLY?!
DING DING! ♬
Re: STAY RIGHT WHERE YOU ARE!!!
TAP TAP TAP TAP!
HANG ON...
We just reached the Future Zone. \(^o^)/
THE FUTURE ZONE?!
JUST KID-DING.
WE'RE IN THE RESORT ZONE!
THERE ARE A WHOLE BUNCH OF PEOPLE HERE!
TAKEO ...!
STOP FOR A SEC.
OH...
WHEW...
OF COURSE.
TEA
AI MUST BE TIRED FROM TRYING TO KEEP UP WITH ME.
OKAY, I'M READY!
AI...

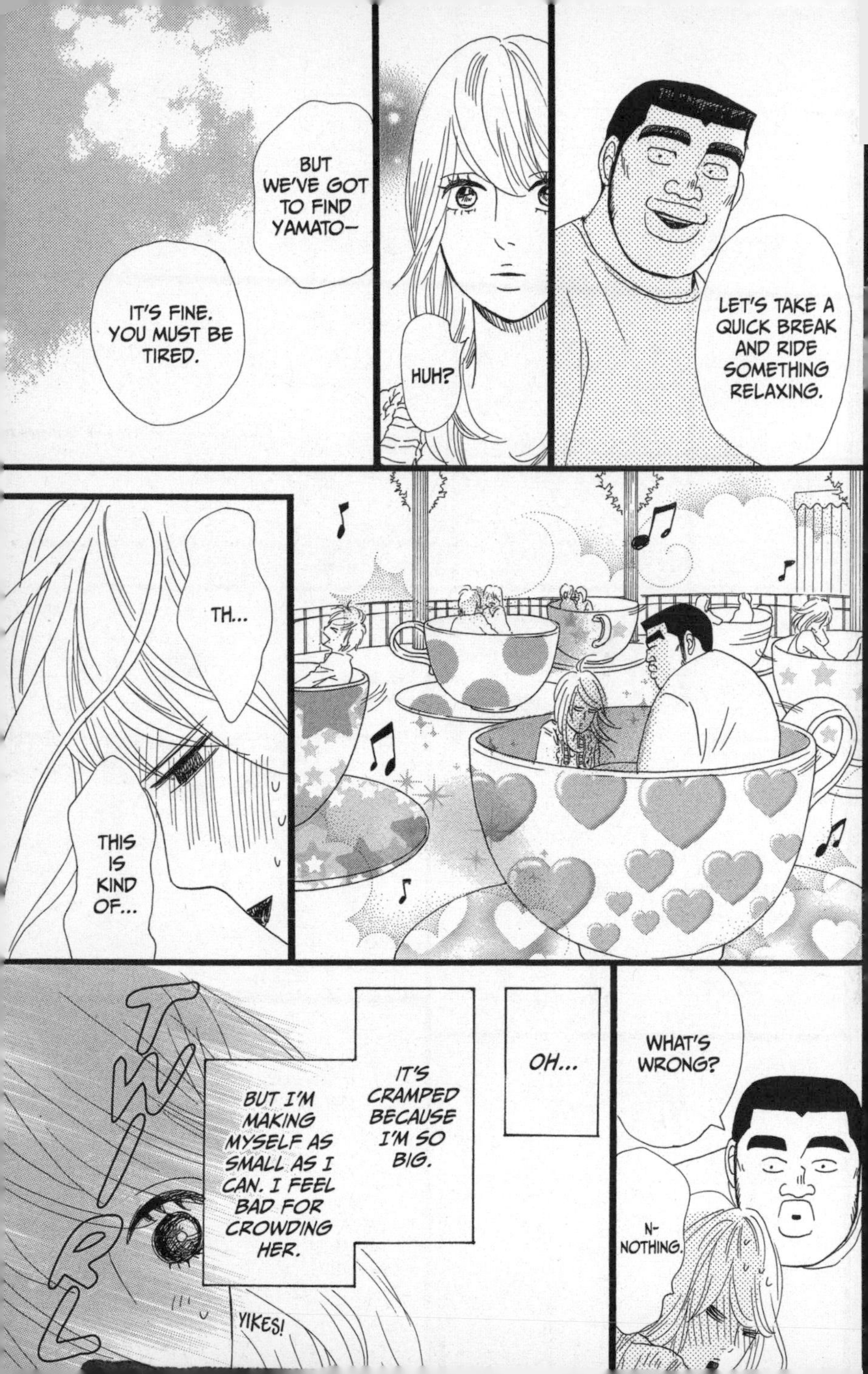
LET'S TAKE A QUICK BREAK AND RIDE SOMETHING RELAXING.
HUH?
BUT WE'VE GOT TO FIND YAMATO—
IT'S FINE. YOU MUST BE TIRED.
TH...
THIS IS KIND OF...
WHAT'S WRONG?
N-NOTHING.
OH...
IT'S CRAMPED BECAUSE I'M SO BIG.
BUT I'M MAKING MYSELF AS SMALL AS I CAN. I FEEL BAD FOR CROWDING HER.
TWIRL
YIKES!

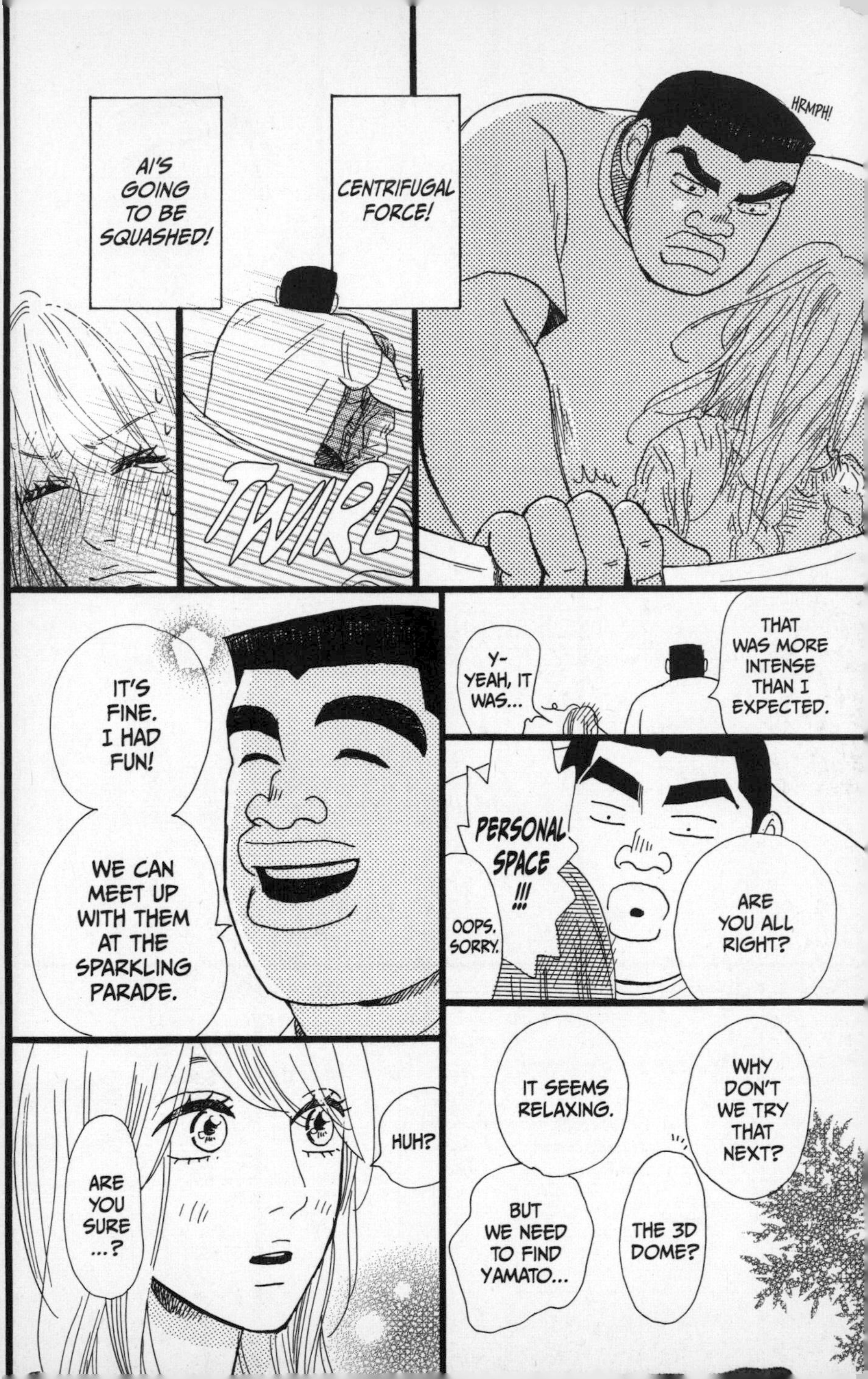
HRMPH!
CENTRIFUGAL FORCE!
TWIRL
AI'S GOING TO BE SQUASHED!
THAT WAS MORE INTENSE THAN I EXPECTED.
Y-YEAH, IT WAS...
ARE YOU ALL RIGHT?
PERSONAL SPACE!!!
OOPS. SORRY.
WHY DON'T WE TRY THAT NEXT?
THE 3D DOME?
IT SEEMS RELAXING.
BUT WE NEED TO FIND YAMATO...
IT'S FINE. I HAD FUN!
WE CAN MEET UP WITH THEM AT THE SPARKLING PARADE.
HUH?
ARE YOU SURE ...?

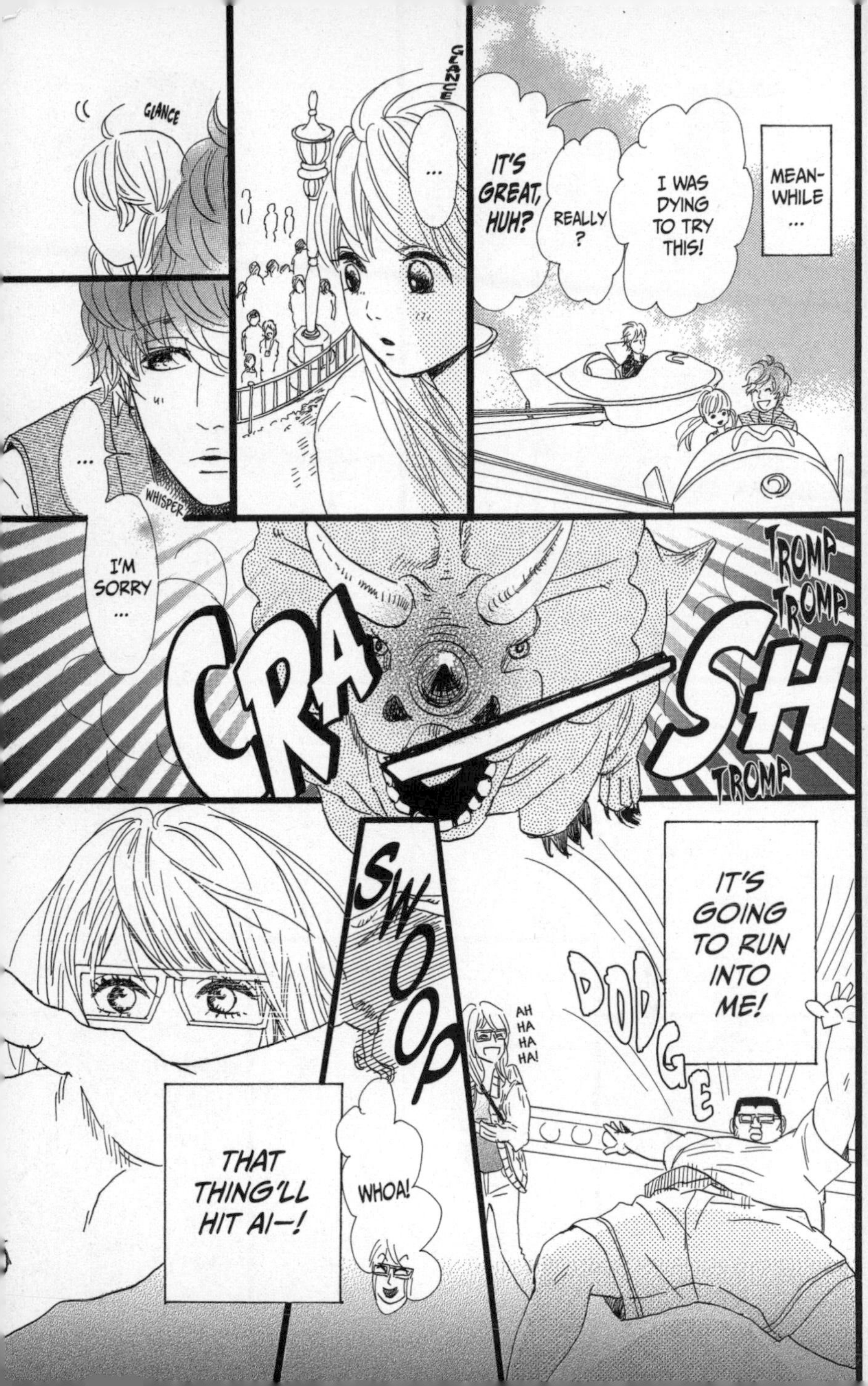
MEAN-WHILE ...
I WAS DYING TO TRY THIS!
REALLY?
IT'S GREAT, HUH?
GLANCE
...
GLANCE
...
WHISPER
I'M SORRY ...
TROMP
TROMP
CRASH
TROMP
IT'S GOING TO RUN INTO ME!
DODGE
AH HA HA HA!
SWOOP
WHOA!
THAT THING'LL HIT AI—!

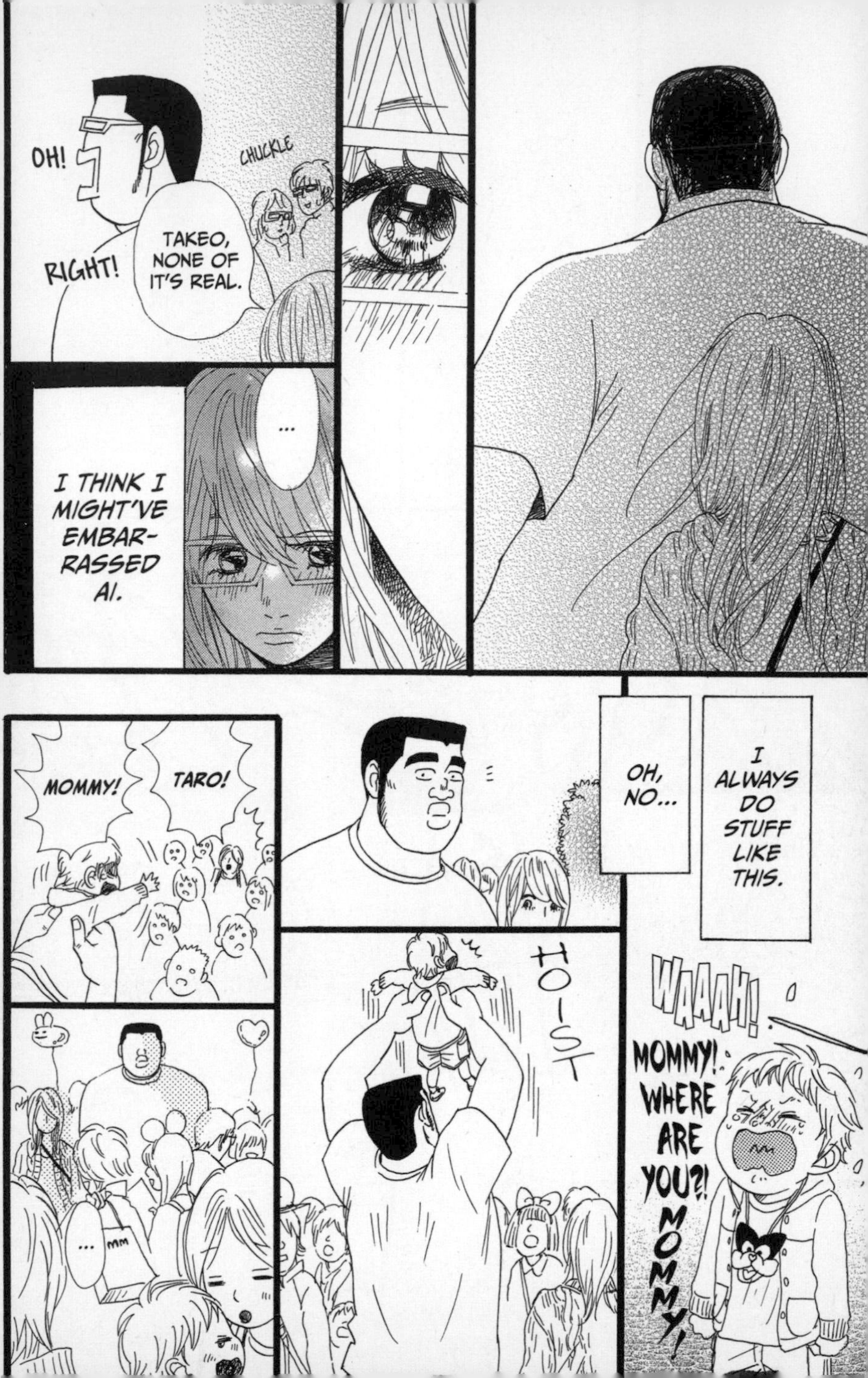
CHUCKLE
TAKEO, NONE OF IT'S REAL.
OH!
RIGHT!
...
I THINK I MIGHT'VE EMBARRASSED AI.
I ALWAYS DO STUFF LIKE THIS.
OH, NO...
WAAAH!
MOMMY! WHERE ARE YOU?!
MOMMY, MOMMY!
HOIST
TARO!
MOMMY!
...
MM

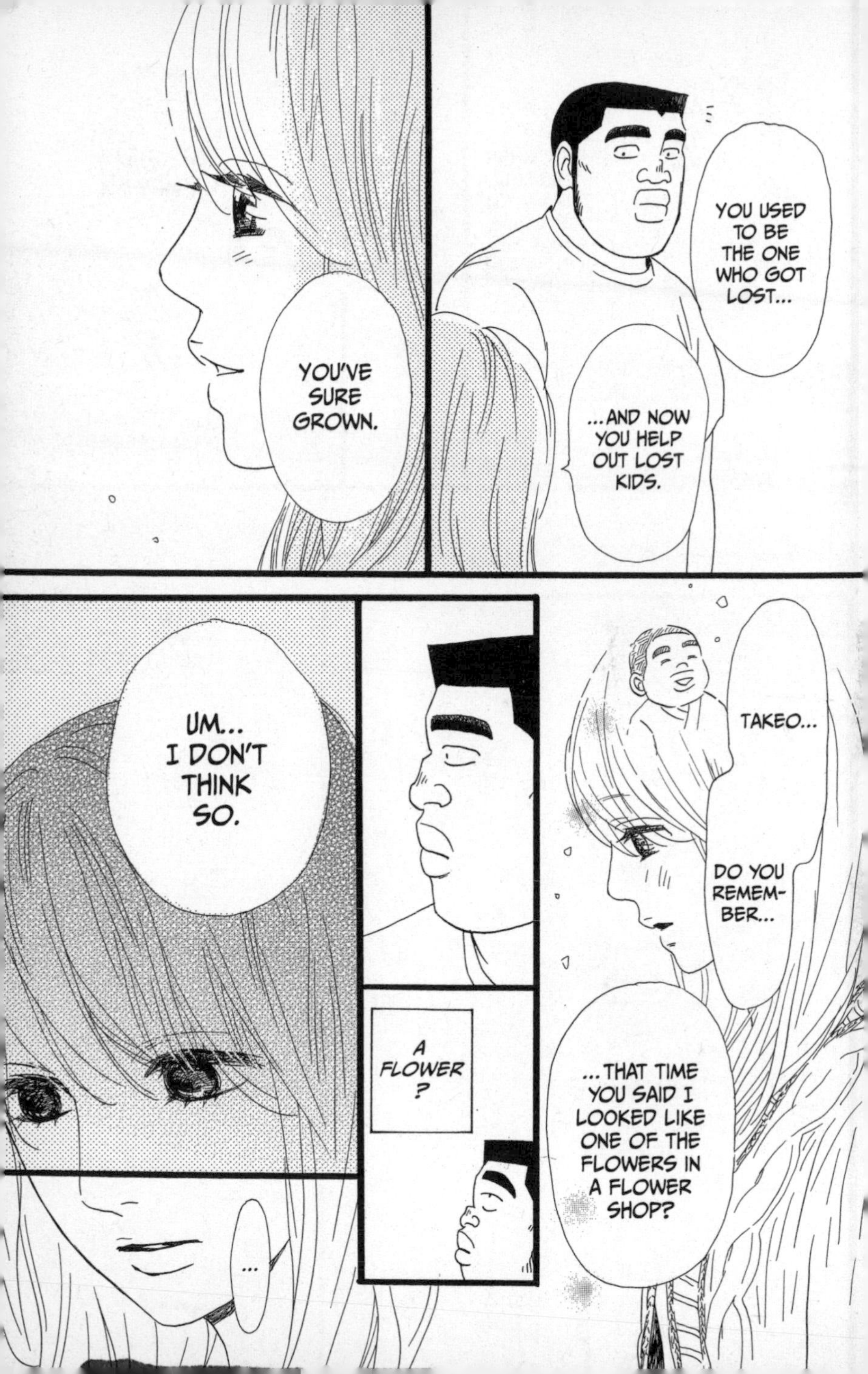
YOU USED TO BE THE ONE WHO GOT LOST...
...AND NOW YOU HELP OUT LOST KIDS.
YOU'VE SURE GROWN.
TAKEO...
DO YOU REMEMBER...
...THAT TIME YOU SAID I LOOKED LIKE ONE OF THE FLOWERS IN A FLOWER SHOP?
A FLOWER?
UM... I DON'T THINK SO.
...

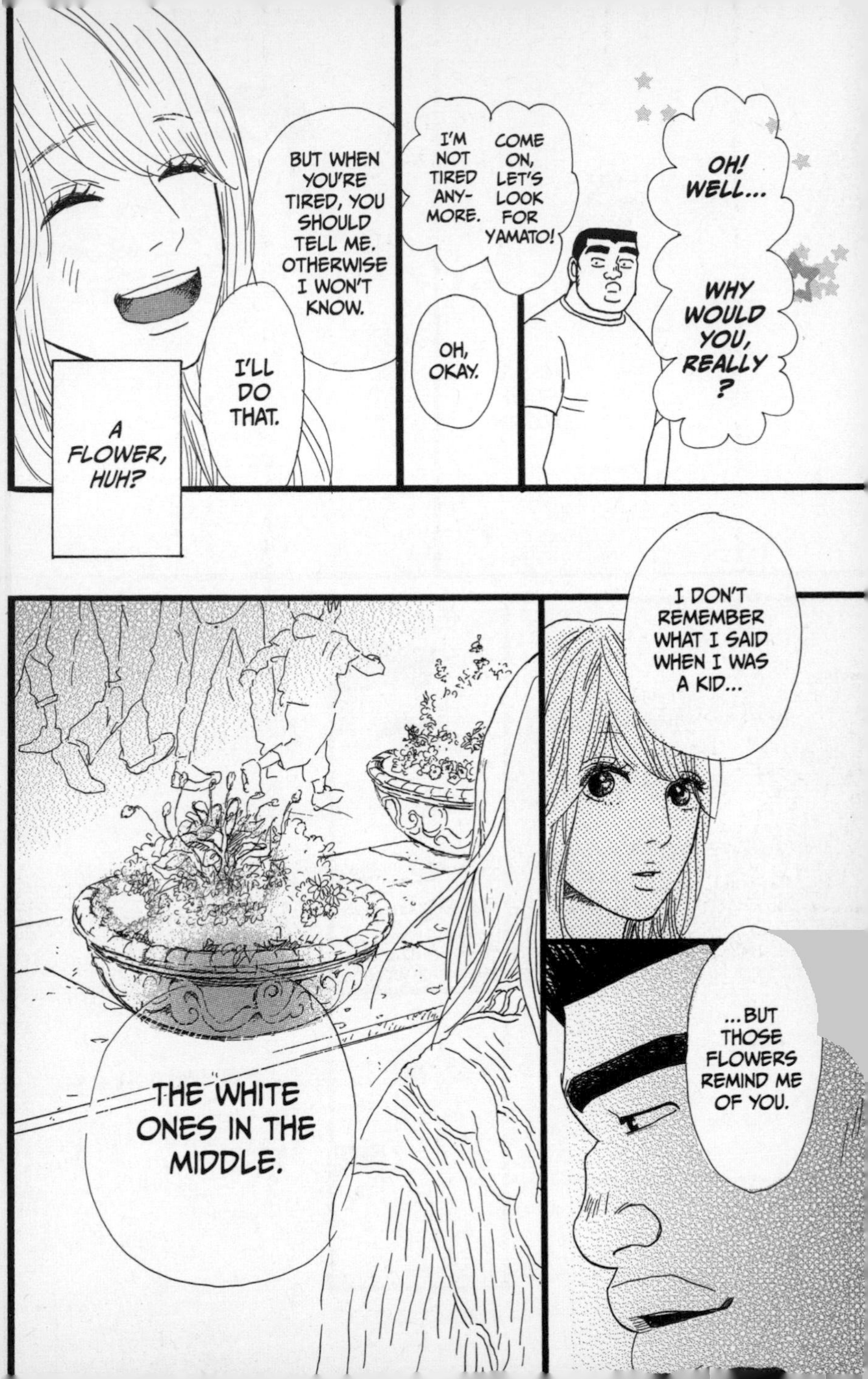
OH! WELL...
WHY WOULD YOU, REALLY?
COME ON, LET'S LOOK FOR YAMATO!
I'M NOT TIRED ANYMORE.
OH, OKAY.
BUT WHEN YOU'RE TIRED, YOU SHOULD TELL ME. OTHERWISE I WON'T KNOW.
I'LL DO THAT.
A FLOWER, HUH?
I DON'T REMEMBER WHAT I SAID WHEN I WAS A KID...
...BUT THOSE FLOWERS REMIND ME OF YOU.
THE WHITE ONES IN THE MIDDLE.

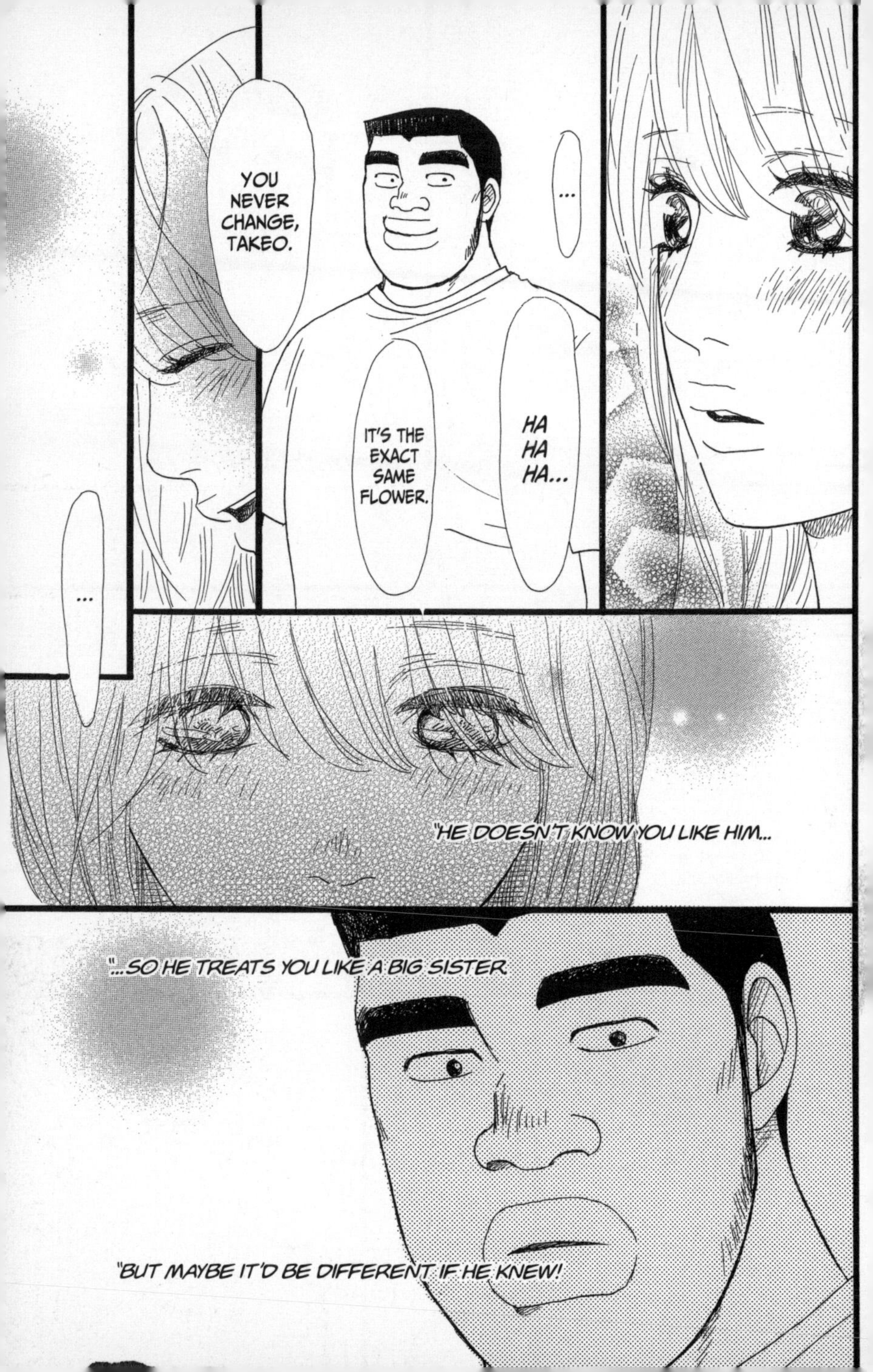
...
HA HA HA...
IT'S THE EXACT SAME FLOWER.
YOU NEVER CHANGE, TAKEO.
...
"HE DOESN'T KNOW YOU LIKE HIM...
"...SO HE TREATS YOU LIKE A BIG SISTER.
"BUT MAYBE IT'D BE DIFFERENT IF HE KNEW!

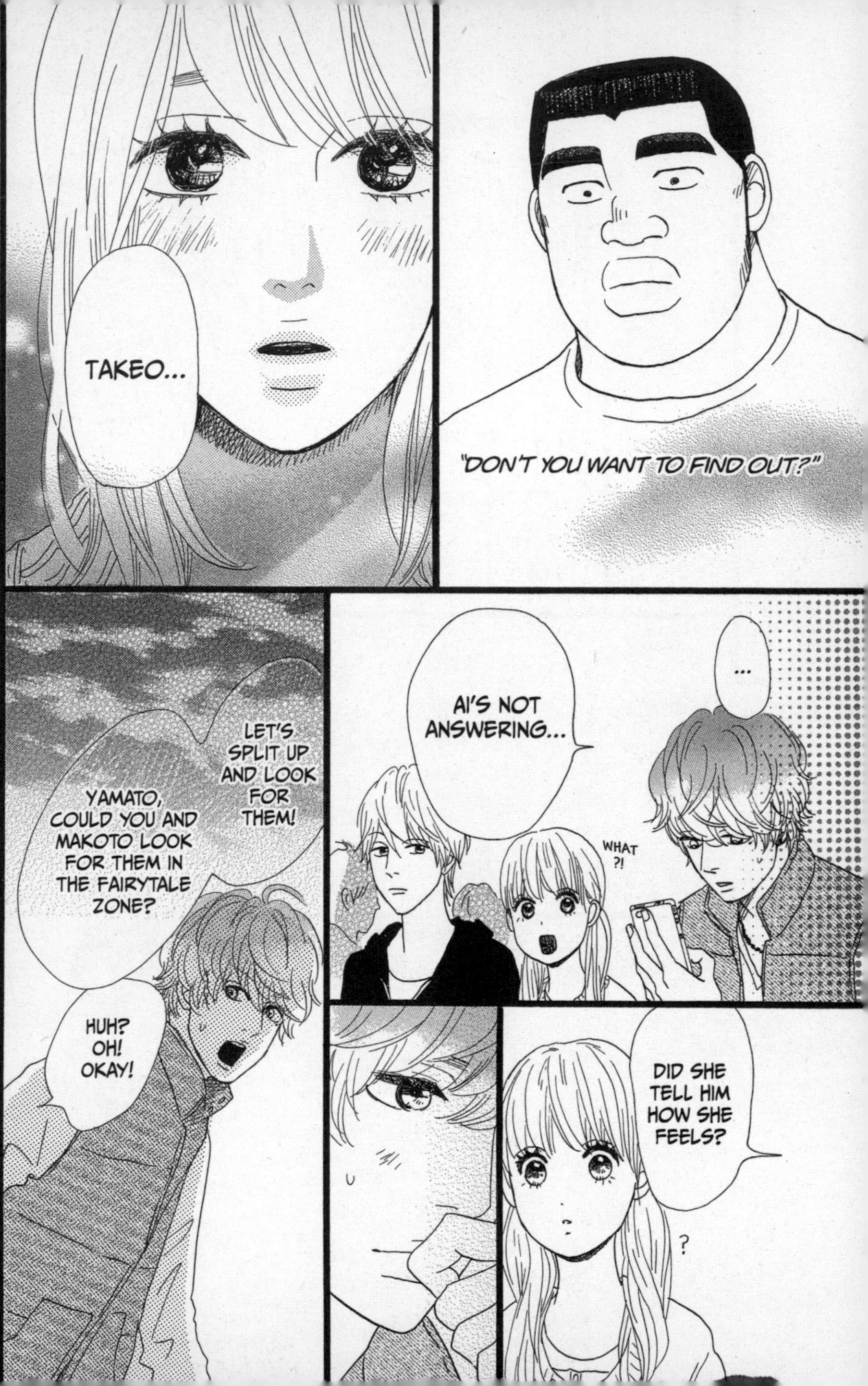
"DON'T YOU WANT TO FIND OUT?"
TAKEO...
...
AI'S NOT ANSWERING...
WHAT ?!
DID SHE TELL HIM HOW SHE FEELS?
?
LET'S SPLIT UP AND LOOK FOR THEM!
YAMATO, COULD YOU AND MAKOTO LOOK FOR THEM IN THE FAIRYTALE ZONE?
HUH? OH! OKAY!

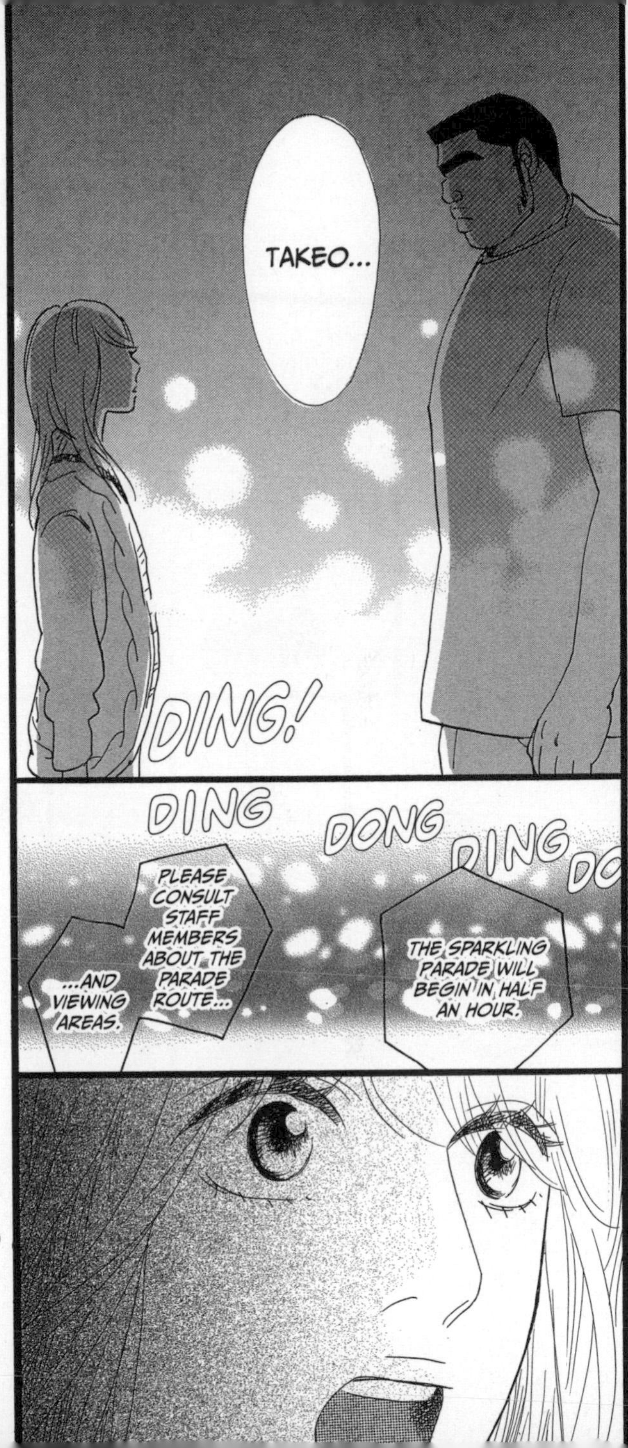
TAKEO...
DING!
DING
DONG
DING
THE SPARKLING PARADE WILL BEGIN IN HALF AN HOUR.
PLEASE CONSULT STAFF MEMBERS ABOUT THE PARADE ROUTE...
...AND VIEWING AREAS.

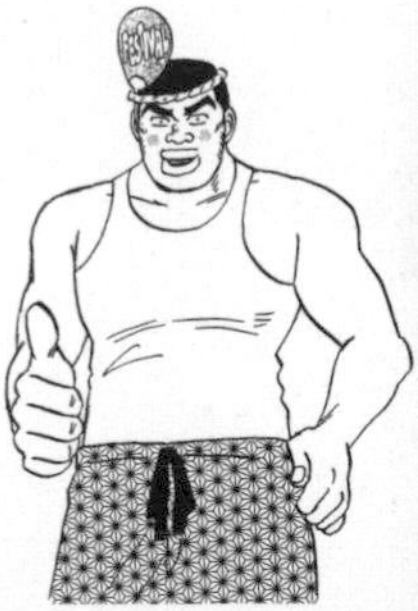

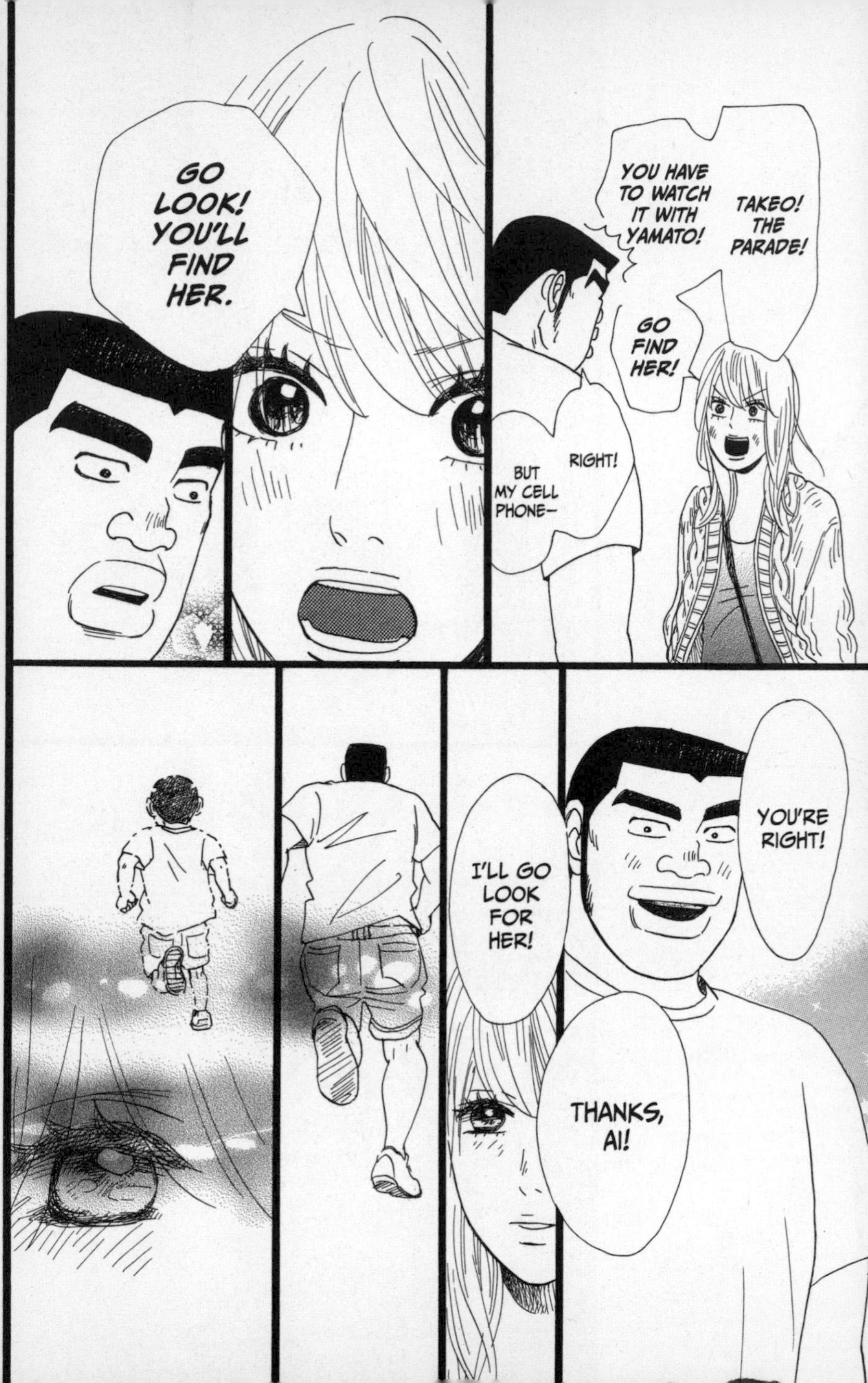
TAKEO! THE PARADE!
YOU HAVE TO WATCH IT WITH YAMATO!
GO FIND HER!
RIGHT!
BUT MY CELL PHONE—
GO LOOK! YOU'LL FIND HER.
YOU'RE RIGHT!
I'LL GO LOOK FOR HER!
THANKS, AI!

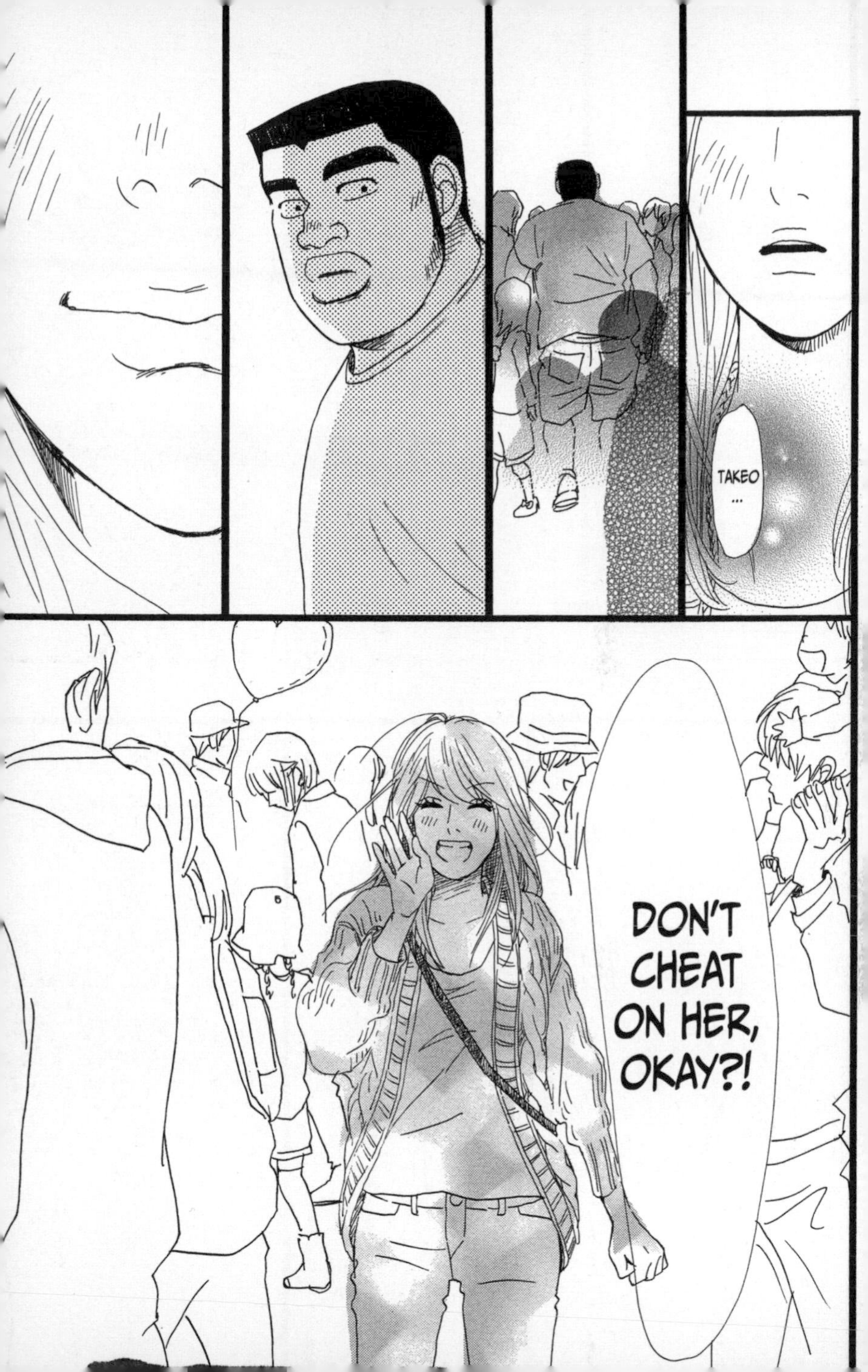
TAKEO ...
DON'T CHEAT ON HER, OKAY?!

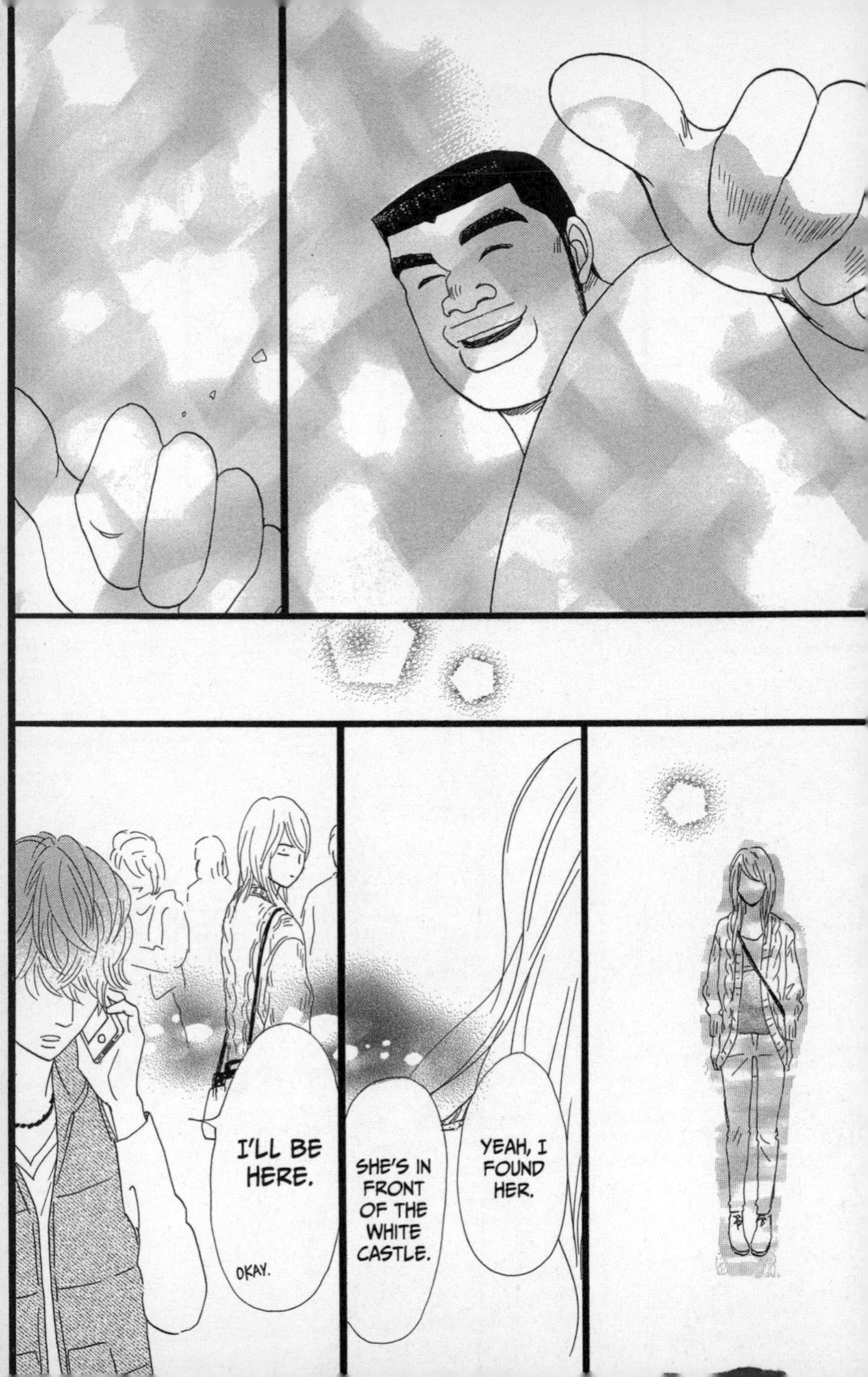
YEAH, I FOUND HER.
SHE'S IN FRONT OF THE WHITE CASTLE.
I'LL BE HERE.
OKAY.

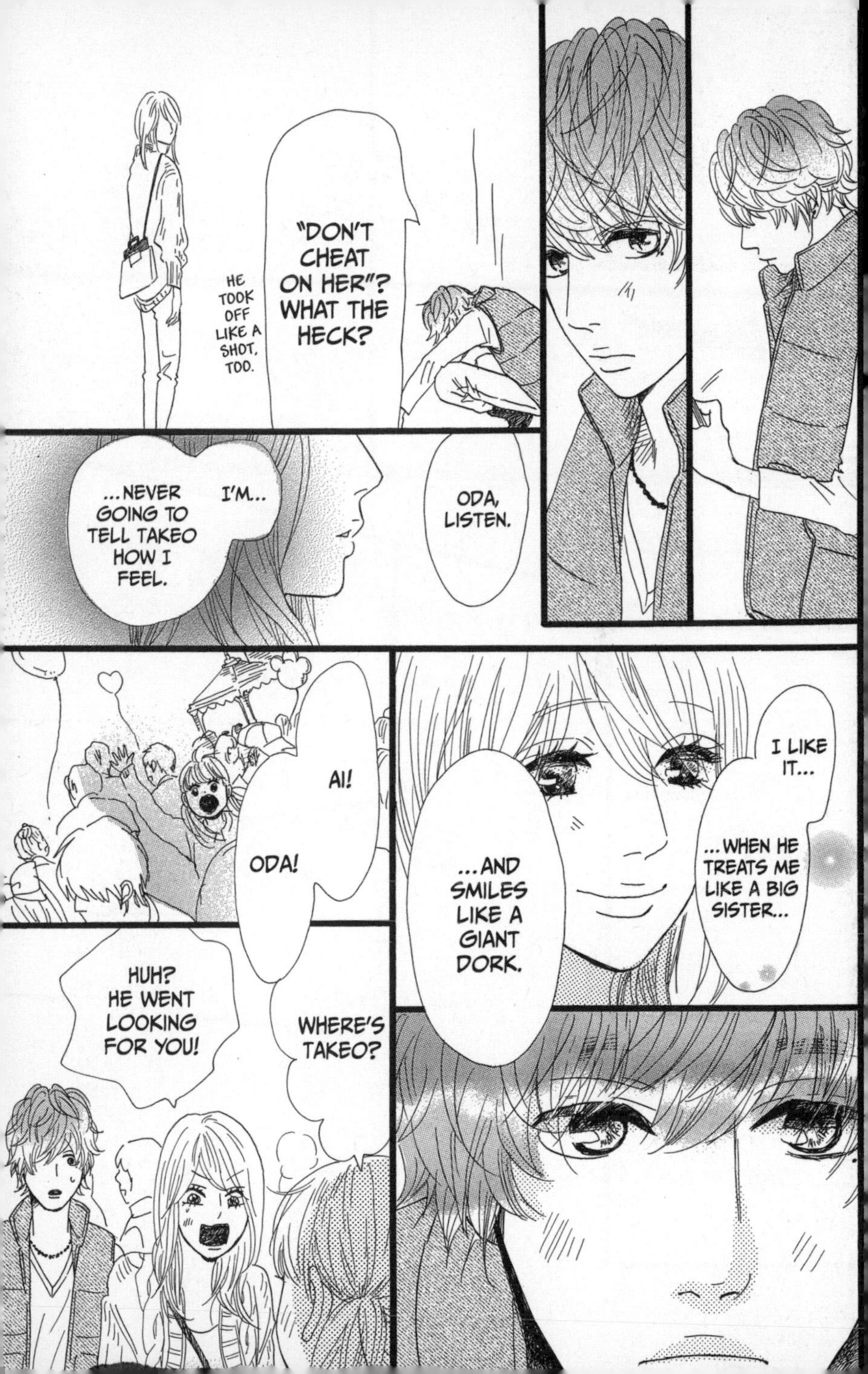

"DON'T CHEAT ON HER"? WHAT THE HECK?
HE TOOK OFF LIKE A SHOT, TOO.
ODA, LISTEN.
I'M...
...NEVER GOING TO TELL TAKEO HOW I FEEL.
I LIKE IT...
...WHEN HE TREATS ME LIKE A BIG SISTER...
...AND SMILES LIKE A GIANT DORK.
AI!
ODA!
WHERE'S TAKEO?
HUH? HE WENT LOOKING FOR YOU!

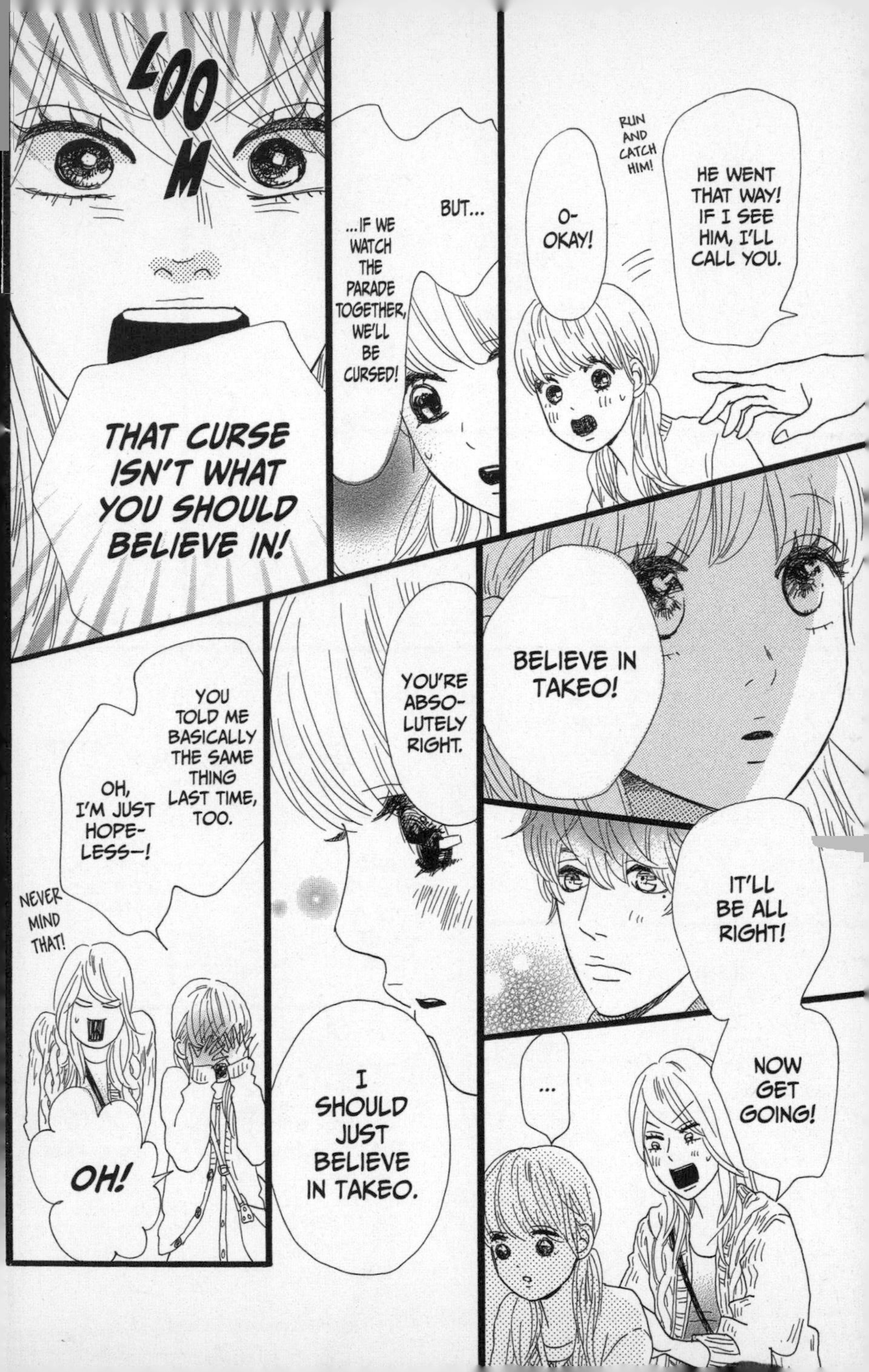
HE WENT THAT WAY! IF I SEE HIM, I'LL CALL YOU.
RUN AND CATCH HIM!
O-OKAY!
BUT...
...IF WE WATCH THE PARADE TOGETHER, WE'LL BE CURSED!
LOOM
THAT CURSE ISN'T WHAT YOU SHOULD BELIEVE IN!
BELIEVE IN TAKEO!
IT'LL BE ALL RIGHT!
NOW GET GOING!
...
YOU'RE ABSOLUTELY RIGHT.
I SHOULD JUST BELIEVE IN TAKEO.
YOU TOLD ME BASICALLY THE SAME THING LAST TIME, TOO.
OH, I'M JUST HOPELESS--!
NEVER MIND THAT!
OH!

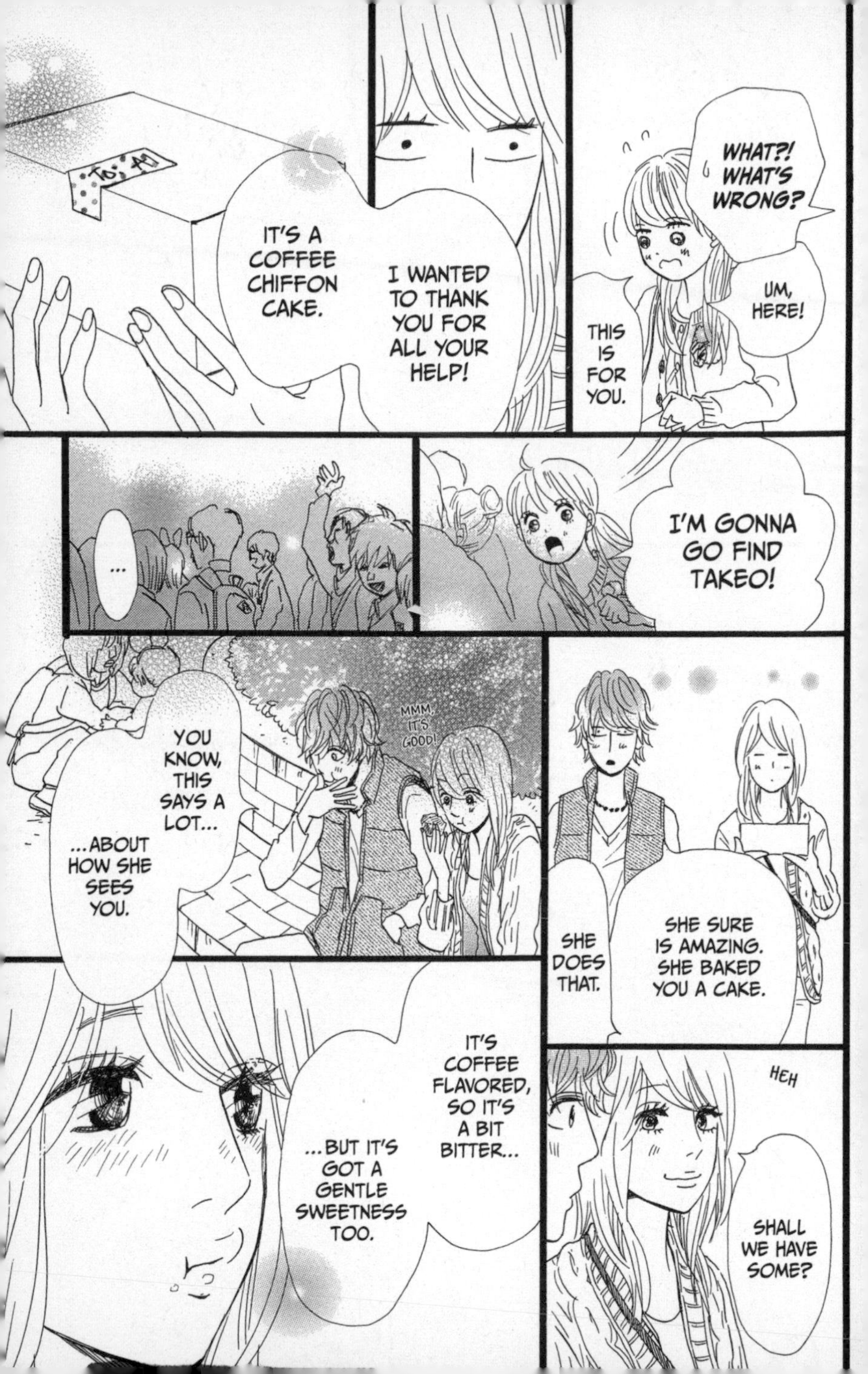
WHAT?! WHAT'S WRONG?
UM, HERE!
THIS IS FOR YOU.
I WANTED TO THANK YOU FOR ALL YOUR HELP!
IT'S A COFFEE CHIFFON CAKE.
I'M GONNA GO FIND TAKEO!
...
SHE SURE IS AMAZING. SHE BAKED YOU A CAKE.
SHE DOES THAT.
MMM, IT'S GOOD!
YOU KNOW, THIS SAYS A LOT...
...ABOUT HOW SHE SEES YOU.
HEH
SHALL WE HAVE SOME?
IT'S COFFEE FLAVORED, SO IT'S A BIT BITTER...
...BUT IT'S GOT A GENTLE SWEETNESS TOO.

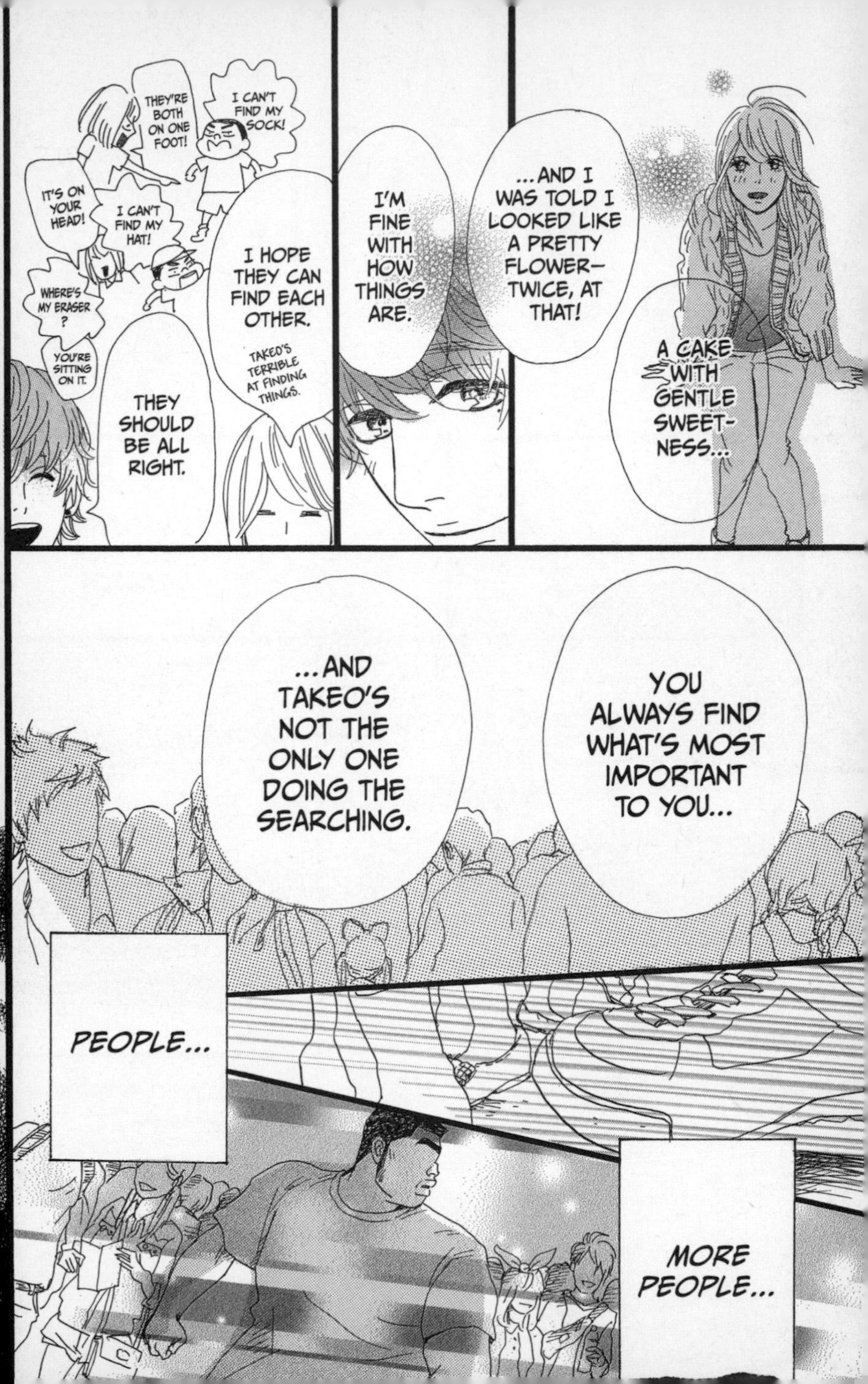
A CAKE WITH GENTLE SWEETNESS...
...AND I WAS TOLD I LOOKED LIKE A PRETTY FLOWER—TWICE, AT THAT!
I'M FINE WITH HOW THINGS ARE.
I HOPE THEY CAN FIND EACH OTHER.
TAKEO'S TERRIBLE AT FINDING THINGS.
I CAN'T FIND MY SOCK!
THEY'RE BOTH ON ONE FOOT!
I CAN'T FIND MY HAT!
IT'S ON YOUR HEAD!
WHERE'S MY ERASER?
YOU'RE SITTING ON IT.
THEY SHOULD BE ALL RIGHT.
YOU ALWAYS FIND WHAT'S MOST IMPORTANT TO YOU...
...AND TAKEO'S NOT THE ONLY ONE DOING THE SEARCHING.
PEOPLE...
MORE PEOPLE...

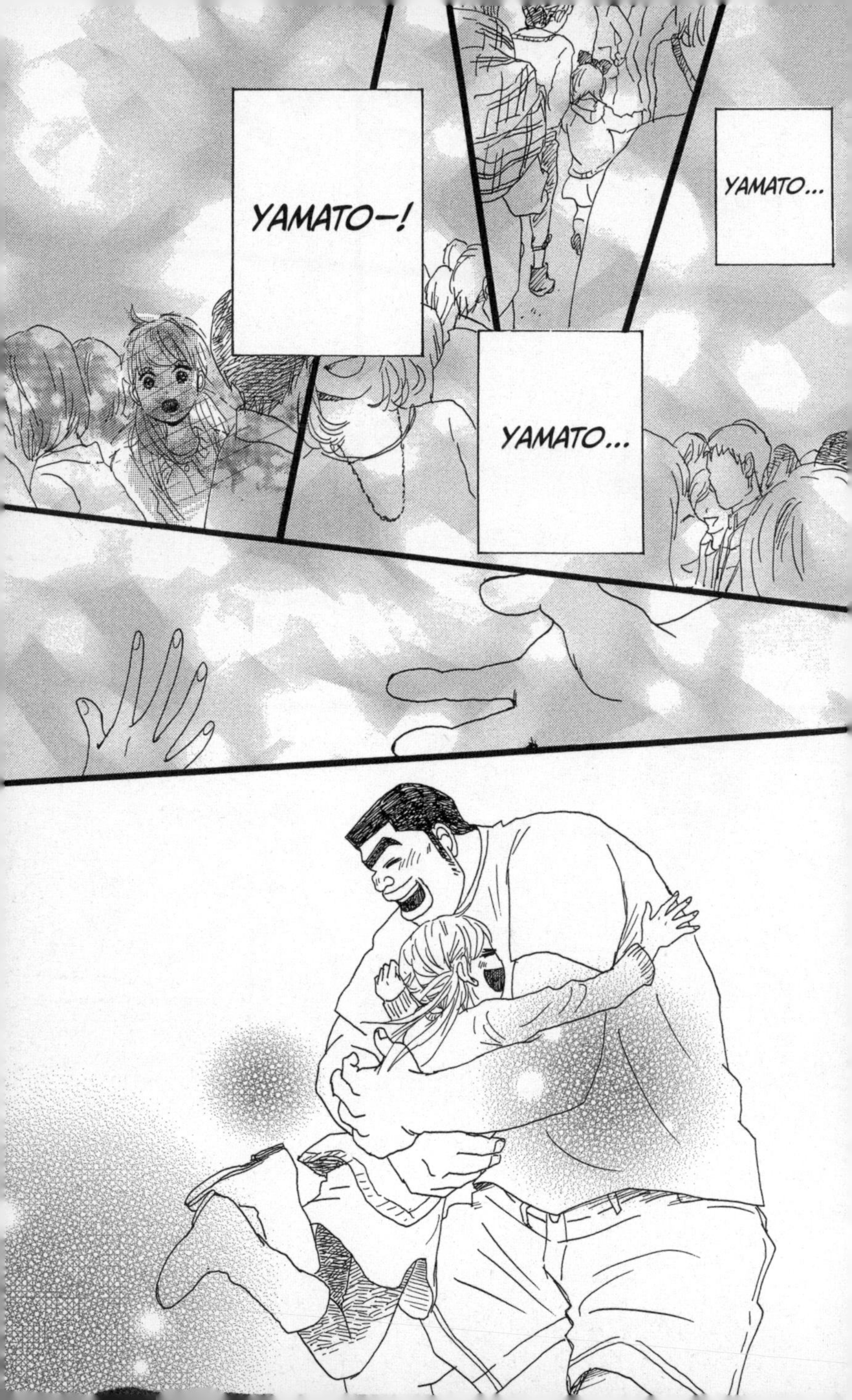
YAMATO...
YAMATO...
YAMATO—!

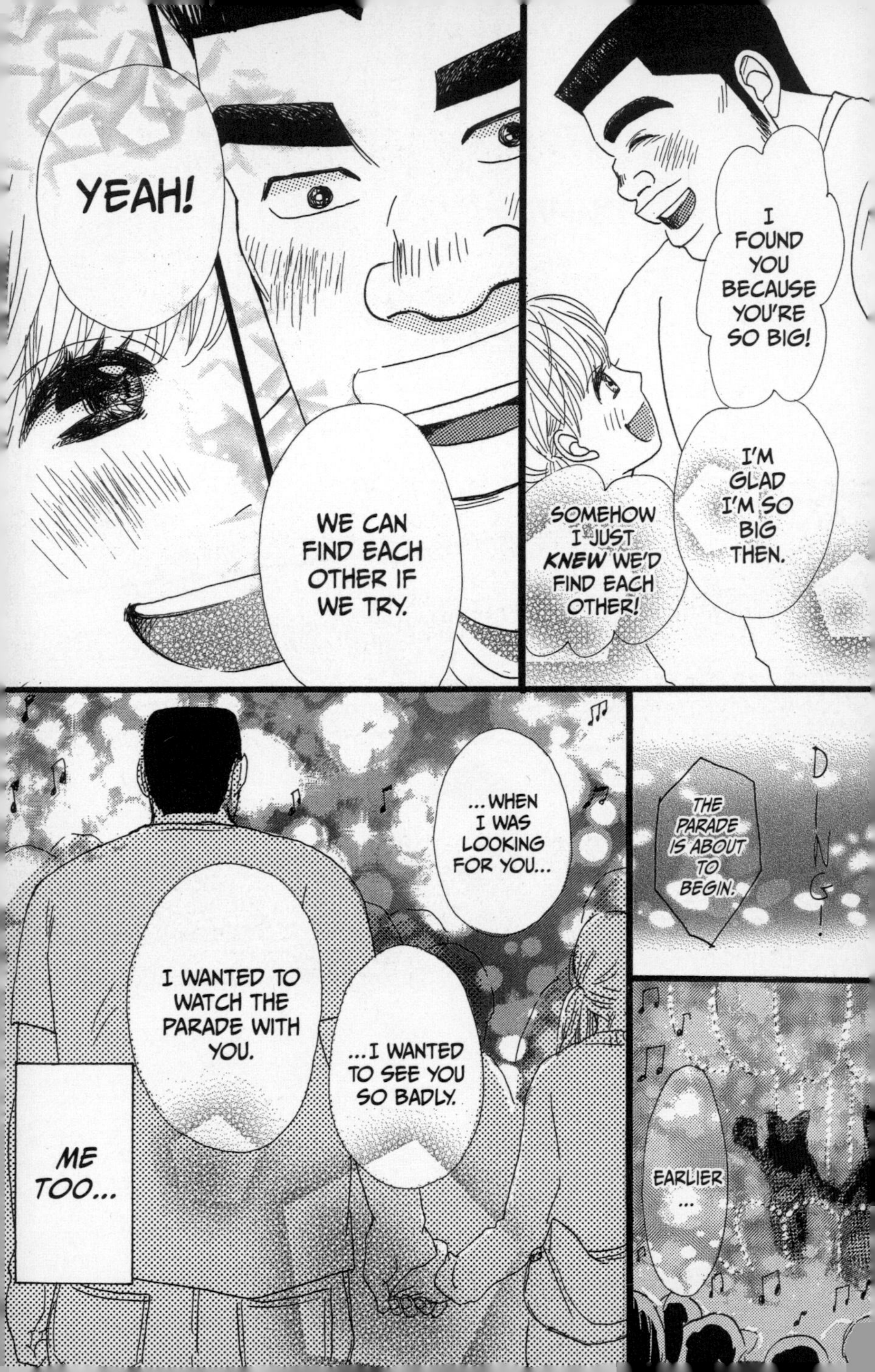
I FOUND YOU BECAUSE YOU'RE SO BIG!
I'M GLAD I'M SO BIG THEN.
SOMEHOW I JUST *KNEW* WE'D FIND EACH OTHER!
WE CAN FIND EACH OTHER IF WE TRY.
YEAH!
DING!
THE PARADE IS ABOUT TO BEGIN.
EARLIER...
...WHEN I WAS LOOKING FOR YOU...
...I WANTED TO SEE YOU SO BADLY.
I WANTED TO WATCH THE PARADE WITH YOU.
ME TOO...

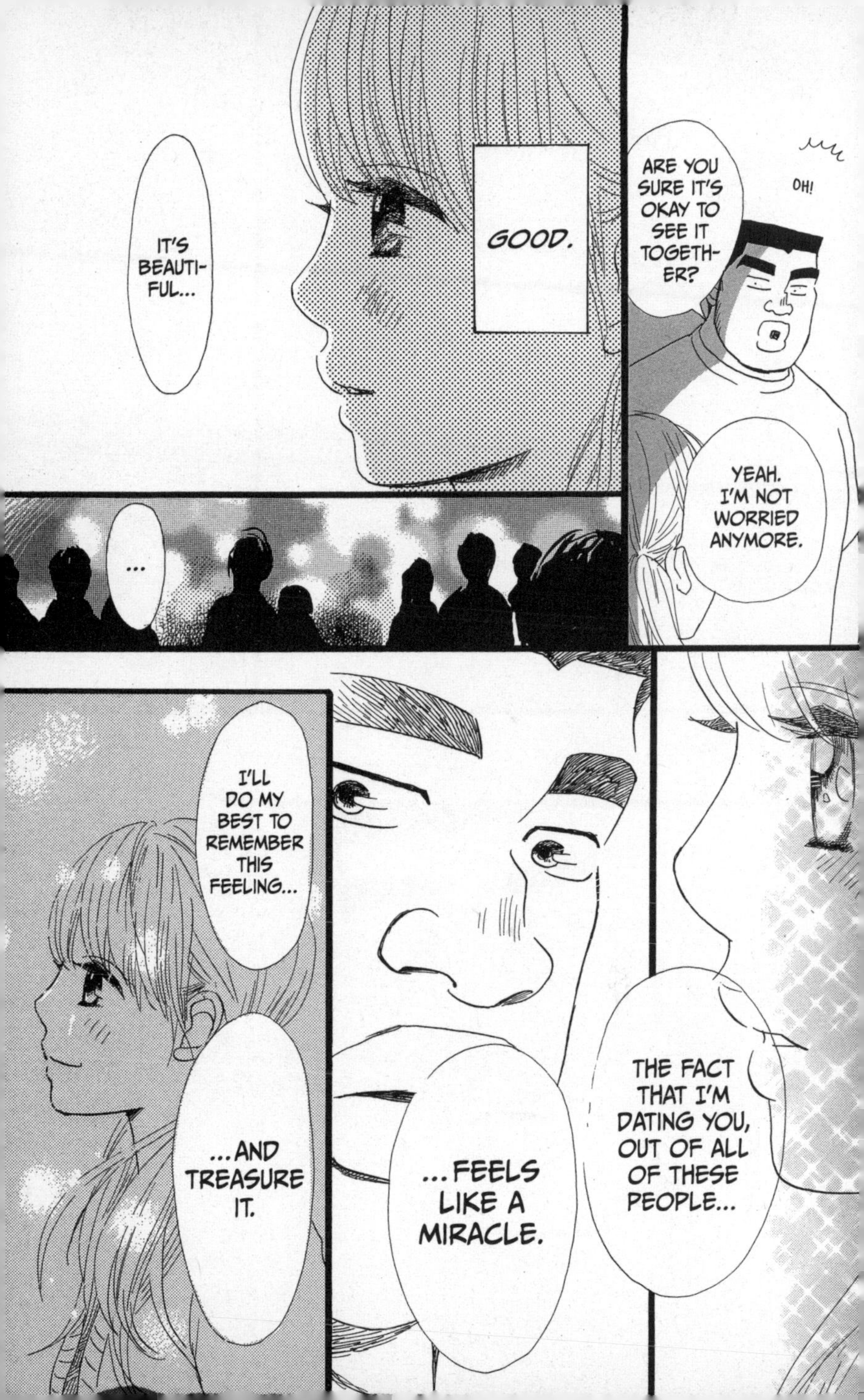
OH!
ARE YOU SURE IT'S OKAY TO SEE IT TOGETHER?
YEAH. I'M NOT WORRIED ANYMORE.
GOOD.
IT'S BEAUTIFUL...
...
THE FACT THAT I'M DATING YOU, OUT OF ALL OF THESE PEOPLE...
...FEELS LIKE A MIRACLE.
I'LL DO MY BEST TO REMEMBER THIS FEELING...
...AND TREASURE IT.

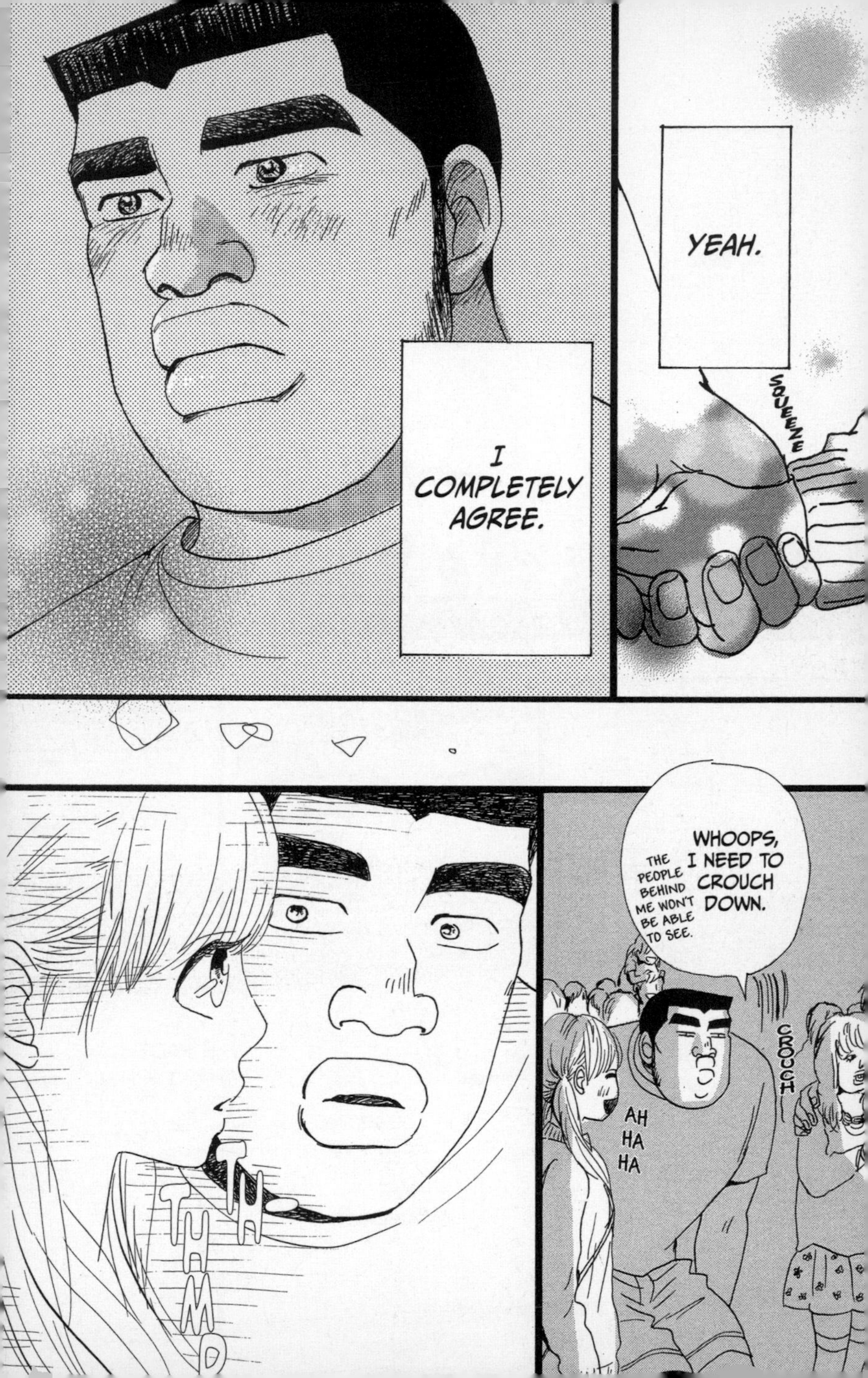
YEAH.
SQUEEZE
I COMPLETELY AGREE.
WHOOPS, I NEED TO CROUCH DOWN.
THE PEOPLE BEHIND ME WON'T BE ABLE TO SEE.
CROUCH
AH HA HA
THUMP

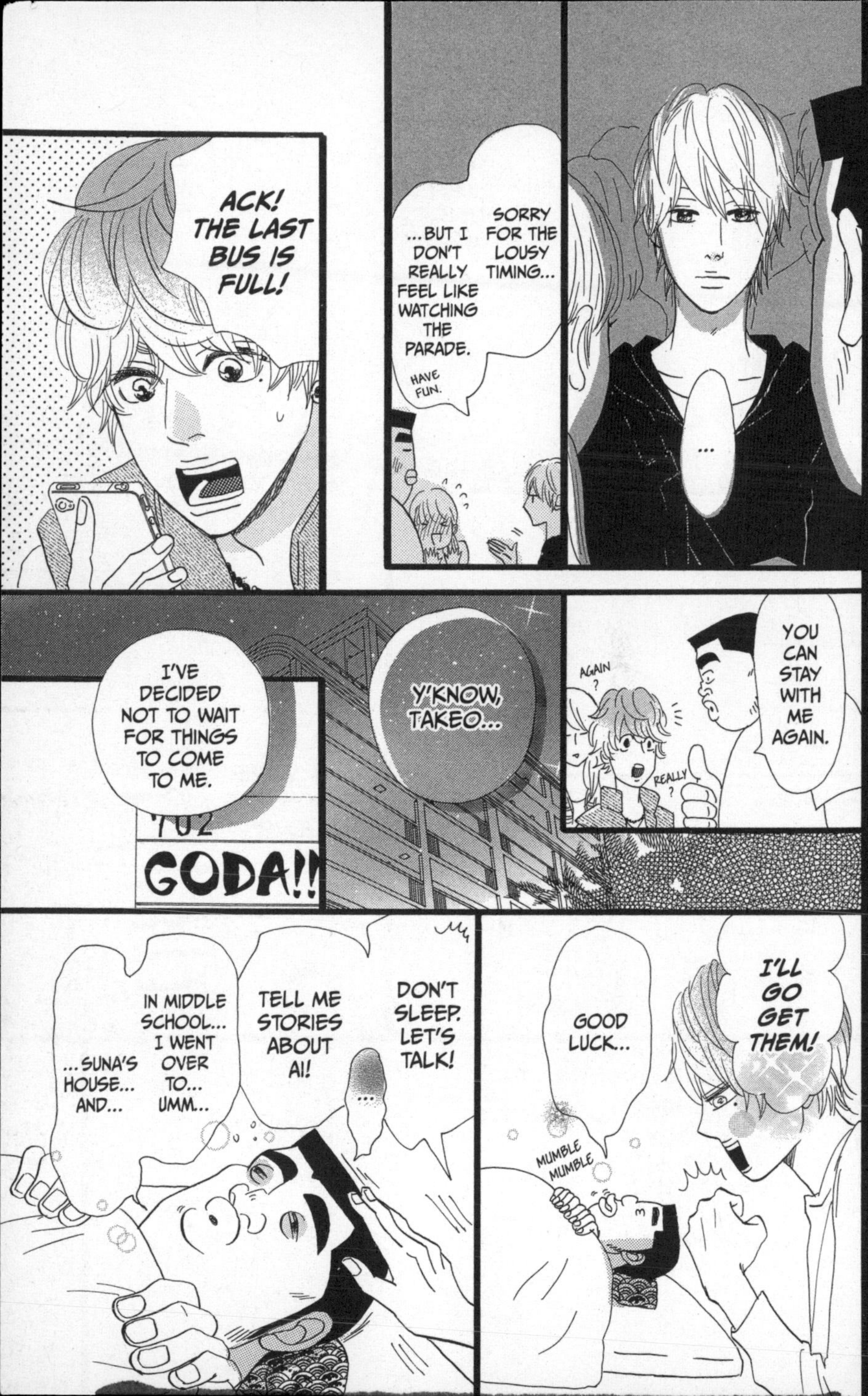
...
SORRY FOR THE LOUSY TIMING...
...BUT I DON'T REALLY FEEL LIKE WATCHING THE PARADE.
HAVE FUN.
ACK! THE LAST BUS IS FULL!
YOU CAN STAY WITH ME AGAIN.
AGAIN?
REALLY?
Y'KNOW, TAKEO...
I'VE DECIDED NOT TO WAIT FOR THINGS TO COME TO ME.
GODA!!
I'LL GO GET THEM!
GOOD LUCK...
MUMBLE MUMBLE
DON'T SLEEP. LET'S TALK!
TELL ME STORIES ABOUT AI!
...
IN MIDDLE SCHOOL... I WENT OVER TO... UMM...
...SUNA'S HOUSE... AND...

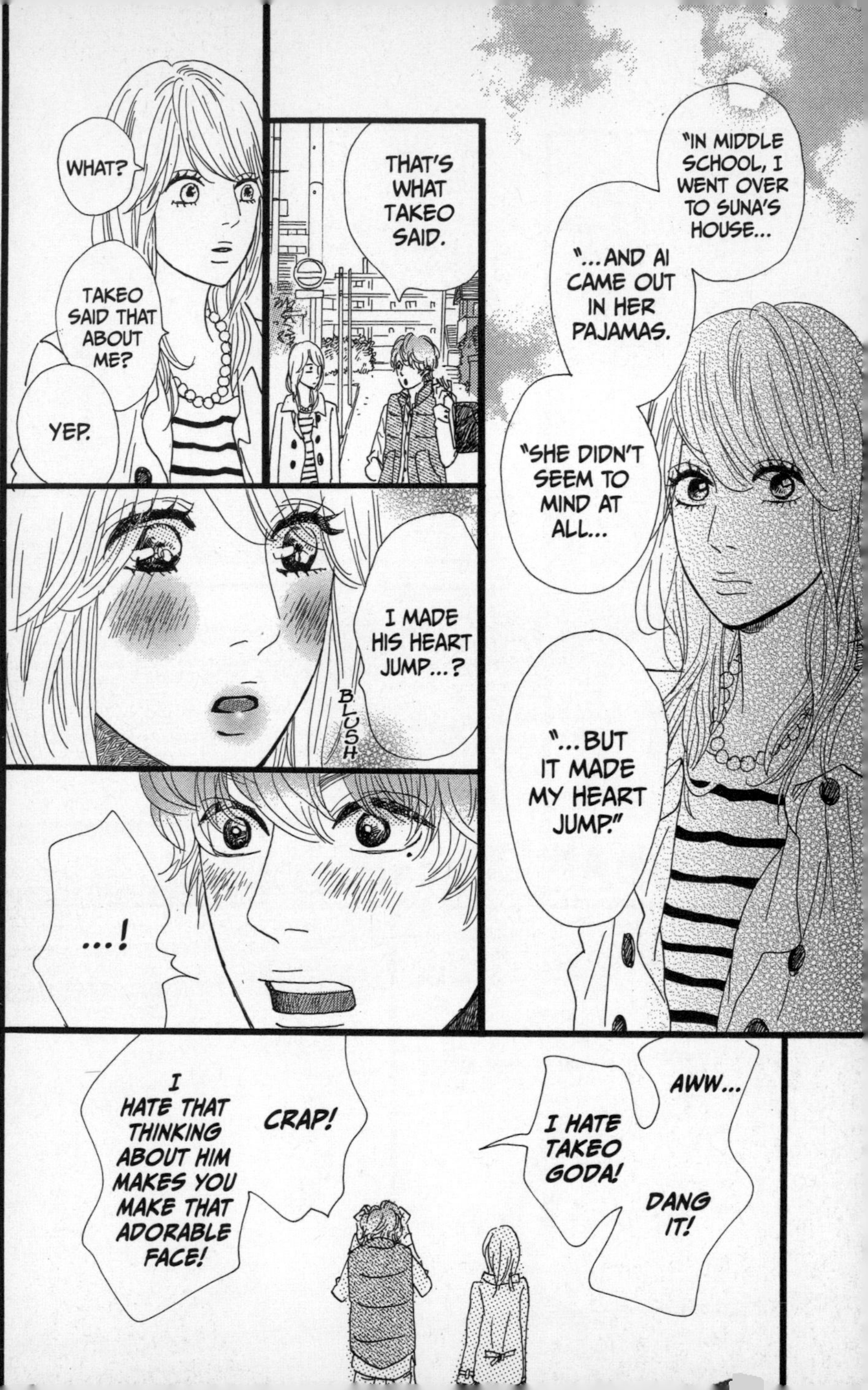
"IN MIDDLE SCHOOL, I WENT OVER TO SUNA'S HOUSE...
"...AND AI CAME OUT IN HER PAJAMAS.
"SHE DIDN'T SEEM TO MIND AT ALL...
"...BUT IT MADE MY HEART JUMP."
THAT'S WHAT TAKEO SAID.
WHAT?
TAKEO SAID THAT ABOUT ME?
YEP.
I MADE HIS HEART JUMP...?
BLUSH
...!
AWW...
"I HATE TAKEO GODA!
DANG IT!
CRAP!
I HATE THAT THINKING ABOUT HIM MAKES YOU MAKE THAT ADORABLE FACE!

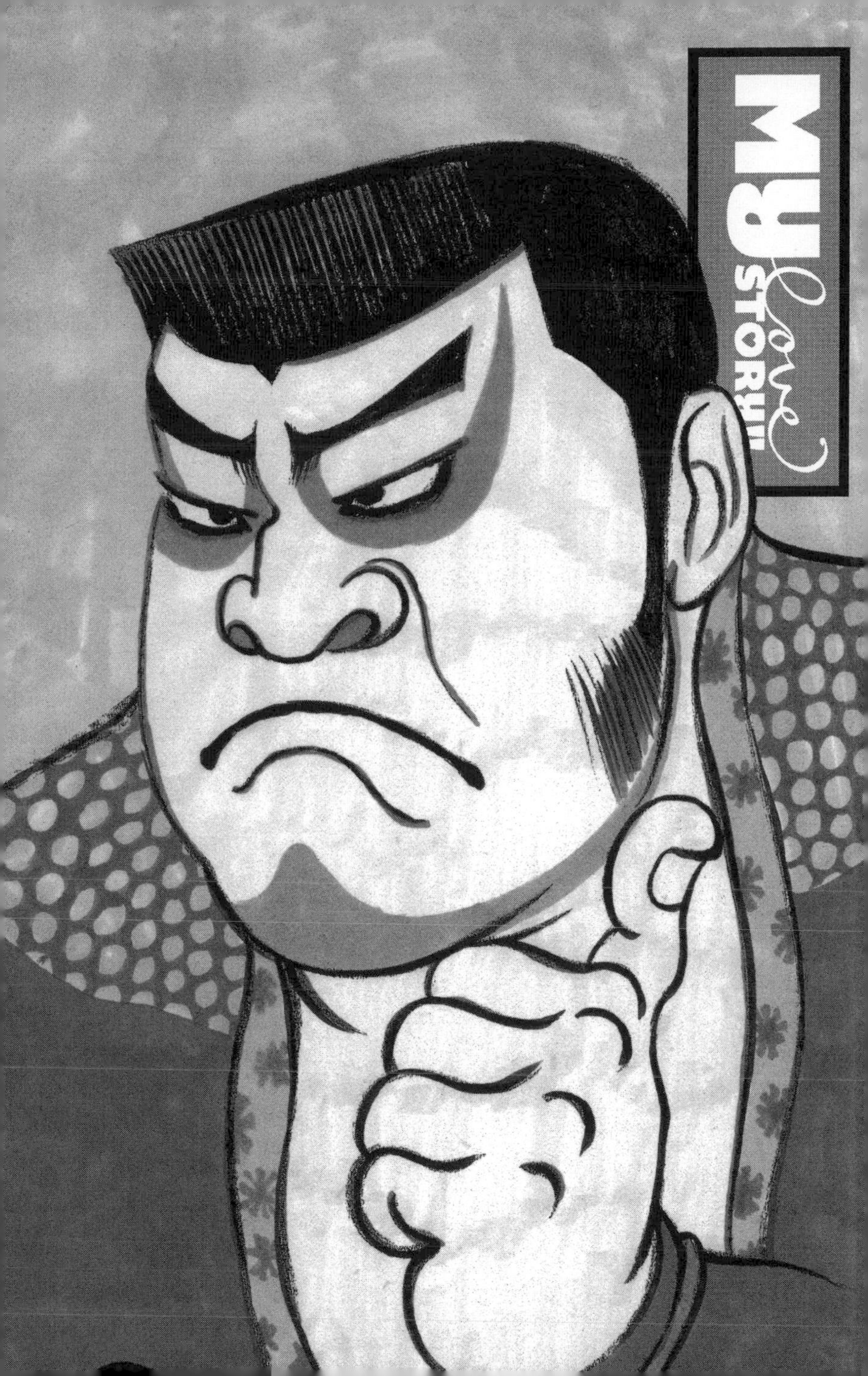
MY love STORY!!

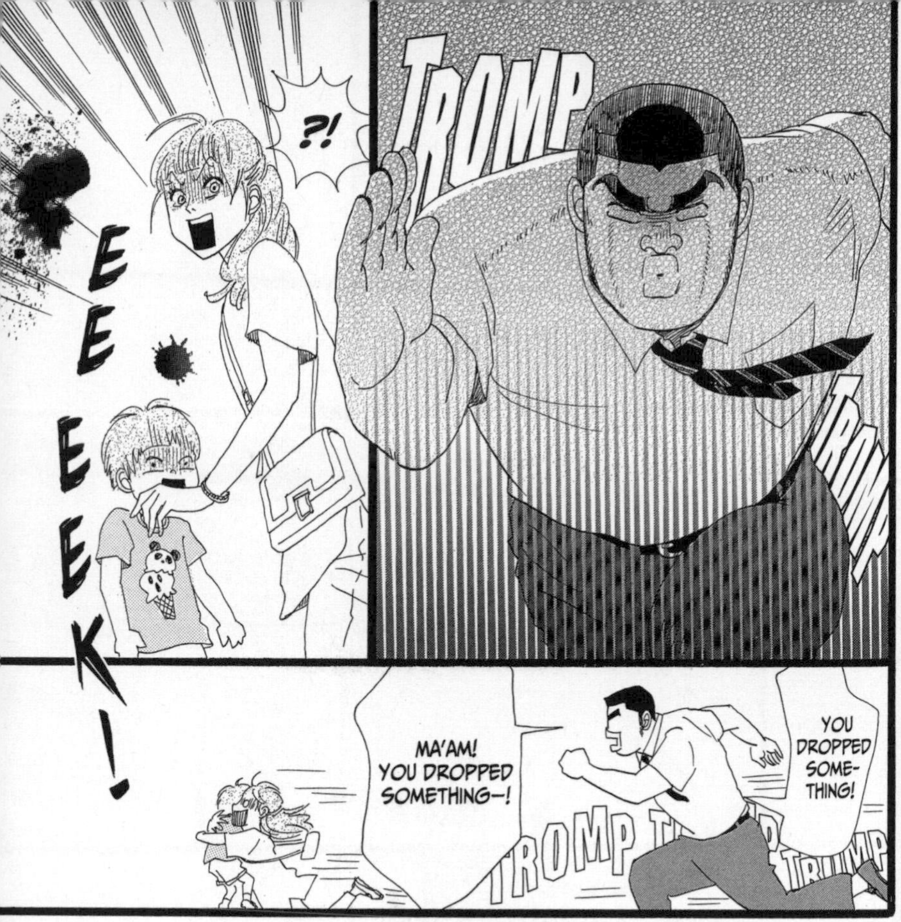
TROMP
TROMP
?!
EEEEEK!
YOU DROPPED SOME-THING!
TROMP
MA'AM! YOU DROPPED SOMETHING—!

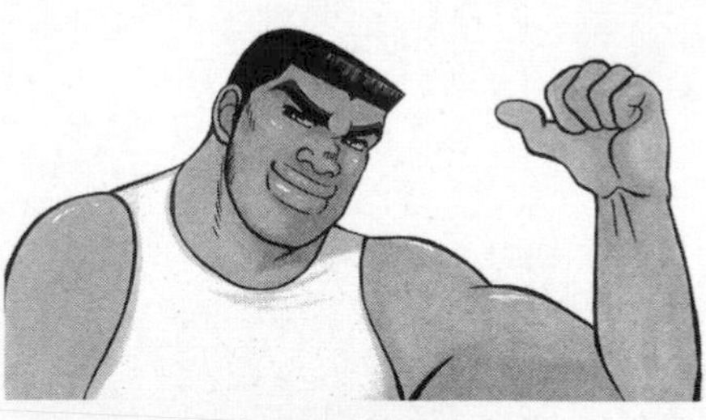

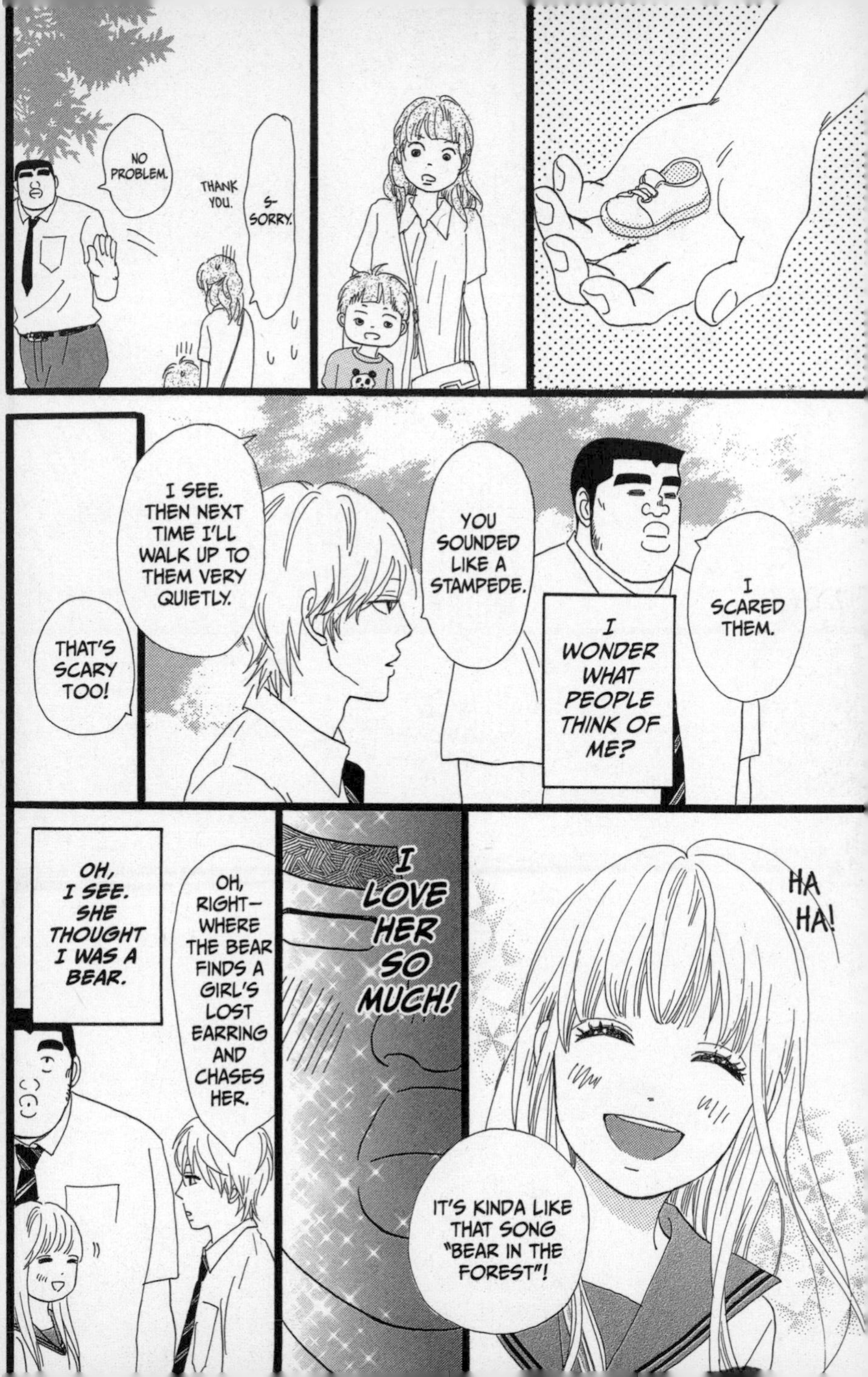
S-SORRY.
THANK YOU.
NO PROBLEM.
I SCARED THEM.
I WONDER WHAT PEOPLE THINK OF ME?
YOU SOUNDED LIKE A STAMPEDE.
I SEE. THEN NEXT TIME I'LL WALK UP TO THEM VERY QUIETLY.
THAT'S SCARY TOO!
HA HA!
IT'S KINDA LIKE THAT SONG "BEAR IN THE FOREST"!
I LOVE HER SO MUCH!
OH, RIGHT— WHERE THE BEAR FINDS A GIRL'S LOST EARRING AND CHASES HER.
OH, I SEE. SHE THOUGHT I WAS A BEAR.

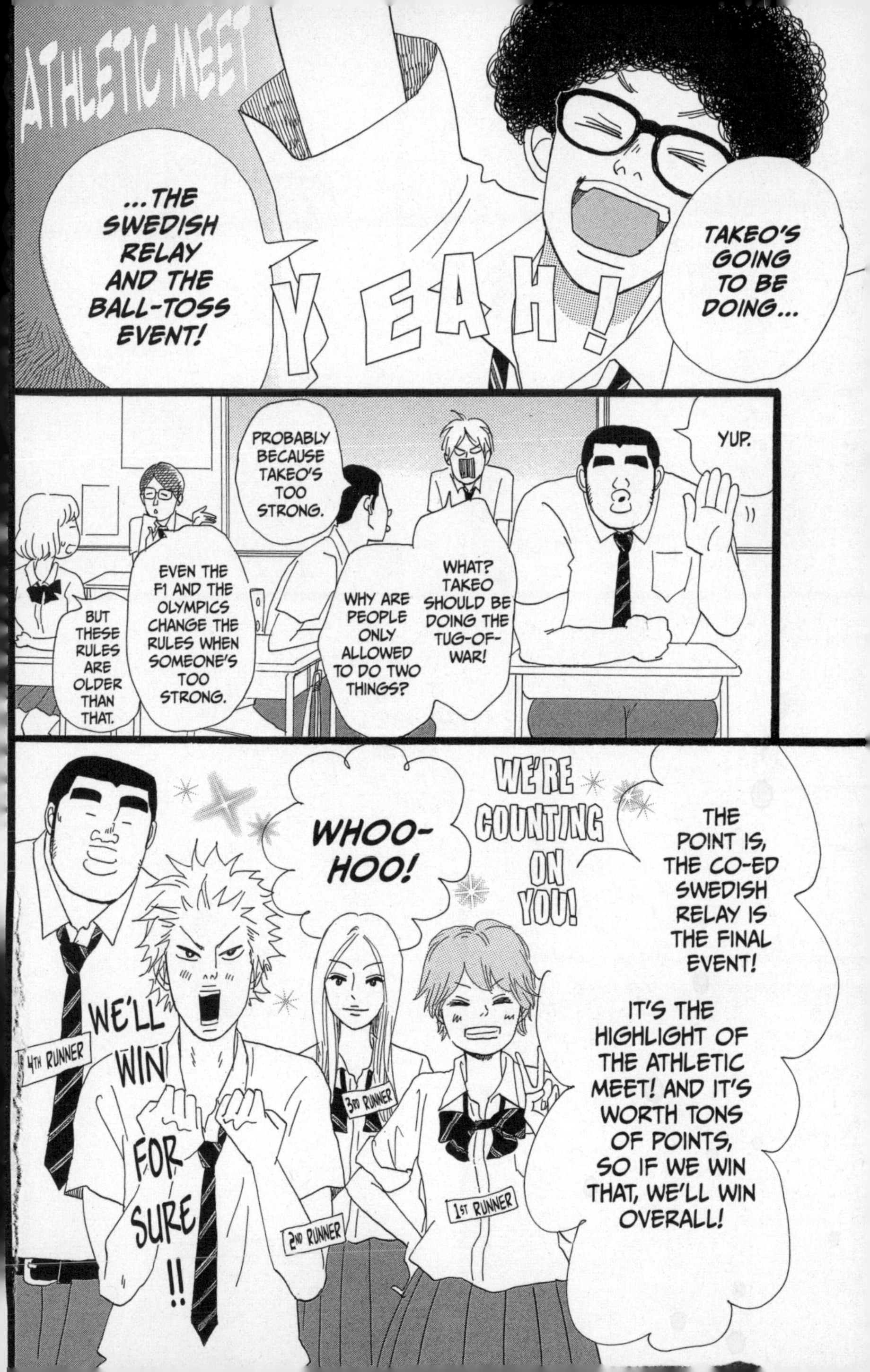
ATHLETIC MEET
TAKEO'S GOING TO BE DOING...
YEAH!
...THE SWEDISH RELAY AND THE BALL-TOSS EVENT!
YUP.
PROBABLY BECAUSE TAKEO'S TOO STRONG.
WHAT? TAKEO SHOULD BE DOING THE TUG-OF-WAR!
WHY ARE PEOPLE ONLY ALLOWED TO DO TWO THINGS?
EVEN THE F1 AND THE OLYMPICS CHANGE THE RULES WHEN SOMEONE'S TOO STRONG.
BUT THESE RULES ARE OLDER THAN THAT.
THE POINT IS, THE CO-ED SWEDISH RELAY IS THE FINAL EVENT!
IT'S THE HIGHLIGHT OF THE ATHLETIC MEET! AND IT'S WORTH TONS OF POINTS, SO IF WE WIN THAT, WE'LL WIN OVERALL!
WE'RE COUNTING ON YOU!
WHOO-HOO!
1ST RUNNER
3RD RUNNER
2ND RUNNER
WE'LL WIN FOR SURE!!
4TH RUNNER

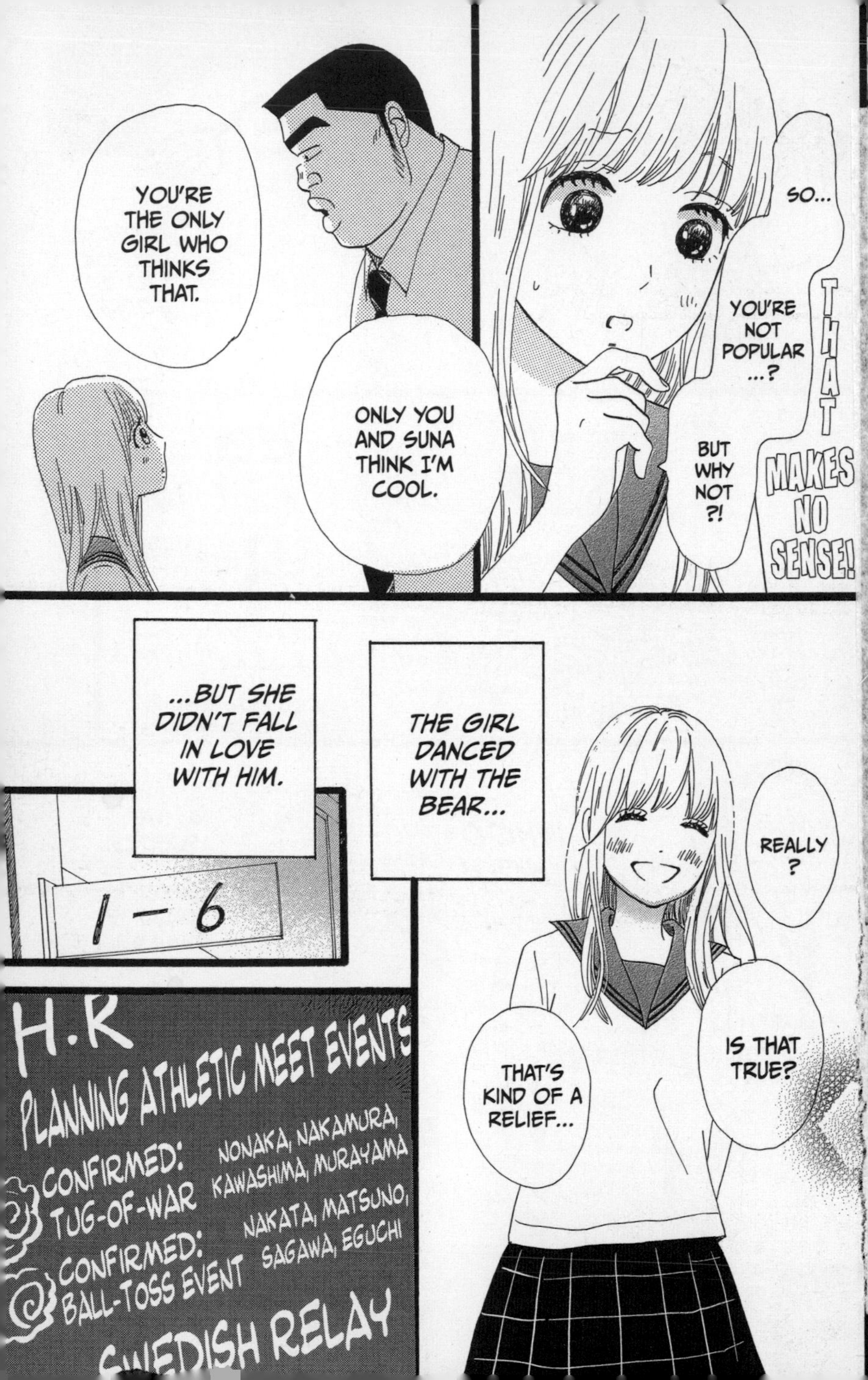
SO...
YOU'RE NOT POPULAR ...?
BUT WHY NOT ?!
THAT MAKES NO SENSE!
YOU'RE THE ONLY GIRL WHO THINKS THAT.
ONLY YOU AND SUNA THINK I'M COOL.
THE GIRL DANCED WITH THE BEAR...
...BUT SHE DIDN'T FALL IN LOVE WITH HIM.
REALLY ?
IS THAT TRUE?
THAT'S KIND OF A RELIEF...
1-6
H.R
PLANNING ATHLETIC MEET EVENTS
CONFIRMED: TUG-OF-WAR NONAKA, NAKAMURA, KAWASHIMA, MURAYAMA
CONFIRMED: BALL-TOSS EVENT NAKATA, MATSUNO, SAGAWA, EGUCHI
SWEDISH RELAY

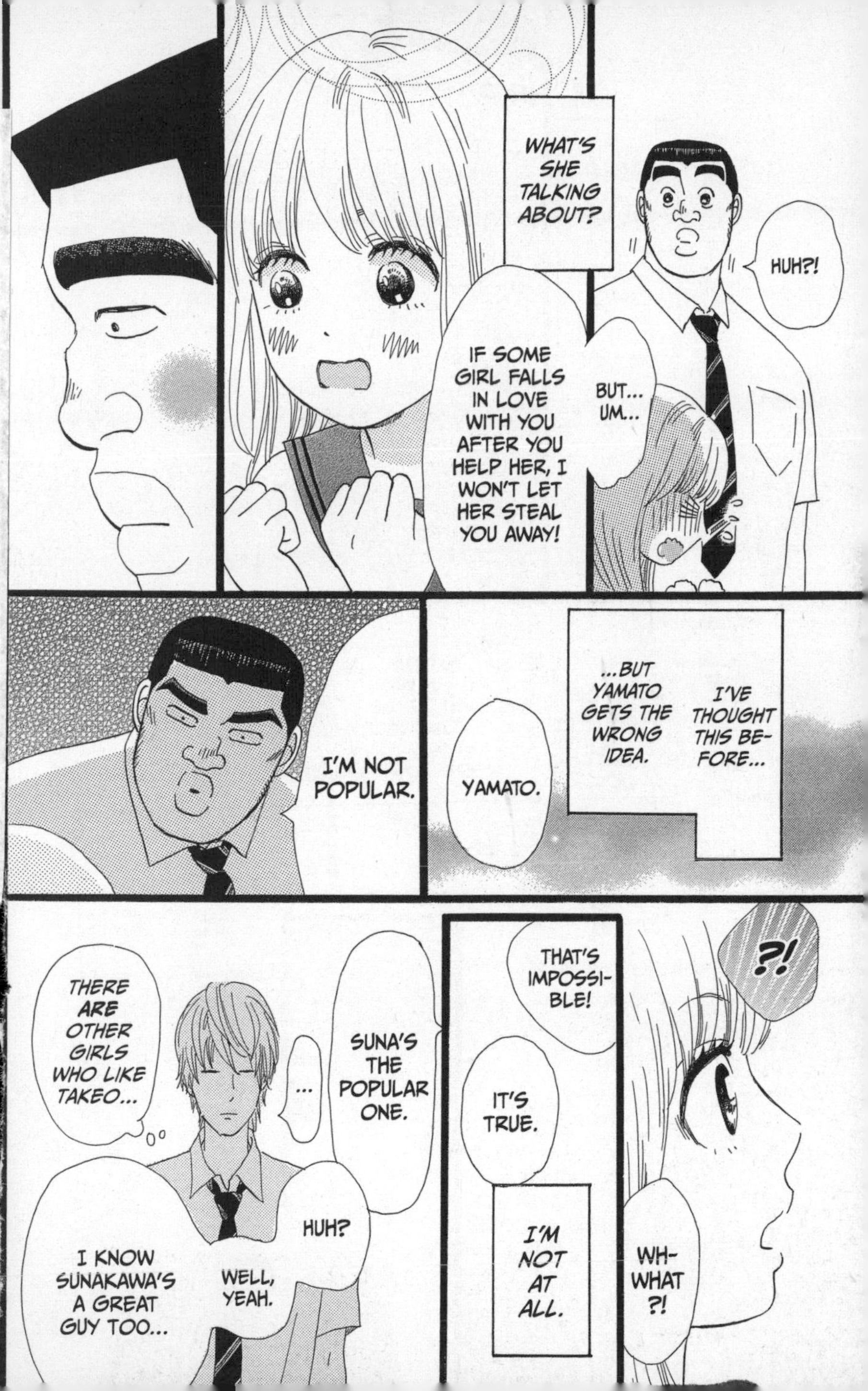
HUH?!
WHAT'S SHE TALKING ABOUT?
BUT... UM...
IF SOME GIRL FALLS IN LOVE WITH YOU AFTER YOU HELP HER, I WON'T LET HER STEAL YOU AWAY!
I'VE THOUGHT THIS BEFORE...
...BUT YAMATO GETS THE WRONG IDEA.
YAMATO.
I'M NOT POPULAR.
?!
THAT'S IMPOSSIBLE!
IT'S TRUE.
WH-WHAT?!
I'M NOT AT ALL.
SUNA'S THE POPULAR ONE.
...
THERE ARE OTHER GIRLS WHO LIKE TAKEO...
HUH?
WELL, YEAH.
I KNOW SUNAKAWA'S A GREAT GUY TOO...

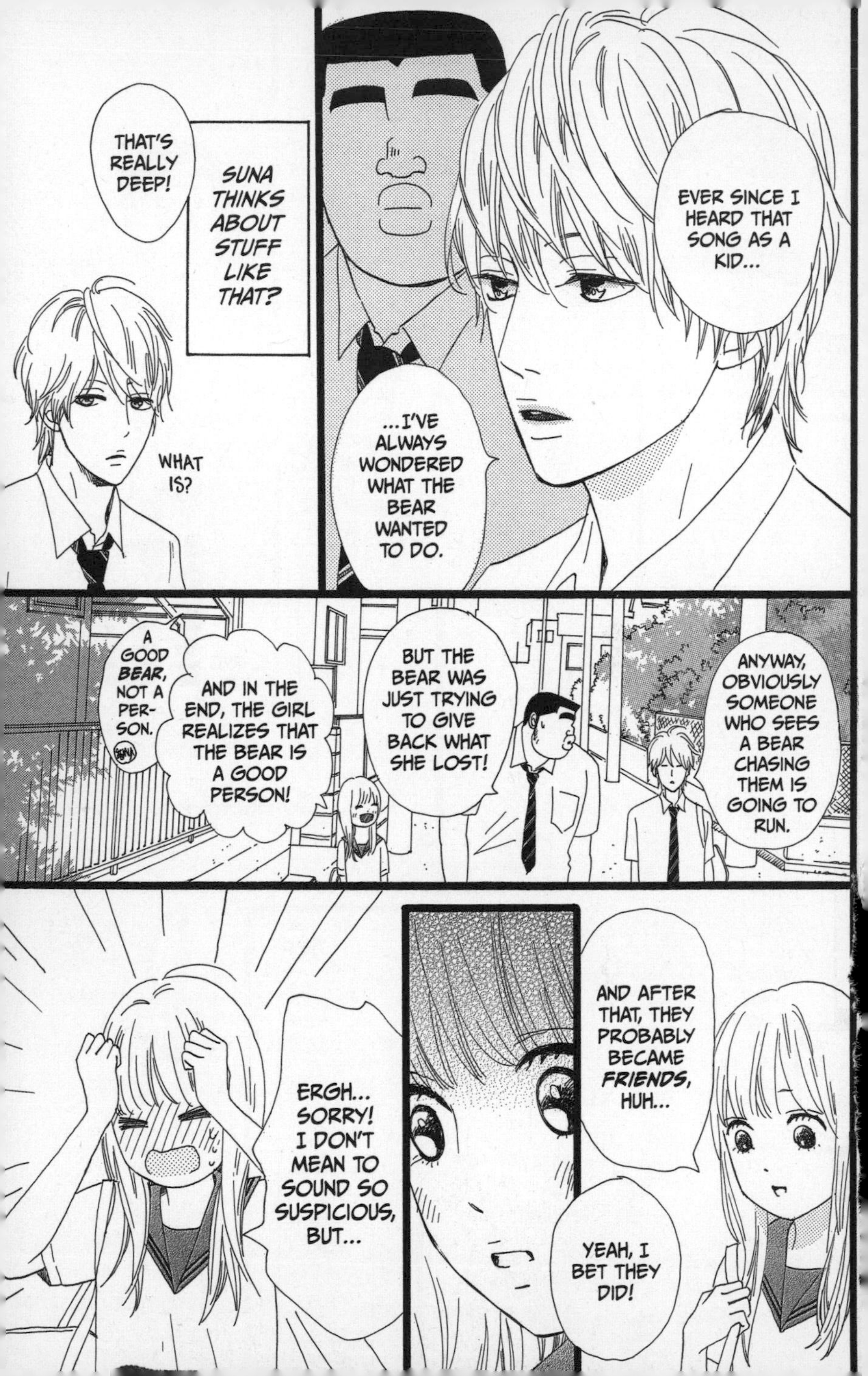
EVER SINCE I HEARD THAT SONG AS A KID...
...I'VE ALWAYS WONDERED WHAT THE BEAR WANTED TO DO.
SUNA THINKS ABOUT STUFF LIKE THAT?
THAT'S REALLY DEEP!
WHAT IS?
ANYWAY, OBVIOUSLY SOMEONE WHO SEES A BEAR CHASING THEM IS GOING TO RUN.
BUT THE BEAR WAS JUST TRYING TO GIVE BACK WHAT SHE LOST!
AND IN THE END, THE GIRL REALIZES THAT THE BEAR IS A GOOD PERSON!
A GOOD *BEAR*, NOT A PER- SON.
SUNA
AND AFTER THAT, THEY PROBABLY BECAME *FRIENDS*, HUH...
YEAH, I BET THEY DID!
ERGH... SORRY! I DON'T MEAN TO SOUND SO SUSPICIOUS, BUT...

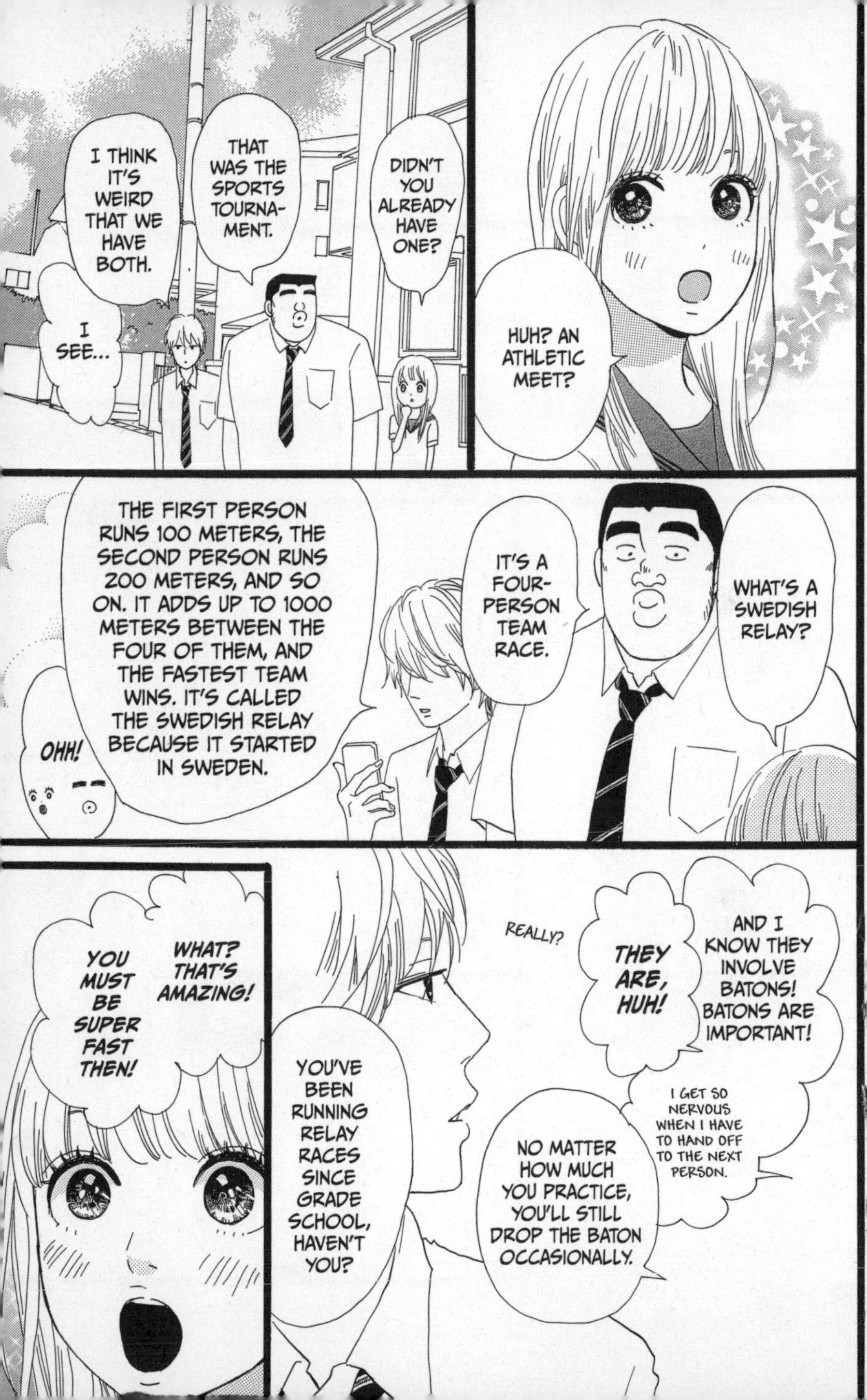
HUH? AN ATHLETIC MEET?
DIDN'T YOU ALREADY HAVE ONE?
THAT WAS THE SPORTS TOURNAMENT.
I THINK IT'S WEIRD THAT WE HAVE BOTH.
I SEE...
WHAT'S A SWEDISH RELAY?
IT'S A FOUR-PERSON TEAM RACE.
THE FIRST PERSON RUNS 100 METERS, THE SECOND PERSON RUNS 200 METERS, AND SO ON. IT ADDS UP TO 1000 METERS BETWEEN THE FOUR OF THEM, AND THE FASTEST TEAM WINS. IT'S CALLED THE SWEDISH RELAY BECAUSE IT STARTED IN SWEDEN.
OHH!
AND I KNOW THEY INVOLVE BATONS! BATONS ARE IMPORTANT!
THEY ARE, HUH!
REALLY?
I GET SO NERVOUS WHEN I HAVE TO HAND OFF TO THE NEXT PERSON.
NO MATTER HOW MUCH YOU PRACTICE, YOU'LL STILL DROP THE BATON OCCASIONALLY.
YOU'VE BEEN RUNNING RELAY RACES SINCE GRADE SCHOOL, HAVEN'T YOU?
WHAT? THAT'S AMAZING!
YOU MUST BE SUPER FAST THEN!

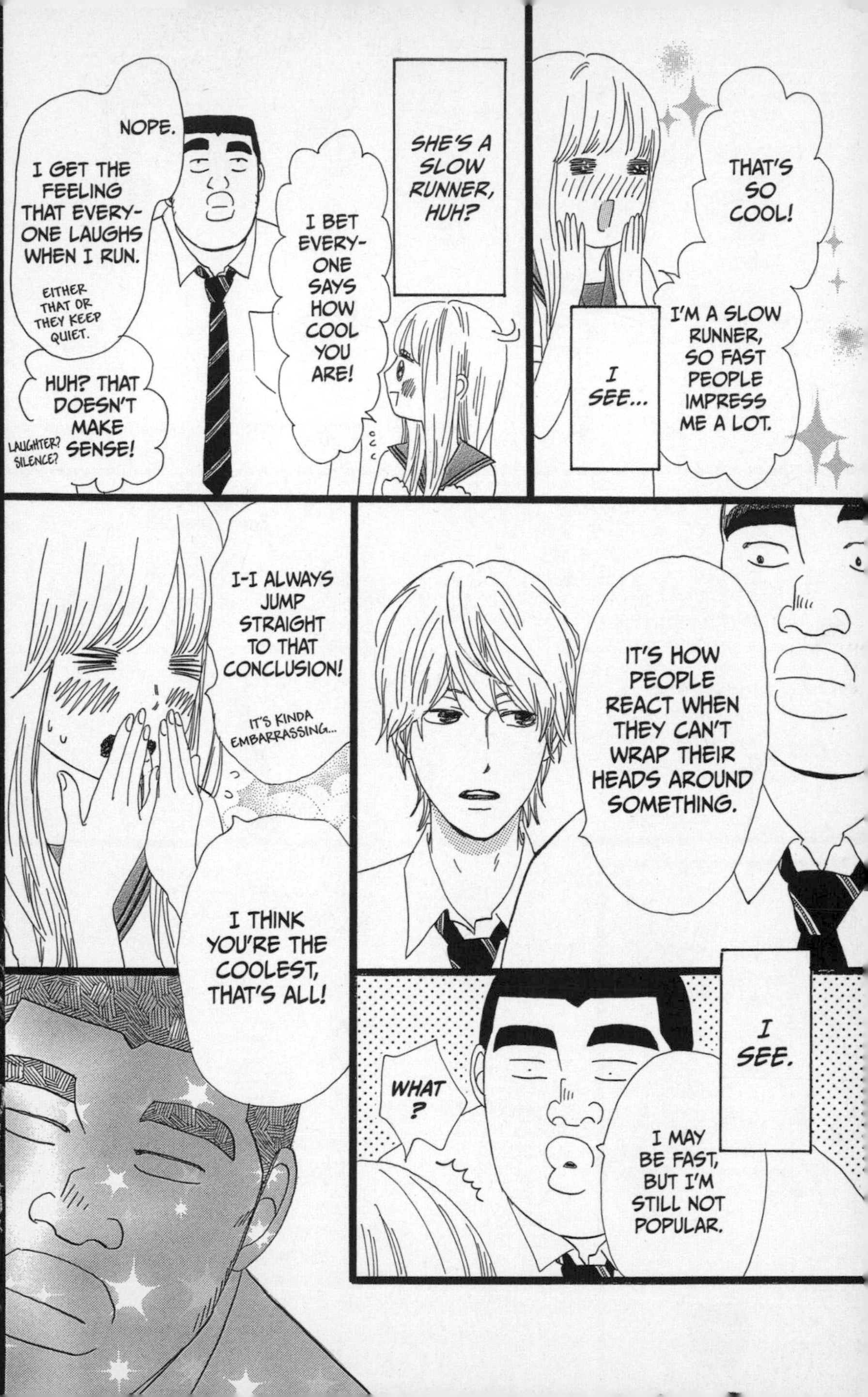
THAT'S SO COOL!
I'M A SLOW RUNNER, SO FAST PEOPLE IMPRESS ME A LOT.
I SEE...
SHE'S A SLOW RUNNER, HUH?
I BET EVERYONE SAYS HOW COOL YOU ARE!
NOPE.
I GET THE FEELING THAT EVERYONE LAUGHS WHEN I RUN.
EITHER THAT OR THEY KEEP QUIET.
HUH? THAT DOESN'T MAKE SENSE!
LAUGHTER? SILENCE?
IT'S HOW PEOPLE REACT WHEN THEY CAN'T WRAP THEIR HEADS AROUND SOMETHING.
I-I ALWAYS JUMP STRAIGHT TO THAT CONCLUSION!
IT'S KINDA EMBARRASSING...
I THINK YOU'RE THE COOLEST, THAT'S ALL!
I SEE.
I MAY BE FAST, BUT I'M STILL NOT POPULAR.
WHAT?

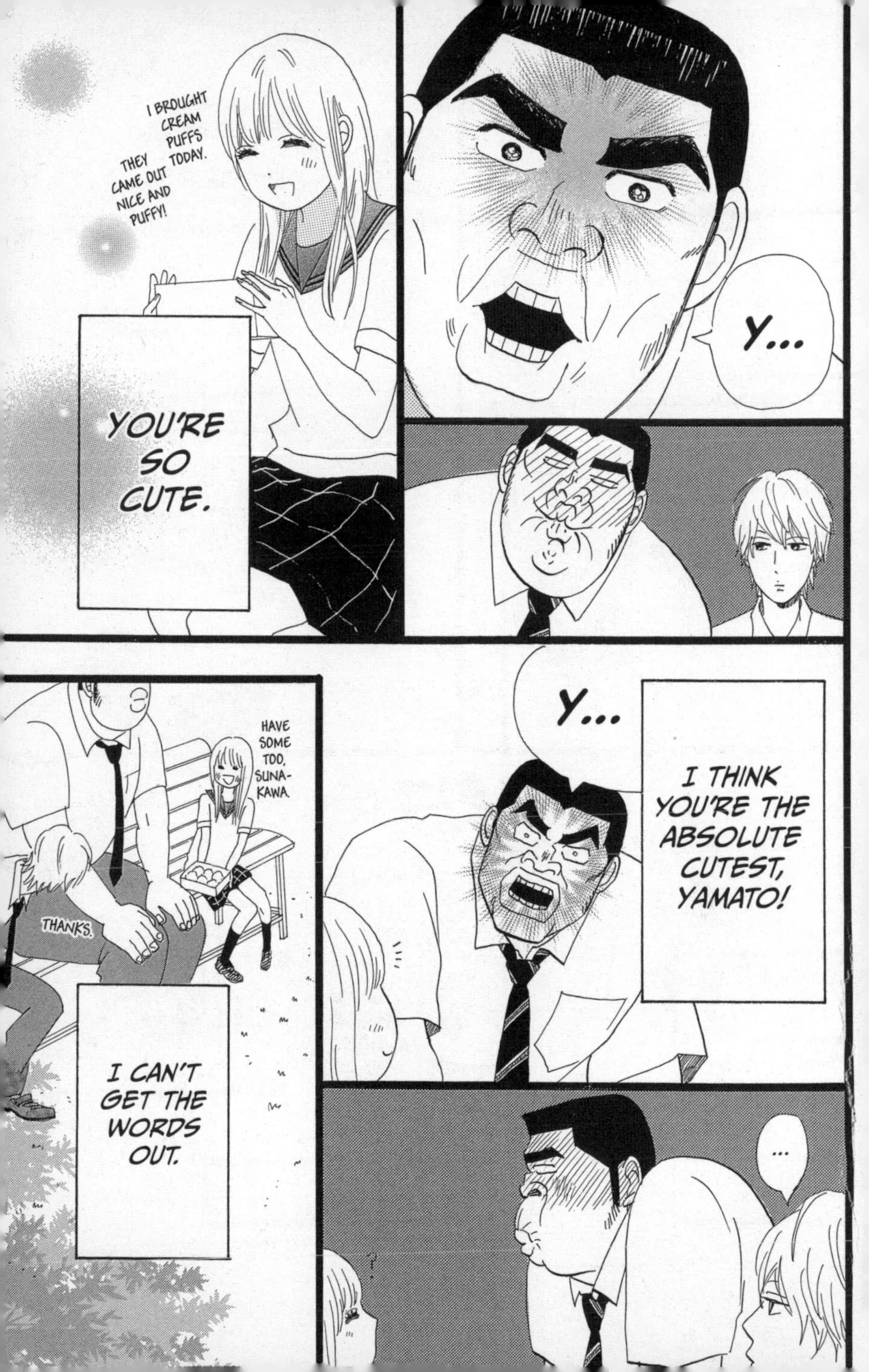
Y...
I BROUGHT CREAM PUFFS TODAY.
THEY CAME OUT NICE AND PUFFY!
YOU'RE SO CUTE.
Y...
I THINK YOU'RE THE ABSOLUTE CUTEST, YAMATO!
...
HAVE SOME TOO, SUNAKAWA.
THANKS.
I CAN'T GET THE WORDS OUT.

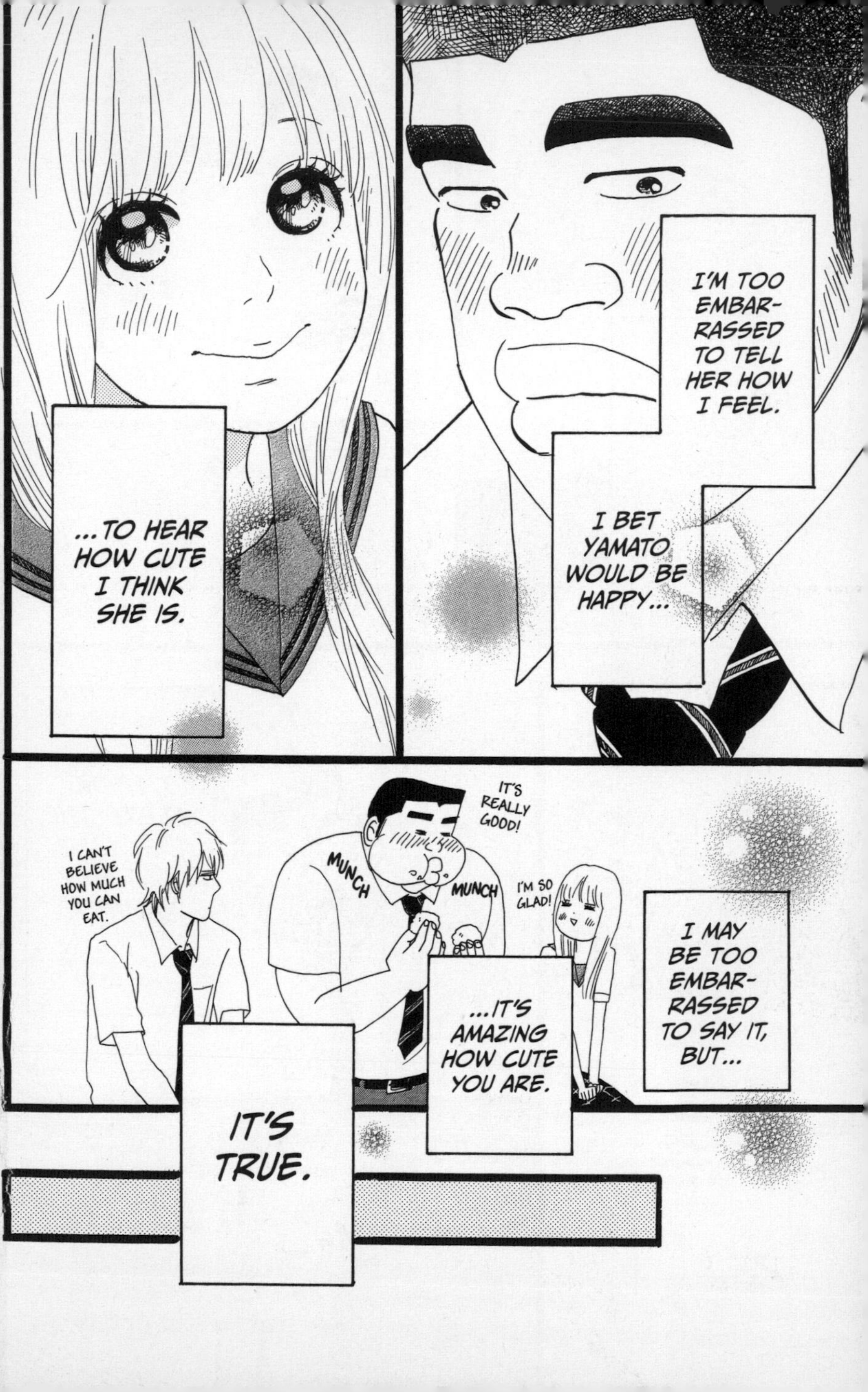
I'M TOO EMBARRASSED TO TELL HER HOW I FEEL.
I BET YAMATO WOULD BE HAPPY...
...TO HEAR HOW CUTE I THINK SHE IS.
I MAY BE TOO EMBARRASSED TO SAY IT, BUT...
IT'S REALLY GOOD!
MUNCH
MUNCH
I'M SO GLAD!
...IT'S AMAZING HOW CUTE YOU ARE.
I CAN'T BELIEVE HOW MUCH YOU CAN EAT.
IT'S TRUE.

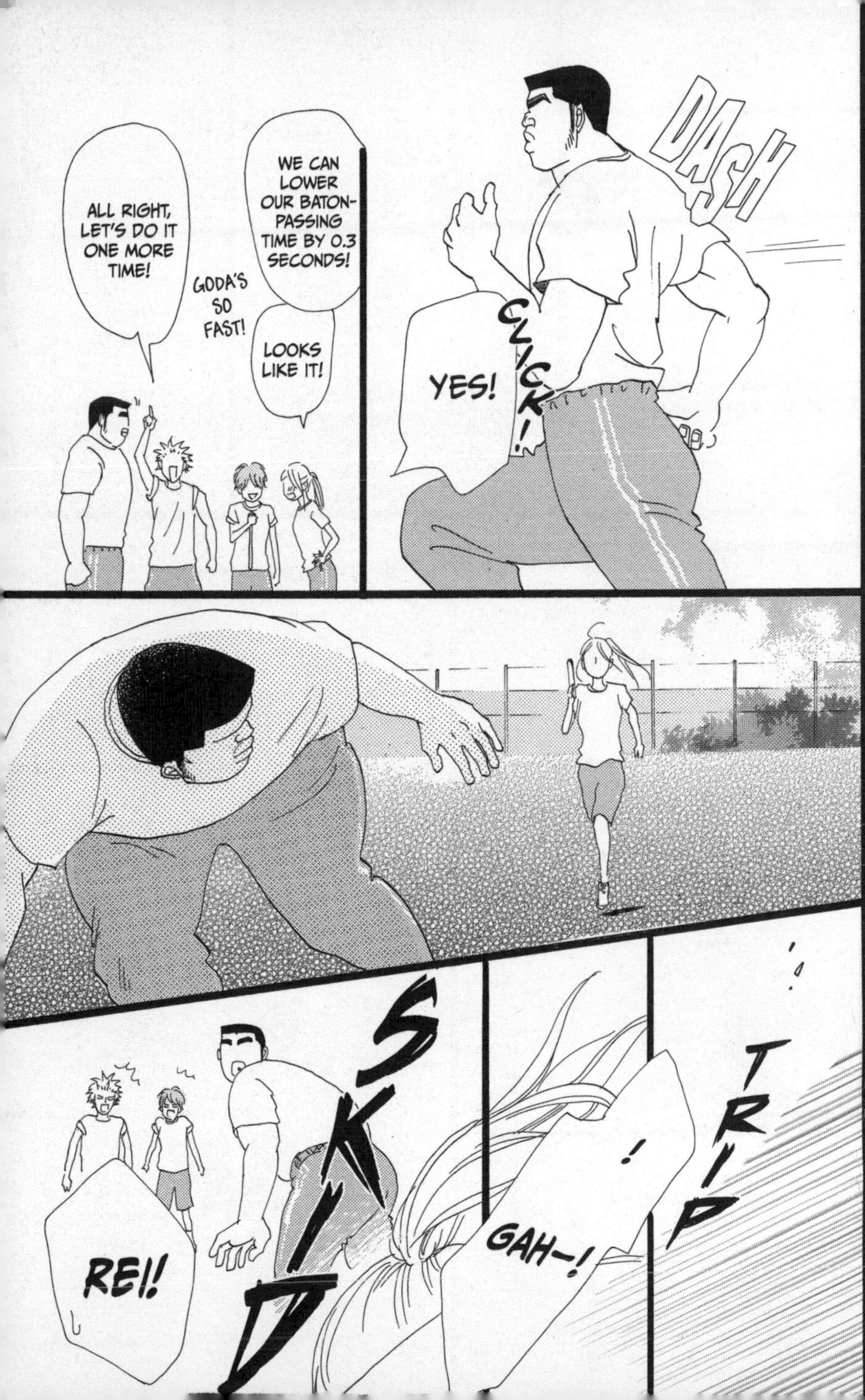
DASH
CLICK!
YES!
WE CAN LOWER OUR BATON-PASSING TIME BY 0.3 SECONDS!
LOOKS LIKE IT!
GODA'S SO FAST!
ALL RIGHT, LET'S DO IT ONE MORE TIME!
TRIP
GAH-!
SKID
REI!

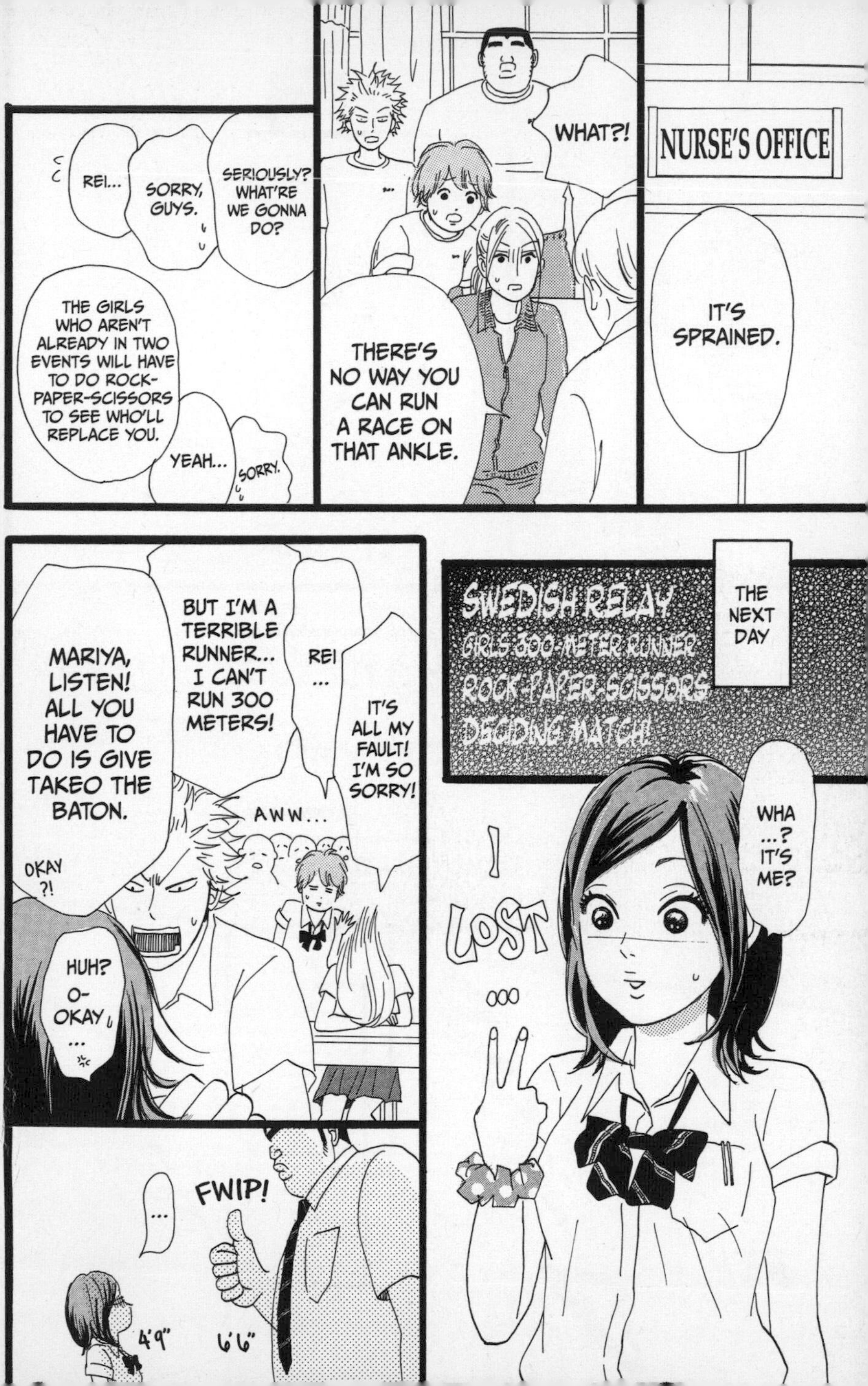
NURSE'S OFFICE
IT'S SPRAINED.
WHAT?!
THERE'S NO WAY YOU CAN RUN A RACE ON THAT ANKLE.
SERIOUSLY? WHAT'RE WE GONNA DO?
SORRY, GUYS.
REI...
THE GIRLS WHO AREN'T ALREADY IN TWO EVENTS WILL HAVE TO DO ROCK-PAPER-SCISSORS TO SEE WHO'LL REPLACE YOU.
YEAH...
SORRY.
THE NEXT DAY
SWEDISH RELAY
GIRLS 300-METER RUNNER
ROCK-PAPER-SCISSORS
DECIDING MATCH!
WHA...? IT'S ME?
I LOST
BUT I'M A TERRIBLE RUNNER... I CAN'T RUN 300 METERS!
REI...
IT'S ALL MY FAULT! I'M SO SORRY!
MARIYA, LISTEN! ALL YOU HAVE TO DO IS GIVE TAKEO THE BATON.
AWW...
OKAY?!
HUH? O-OKAY...
FWIP!
...
4'9"
6'6"

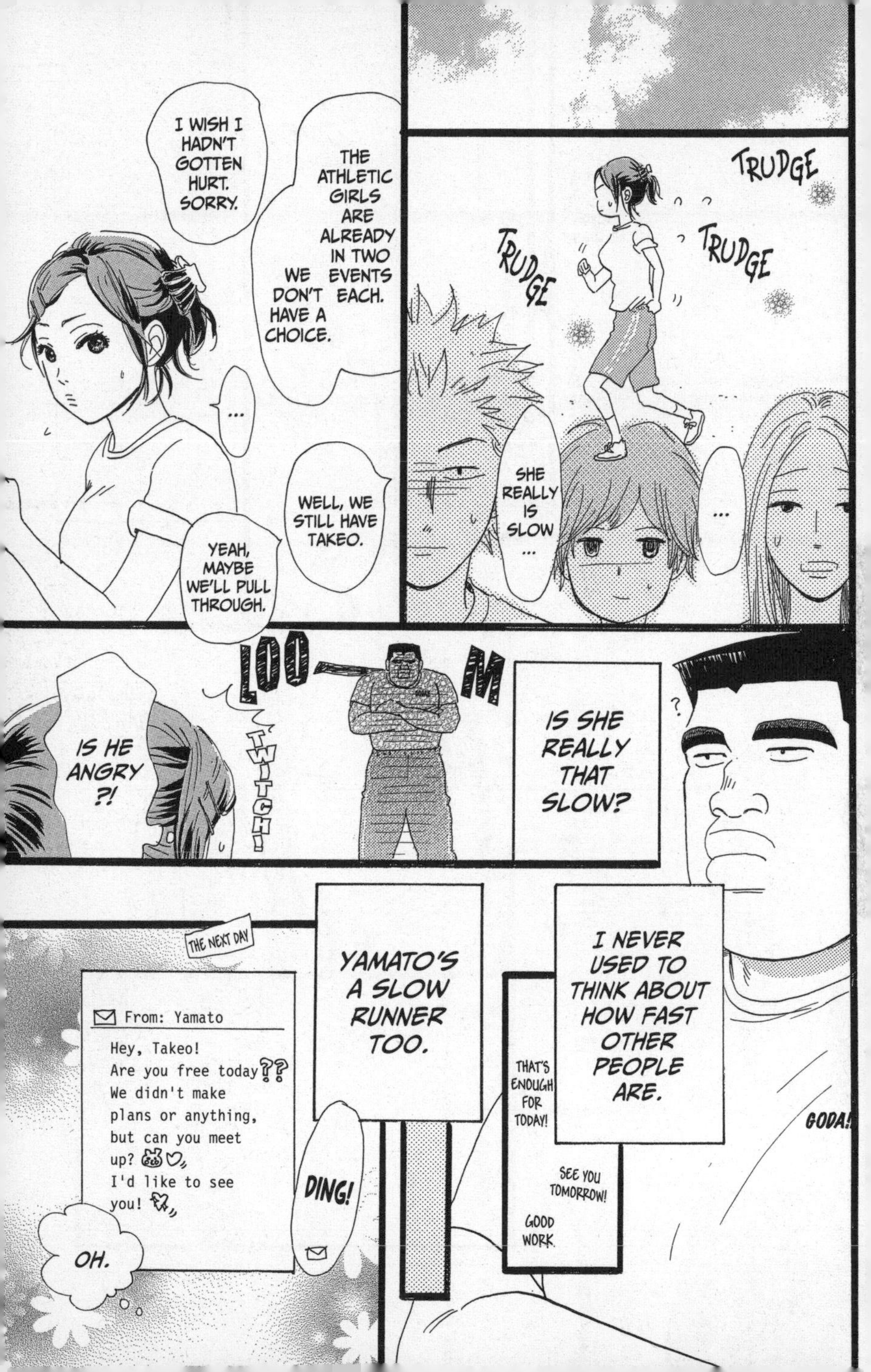
TRUDGE
TRUDGE
TRUDGE
...
SHE REALLY IS SLOW...
THE ATHLETIC GIRLS ARE ALREADY IN TWO EVENTS EACH. WE DON'T HAVE A CHOICE.
I WISH I HADN'T GOTTEN HURT. SORRY.
...
WELL, WE STILL HAVE TAKEO.
YEAH, MAYBE WE'LL PULL THROUGH.
?
IS SHE REALLY THAT SLOW?
LOOOM
TWITCH!
IS HE ANGRY?!
GODA!
I NEVER USED TO THINK ABOUT HOW FAST OTHER PEOPLE ARE.
THAT'S ENOUGH FOR TODAY!
SEE YOU TOMORROW!
GOOD WORK.
YAMATO'S A SLOW RUNNER TOO.
DING!
THE NEXT DAY
From: Yamato
Hey, Takeo!
Are you free today??
We didn't make plans or anything, but can you meet up?
I'd like to see you!
OH.

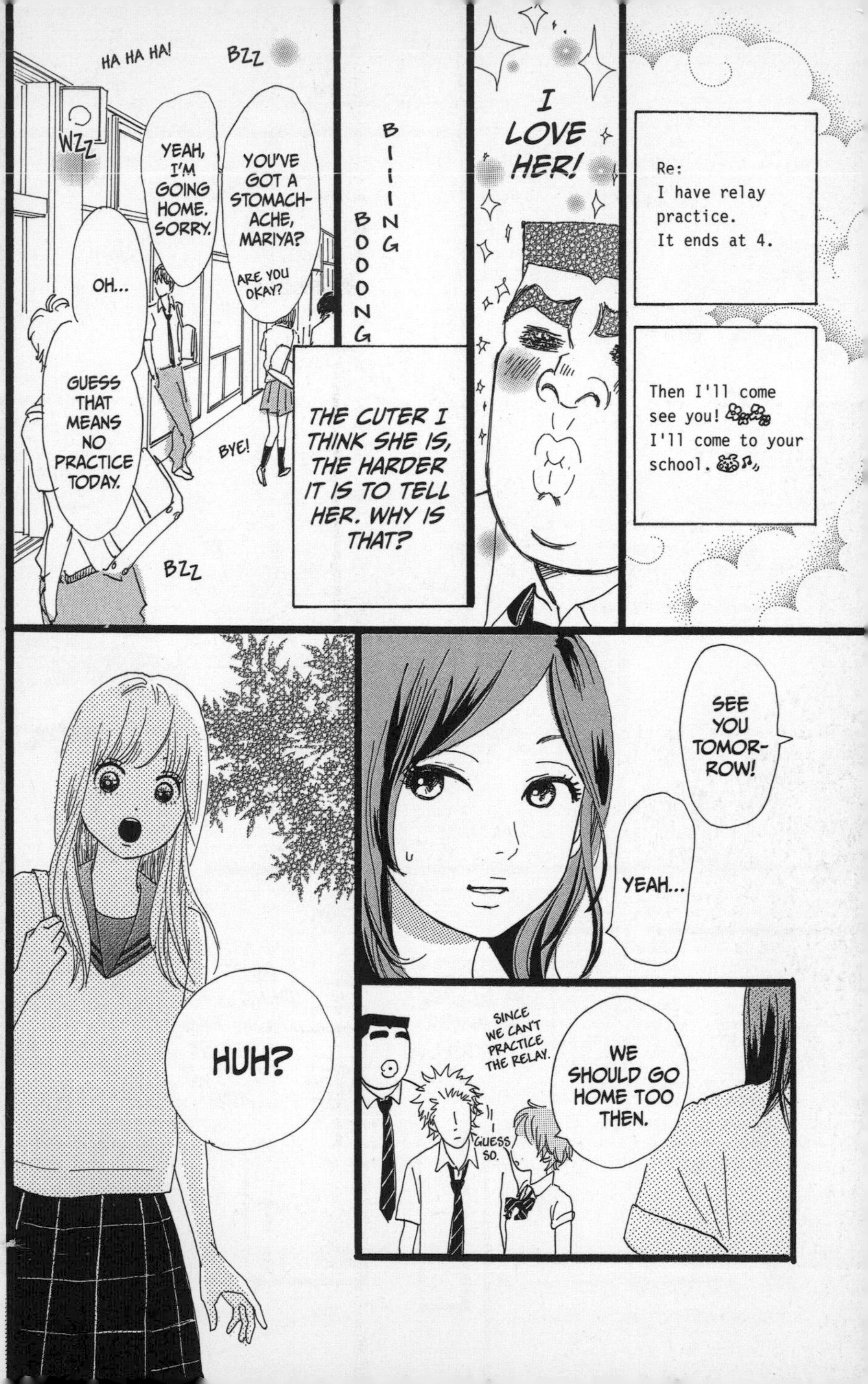
Re:
I have relay practice.
It ends at 4.
Then I'll come see you!
I'll come to your school.
I LOVE HER!
BIIING
BOOONG
THE CUTER I THINK SHE IS, THE HARDER IT IS TO TELL HER. WHY IS THAT?
BZZ
HA HA HA!
YOU'VE GOT A STOMACHACHE, MARIYA?
ARE YOU OKAY?
YEAH, I'M GOING HOME. SORRY.
WZZ
BYE!
OH...
GUESS THAT MEANS NO PRACTICE TODAY.
BZZ
SEE YOU TOMORROW!
YEAH...
WE SHOULD GO HOME TOO THEN.
SINCE WE CAN'T PRACTICE THE RELAY.
I GUESS SO.
HUH?

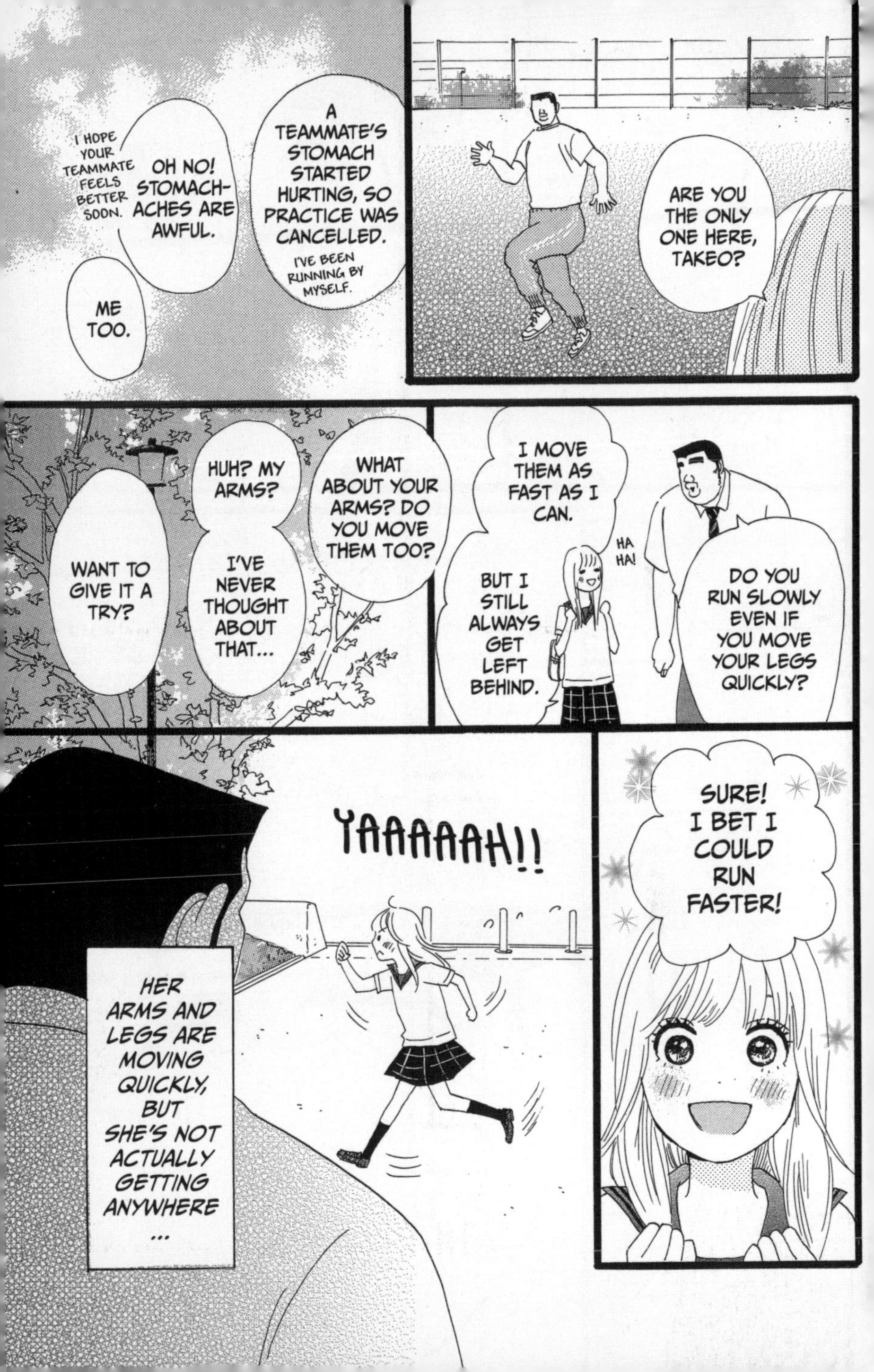
ARE YOU THE ONLY ONE HERE, TAKEO?
A TEAMMATE'S STOMACH STARTED HURTING, SO PRACTICE WAS CANCELLED.
I'VE BEEN RUNNING BY MYSELF.
OH NO! STOMACH-ACHES ARE AWFUL.
I HOPE YOUR TEAMMATE FEELS BETTER SOON.
ME TOO.
DO YOU RUN SLOWLY EVEN IF YOU MOVE YOUR LEGS QUICKLY?
HA HA!
I MOVE THEM AS FAST AS I CAN.
BUT I STILL ALWAYS GET LEFT BEHIND.
WHAT ABOUT YOUR ARMS? DO YOU MOVE THEM TOO?
HUH? MY ARMS?
I'VE NEVER THOUGHT ABOUT THAT...
WANT TO GIVE IT A TRY?
SURE! I BET I COULD RUN FASTER!
YAAAAAH!!
HER ARMS AND LEGS ARE MOVING QUICKLY, BUT SHE'S NOT ACTUALLY GETTING ANYWHERE...

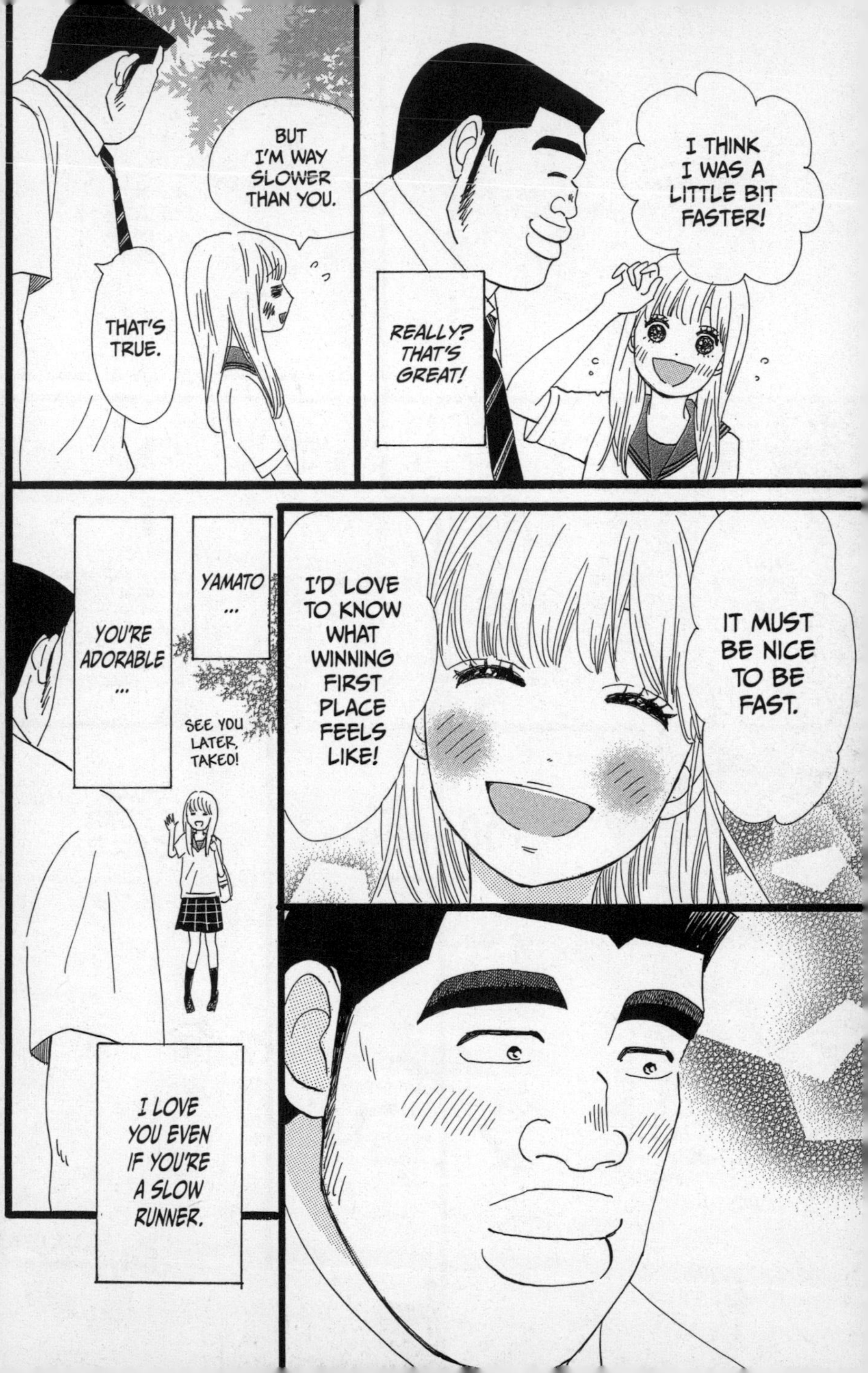
I THINK I WAS A LITTLE BIT FASTER!
REALLY? THAT'S GREAT!
BUT I'M WAY SLOWER THAN YOU.
THAT'S TRUE.
IT MUST BE NICE TO BE FAST.
I'D LOVE TO KNOW WHAT WINNING FIRST PLACE FEELS LIKE!
YAMATO ...
YOU'RE ADORABLE ...
SEE YOU LATER, TAKEO!
I LOVE YOU EVEN IF YOU'RE A SLOW RUNNER.

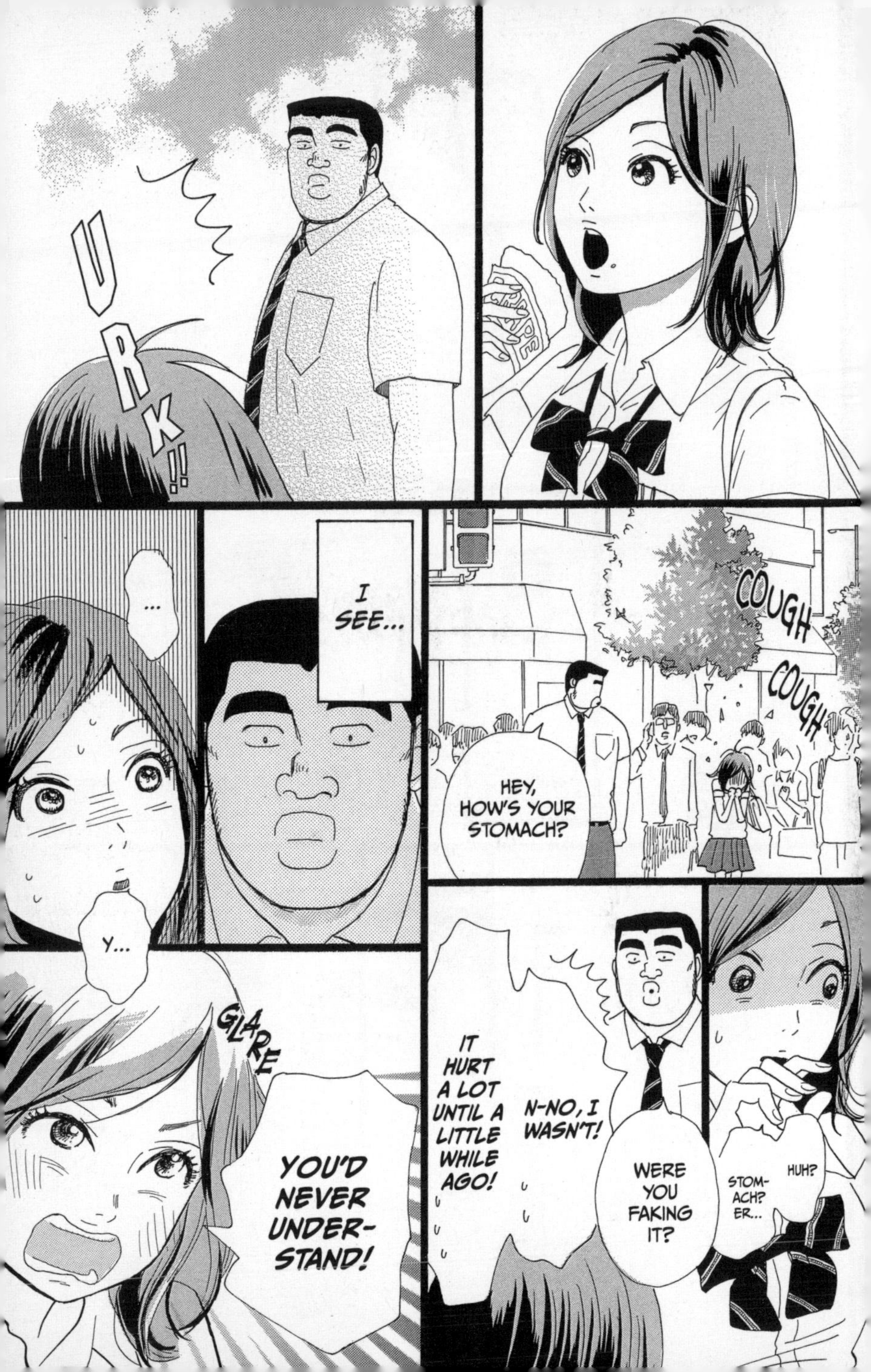
URK!!
COUGH
COUGH
HEY, HOW'S YOUR STOMACH?
HUH?
STOM-ACH? ER...
WERE YOU FAKING IT?
N-NO, I WASN'T!
IT HURT A LOT UNTIL A LITTLE WHILE AGO!
I SEE...
...
Y...
GLARE
YOU'D NEVER UNDER-STAND!

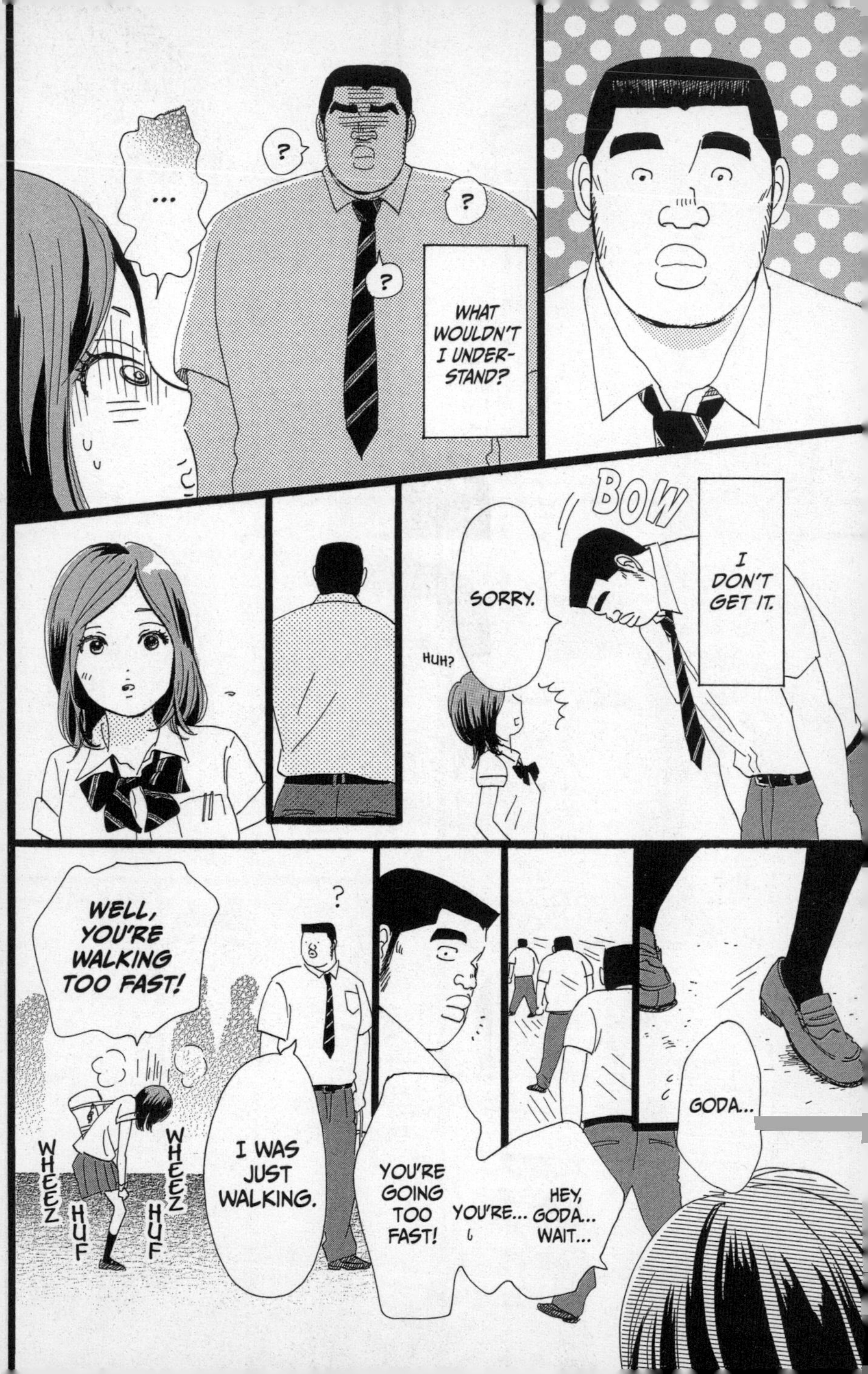
WHAT WOULDN'T I UNDER-STAND?
?
?
?
...
BOW
I DON'T GET IT.
SORRY.
HUH?
GODA...
HEY, GODA... WAIT...
YOU'RE...
YOU'RE GOING TOO FAST!
?
I WAS JUST WALKING.
WELL, YOU'RE WALKING TOO FAST!
WHEEZ
WHEEZ
HUF
HUF

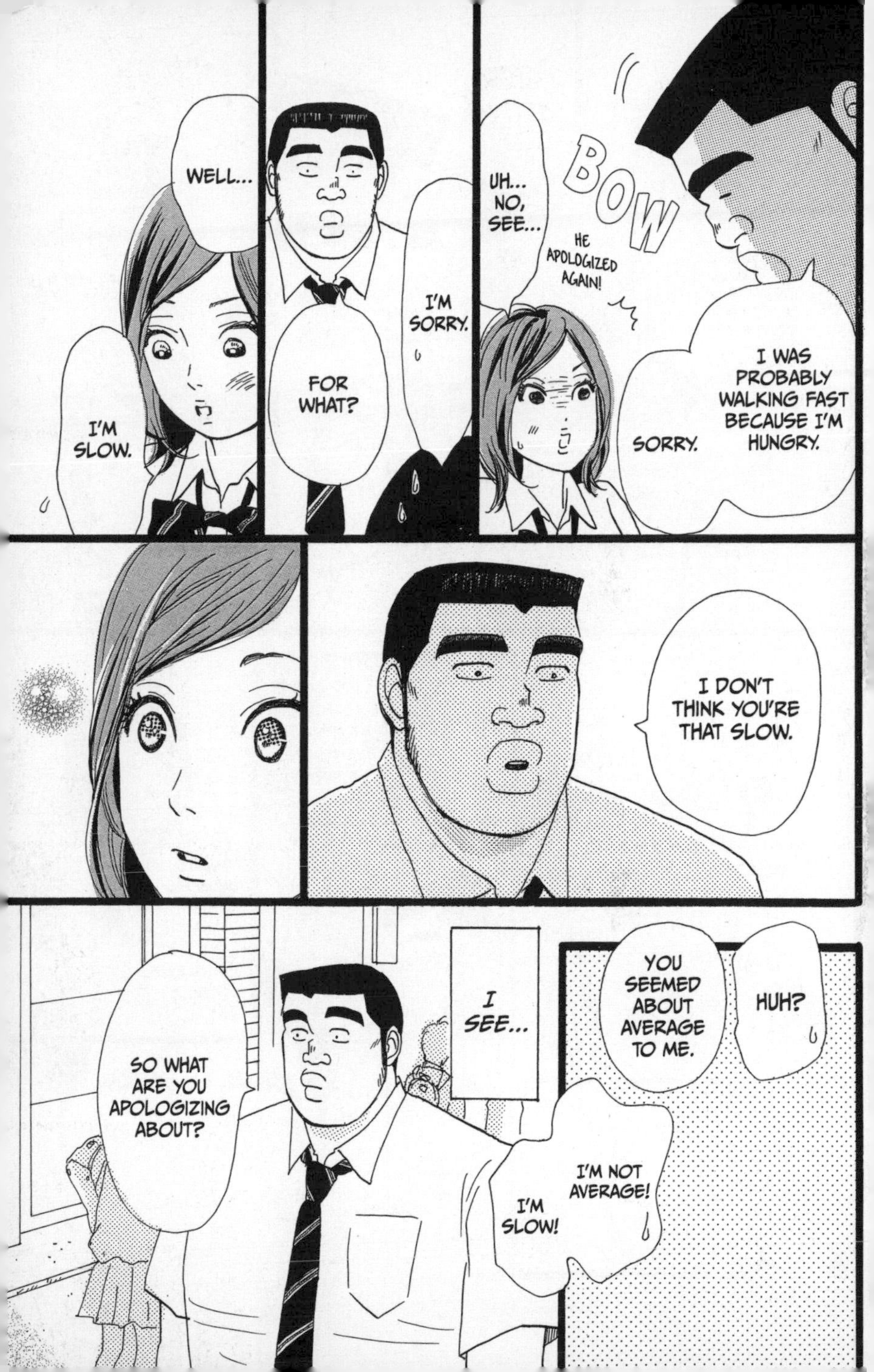
BOW
I WAS PROBABLY WALKING FAST BECAUSE I'M HUNGRY.
SORRY.
HE APOLOGIZED AGAIN!
UH... NO, SEE...
I'M SORRY.
FOR WHAT?
WELL...
I'M SLOW.
I DON'T THINK YOU'RE THAT SLOW.
HUH?
YOU SEEMED ABOUT AVERAGE TO ME.
I'M NOT AVERAGE!
I'M SLOW!
I SEE...
SO WHAT ARE YOU APOLOGIZING ABOUT?

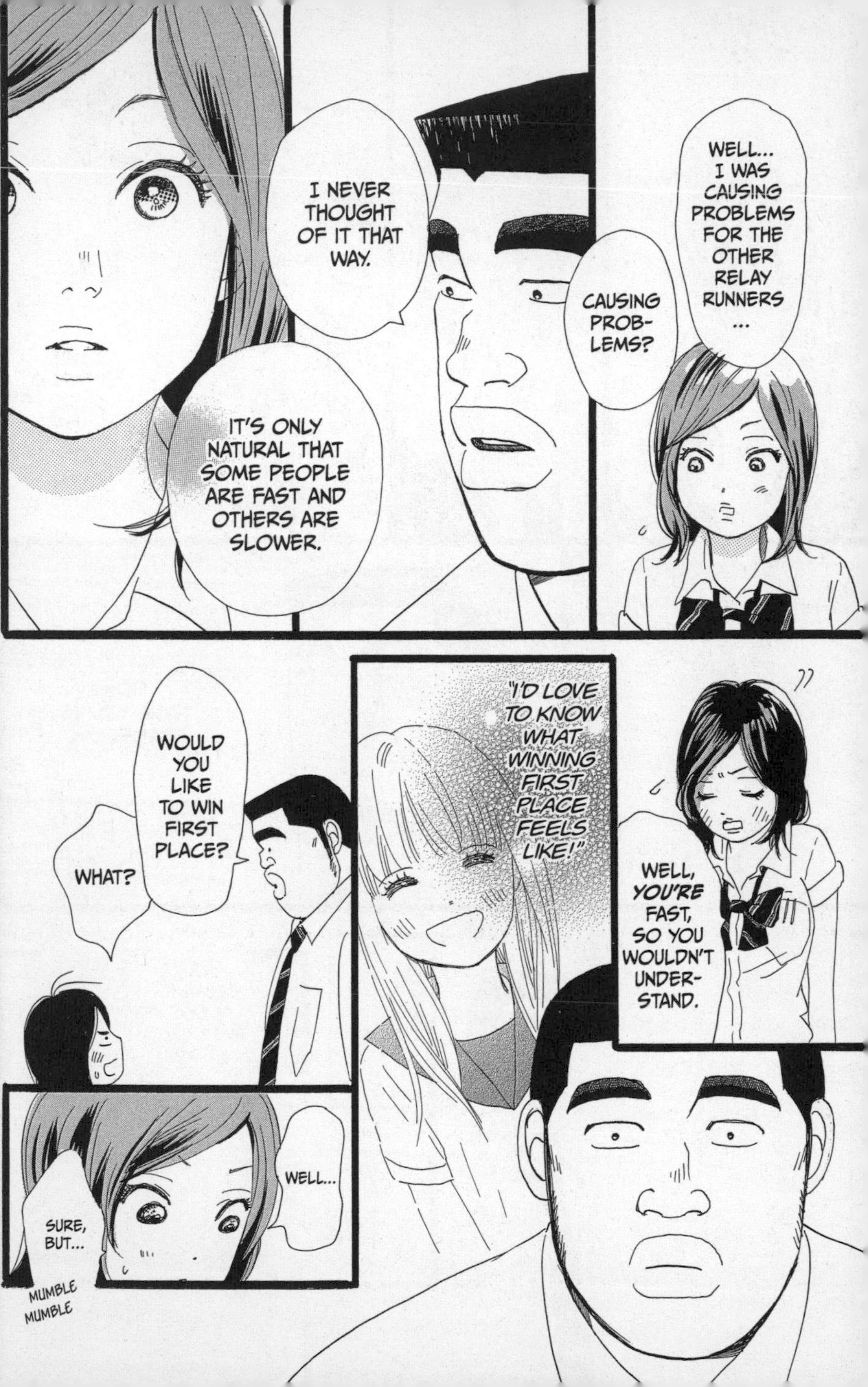

WELL... I WAS CAUSING PROBLEMS FOR THE OTHER RELAY RUNNERS...
CAUSING PROB-LEMS?
I NEVER THOUGHT OF IT THAT WAY.
IT'S ONLY NATURAL THAT SOME PEOPLE ARE FAST AND OTHERS ARE SLOWER.
WELL, *YOU'RE* FAST, SO YOU WOULDN'T UNDER-STAND.
"I'D LOVE TO KNOW WHAT WINNING FIRST PLACE FEELS LIKE!"
WOULD YOU LIKE TO WIN FIRST PLACE?
WHAT?
WELL...
SURE, BUT...
MUMBLE MUMBLE

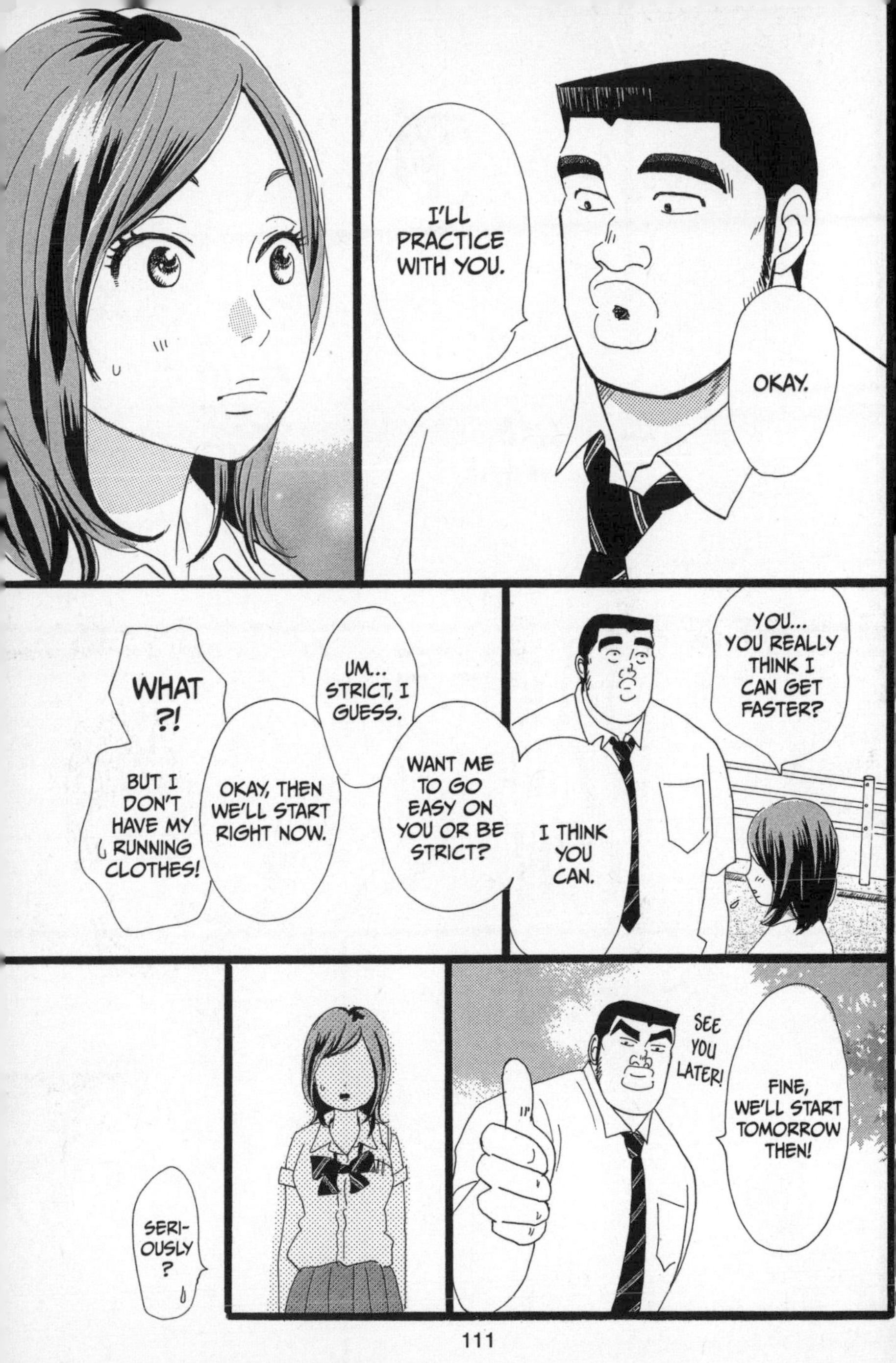
OKAY.
I'LL PRACTICE WITH YOU.
YOU... YOU REALLY THINK I CAN GET FASTER?
I THINK YOU CAN.
WANT ME TO GO EASY ON YOU OR BE STRICT?
UM... STRICT, I GUESS.
OKAY, THEN WE'LL START RIGHT NOW.
WHAT?!
BUT I DON'T HAVE MY RUNNING CLOTHES!
FINE, WE'LL START TOMORROW THEN!
SEE YOU LATER!
SERI-OUSLY?

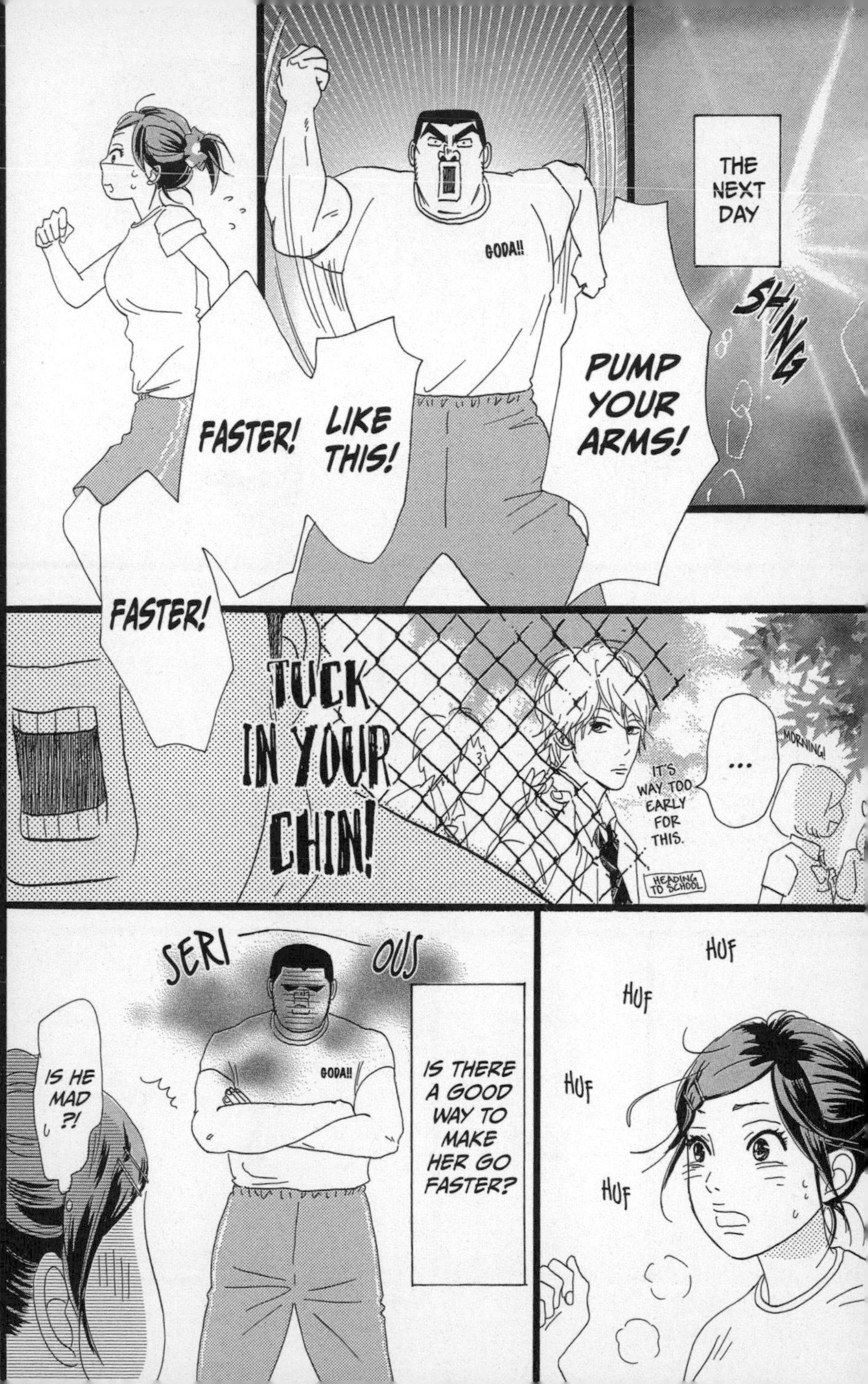
THE NEXT DAY
SHING
PUMP YOUR ARMS!
GODA!!
LIKE THIS!
FASTER!
FASTER!
MORNING!
...
IT'S WAY TOO EARLY FOR THIS.
HEADING TO SCHOOL
TUCK IN YOUR CHIN!
HUF
HUF
HUF
HUF
SERI
OUS
IS THERE A GOOD WAY TO MAKE HER GO FASTER?
GODA!!
IS HE MAD ?!

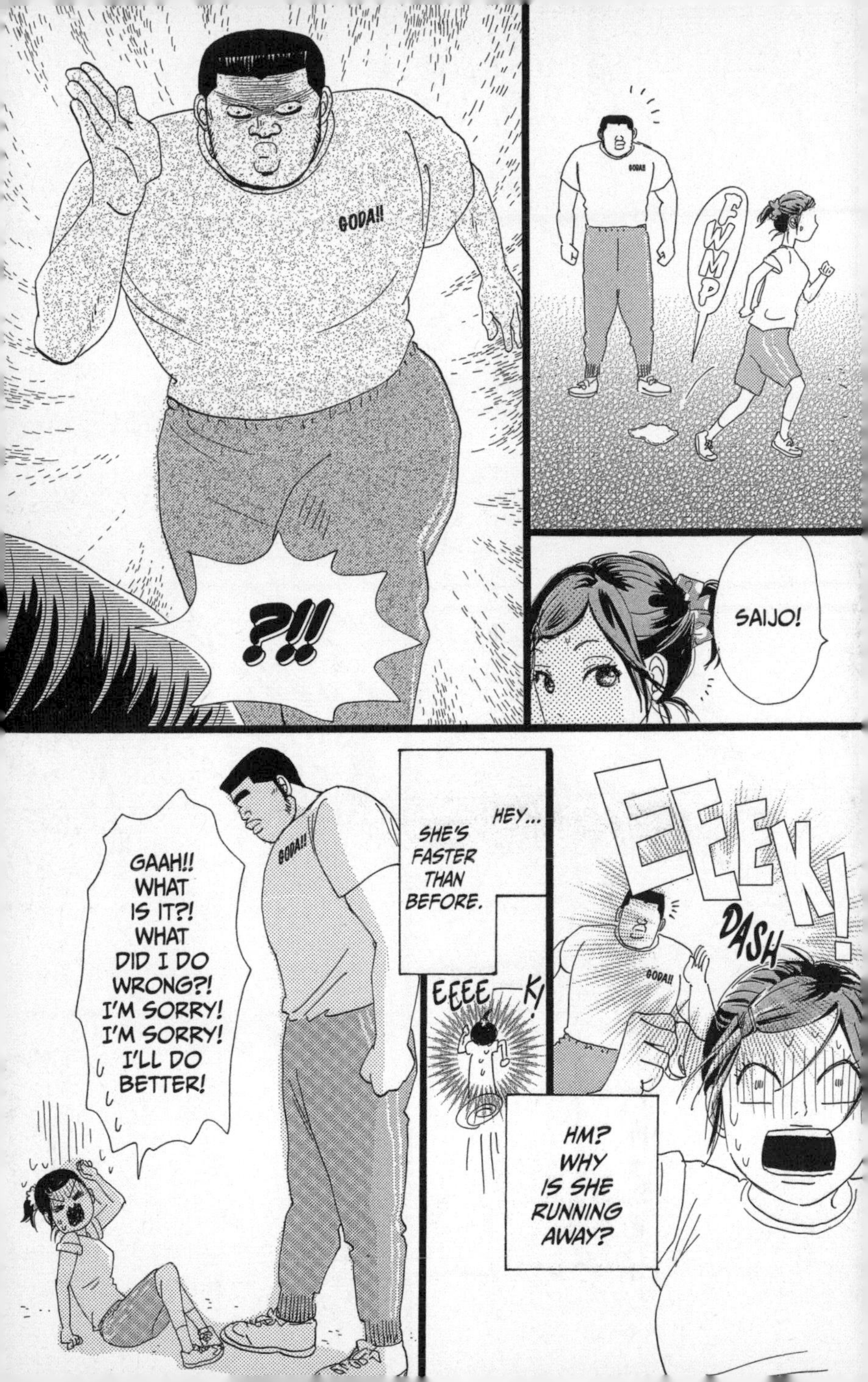
GODA!!
FWMP
SAIJO!
GODA!!
?!!
EEEEK!
DASH
GODA!!
HM? WHY IS SHE RUNNING AWAY?
HEY...
SHE'S FASTER THAN BEFORE.
EEEE—K!
GODA!!
GAAH!! WHAT IS IT?! WHAT DID I DO WRONG?! I'M SORRY! I'M SORRY! I'LL DO BETTER!

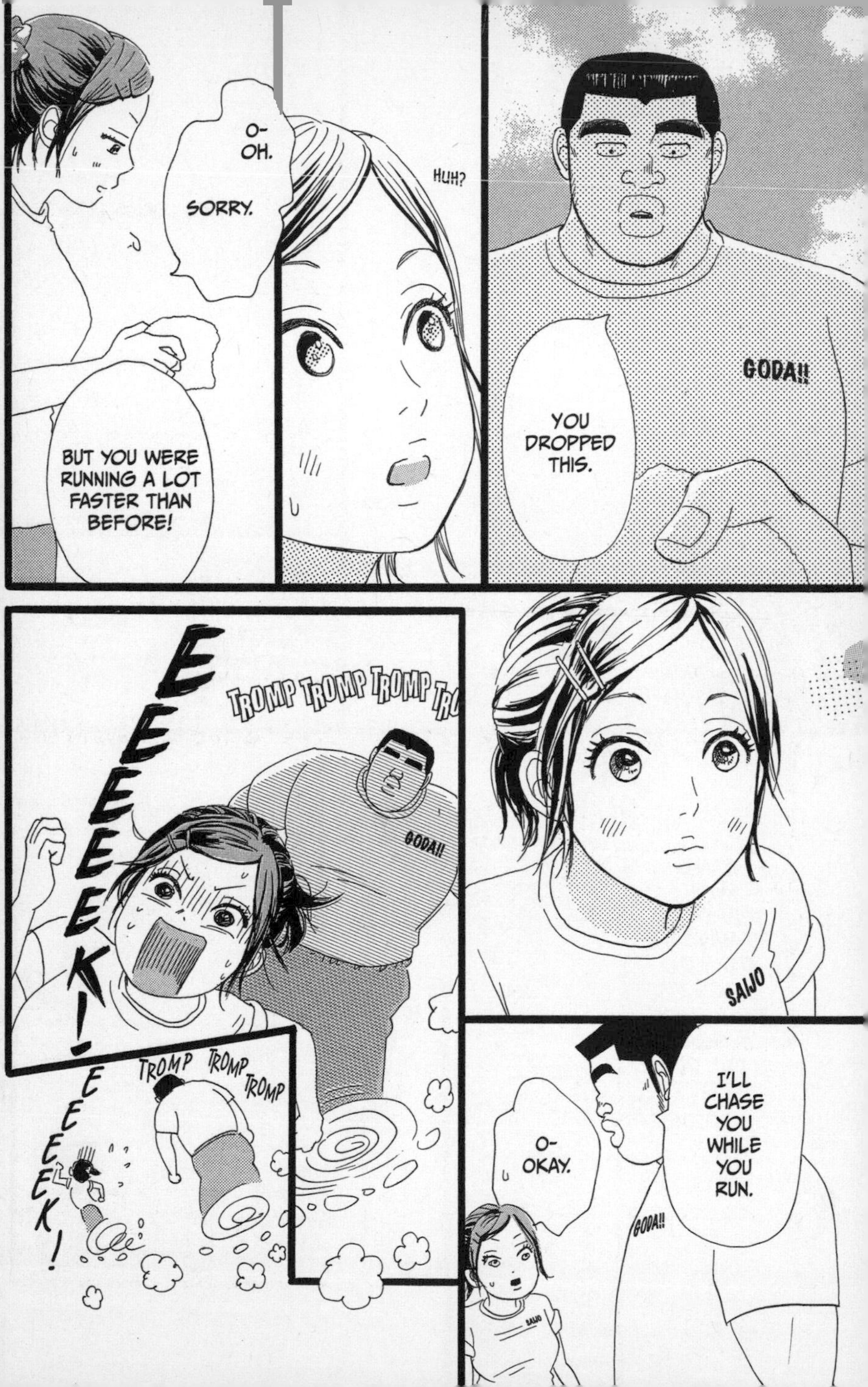
GODA!!
YOU DROPPED THIS.
HUH?
O- OH.
SORRY.
BUT YOU WERE RUNNING A LOT FASTER THAN BEFORE!
SAIJO
I'LL CHASE YOU WHILE YOU RUN.
O- OKAY.
GODA!!
SAIJO
EEEEEEEEK!
TROMP TROMP TROMP TRO
GODA!!
TROMP TROMP TROMP
EEEEEK!

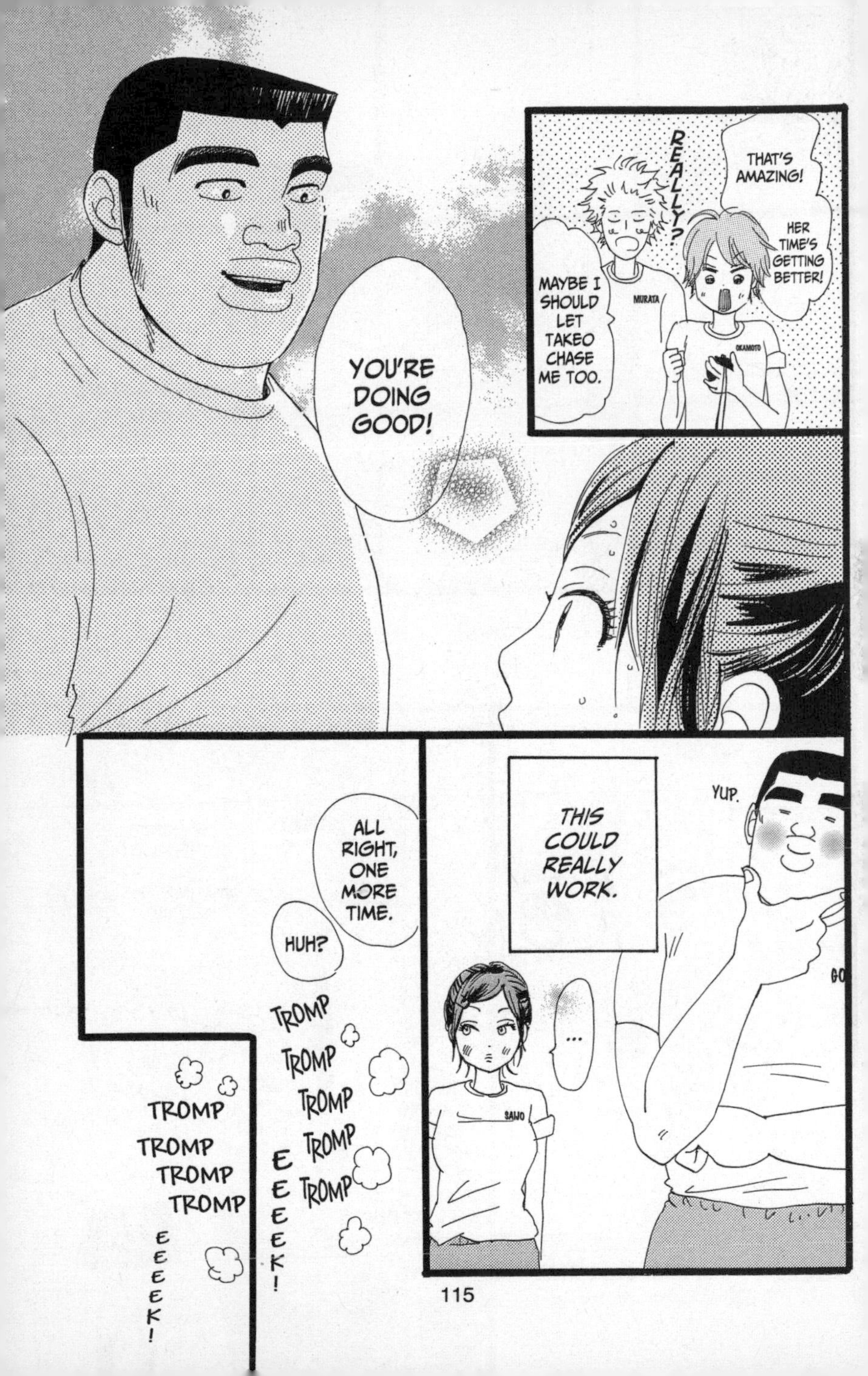
THAT'S AMAZING!
HER TIME'S GETTING BETTER!
REALLY?
MAYBE I SHOULD LET TAKEO CHASE ME TOO.
YOU'RE DOING GOOD!
YUP.
THIS COULD REALLY WORK.
...
ALL RIGHT, ONE MORE TIME.
HUH?
TROMP TROMP TROMP TROMP TROMP
EEEEEK!
TROMP TROMP TROMP TROMP
EEEEEK!

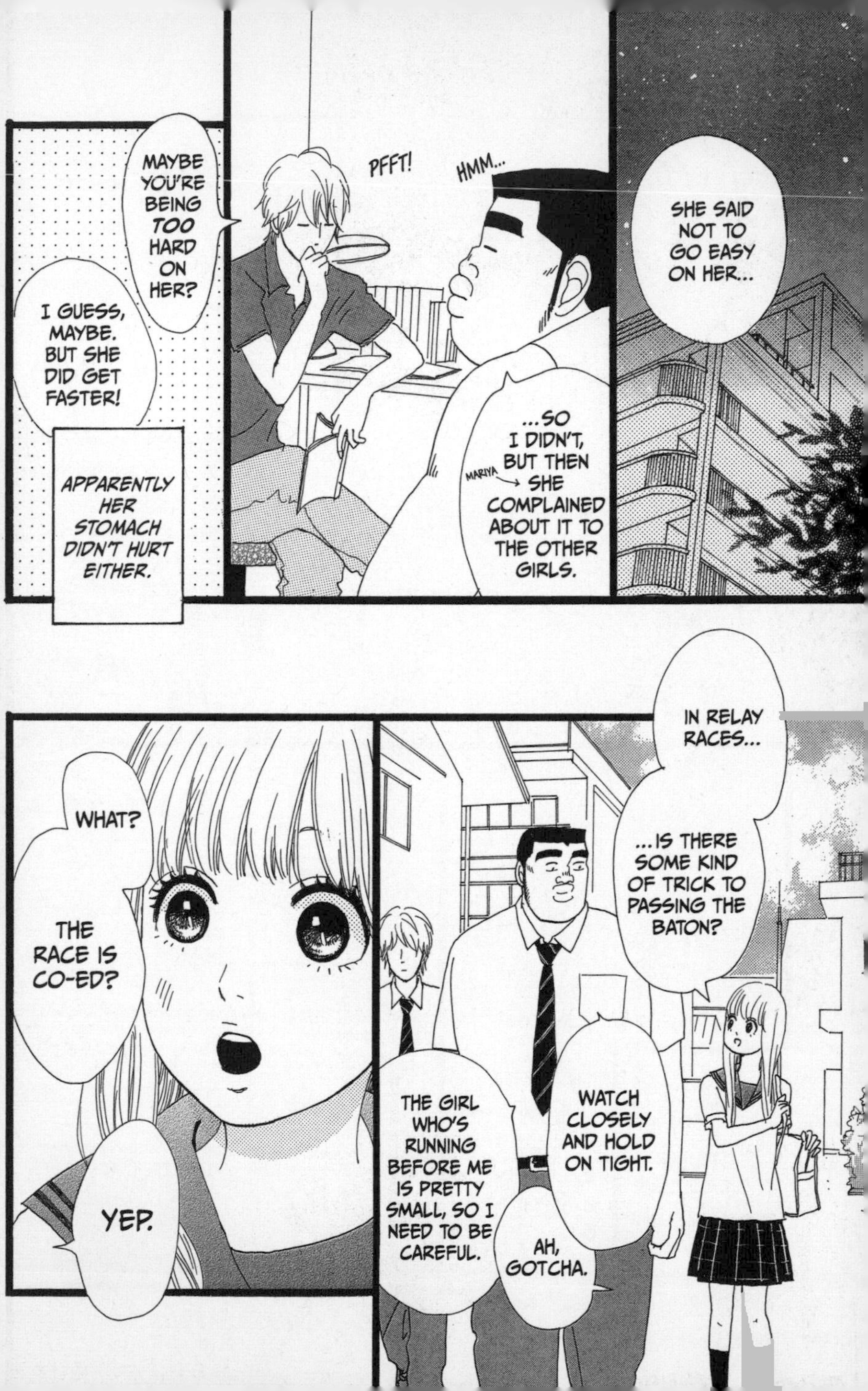
SHE SAID NOT TO GO EASY ON HER...
HMM...
PFFT!
...SO I DIDN'T, BUT THEN SHE COMPLAINED ABOUT IT TO THE OTHER GIRLS.
MARIYA →
MAYBE YOU'RE BEING *TOO* HARD ON HER?
I GUESS, MAYBE. BUT SHE DID GET FASTER!
APPARENTLY HER STOMACH DIDN'T HURT EITHER.
IN RELAY RACES...
...IS THERE SOME KIND OF TRICK TO PASSING THE BATON?
WATCH CLOSELY AND HOLD ON TIGHT.
THE GIRL WHO'S RUNNING BEFORE ME IS PRETTY SMALL, SO I NEED TO BE CAREFUL.
AH, GOTCHA.
WHAT?
THE RACE IS CO-ED?
YEP.

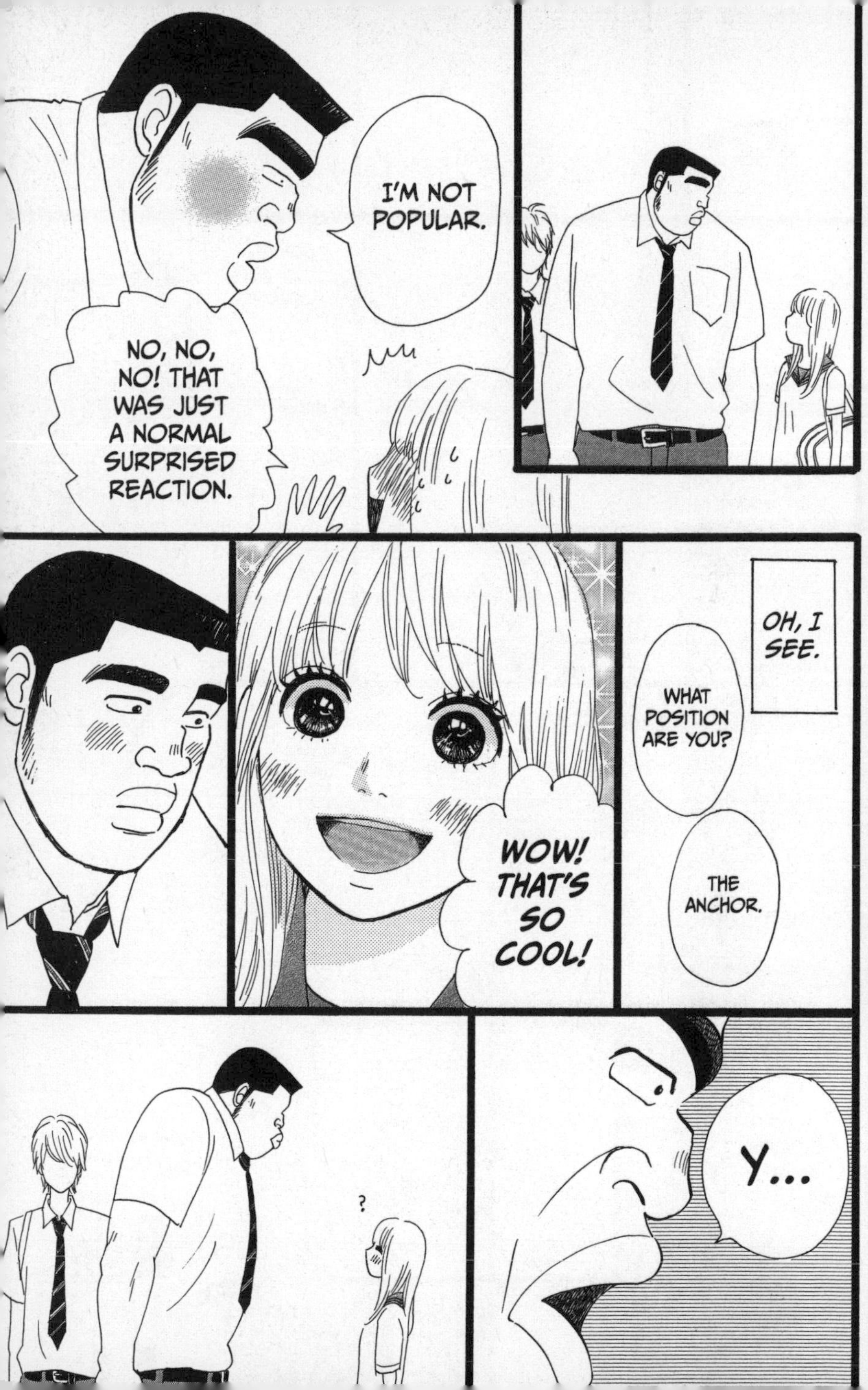
I'M NOT POPULAR.
NO, NO, NO! THAT WAS JUST A NORMAL SURPRISED REACTION.
OH, I SEE.
WHAT POSITION ARE YOU?
THE ANCHOR.
WOW! THAT'S SO COOL!
Y...
?

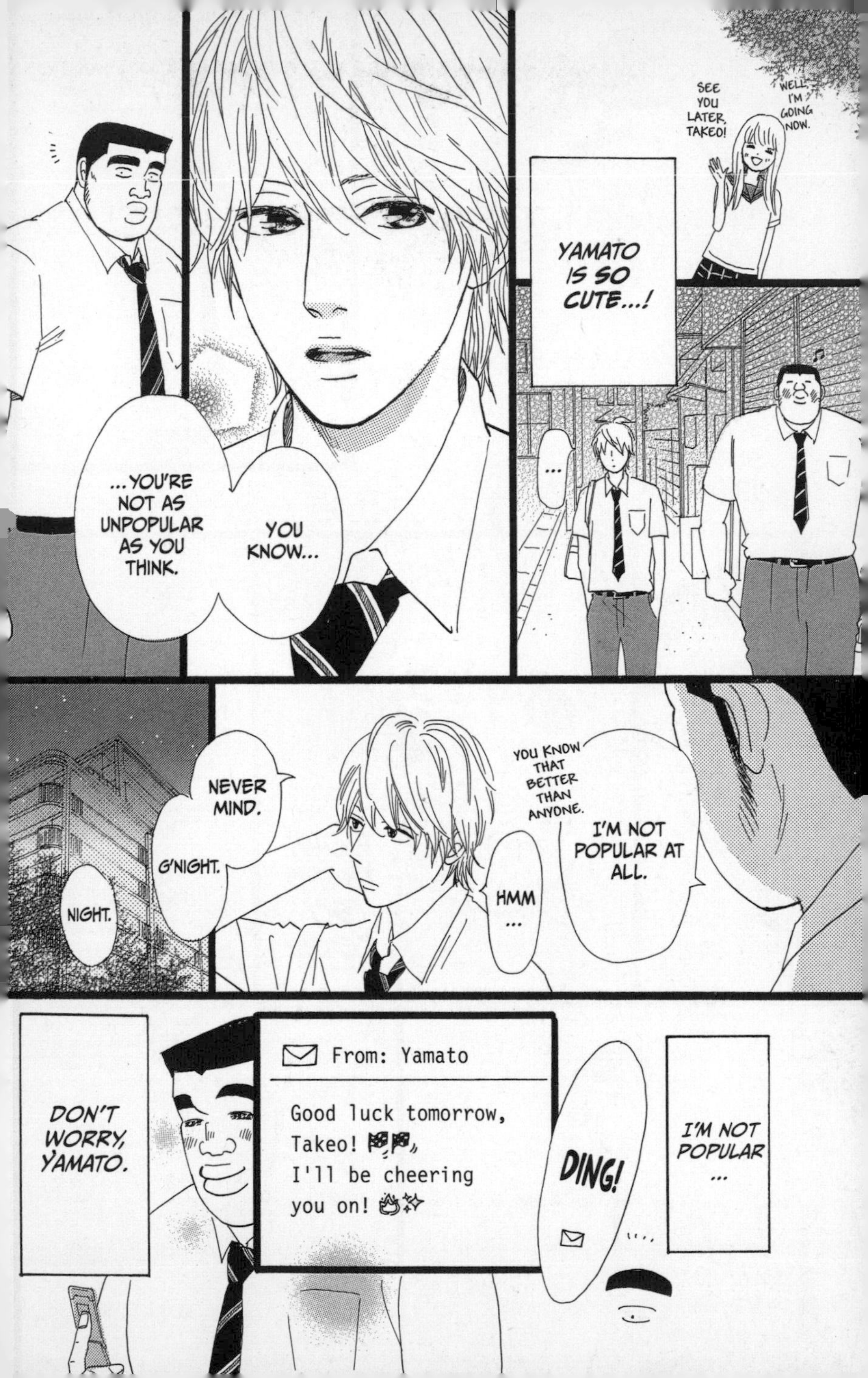
WELL, I'M GOING NOW.
SEE YOU LATER, TAKEO!
YAMATO IS SO CUTE...!
...
YOU KNOW...
...YOU'RE NOT AS UNPOPULAR AS YOU THINK.
YOU KNOW THAT BETTER THAN ANYONE.
I'M NOT POPULAR AT ALL.
HMM...
NEVER MIND.
G'NIGHT.
NIGHT.
I'M NOT POPULAR...
DING!
...,
From: Yamato
Good luck tomorrow, Takeo!
I'll be cheering you on!
DON'T WORRY, YAMATO.

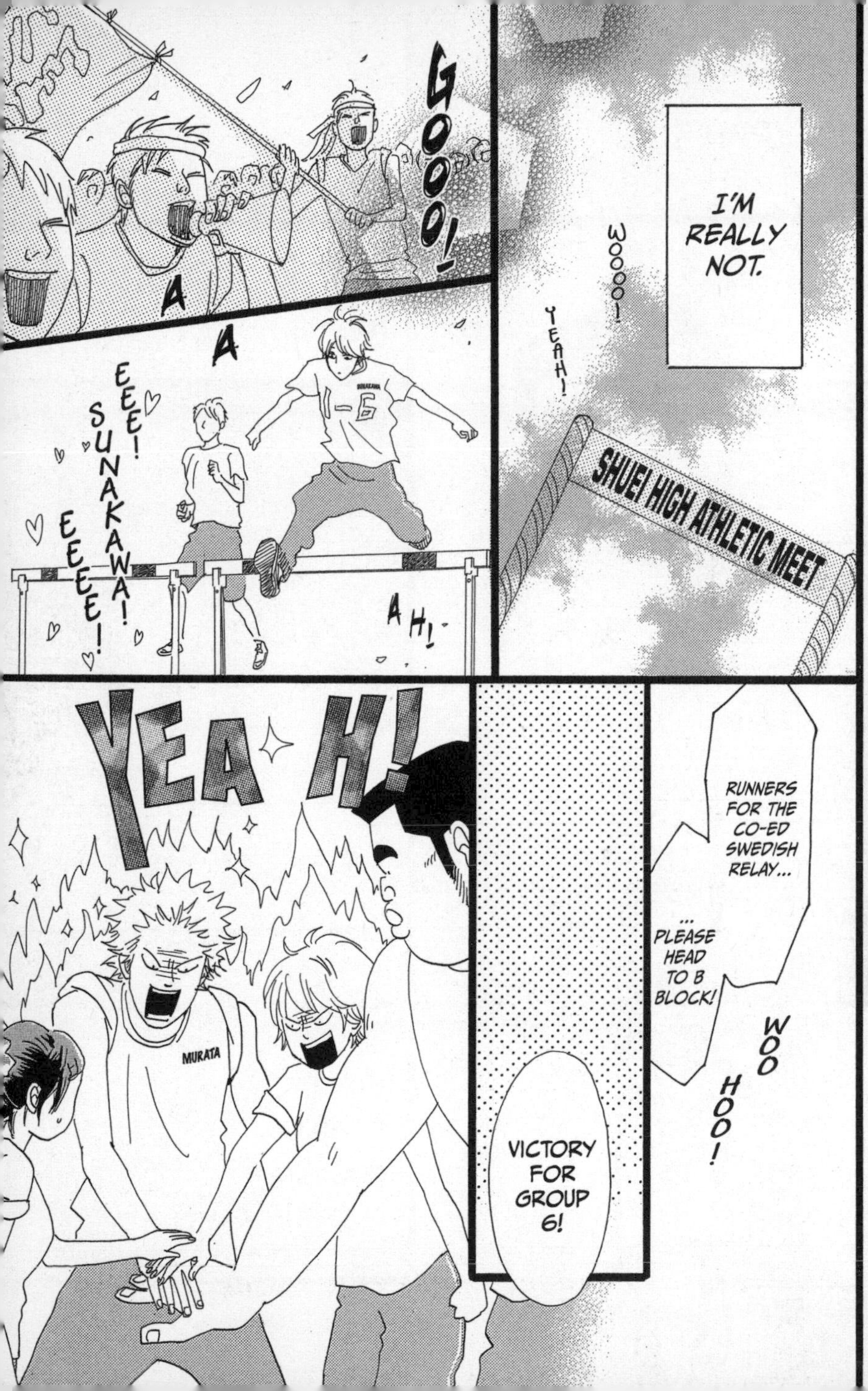
I'M REALLY NOT.
WOOOO!
YEAH!
SHUEI HIGH ATHLETIC MEET
GOOOO!
A
A
EEE!
SUNAKAWA!
EEEE!
AH!
RUNNERS FOR THE CO-ED SWEDISH RELAY...
...PLEASE HEAD TO B BLOCK!
WOO HOO!
VICTORY FOR GROUP 6!
YEAH!

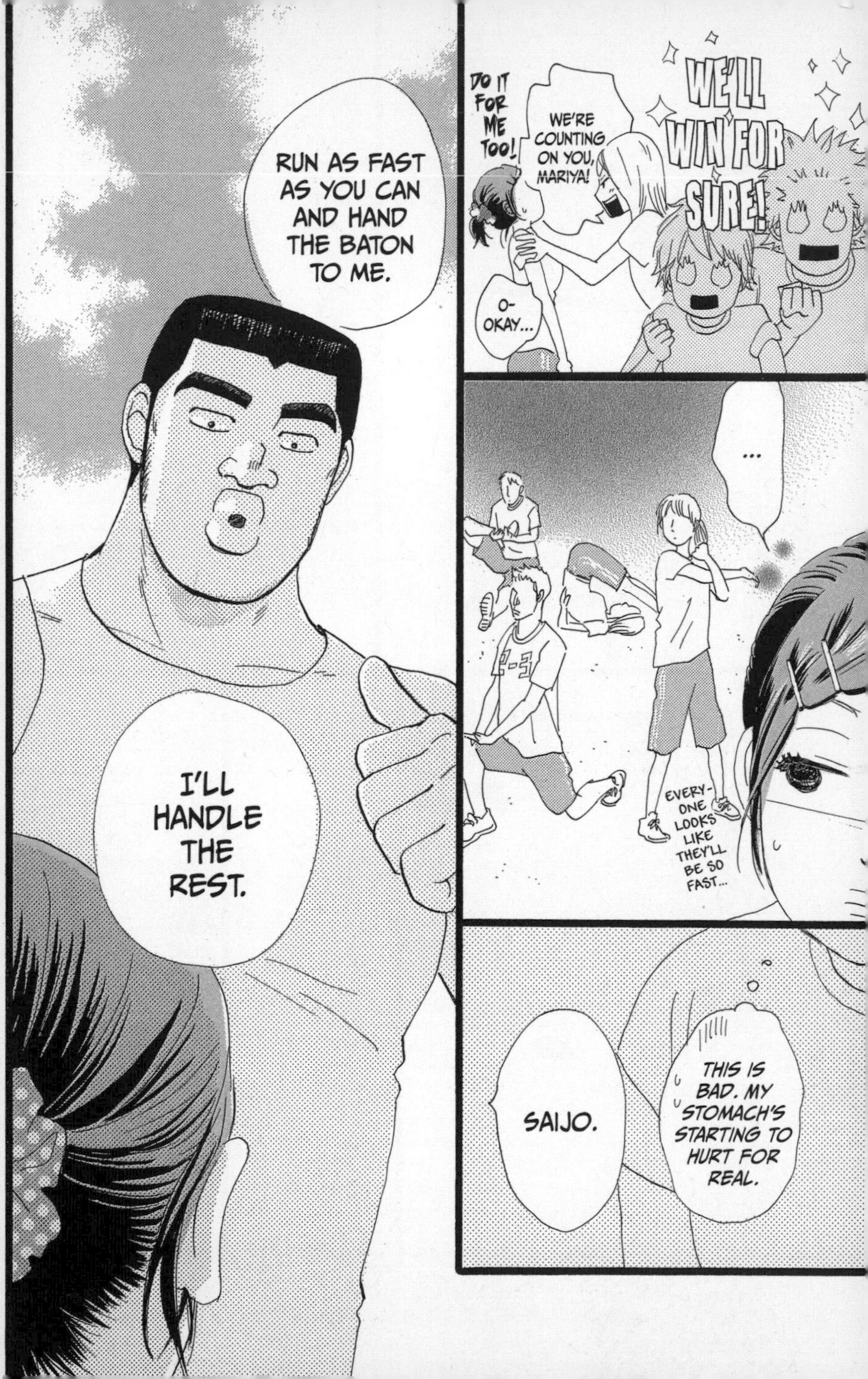
WE'LL WIN FOR SURE!
WE'RE COUNTING ON YOU, MARIYA!
DO IT FOR ME TOO!
O-OKAY...
...
EVERY-ONE LOOKS LIKE THEY'LL BE SO FAST...
THIS IS BAD. MY STOMACH'S STARTING TO HURT FOR REAL.
SAIJO.
RUN AS FAST AS YOU CAN AND HAND THE BATON TO ME.
I'LL HANDLE THE REST.

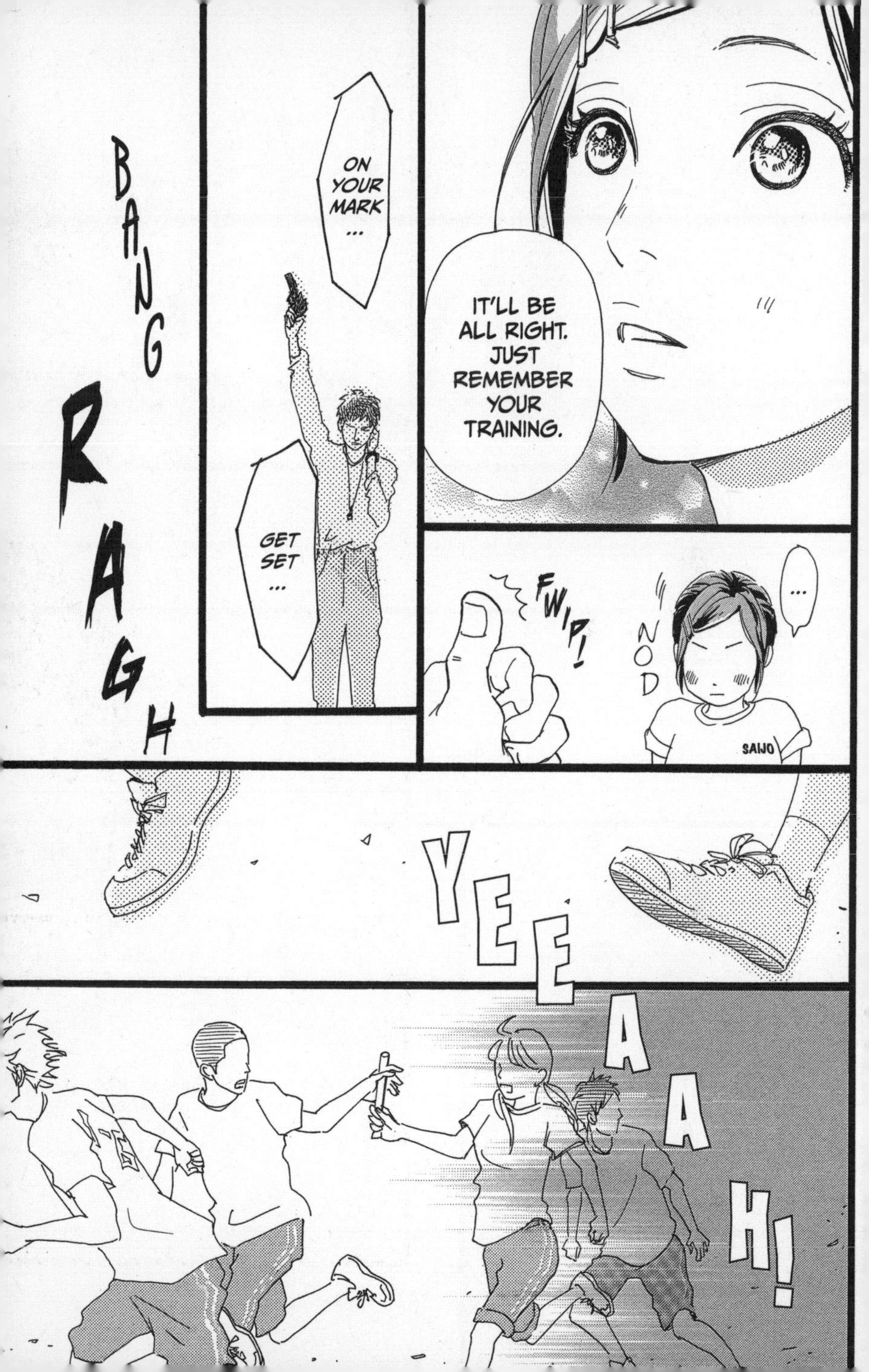
IT'LL BE ALL RIGHT. JUST REMEMBER YOUR TRAINING.
FWIP!
NOD
...
ON YOUR MARK...
GET SET...
BANG
RAGH
SAIJO
YEEAAH!

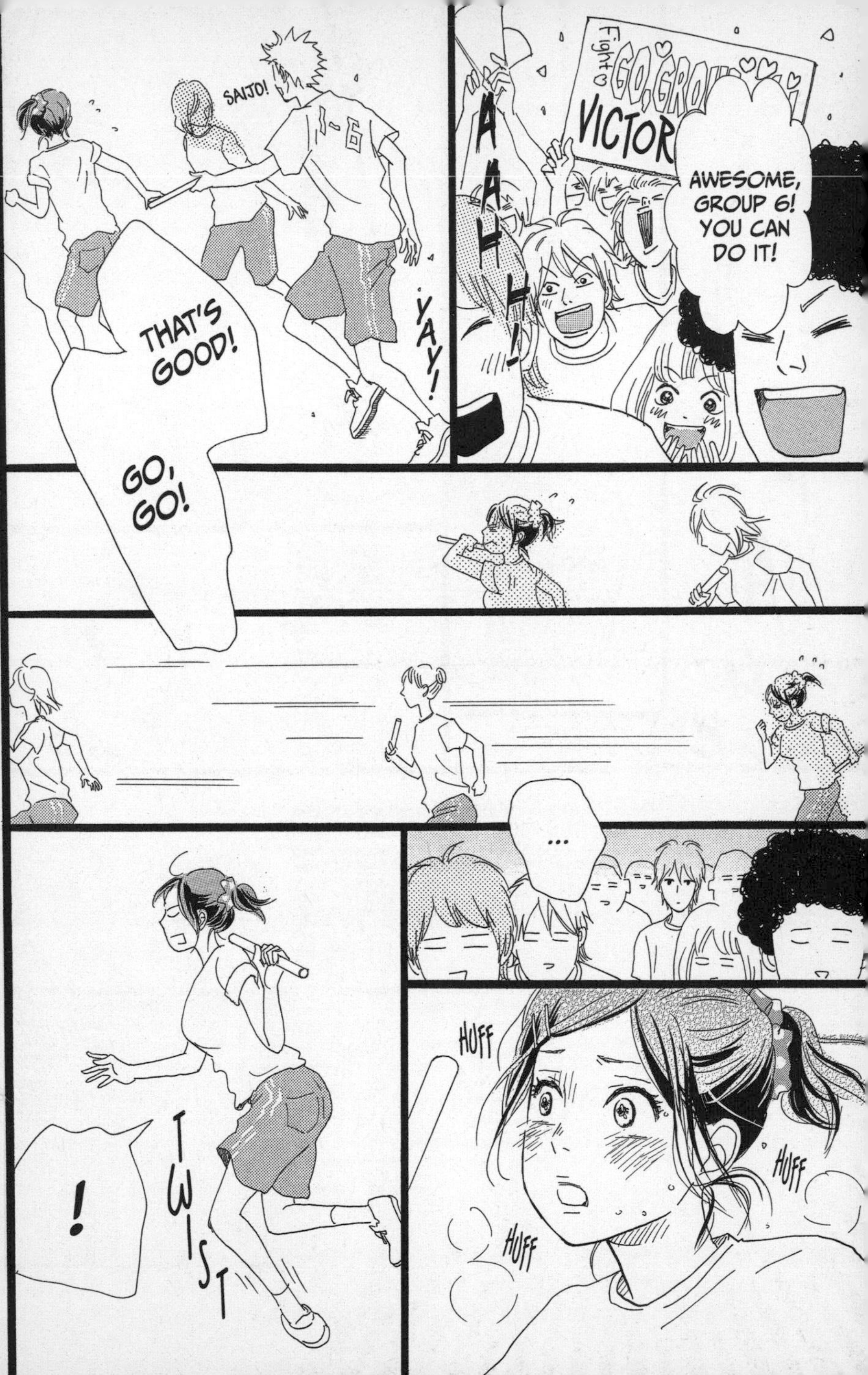
AAHH!
AWESOME, GROUP 6! YOU CAN DO IT!
SAIJO!
YAY!
THAT'S GOOD!
GO, GO!
...
HUFF
HUFF
HUFF
!
TWIST

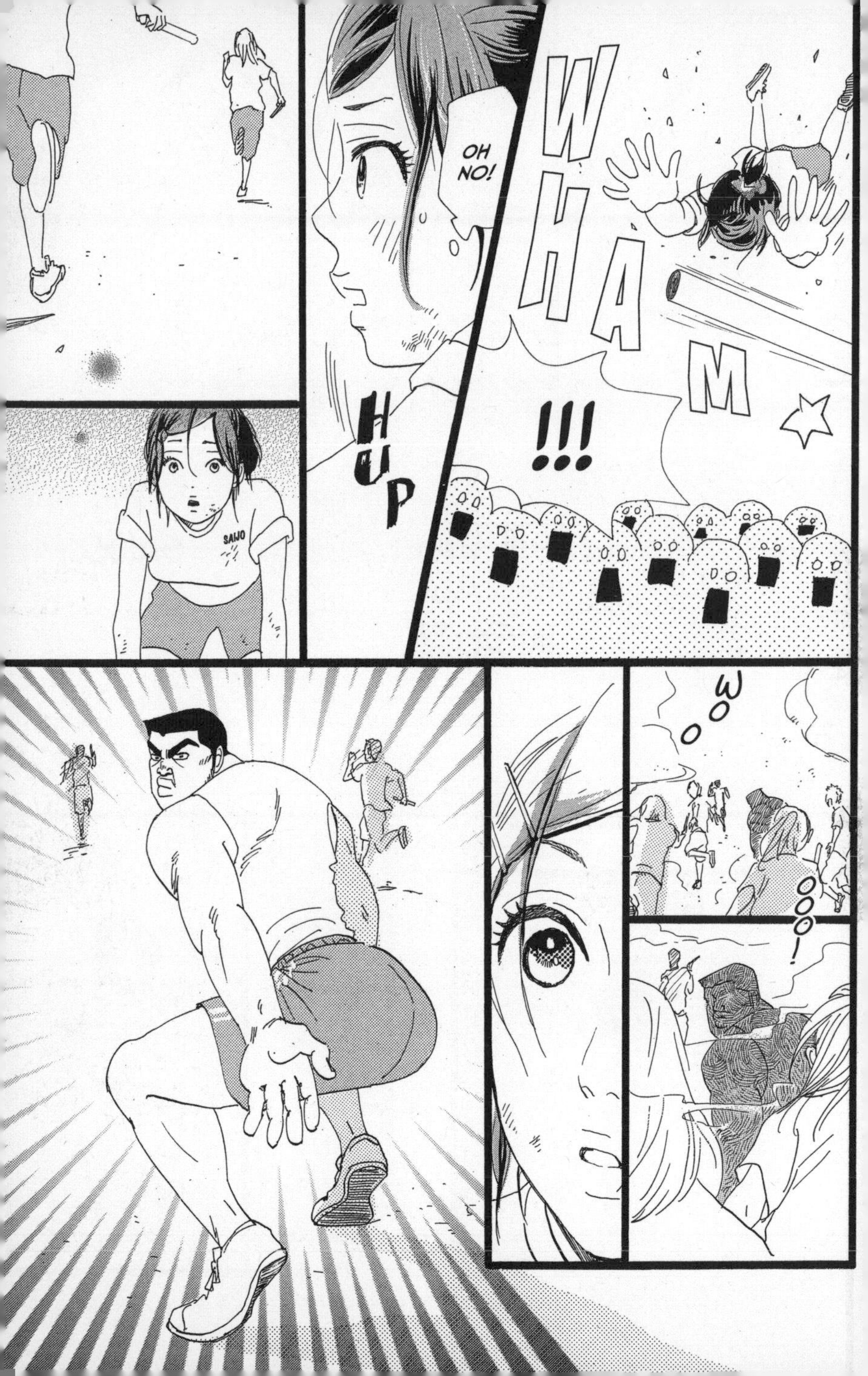
WHAM
!!!
OH NO!
HUP
SAIJO
WOOO
OOOO!

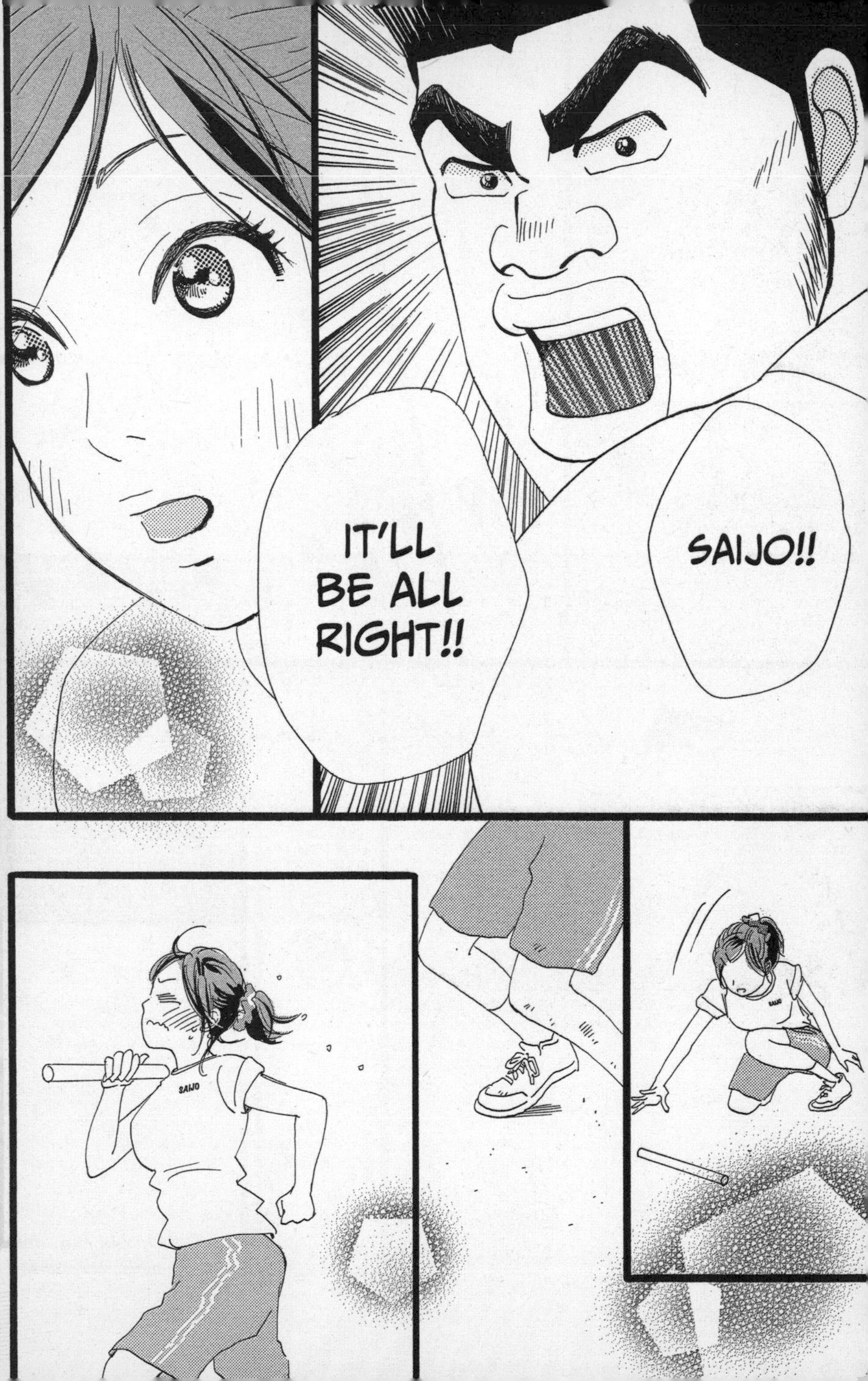
SAIJO!!
IT'LL BE ALL RIGHT!!

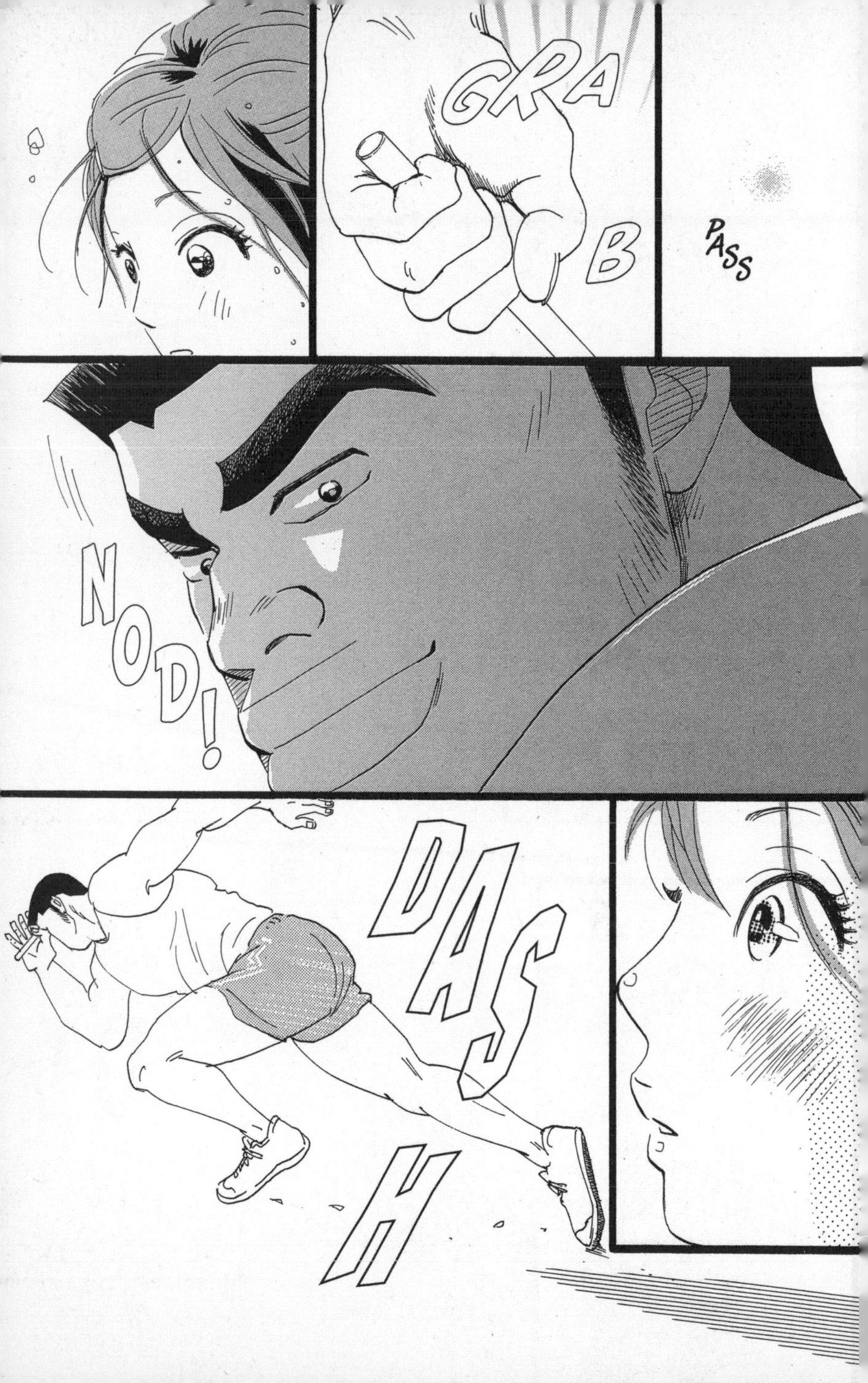
PASS
GRAB
NOD!
DASH

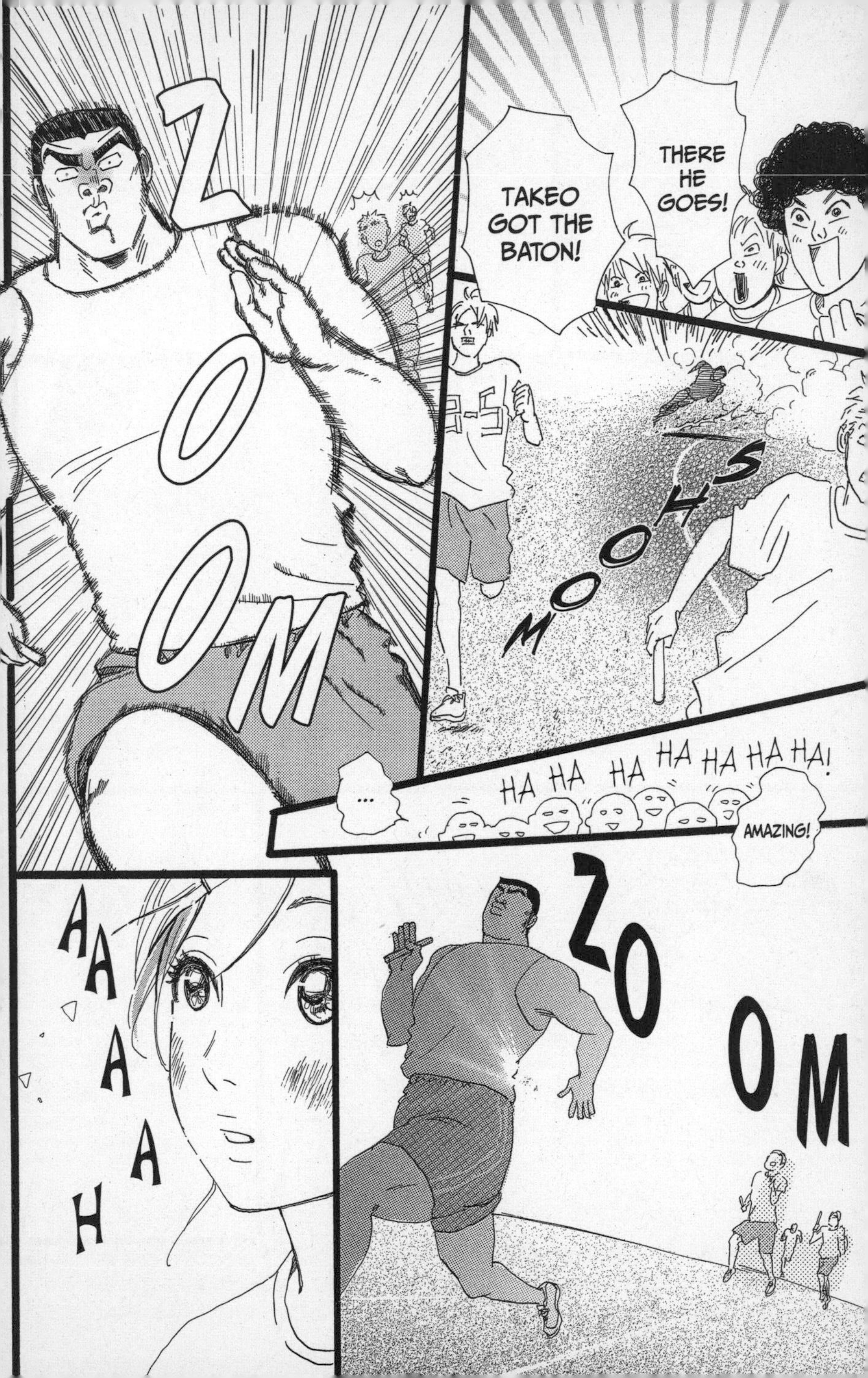
THERE HE GOES!
TAKEO GOT THE BATON!
SHOOOM
HA HA HA HA HA HA HA!
AMAZING!
...
ZOOOM
ZOOOM
AAAAAH

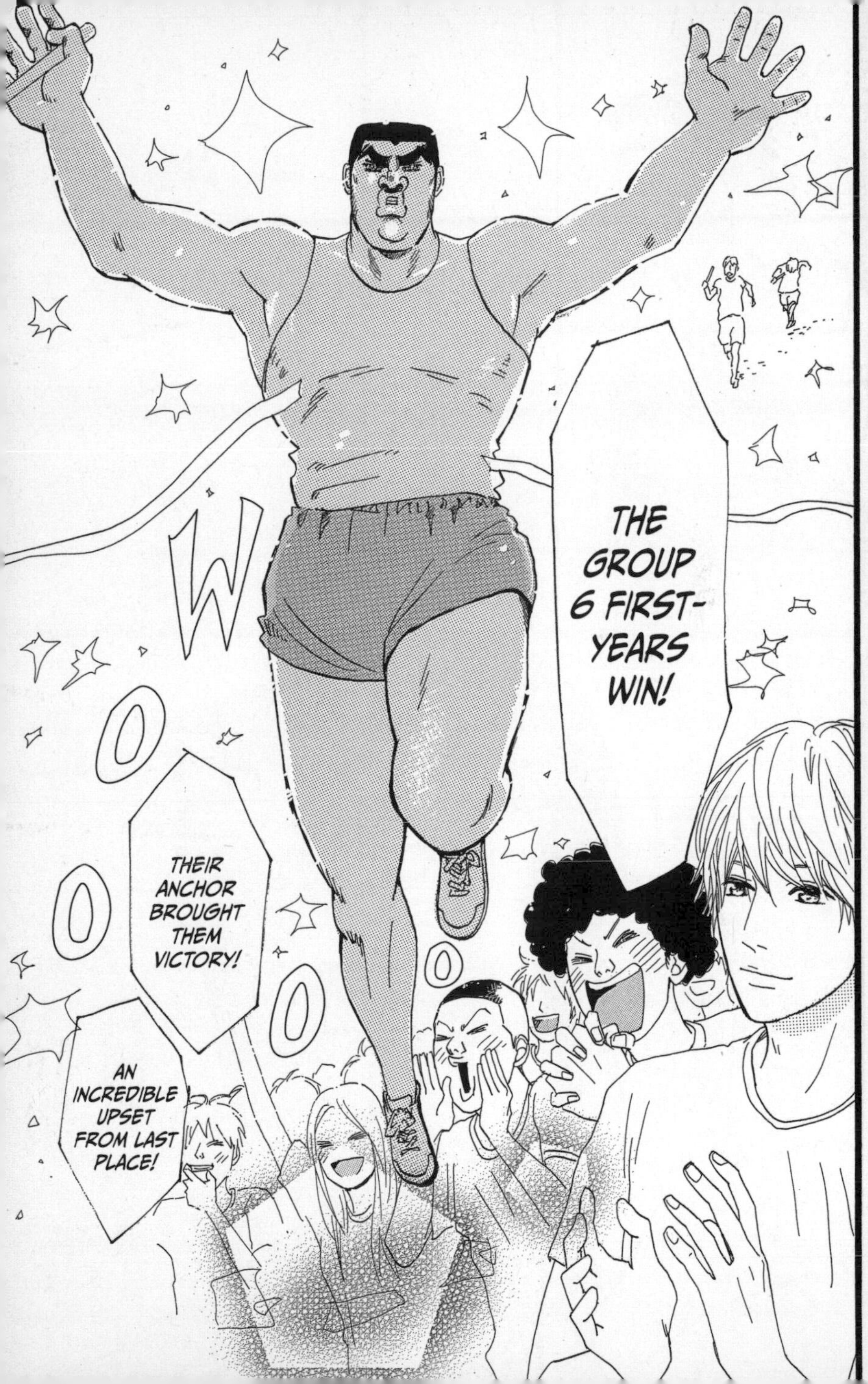
THE GROUP 6 FIRST-YEARS WIN!
WOOOO
THEIR ANCHOR BROUGHT THEM VICTORY!
AN INCREDIBLE UPSET FROM LAST PLACE!

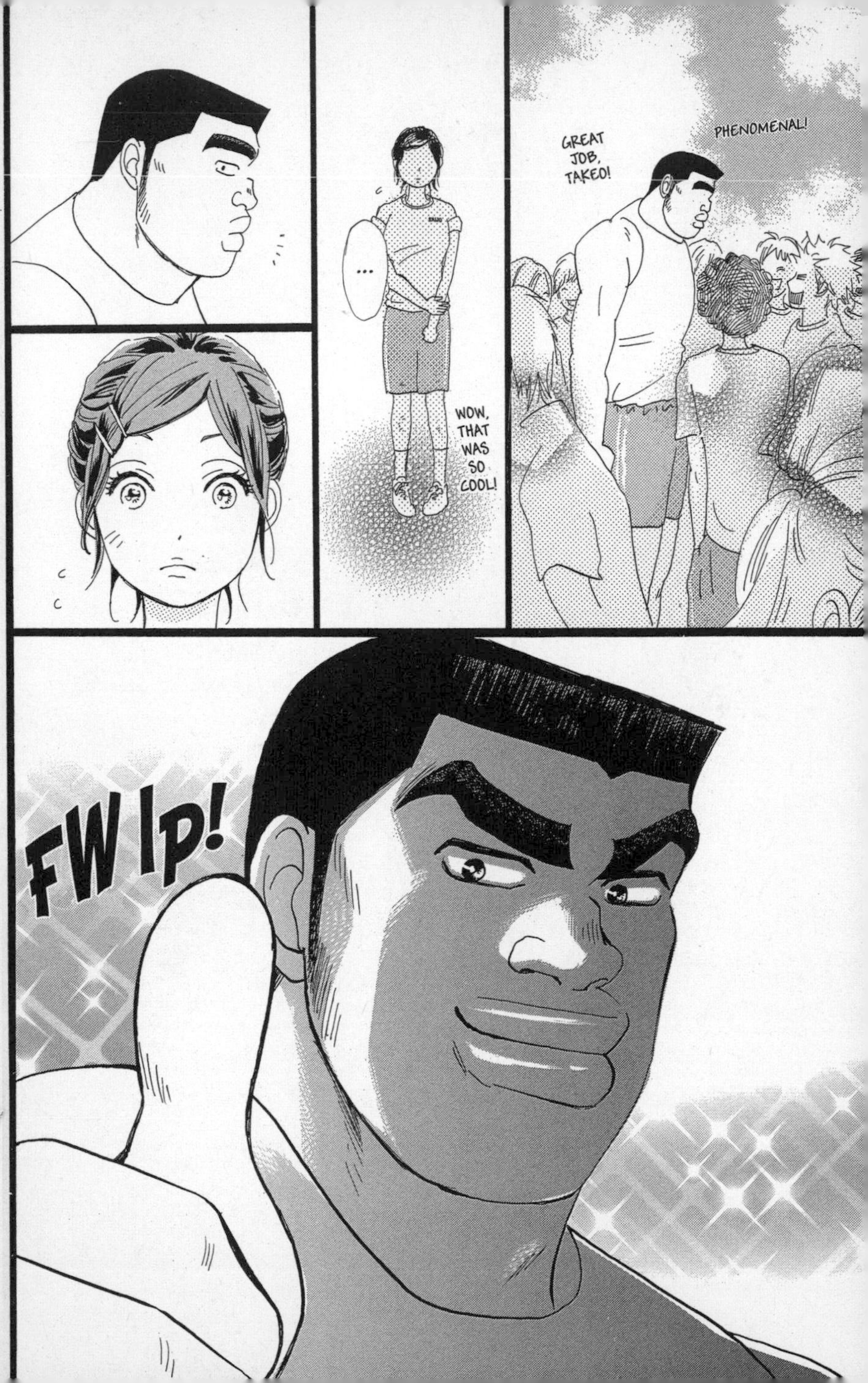
PHENOMENAL!
GREAT JOB, TAKEO!
...
WOW, THAT WAS SO COOL!
FWIP!

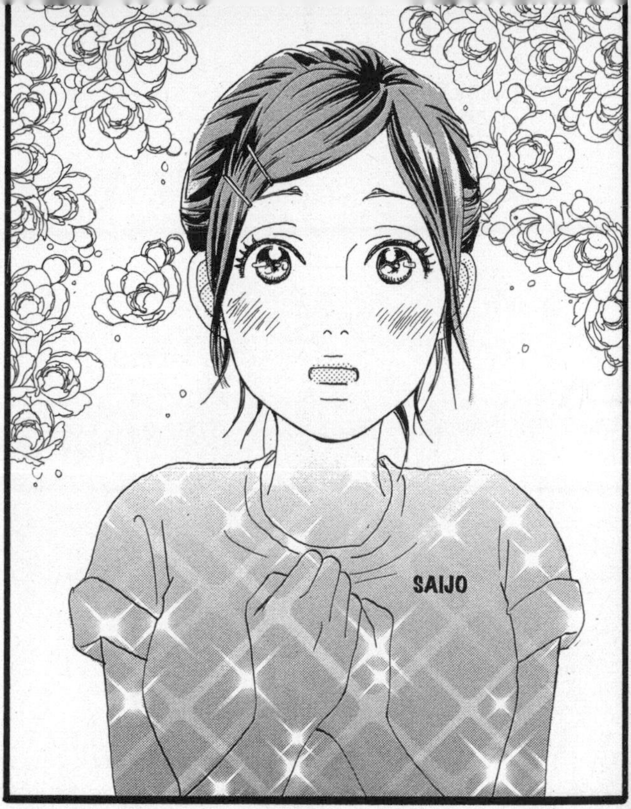
SAIJO
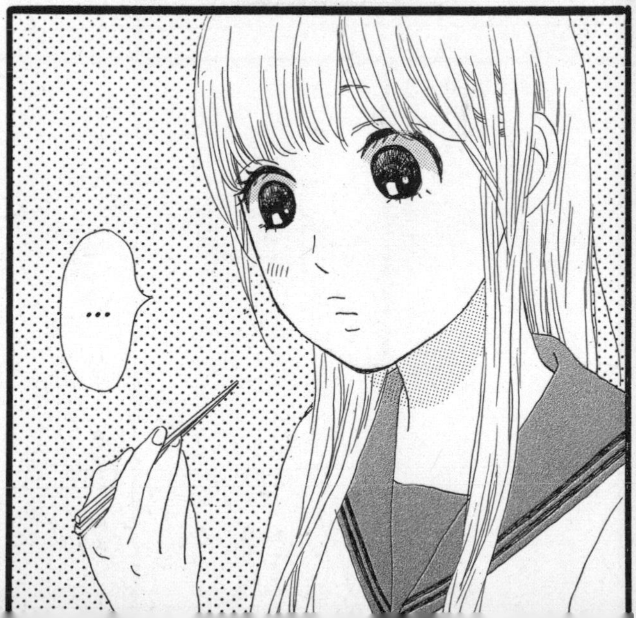
...
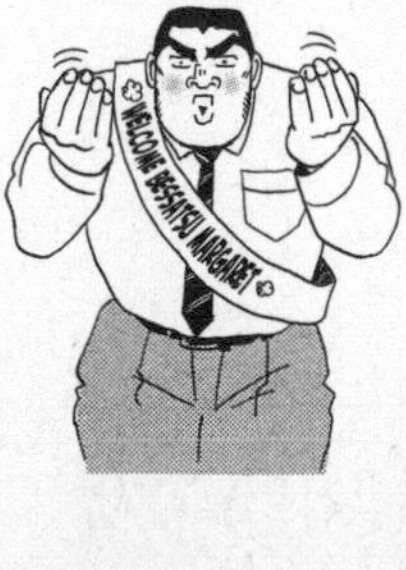
WELCOME BESSATSU MARGARET

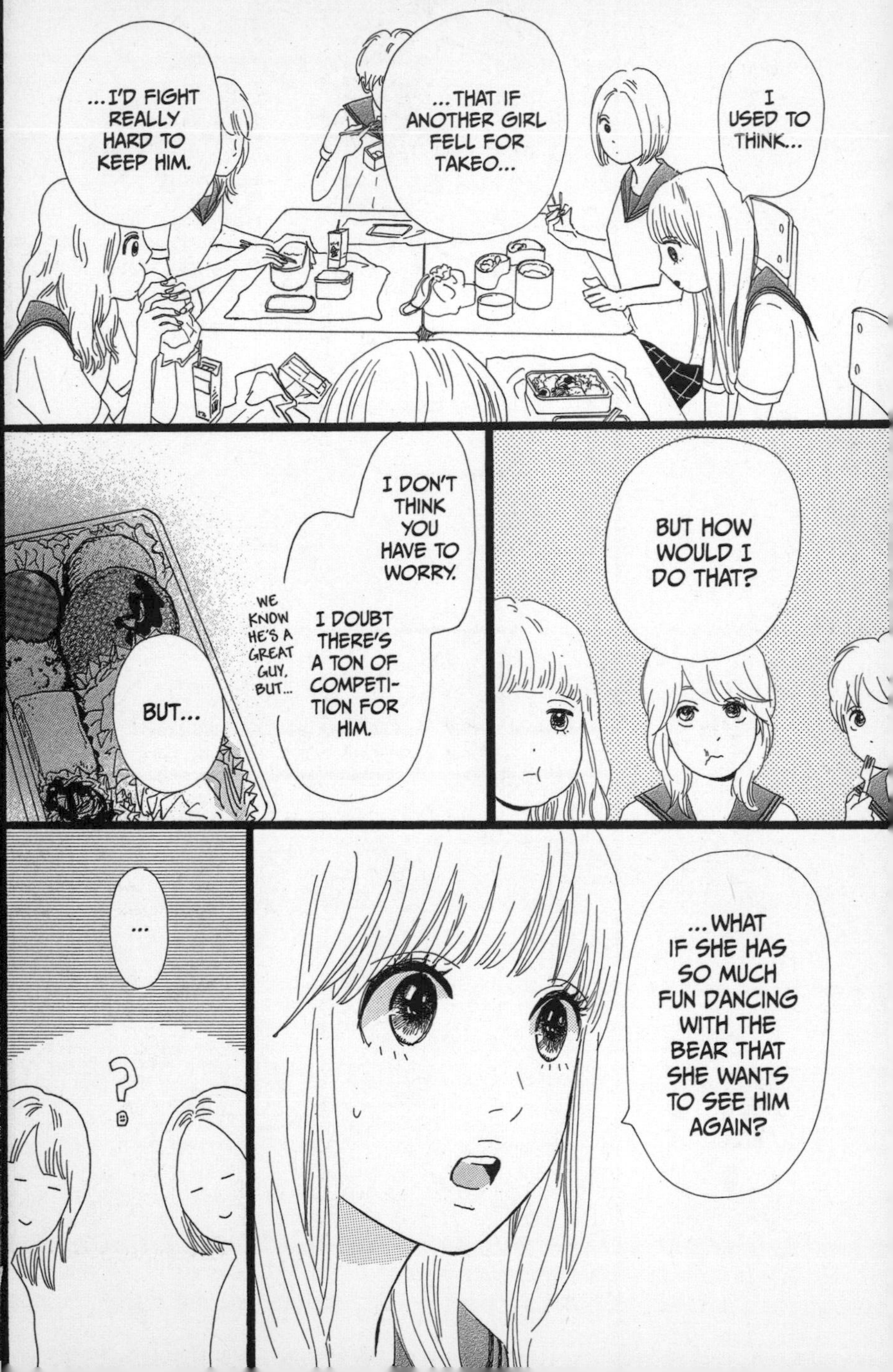
I USED TO THINK...
...THAT IF ANOTHER GIRL FELL FOR TAKEO...
...I'D FIGHT REALLY HARD TO KEEP HIM.
BUT HOW WOULD I DO THAT?
I DON'T THINK YOU HAVE TO WORRY.
I DOUBT THERE'S A TON OF COMPETITION FOR HIM.
WE KNOW HE'S A GREAT GUY, BUT...
BUT...
...WHAT IF SHE HAS SO MUCH FUN DANCING WITH THE BEAR THAT SHE WANTS TO SEE HIM AGAIN?
...
?

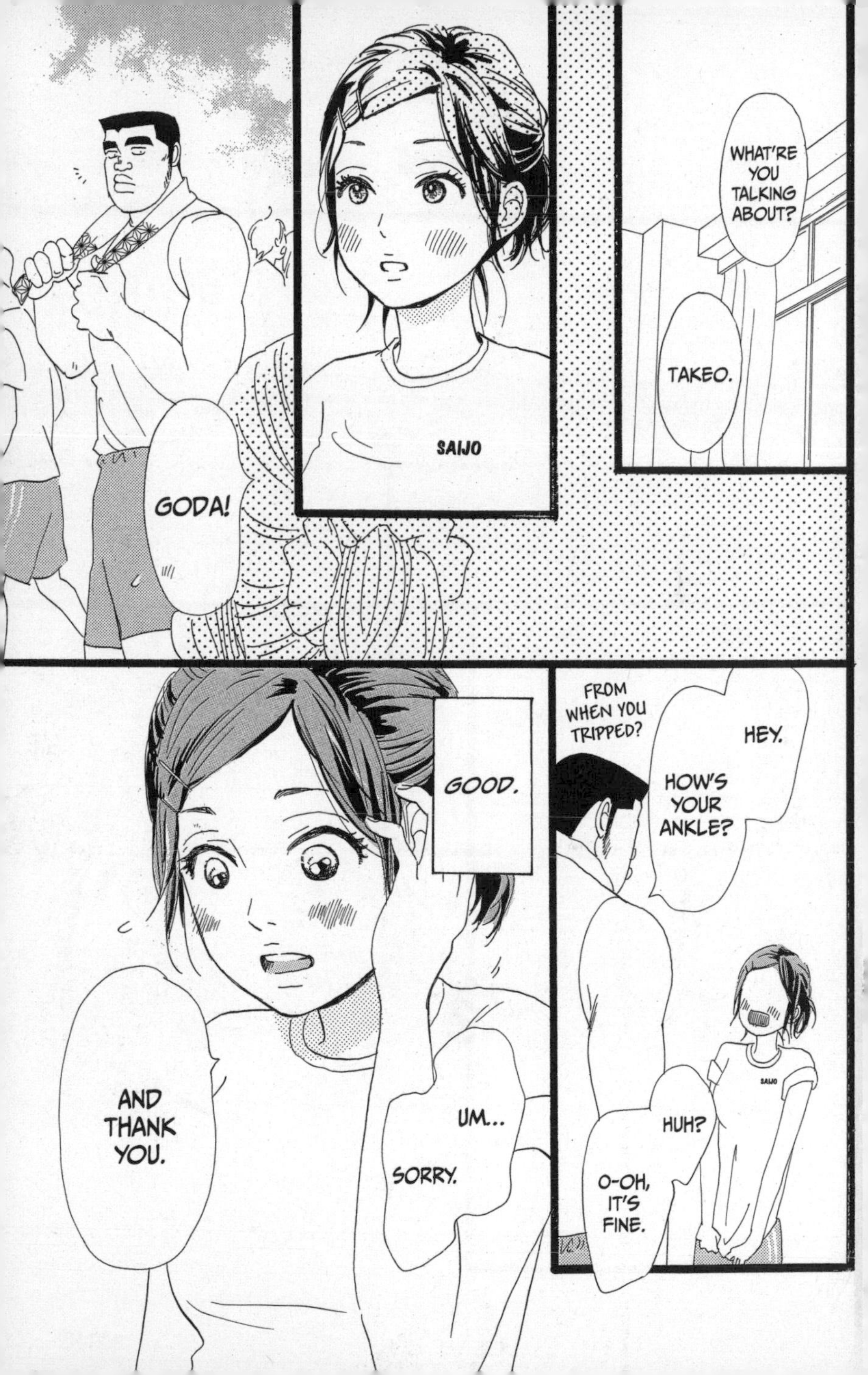
WHAT'RE YOU TALKING ABOUT?
TAKEO.
SAIJO
GODA!
HEY.
HOW'S YOUR ANKLE?
FROM WHEN YOU TRIPPED?
HUH?
O-OH, IT'S FINE.
SAIJO
GOOD.
UM...
SORRY.
AND THANK YOU.

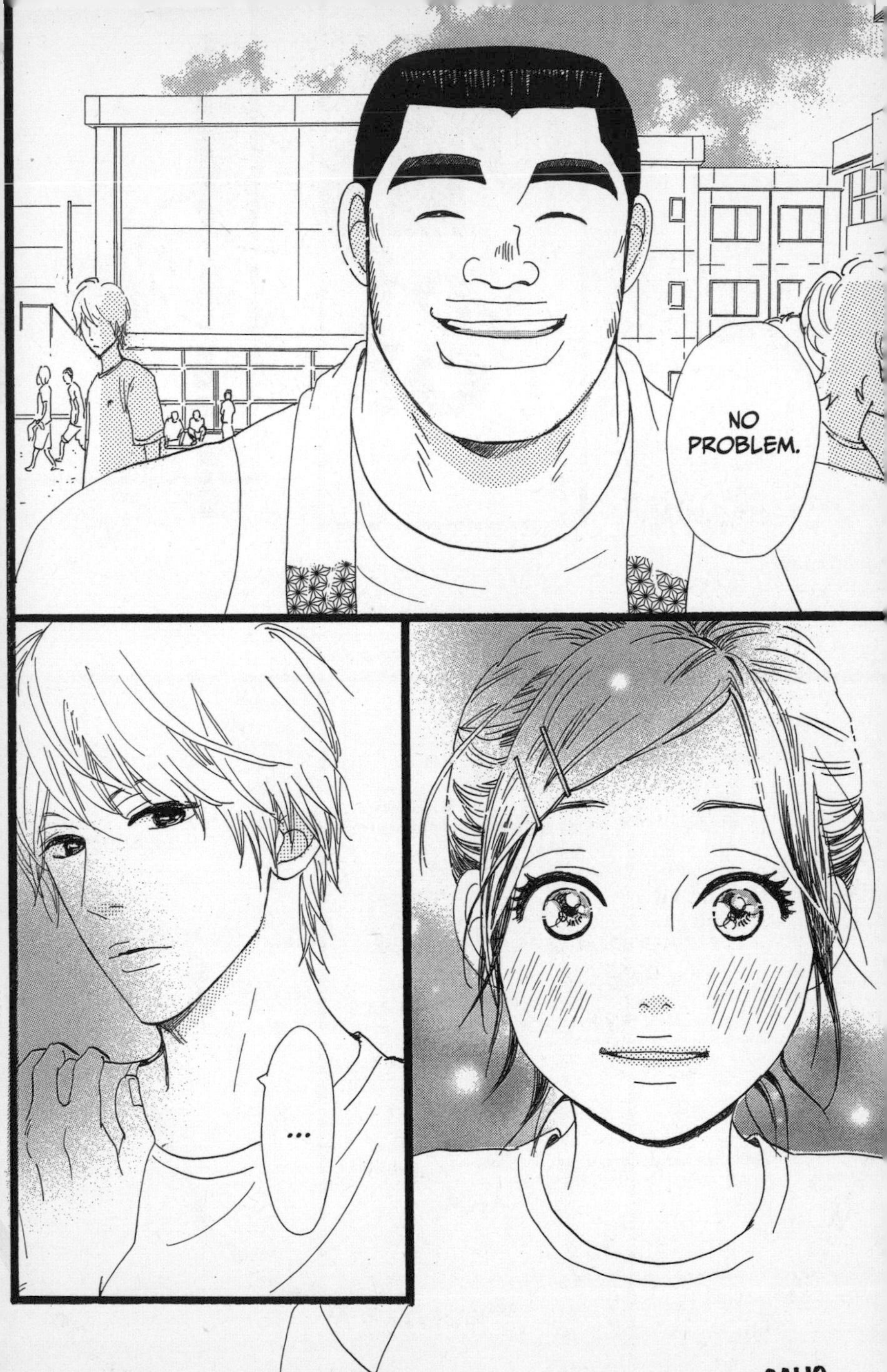
NO PROBLEM.
...
SAIJO

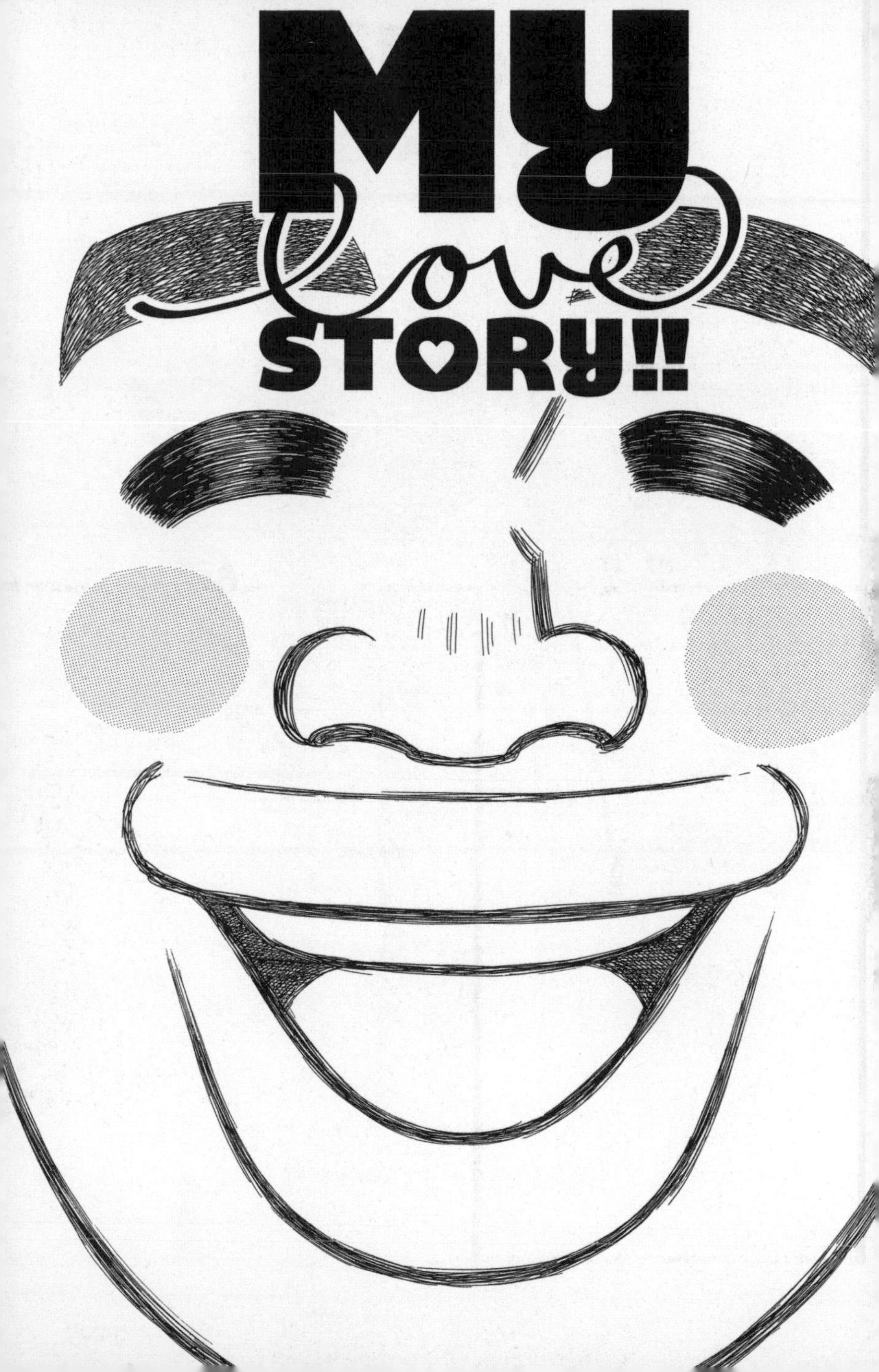
MY
Love
STORY!!

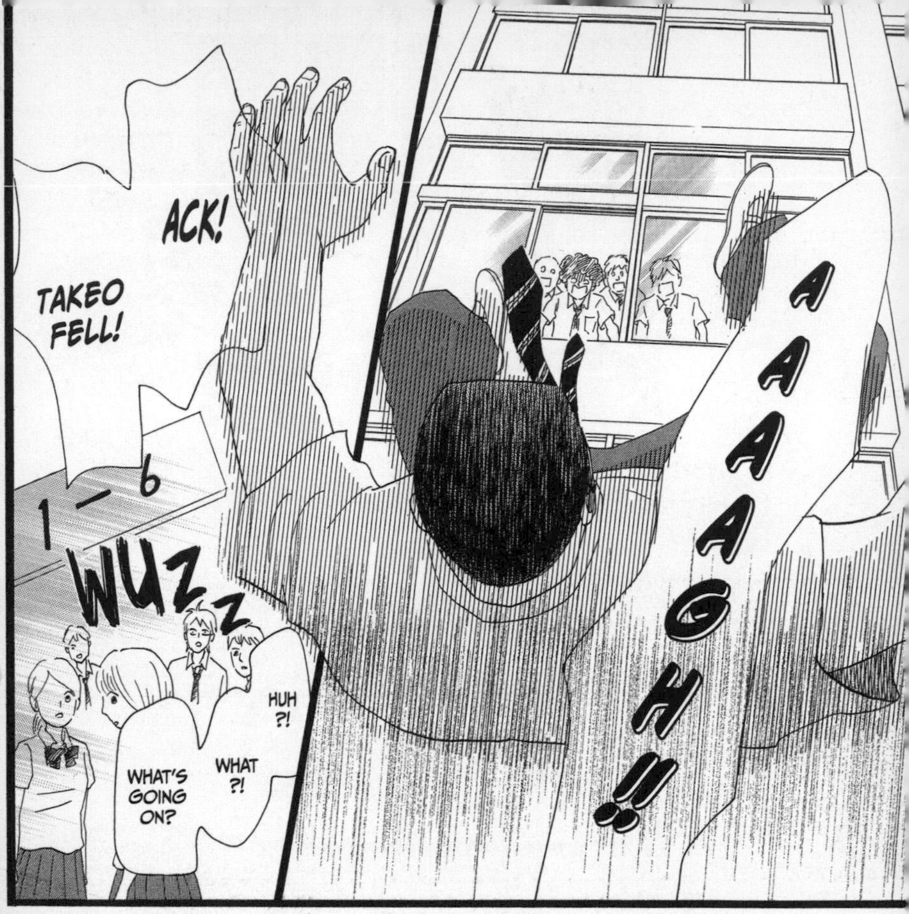
AAAAAGH!!
ACK!
TAKEO FELL!
1-6
WUZZ
HUH?!
WHAT?!
WHAT'S GOING ON?

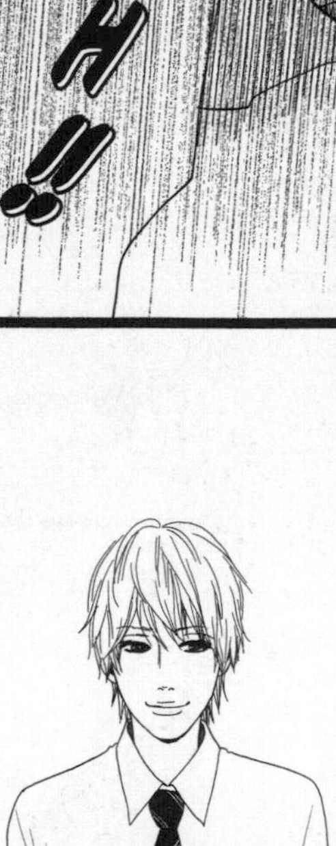

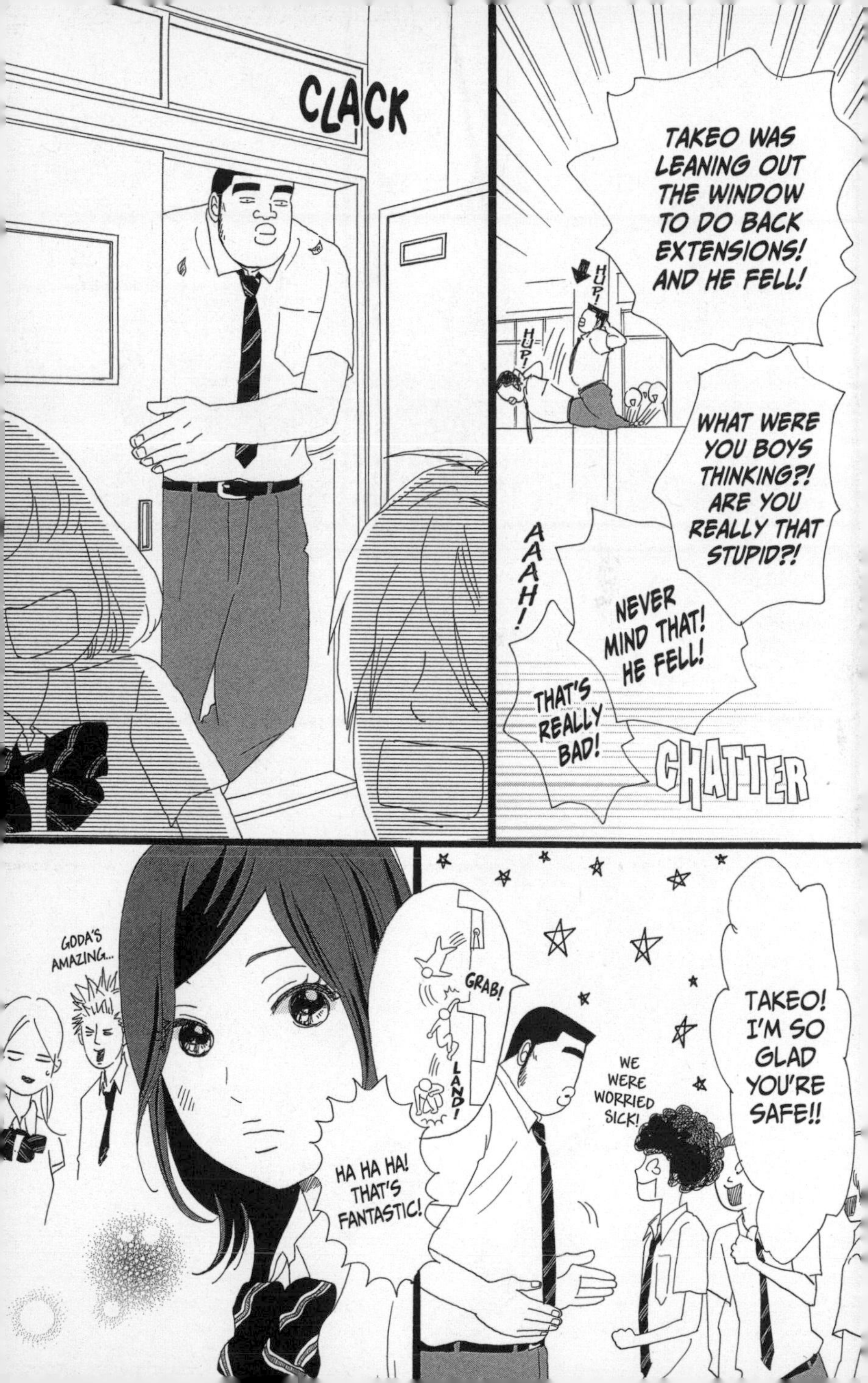
TAKEO WAS LEANING OUT THE WINDOW TO DO BACK EXTENSIONS! AND HE FELL!
HUP!
HUP!
WHAT WERE YOU BOYS THINKING?! ARE YOU REALLY THAT STUPID?!
NEVER MIND THAT! HE FELL!
AAAAH!
THAT'S REALLY BAD!
CHATTER
CLACK
TAKEO! I'M SO GLAD YOU'RE SAFE!!
WE WERE WORRIED SICK!
GRAB!
LAND!
HA HA HA! THAT'S FANTASTIC!
GODA'S AMAZING...

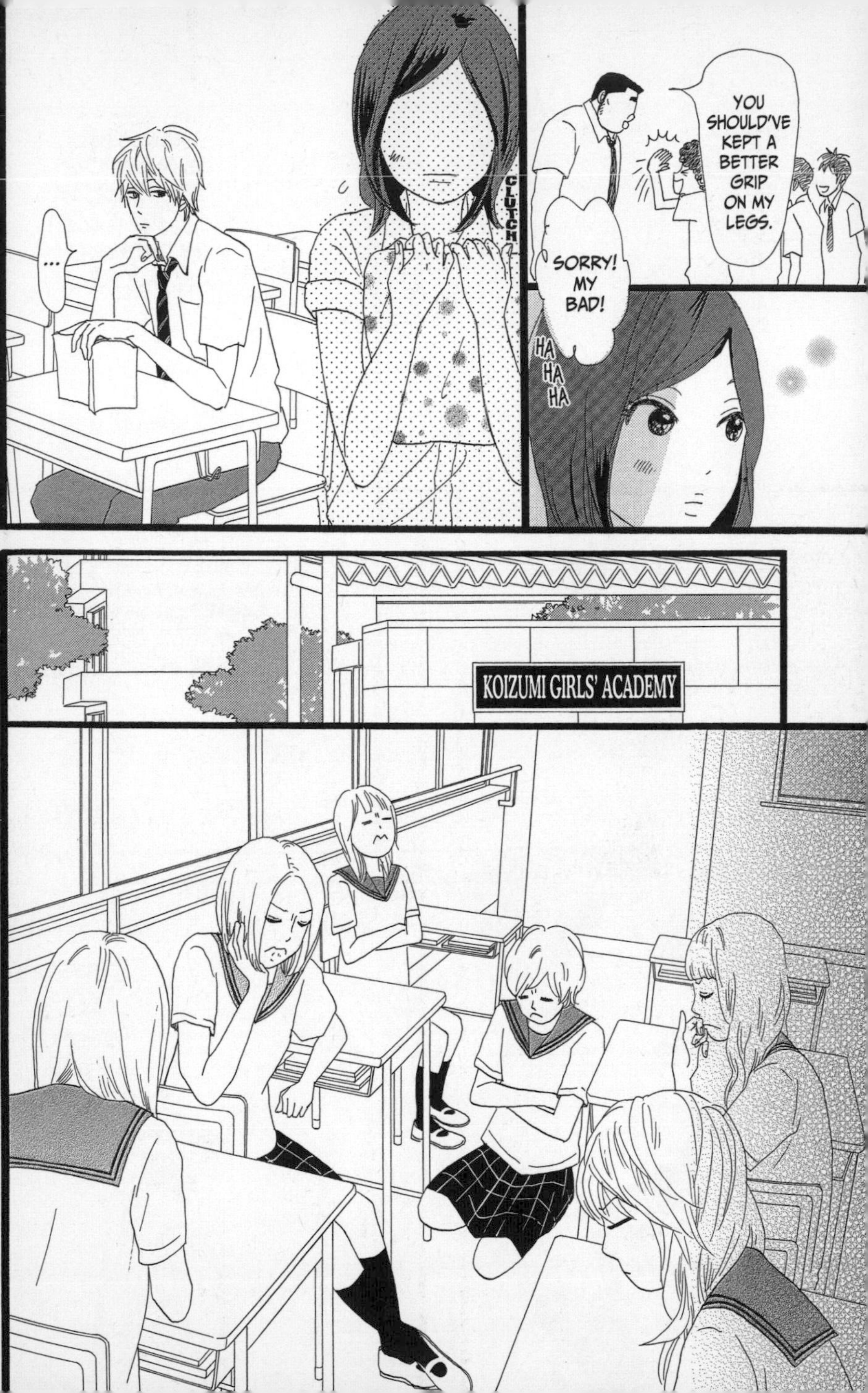
YOU SHOULD'VE KEPT A BETTER GRIP ON MY LEGS.
SORRY! MY BAD!
HA HA HA
CLUTCH
...
KOIZUMI GIRLS' ACADEMY

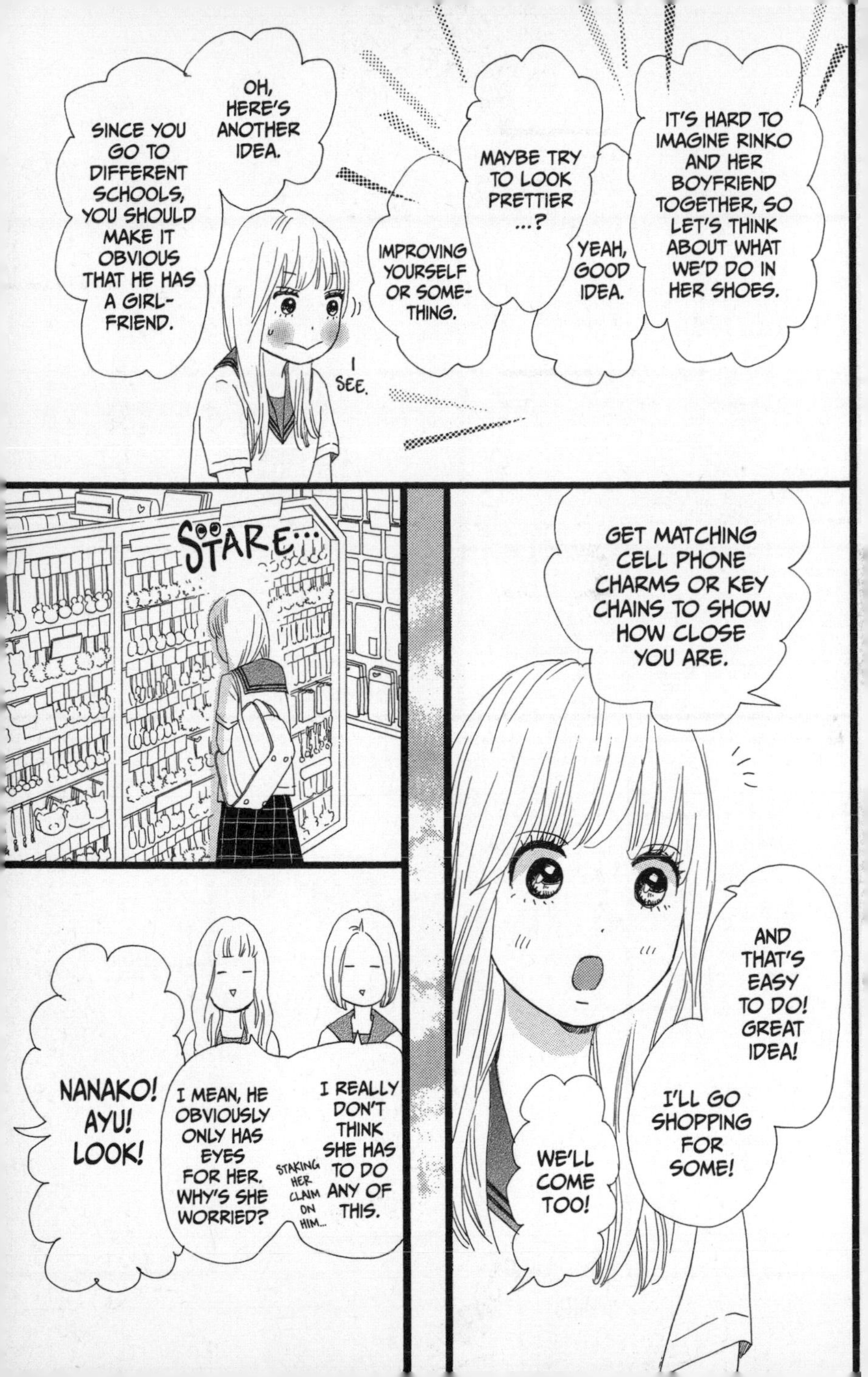
IT'S HARD TO IMAGINE RINKO AND HER BOYFRIEND TOGETHER, SO LET'S THINK ABOUT WHAT WE'D DO IN HER SHOES.
YEAH, GOOD IDEA.
MAYBE TRY TO LOOK PRETTIER ...?
IMPROVING YOURSELF OR SOMETHING.
I SEE.
OH, HERE'S ANOTHER IDEA.
SINCE YOU GO TO DIFFERENT SCHOOLS, YOU SHOULD MAKE IT OBVIOUS THAT HE HAS A GIRLFRIEND.
GET MATCHING CELL PHONE CHARMS OR KEY CHAINS TO SHOW HOW CLOSE YOU ARE.
AND THAT'S EASY TO DO! GREAT IDEA!
I'LL GO SHOPPING FOR SOME!
WE'LL COME TOO!
STARE...
I REALLY DON'T THINK SHE HAS TO DO ANY OF THIS.
STAKING HER CLAIM ON HIM...
I MEAN, HE OBVIOUSLY ONLY HAS EYES FOR HER. WHY'S SHE WORRIED?
NANAKO! AYU! LOOK!

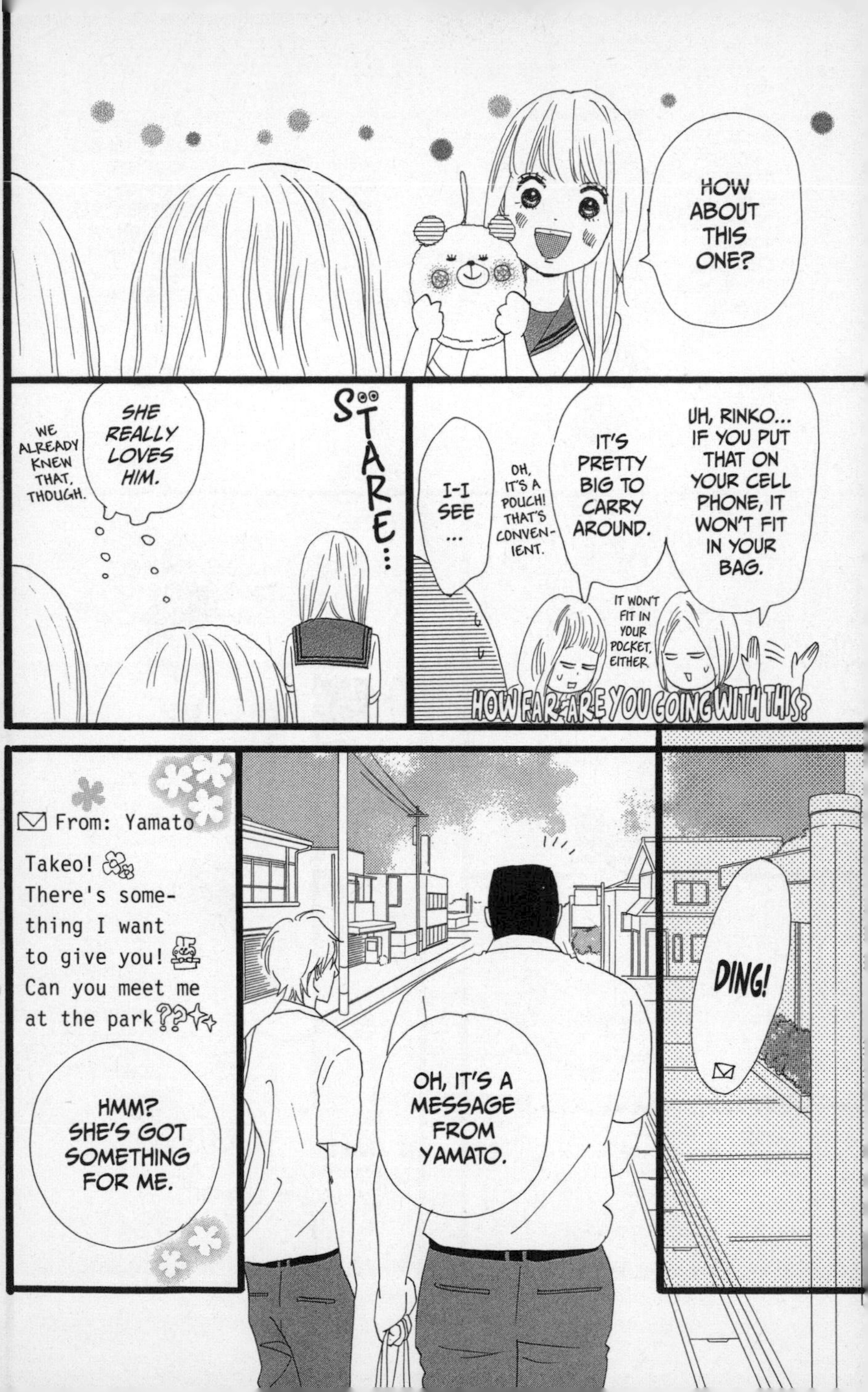
HOW ABOUT THIS ONE?
UH, RINKO... IF YOU PUT THAT ON YOUR CELL PHONE, IT WON'T FIT IN YOUR BAG.
IT WON'T FIT IN YOUR POCKET, EITHER.
IT'S PRETTY BIG TO CARRY AROUND.
OH, IT'S A POUCH! THAT'S CONVEN-IENT.
I-I SEE...
HOW FAR ARE YOU GOING WITH THIS?
STARE...
SHE REALLY LOVES HIM.
WE ALREADY KNEW THAT, THOUGH.
DING!
OH, IT'S A MESSAGE FROM YAMATO.
From: Yamato
Takeo! There's some-thing I want to give you! Can you meet me at the park??
HMM? SHE'S GOT SOMETHING FOR ME.

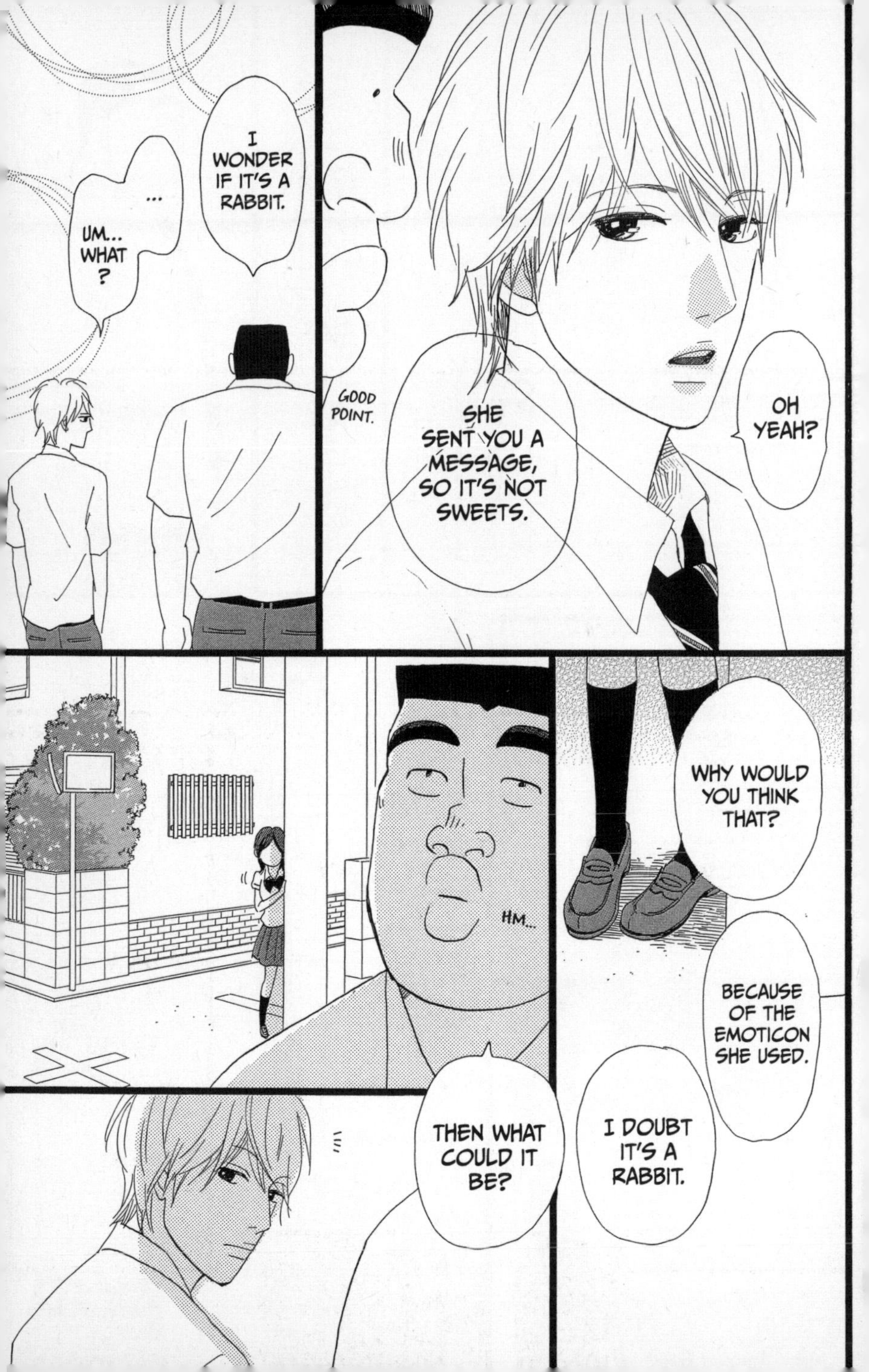
OH YEAH?
SHE SENT YOU A MESSAGE, SO IT'S NOT SWEETS.
GOOD POINT.
I WONDER IF IT'S A RABBIT.
...
UM... WHAT?
WHY WOULD YOU THINK THAT?
BECAUSE OF THE EMOTICON SHE USED.
I DOUBT IT'S A RABBIT.
HM...
THEN WHAT COULD IT BE?

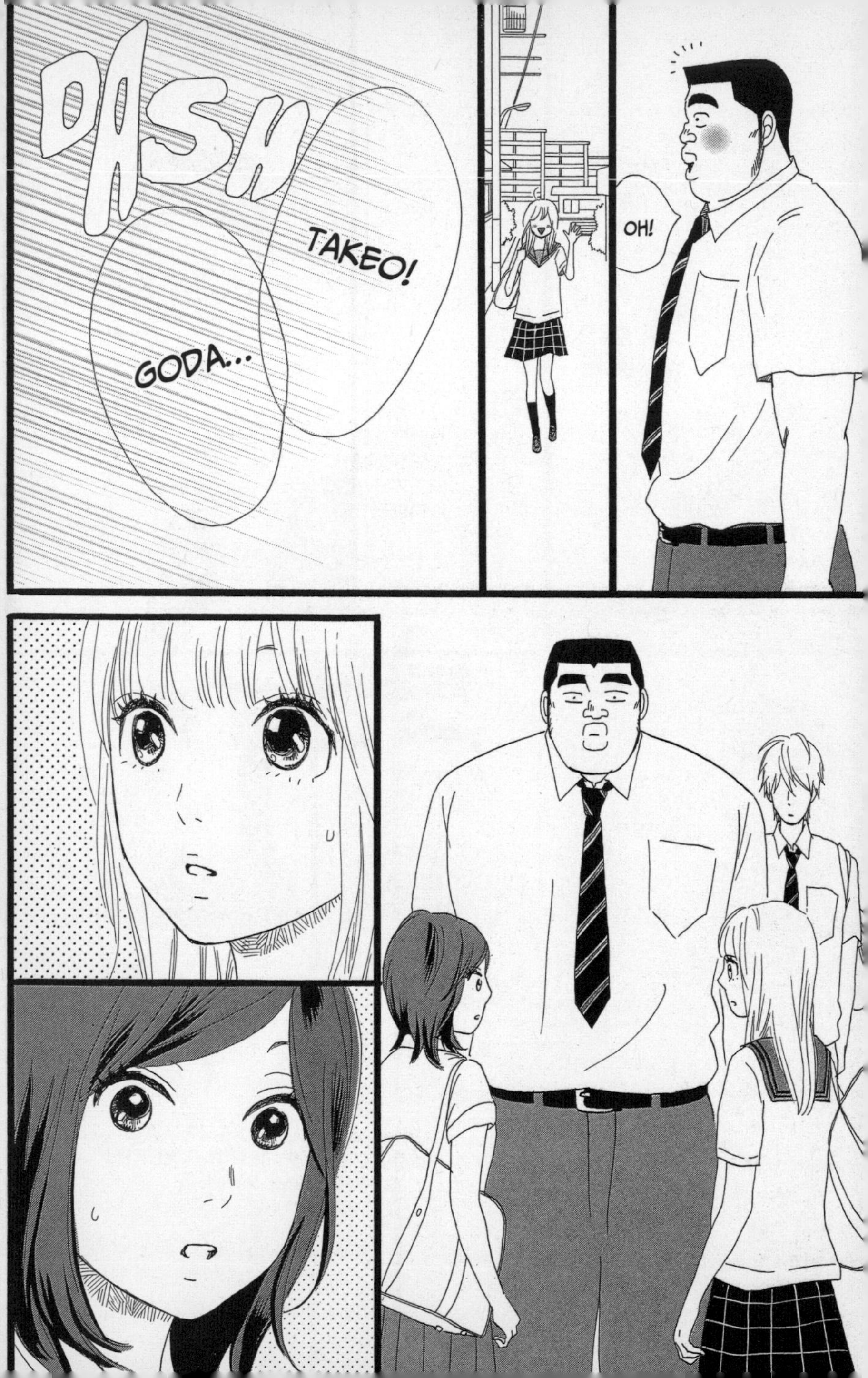
OH!
DASH
TAKEO!
GODA...

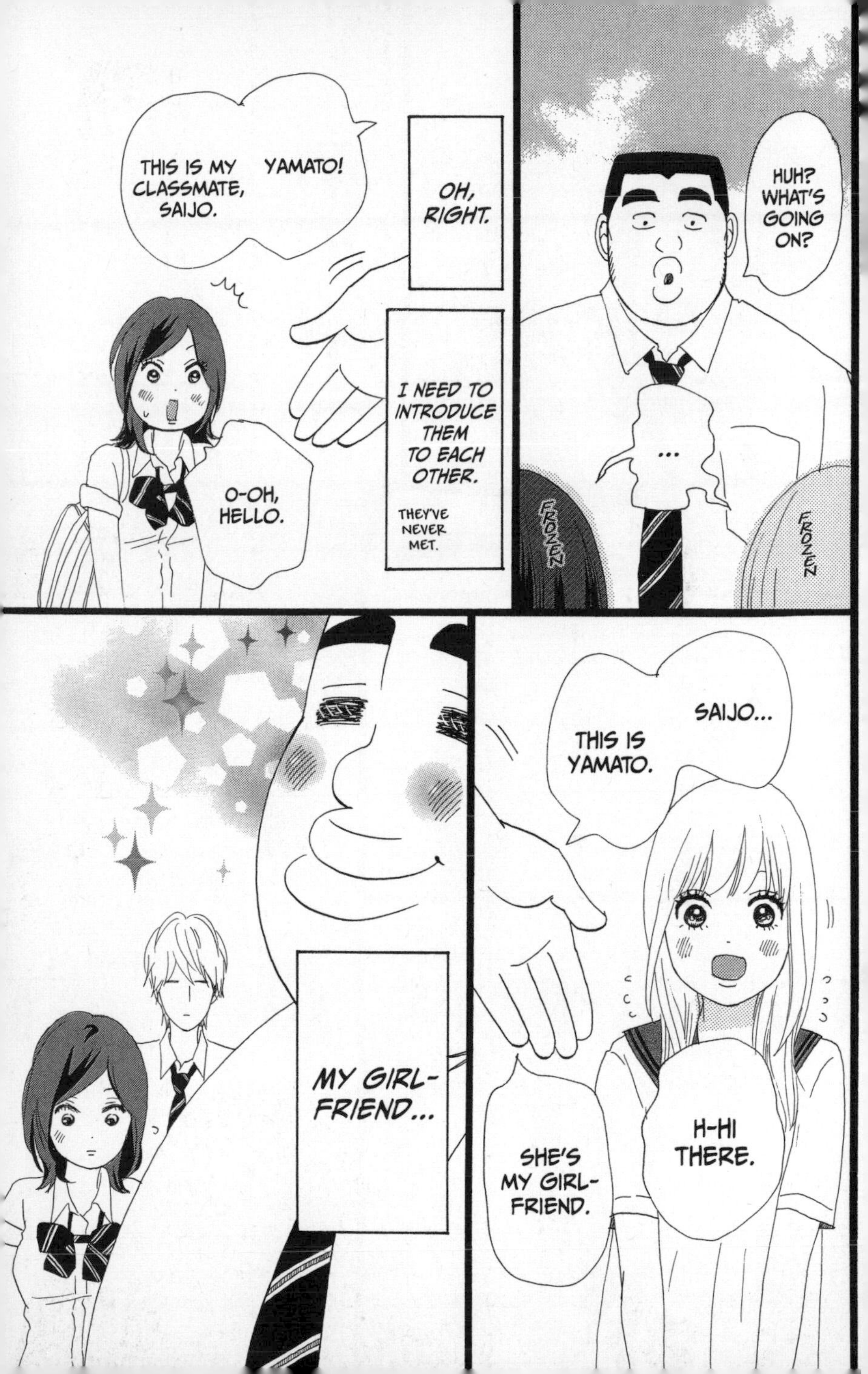
HUH? WHAT'S GOING ON?
...
FROZEN
FROZEN
OH, RIGHT.
I NEED TO INTRODUCE THEM TO EACH OTHER.
THEY'VE NEVER MET.
YAMATO!
THIS IS MY CLASSMATE, SAIJO.
O-OH, HELLO.
SAIJO...
THIS IS YAMATO.
H-HI THERE.
SHE'S MY GIRL-FRIEND.
MY GIRL-FRIEND...

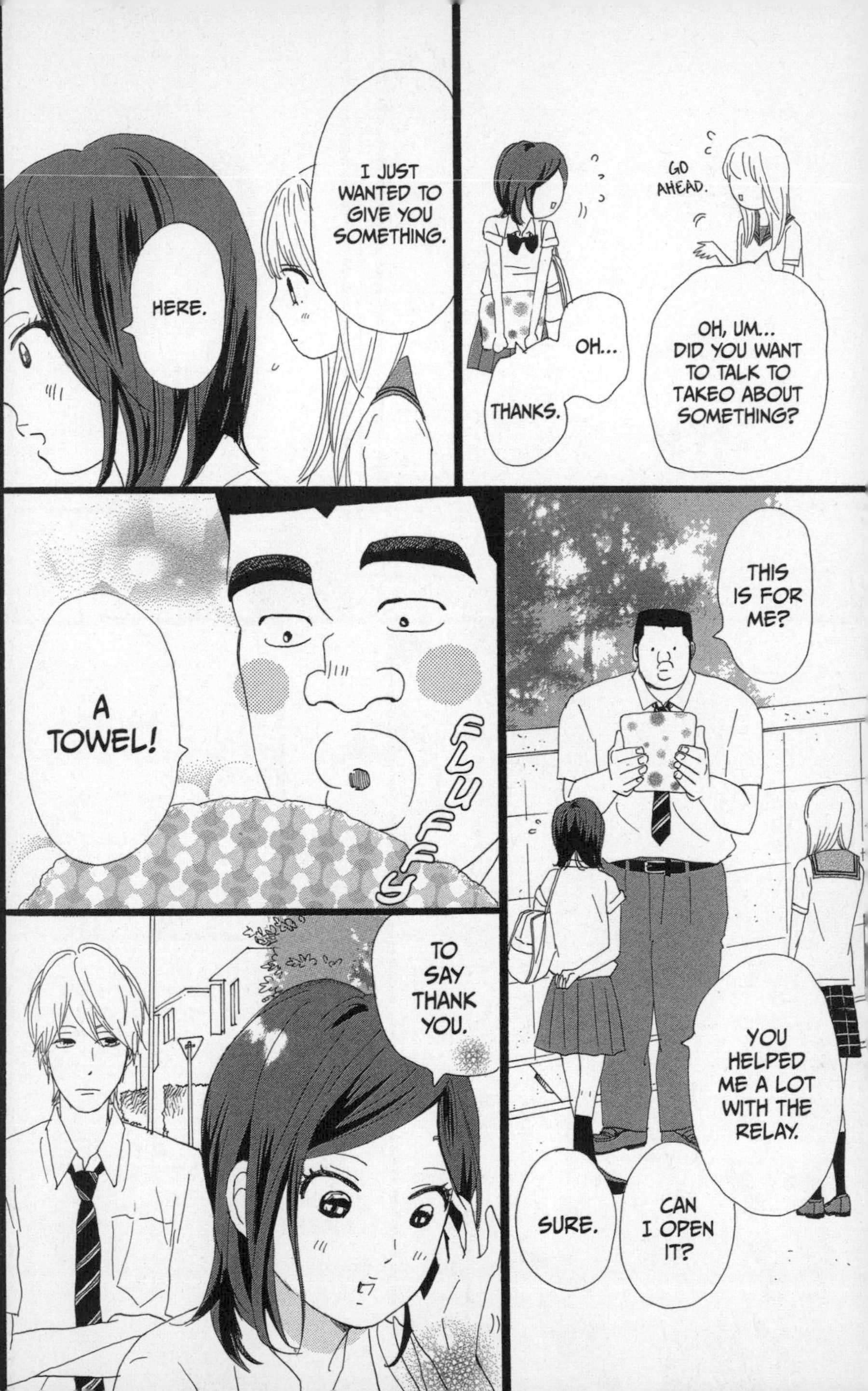
GO AHEAD.
OH, UM... DID YOU WANT TO TALK TO TAKEO ABOUT SOMETHING?
OH...
THANKS.
I JUST WANTED TO GIVE YOU SOMETHING.
HERE.
THIS IS FOR ME?
YOU HELPED ME A LOT WITH THE RELAY.
CAN I OPEN IT?
SURE.
FLUFF
A TOWEL!
TO SAY THANK YOU.

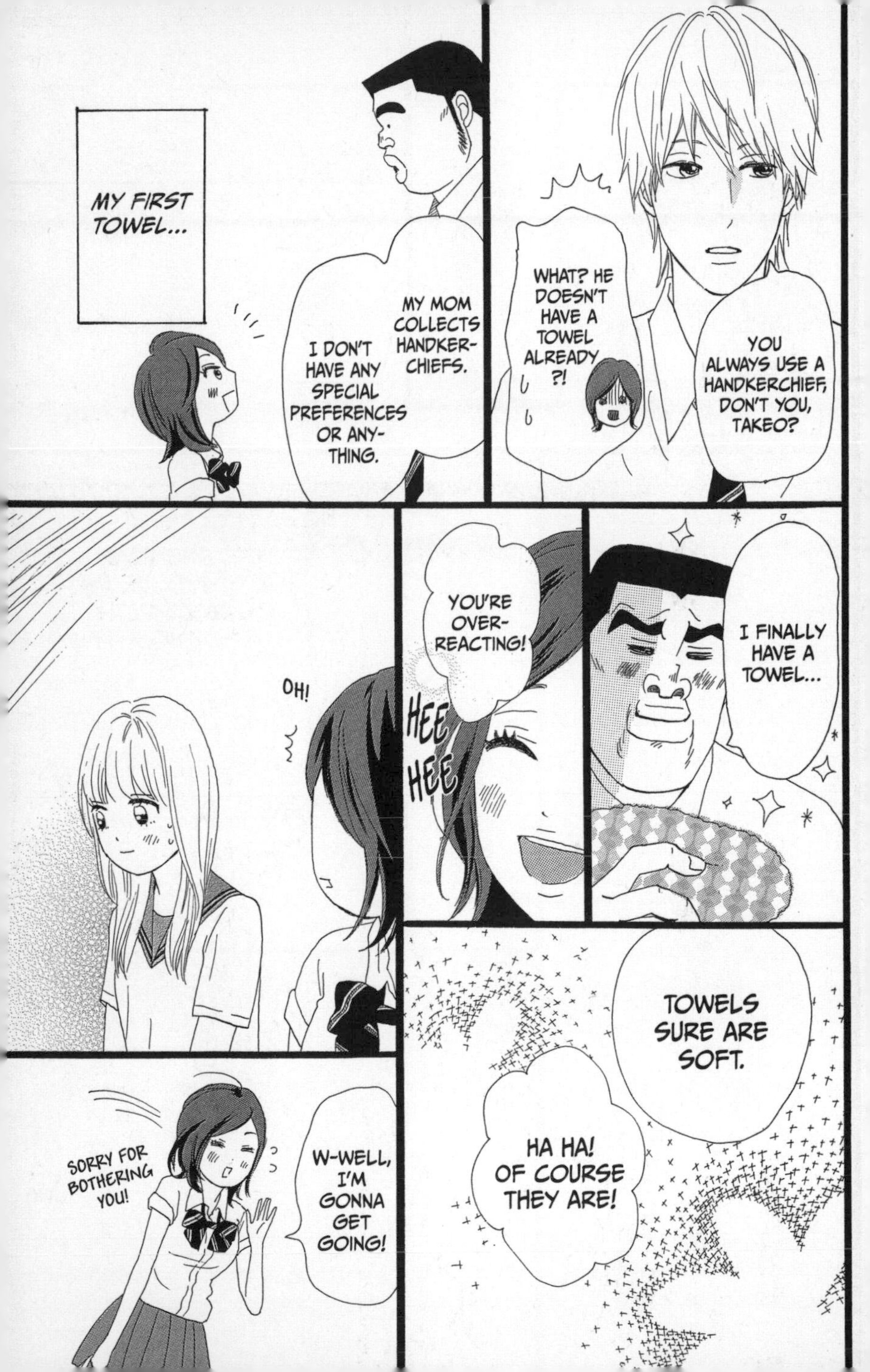
YOU ALWAYS USE A HANDKERCHIEF, DON'T YOU, TAKEO?
WHAT? HE DOESN'T HAVE A TOWEL ALREADY ?!
MY MOM COLLECTS HANDKER-CHIEFS.
I DON'T HAVE ANY SPECIAL PREFERENCES OR ANY-THING.
MY FIRST TOWEL...
I FINALLY HAVE A TOWEL...
YOU'RE OVER-REACTING!
HEE HEE
TOWELS SURE ARE SOFT.
HA HA! OF COURSE THEY ARE!
OH!
W-WELL, I'M GONNA GET GOING!
SORRY FOR BOTHERING YOU!

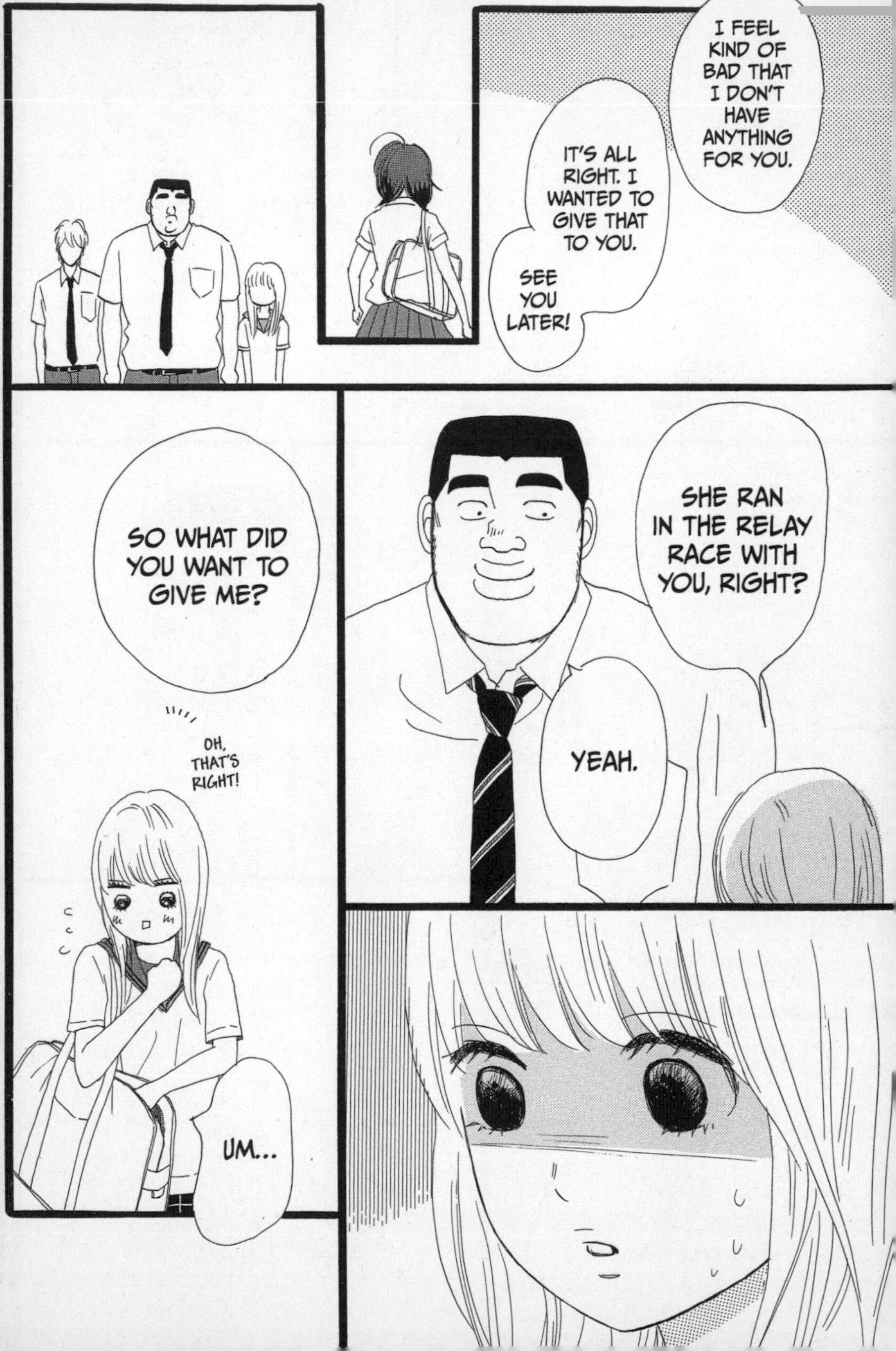
I FEEL KIND OF BAD THAT I DON'T HAVE ANYTHING FOR YOU.
IT'S ALL RIGHT. I WANTED TO GIVE THAT TO YOU.
SEE YOU LATER!
SHE RAN IN THE RELAY RACE WITH YOU, RIGHT?
YEAH.
SO WHAT DID YOU WANT TO GIVE ME?
OH, THAT'S RIGHT!
UM...

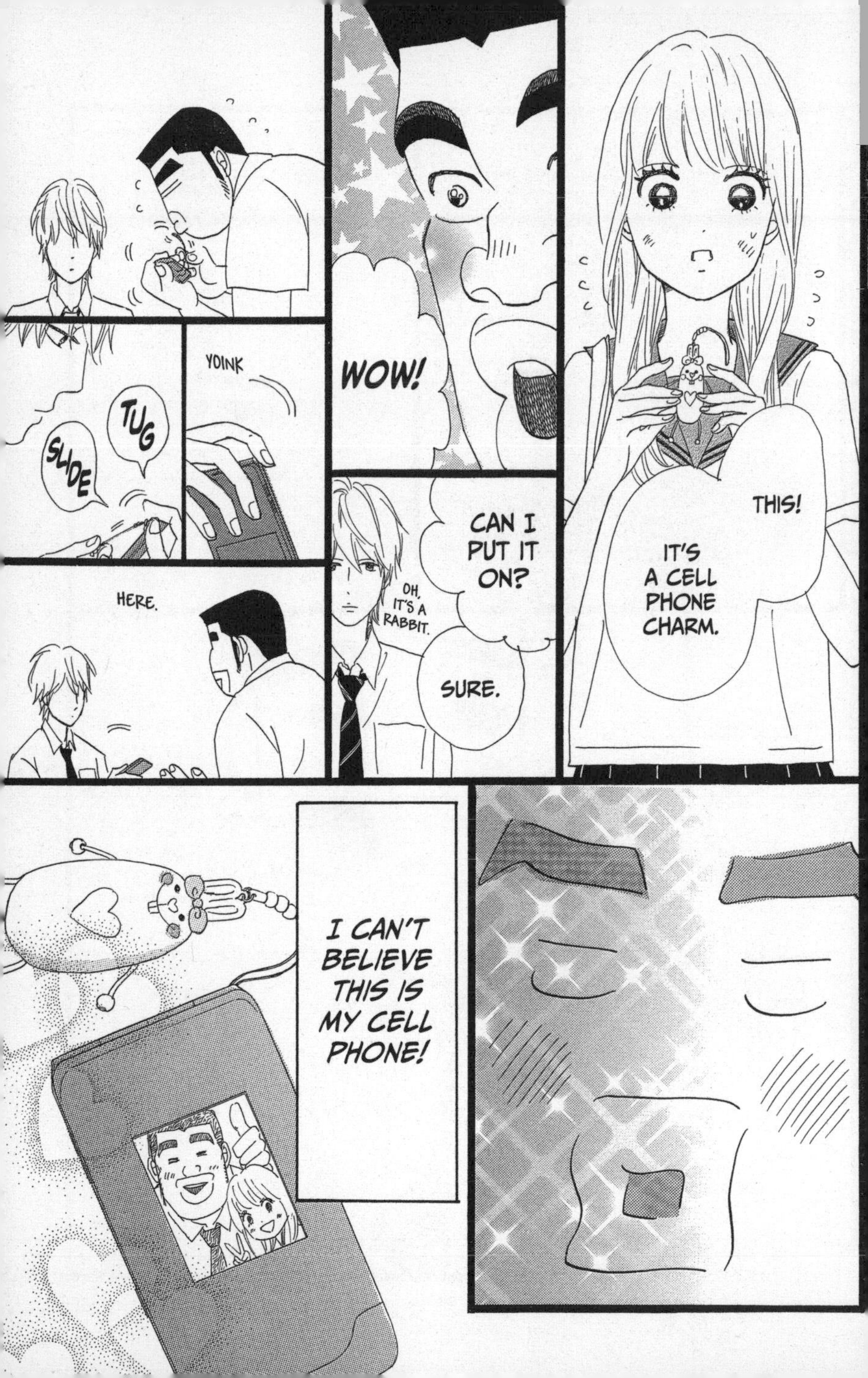
THIS!
IT'S A CELL PHONE CHARM.
WOW!
CAN I PUT IT ON?
OH, IT'S A RABBIT.
SURE.
YOINK
TUG
SLIDE
HERE.
I CAN'T BELIEVE THIS IS MY CELL PHONE!

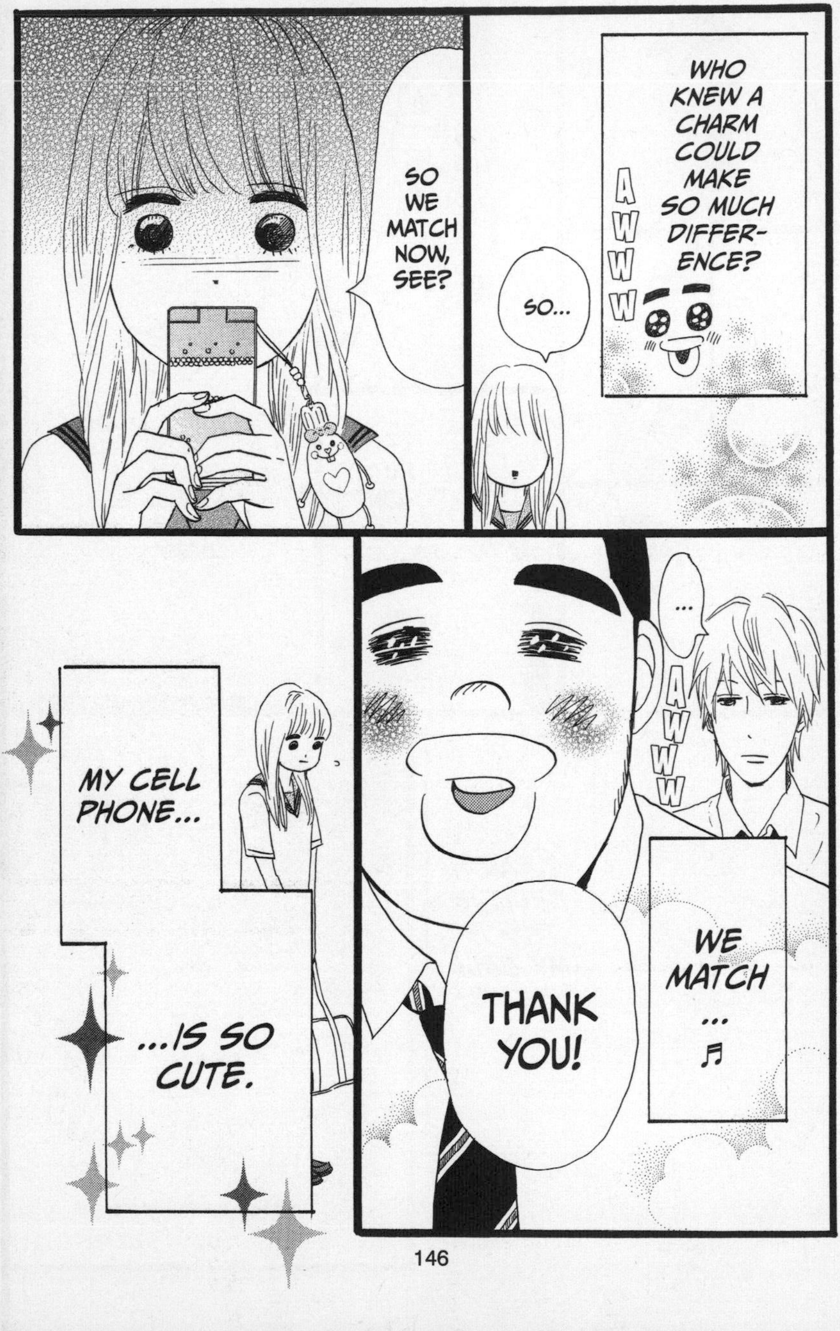
WHO KNEW A CHARM COULD MAKE SO MUCH DIFFER-ENCE?
AWWW
SO...
SO WE MATCH NOW, SEE?
...
AWWWW
WE MATCH ... ♬
THANK YOU!
MY CELL PHONE...
...IS SO CUTE.

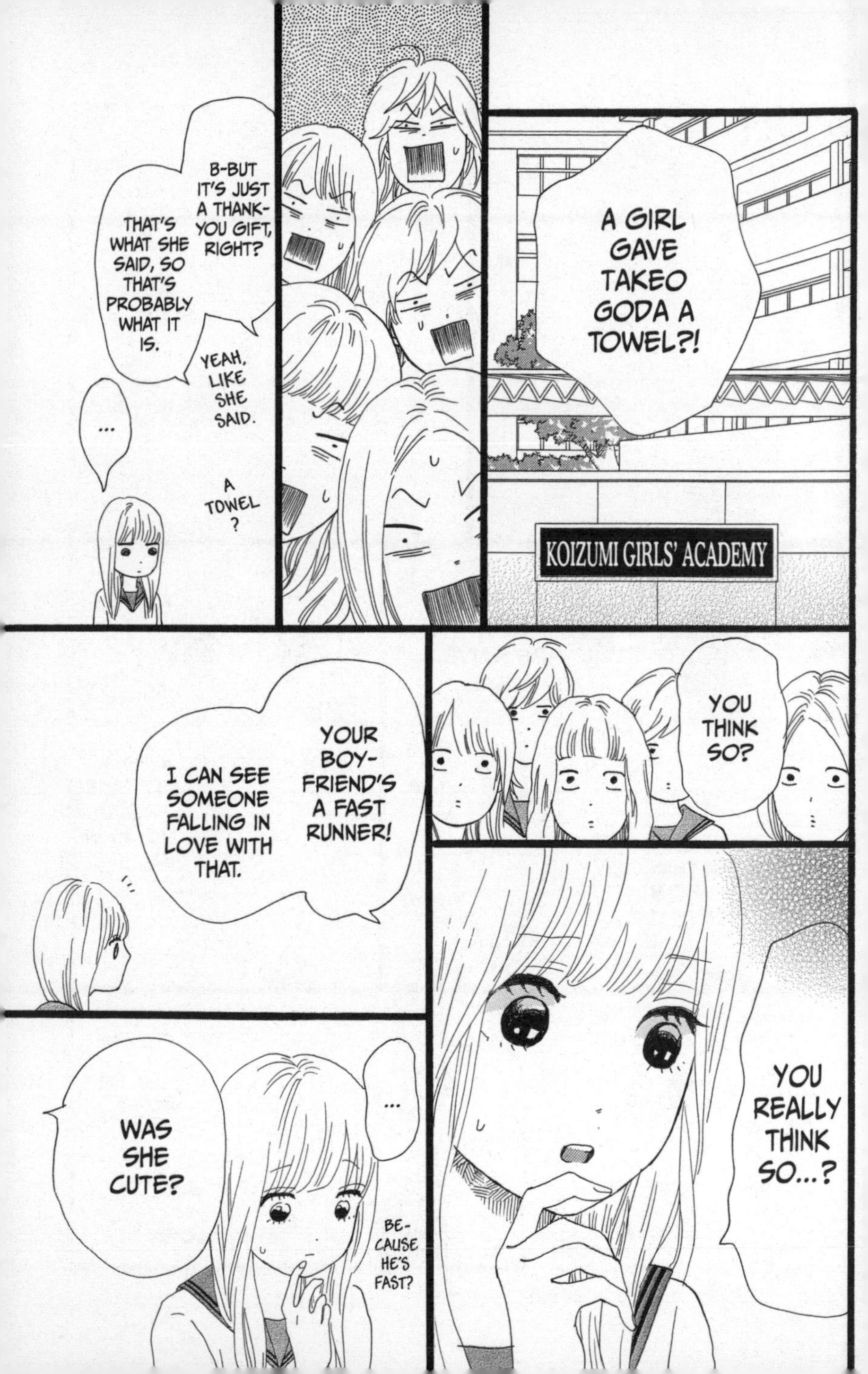
A GIRL GAVE TAKEO GODA A TOWEL?!
KOIZUMI GIRLS' ACADEMY
B-BUT IT'S JUST A THANK-YOU GIFT, RIGHT?
YEAH, LIKE SHE SAID.
THAT'S WHAT SHE SAID, SO THAT'S PROBABLY WHAT IT IS.
...
A TOWEL?
YOU THINK SO?
YOU REALLY THINK SO...?
YOUR BOY-FRIEND'S A FAST RUNNER!
I CAN SEE SOMEONE FALLING IN LOVE WITH THAT.
...
BE-CAUSE HE'S FAST?
WAS SHE CUTE?

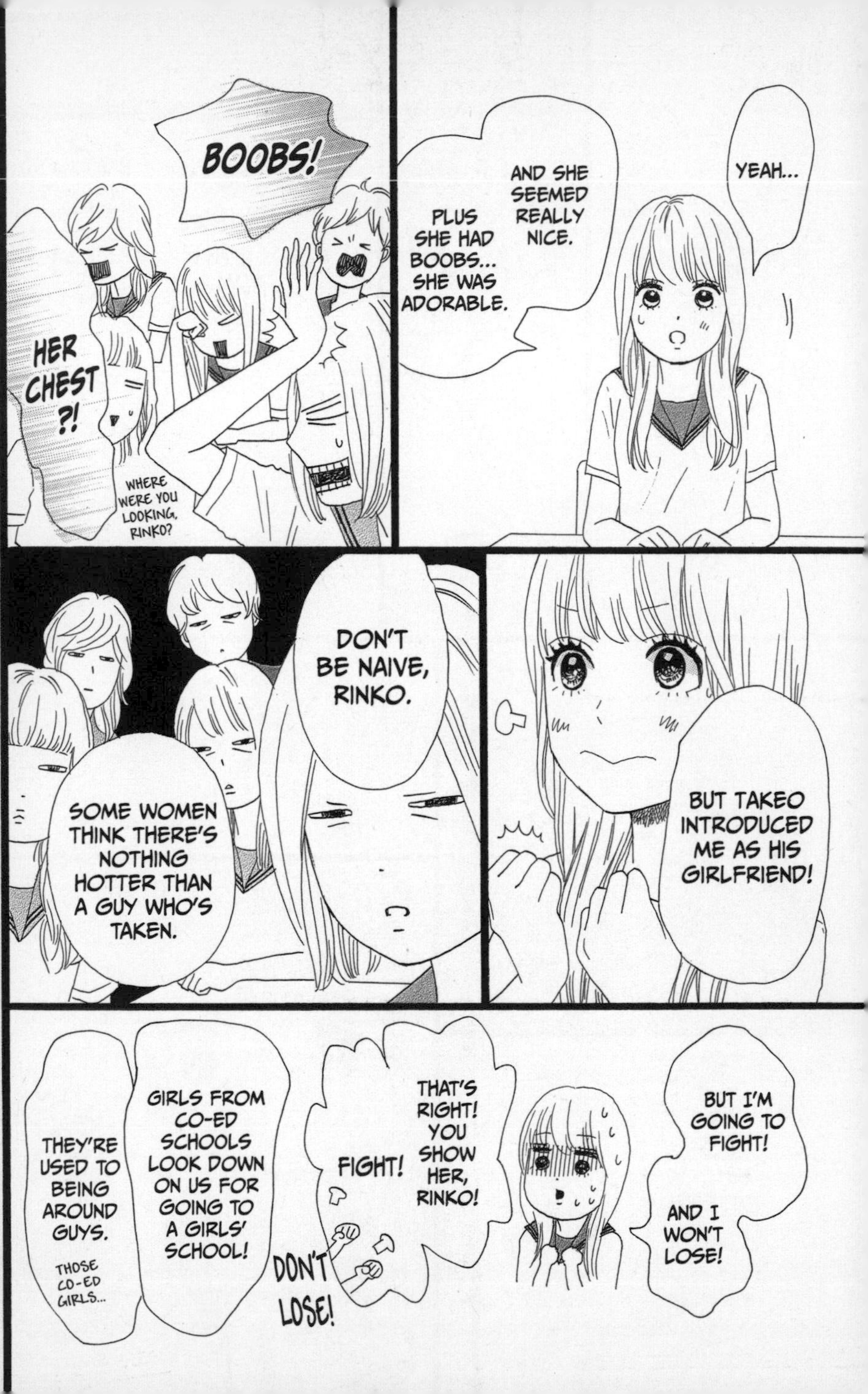
YEAH...
AND SHE SEEMED REALLY NICE.
PLUS SHE HAD BOOBS... SHE WAS ADORABLE.
BOOBS!
HER CHEST ?!
WHERE WERE YOU LOOKING, RINKO?
BUT TAKEO INTRODUCED ME AS HIS GIRLFRIEND!
DON'T BE NAIVE, RINKO.
SOME WOMEN THINK THERE'S NOTHING HOTTER THAN A GUY WHO'S TAKEN.
BUT I'M GOING TO FIGHT!
AND I WON'T LOSE!
THAT'S RIGHT! YOU SHOW HER, RINKO!
FIGHT!
DON'T LOSE!
GIRLS FROM CO-ED SCHOOLS LOOK DOWN ON US FOR GOING TO A GIRLS' SCHOOL!
THEY'RE USED TO BEING AROUND GUYS.
THOSE CO-ED GIRLS...

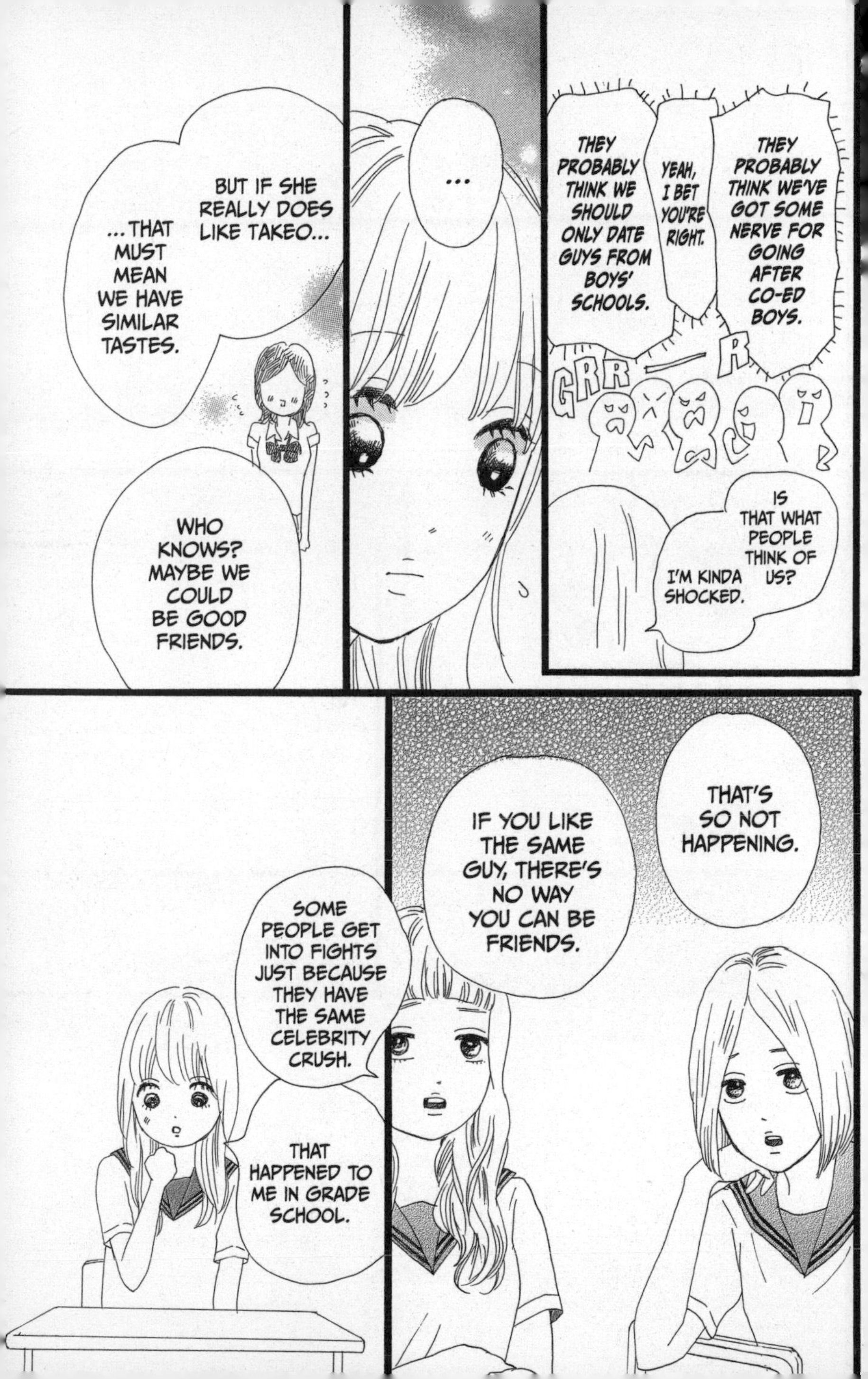
THEY PROBABLY THINK WE'VE GOT SOME NERVE FOR GOING AFTER CO-ED BOYS.
YEAH, I BET YOU'RE RIGHT.
THEY PROBABLY THINK WE SHOULD ONLY DATE GUYS FROM BOYS' SCHOOLS.
GRR—R
IS THAT WHAT PEOPLE THINK OF US?
I'M KINDA SHOCKED.
...
BUT IF SHE REALLY DOES LIKE TAKEO...
...THAT MUST MEAN WE HAVE SIMILAR TASTES.
WHO KNOWS? MAYBE WE COULD BE GOOD FRIENDS.
THAT'S SO NOT HAPPENING.
IF YOU LIKE THE SAME GUY, THERE'S NO WAY YOU CAN BE FRIENDS.
SOME PEOPLE GET INTO FIGHTS JUST BECAUSE THEY HAVE THE SAME CELEBRITY CRUSH.
THAT HAPPENED TO ME IN GRADE SCHOOL.

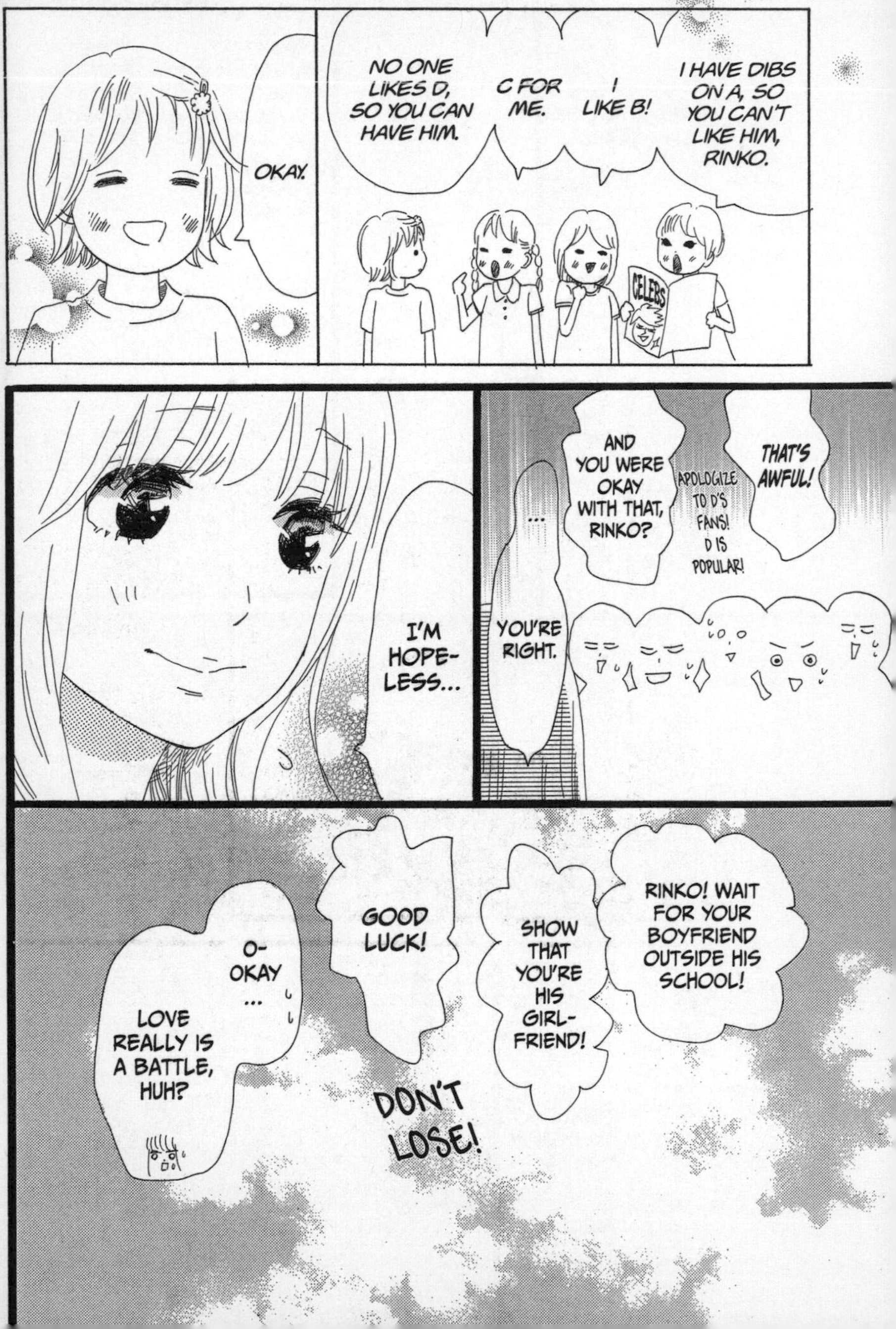
I HAVE DIBS ON A, SO YOU CAN'T LIKE HIM, RINKO.
I LIKE B!
C FOR ME.
NO ONE LIKES D, SO YOU CAN HAVE HIM.
CELEBS
OKAY.
THAT'S AWFUL!
APOLOGIZE TO D'S FANS! D IS POPULAR!
AND YOU WERE OKAY WITH THAT, RINKO?
...
YOU'RE RIGHT.
I'M HOPE-LESS...
RINKO! WAIT FOR YOUR BOYFRIEND OUTSIDE HIS SCHOOL!
SHOW THAT YOU'RE HIS GIRL-FRIEND!
GOOD LUCK!
DON'T LOSE!
O-OKAY...
LOVE REALLY IS A BATTLE, HUH?

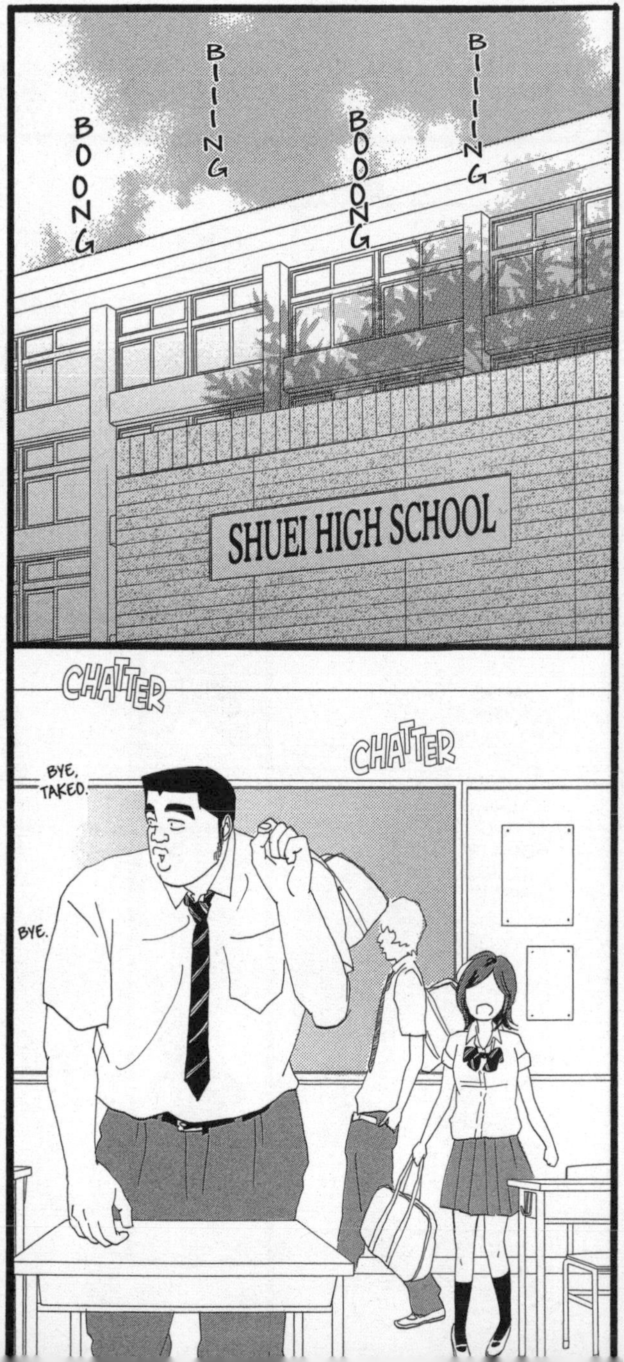
BIIING
BOOONG
BIIING
BOONG
SHUEI HIGH SCHOOL
CHATTER
CHATTER
BYE, TAKEO.
BYE.

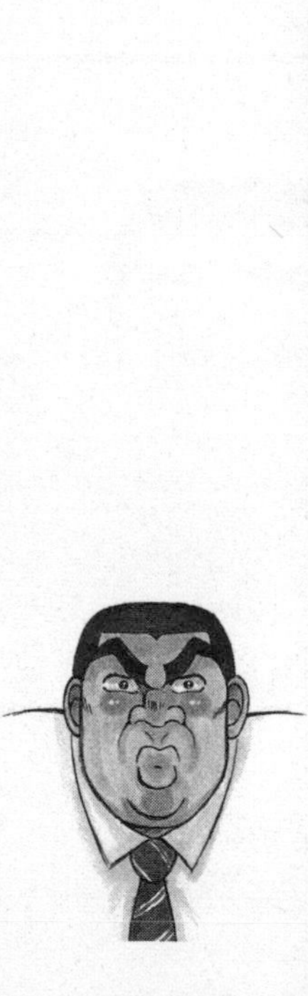

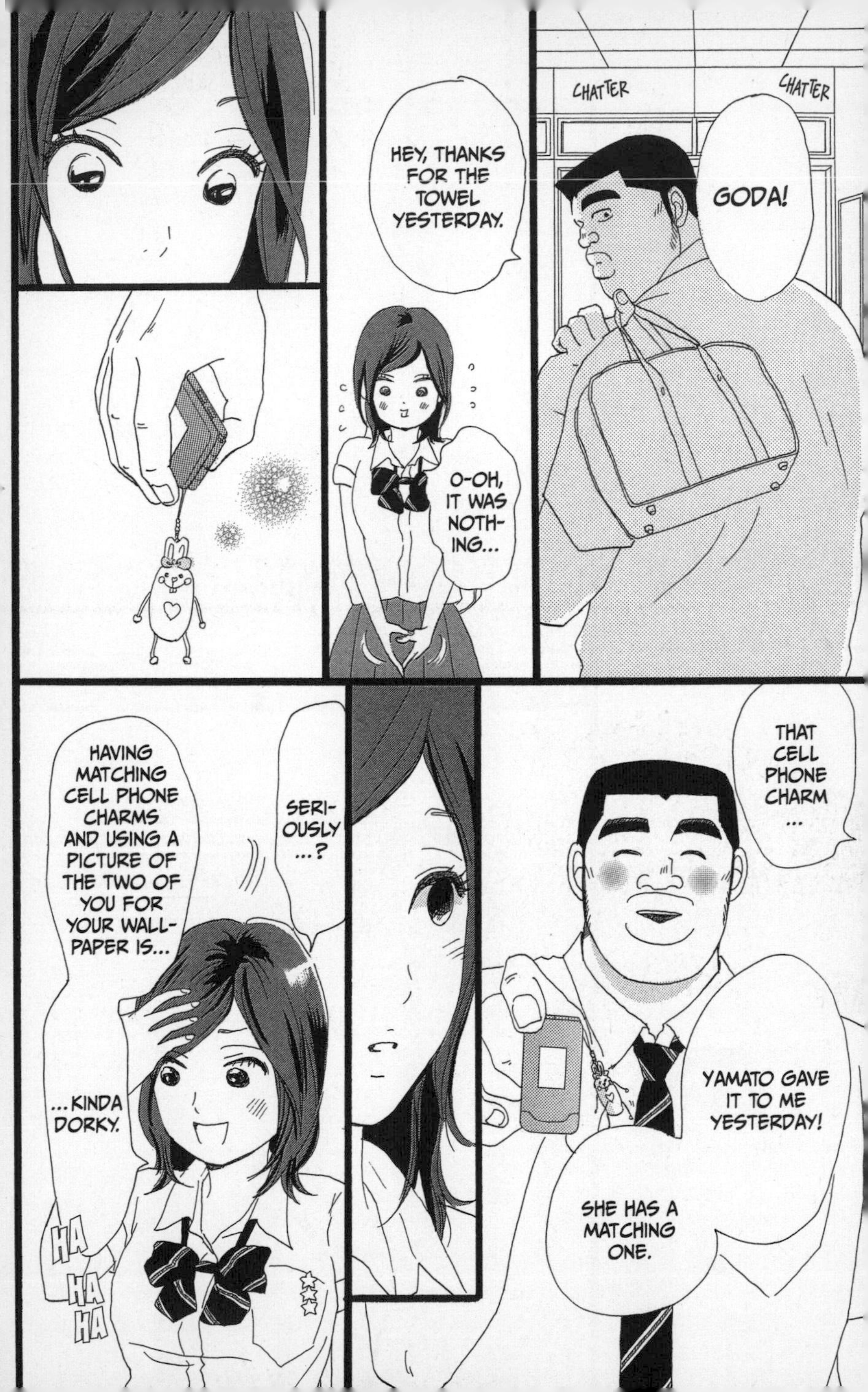
CHATTER
CHATTER
GODA!
HEY, THANKS FOR THE TOWEL YESTERDAY.
O-OH, IT WAS NOTHING...
THAT CELL PHONE CHARM...
YAMATO GAVE IT TO ME YESTERDAY!
SHE HAS A MATCHING ONE.
SERIOUSLY...?
HAVING MATCHING CELL PHONE CHARMS AND USING A PICTURE OF THE TWO OF YOU FOR YOUR WALLPAPER IS...
...KINDA DORKY.
HA HA HA

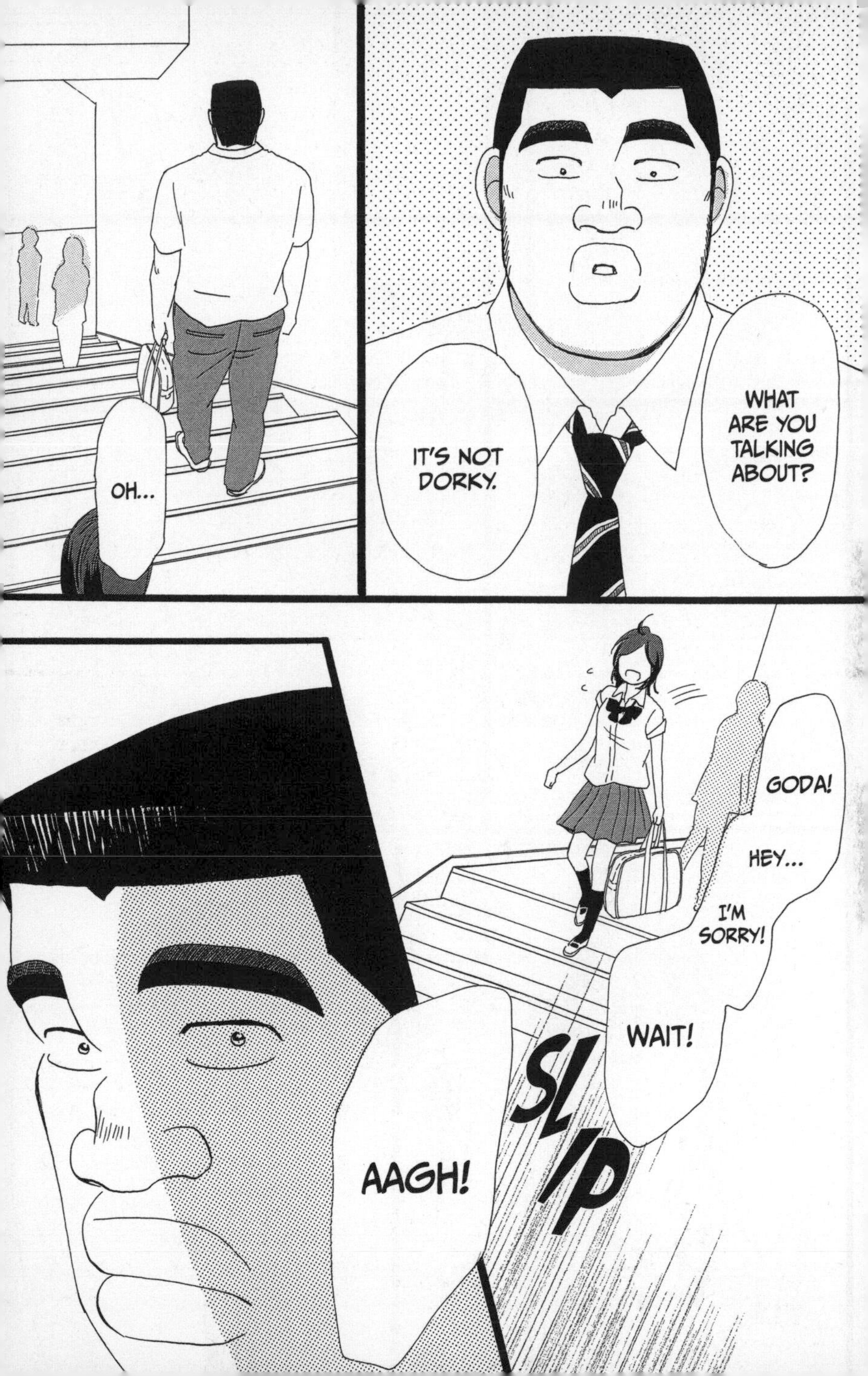
WHAT ARE YOU TALKING ABOUT?
IT'S NOT DORKY.
OH...
GODA!
HEY...
I'M SORRY!
WAIT!
SLIP
AAGH!

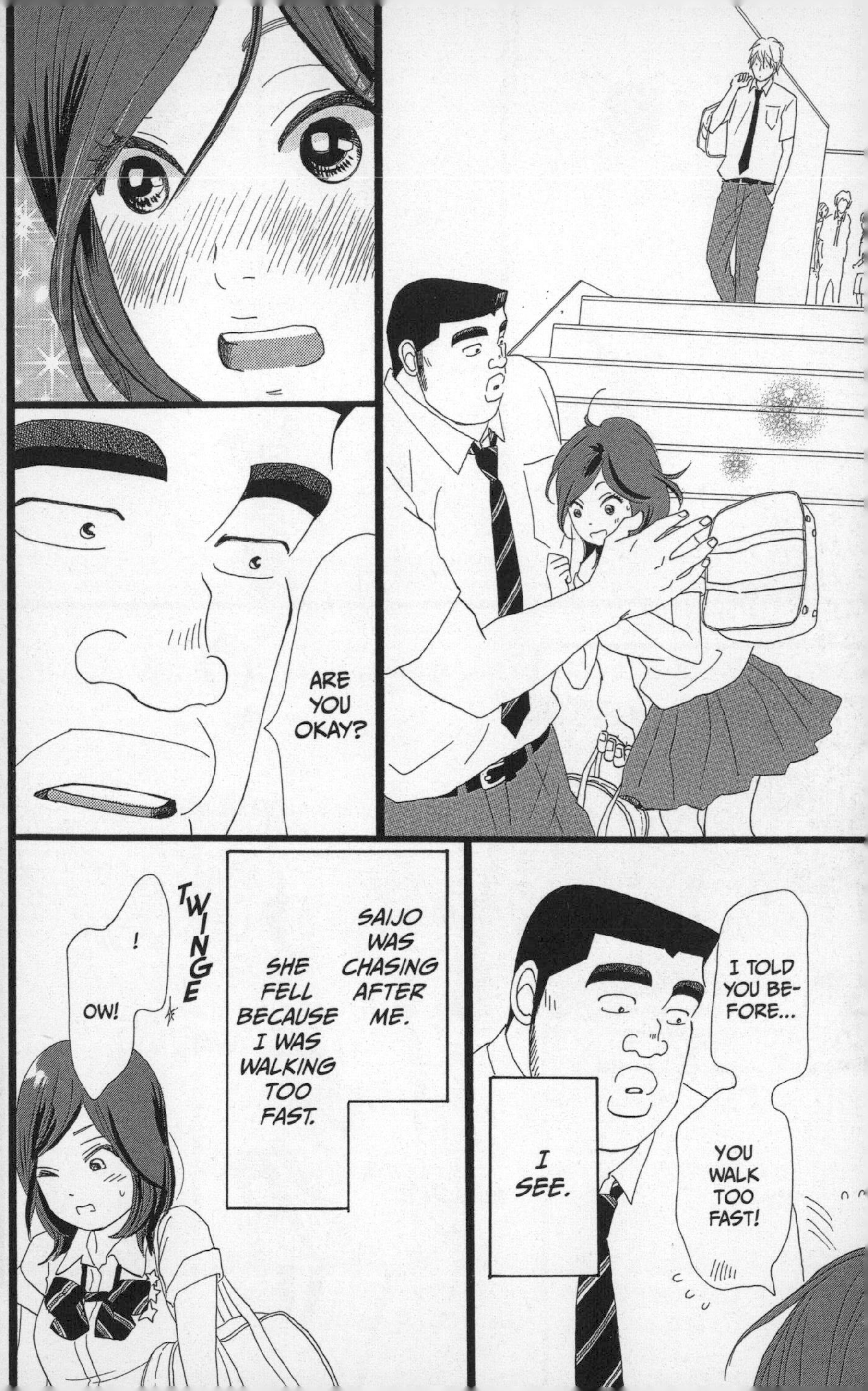
ARE YOU OKAY?
I TOLD YOU BE-FORE...
YOU WALK TOO FAST!
I SEE.
SAIJO WAS CHASING AFTER ME.
SHE FELL BECAUSE I WAS WALKING TOO FAST.
TWINGE
!
OW!

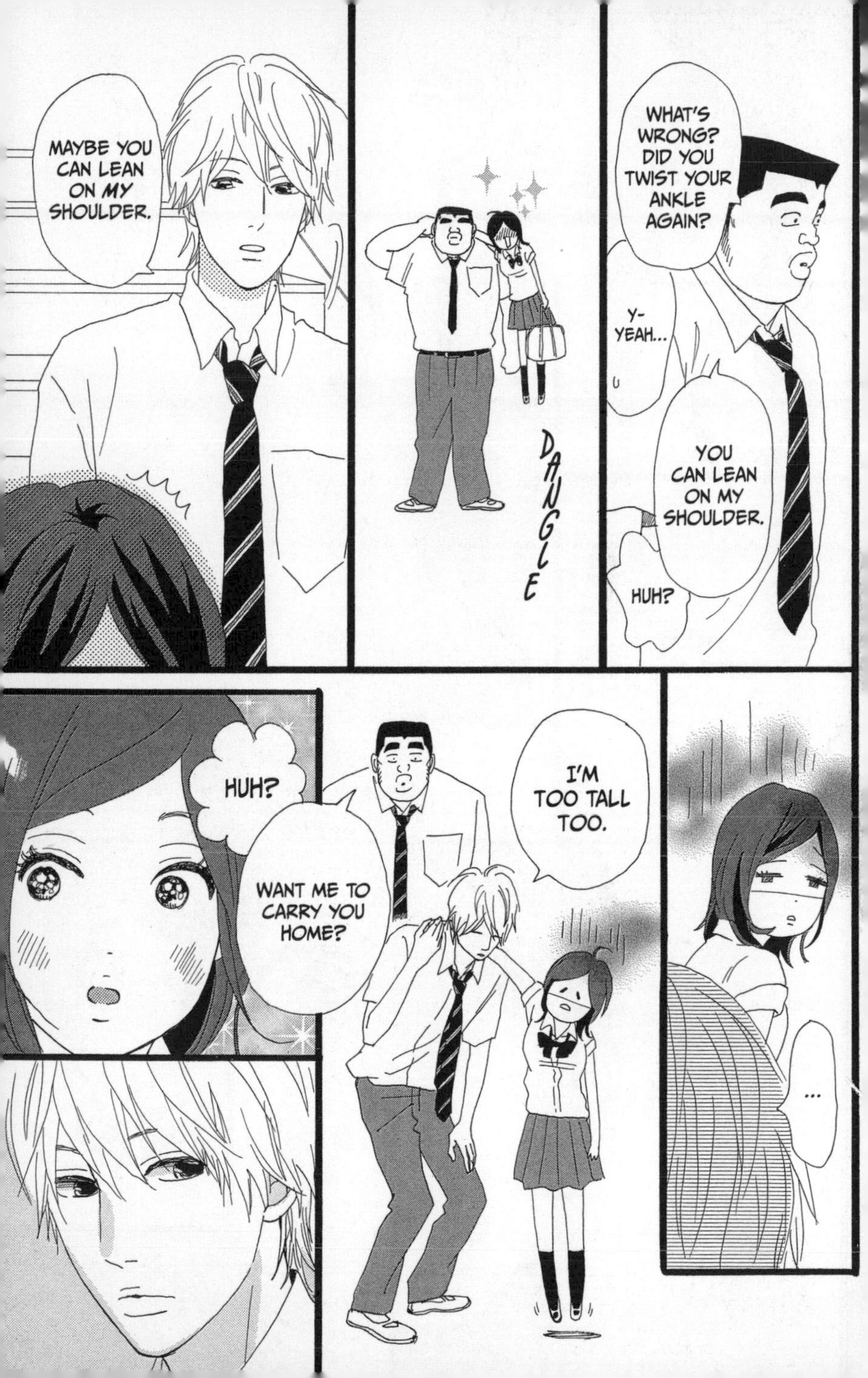
WHAT'S WRONG? DID YOU TWIST YOUR ANKLE AGAIN?
Y-YEAH...
YOU CAN LEAN ON MY SHOULDER.
HUH?
DANGLE
MAYBE YOU CAN LEAN ON MY SHOULDER.
...
I'M TOO TALL TOO.
WANT ME TO CARRY YOU HOME?
HUH?

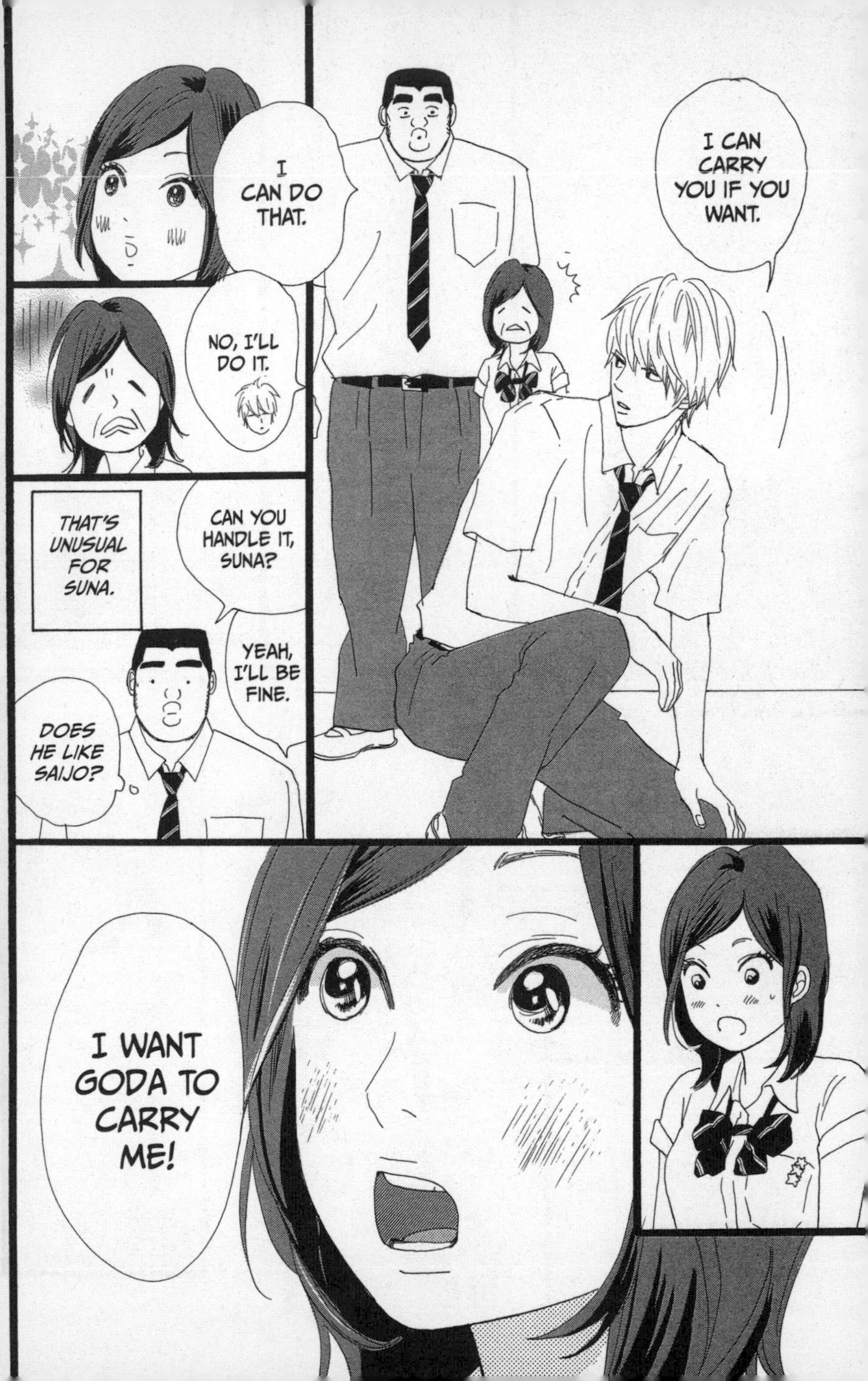
I CAN CARRY YOU IF YOU WANT.
I CAN DO THAT.
NO, I'LL DO IT.
CAN YOU HANDLE IT, SUNA?
THAT'S UNUSUAL FOR SUNA.
YEAH, I'LL BE FINE.
DOES HE LIKE SAIJO?
I WANT GODA TO CARRY ME!

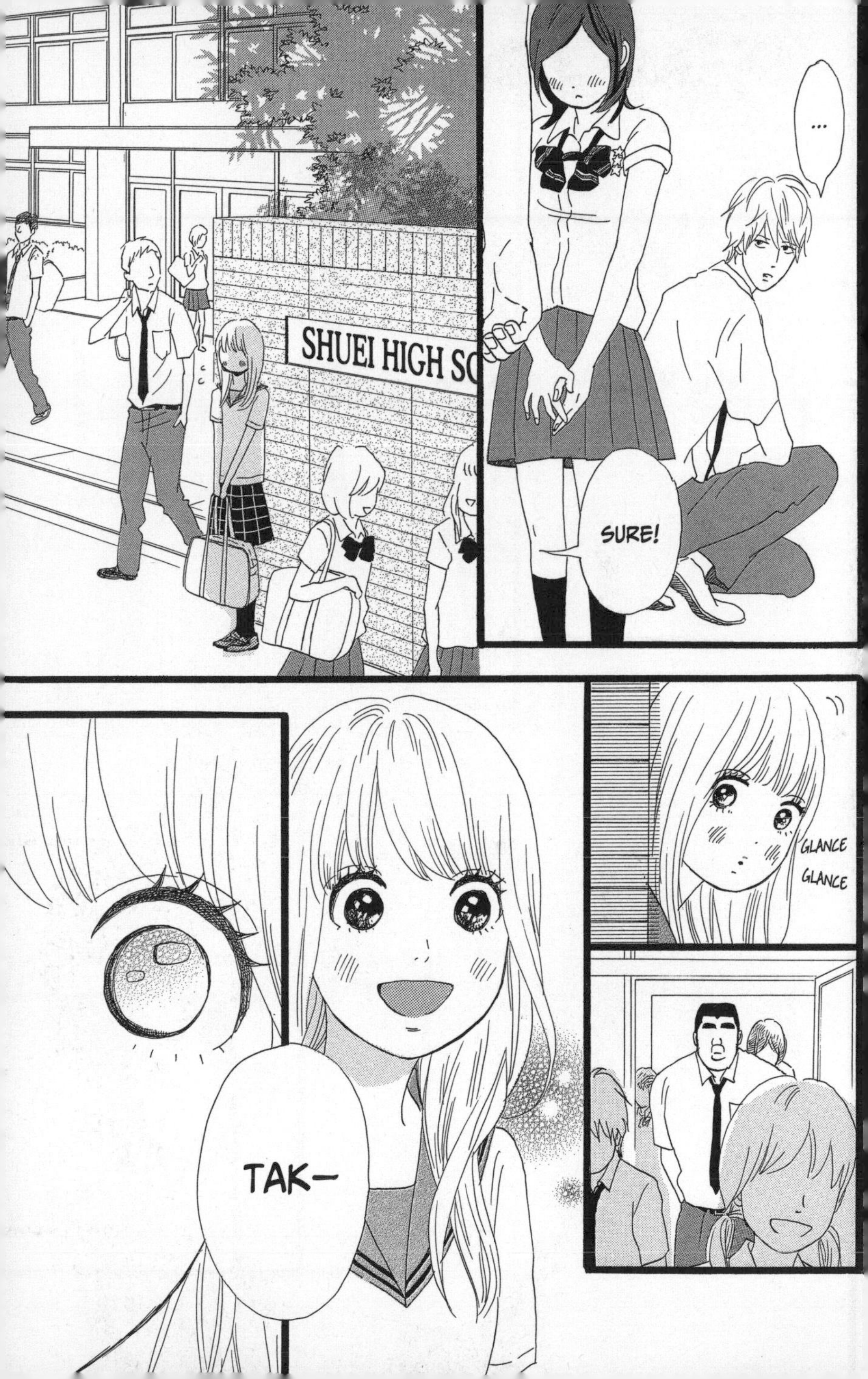
...
SURE!
SHUEI HIGH SC
GLANCE
GLANCE
TAK—

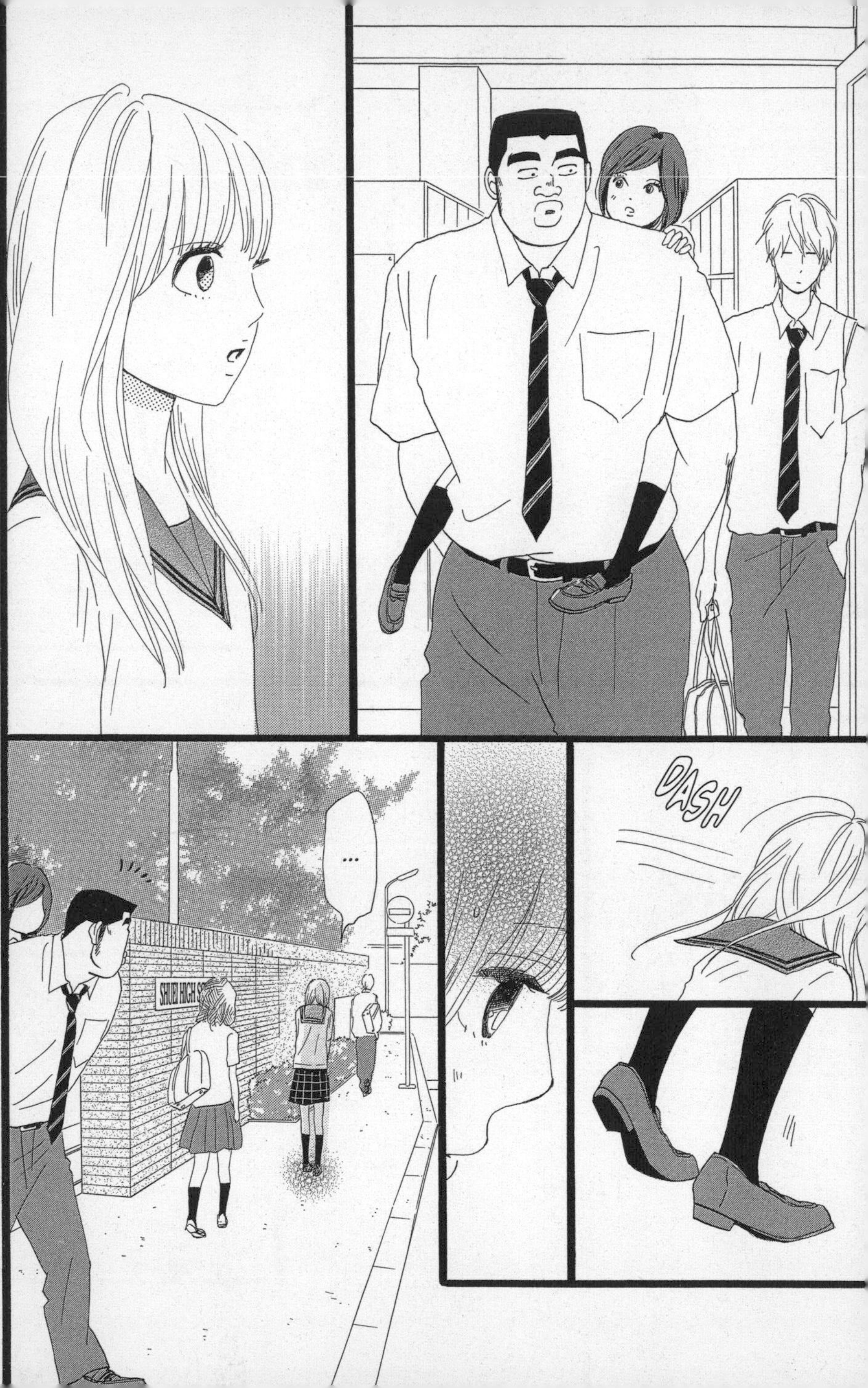
DASH
...

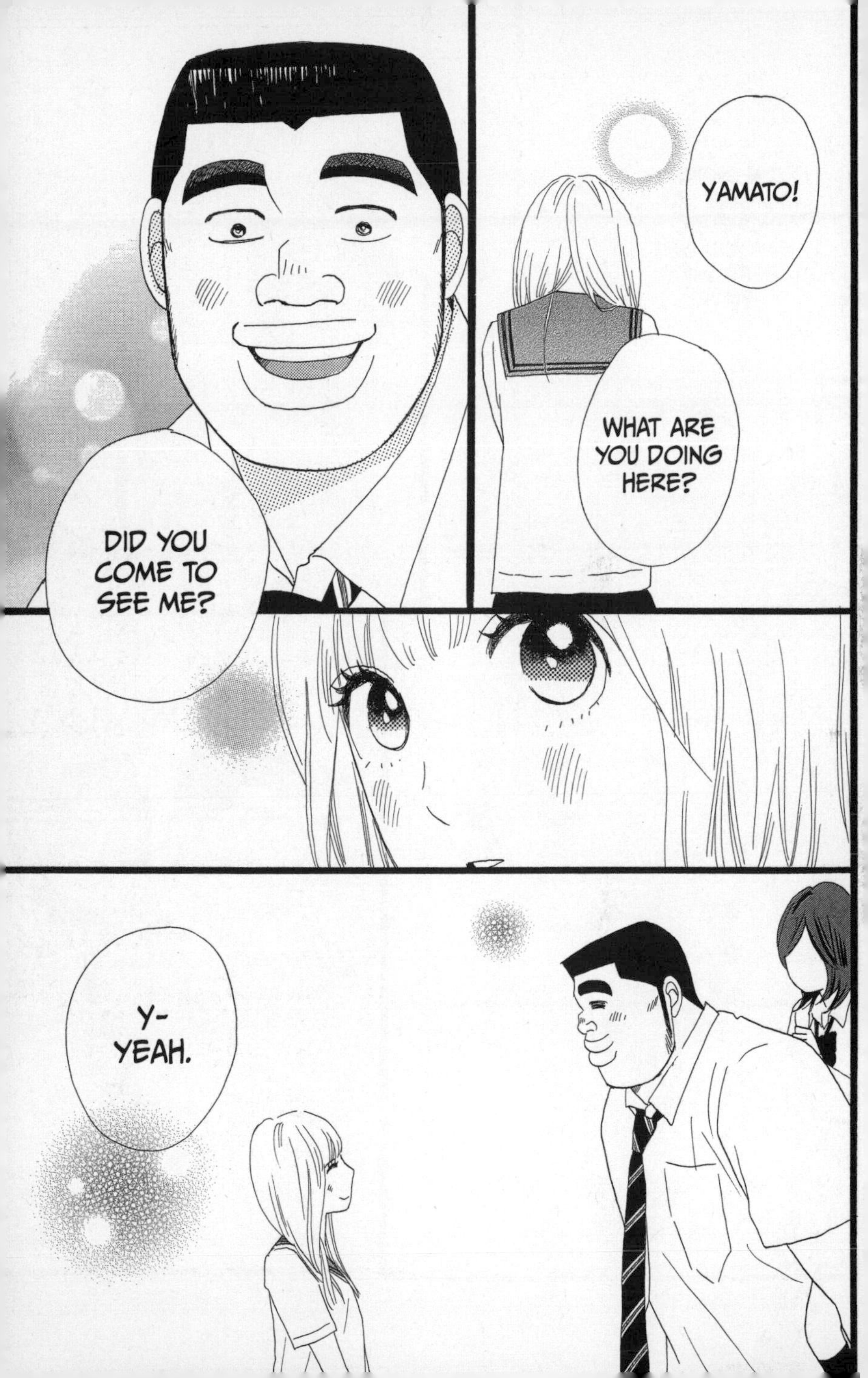
YAMATO!
WHAT ARE YOU DOING HERE?
DID YOU COME TO SEE ME?
Y-YEAH.

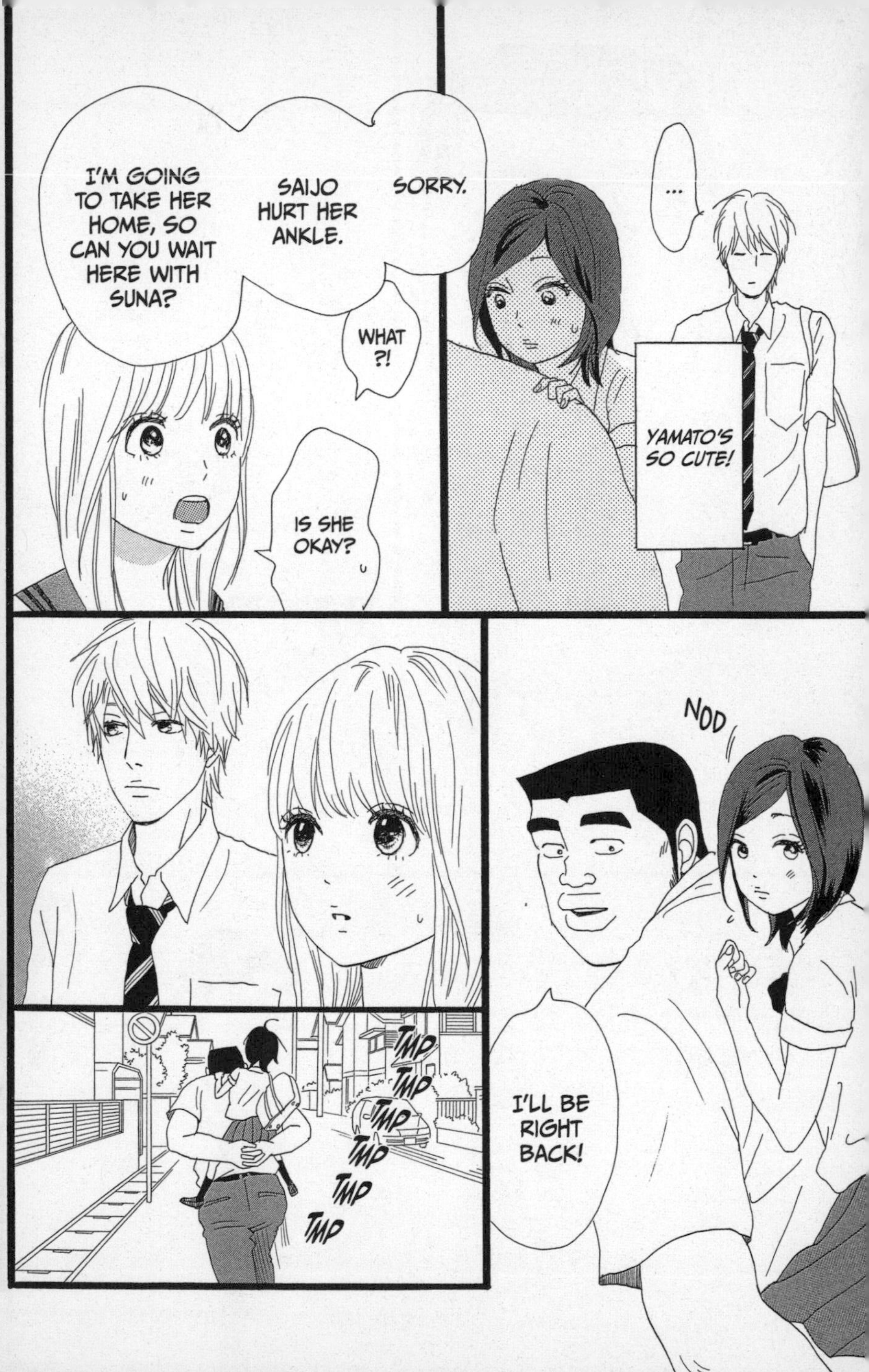
...
YAMATO'S SO CUTE!
SORRY.
SAIJO HURT HER ANKLE.
I'M GOING TO TAKE HER HOME, SO CAN YOU WAIT HERE WITH SUNA?
WHAT ?!
IS SHE OKAY?
NOD
I'LL BE RIGHT BACK!
TMP TMP TMP TMP TMP TMP

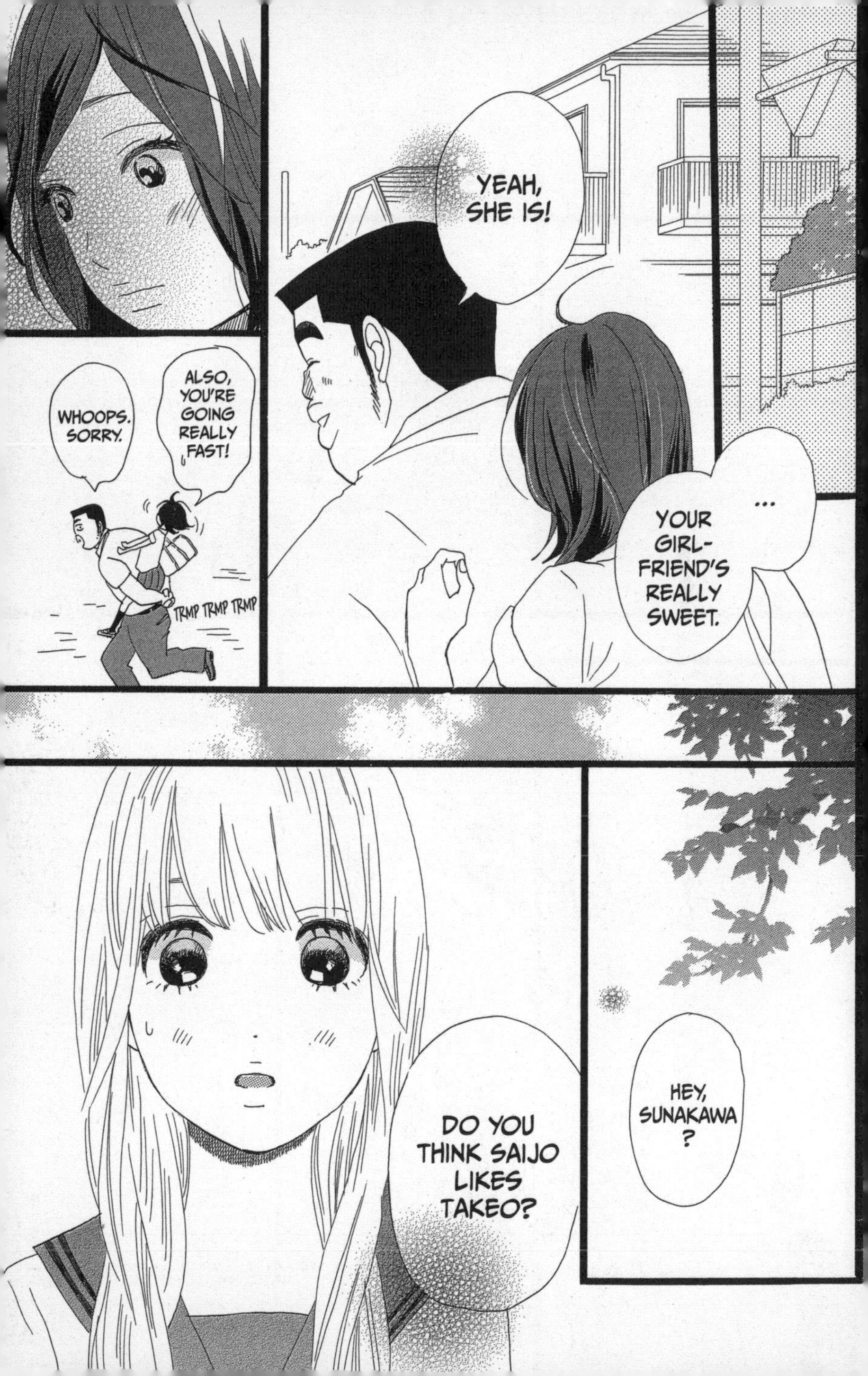

... YOUR GIRLFRIEND'S REALLY SWEET.
YEAH, SHE IS!
ALSO, YOU'RE GOING REALLY FAST!
WHOOPS. SORRY.
TRMP TRMP TRMP
HEY, SUNAKAWA?
DO YOU THINK SAIJO LIKES TAKEO?

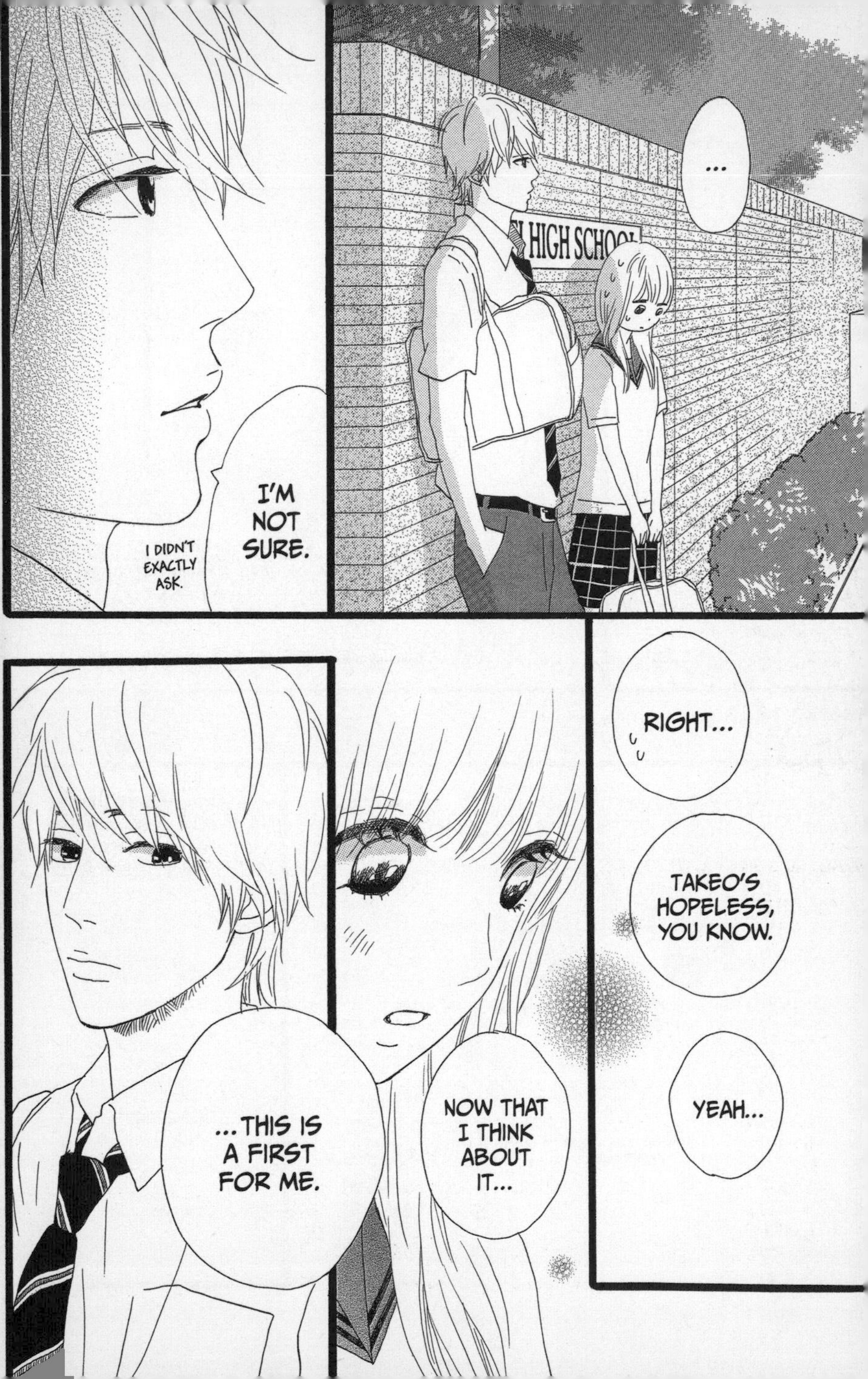
...
I'M NOT SURE.
I DIDN'T EXACTLY ASK.
RIGHT...
TAKEO'S HOPELESS, YOU KNOW.
YEAH...
NOW THAT I THINK ABOUT IT...
...THIS IS A FIRST FOR ME.

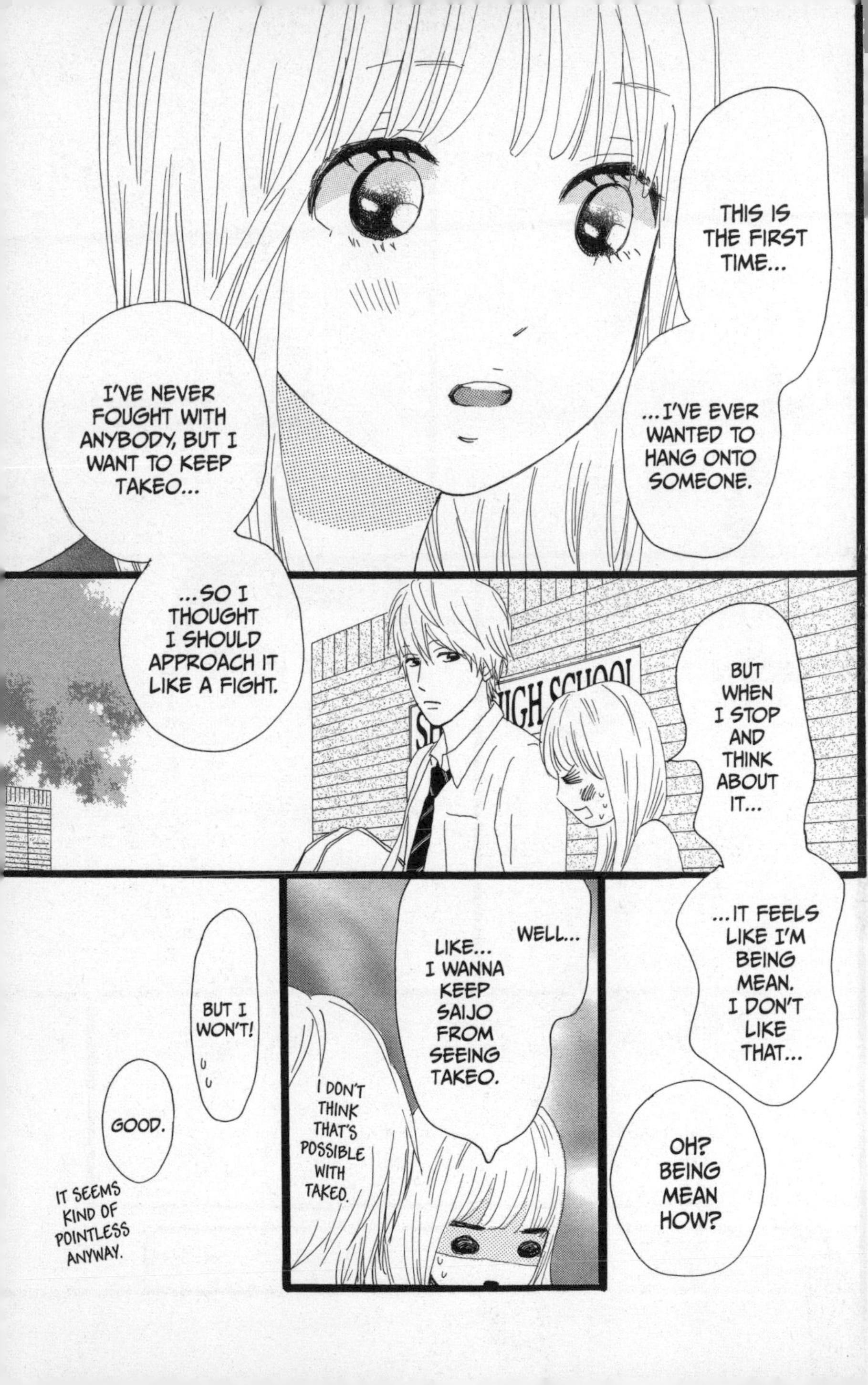
THIS IS THE FIRST TIME...
...I'VE EVER WANTED TO HANG ONTO SOMEONE.
I'VE NEVER FOUGHT WITH ANYBODY, BUT I WANT TO KEEP TAKEO...
...SO I THOUGHT I SHOULD APPROACH IT LIKE A FIGHT.
BUT WHEN I STOP AND THINK ABOUT IT...
...IT FEELS LIKE I'M BEING MEAN. I DON'T LIKE THAT...
OH? BEING MEAN HOW?
WELL...
LIKE... I WANNA KEEP SAIJO FROM SEEING TAKEO.
I DON'T THINK THAT'S POSSIBLE WITH TAKEO.
BUT I WON'T!
GOOD.
IT SEEMS KIND OF POINTLESS ANYWAY.

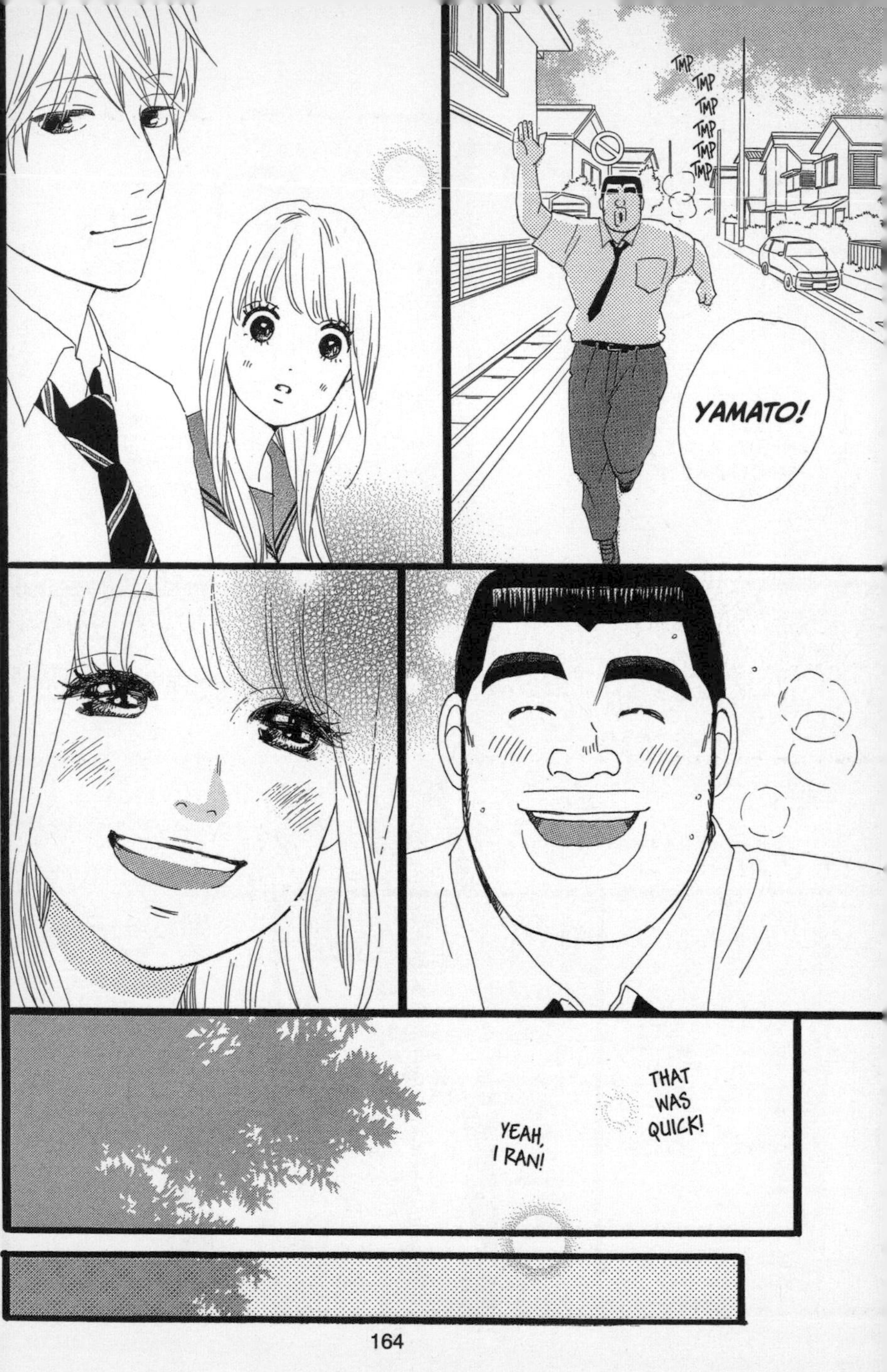
TMP TMP TMP TMP TMP TMP
YAMATO!
THAT WAS QUICK!
YEAH, I RAN!

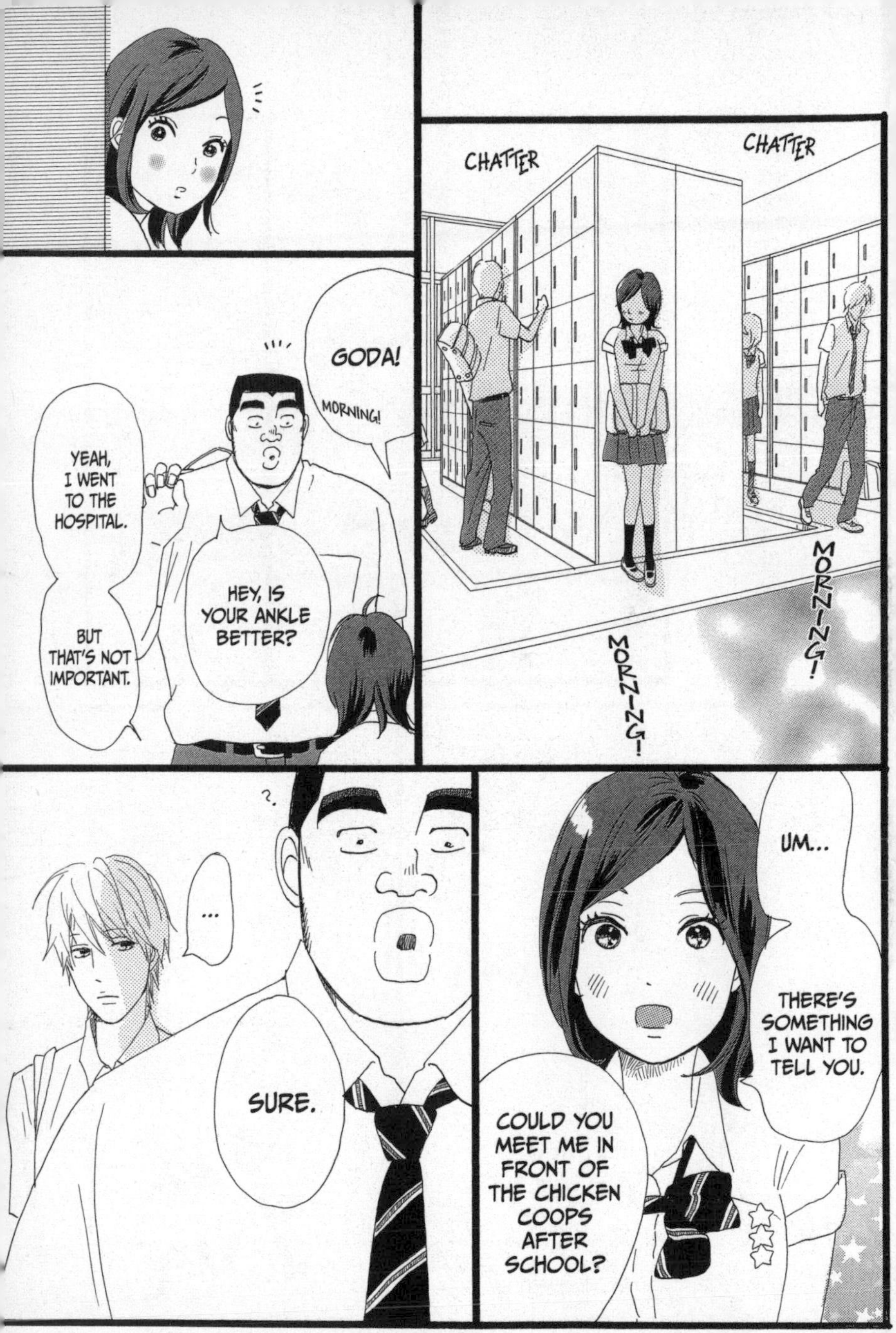
CHATTER
CHATTER
MORNING!
MORNING!
GODA!
MORNING!
HEY, IS YOUR ANKLE BETTER?
YEAH, I WENT TO THE HOSPITAL.
BUT THAT'S NOT IMPORTANT.
UM...
THERE'S SOMETHING I WANT TO TELL YOU.
COULD YOU MEET ME IN FRONT OF THE CHICKEN COOPS AFTER SCHOOL?
...
SURE.

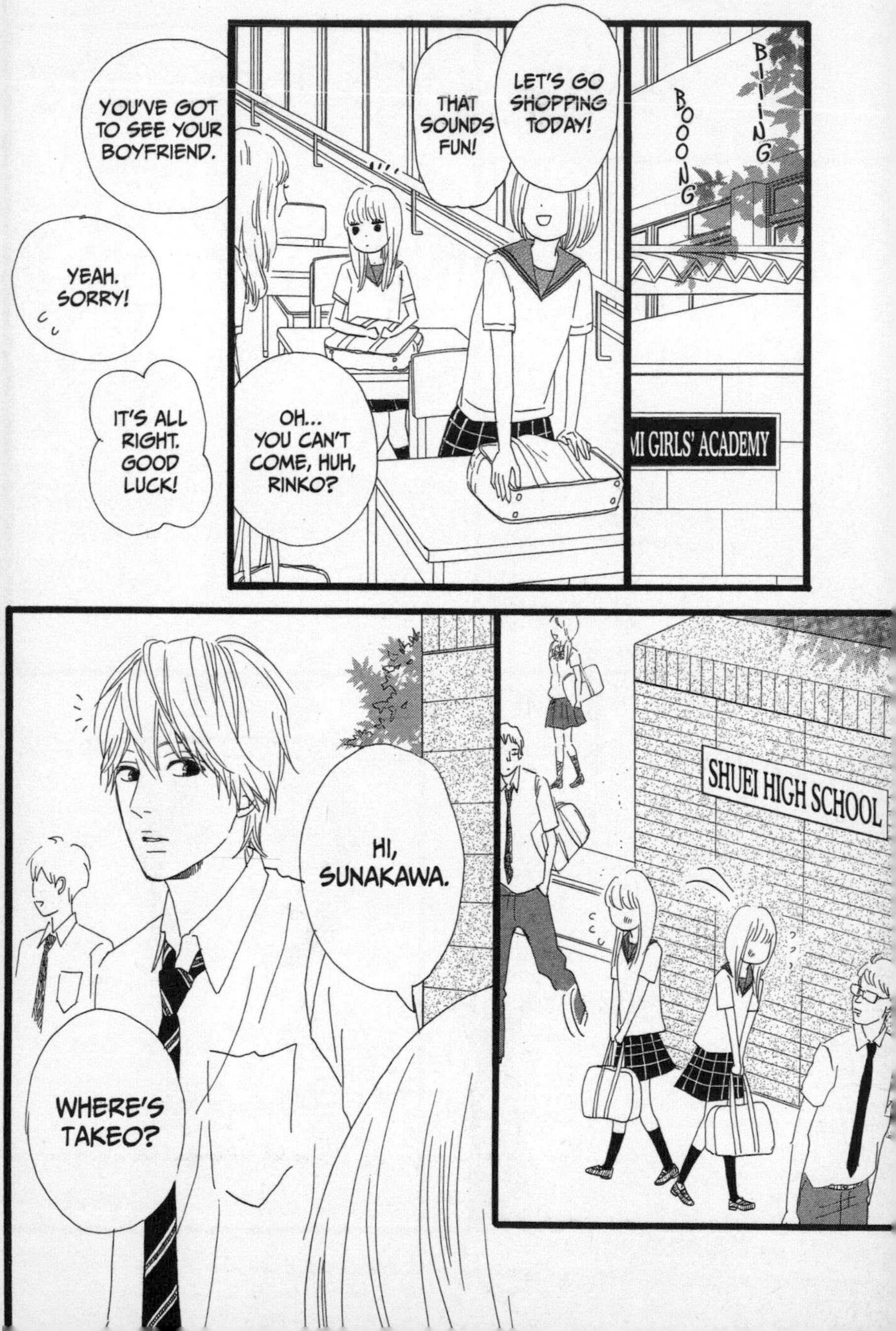
BIIING
BOOONG
MI GIRLS' ACADEMY
LET'S GO SHOPPING TODAY!
THAT SOUNDS FUN!
OH... YOU CAN'T COME, HUH, RINKO?
YOU'VE GOT TO SEE YOUR BOYFRIEND.
YEAH. SORRY!
IT'S ALL RIGHT. GOOD LUCK!
SHUEI HIGH SCHOOL
HI, SUNAKAWA.
WHERE'S TAKEO?

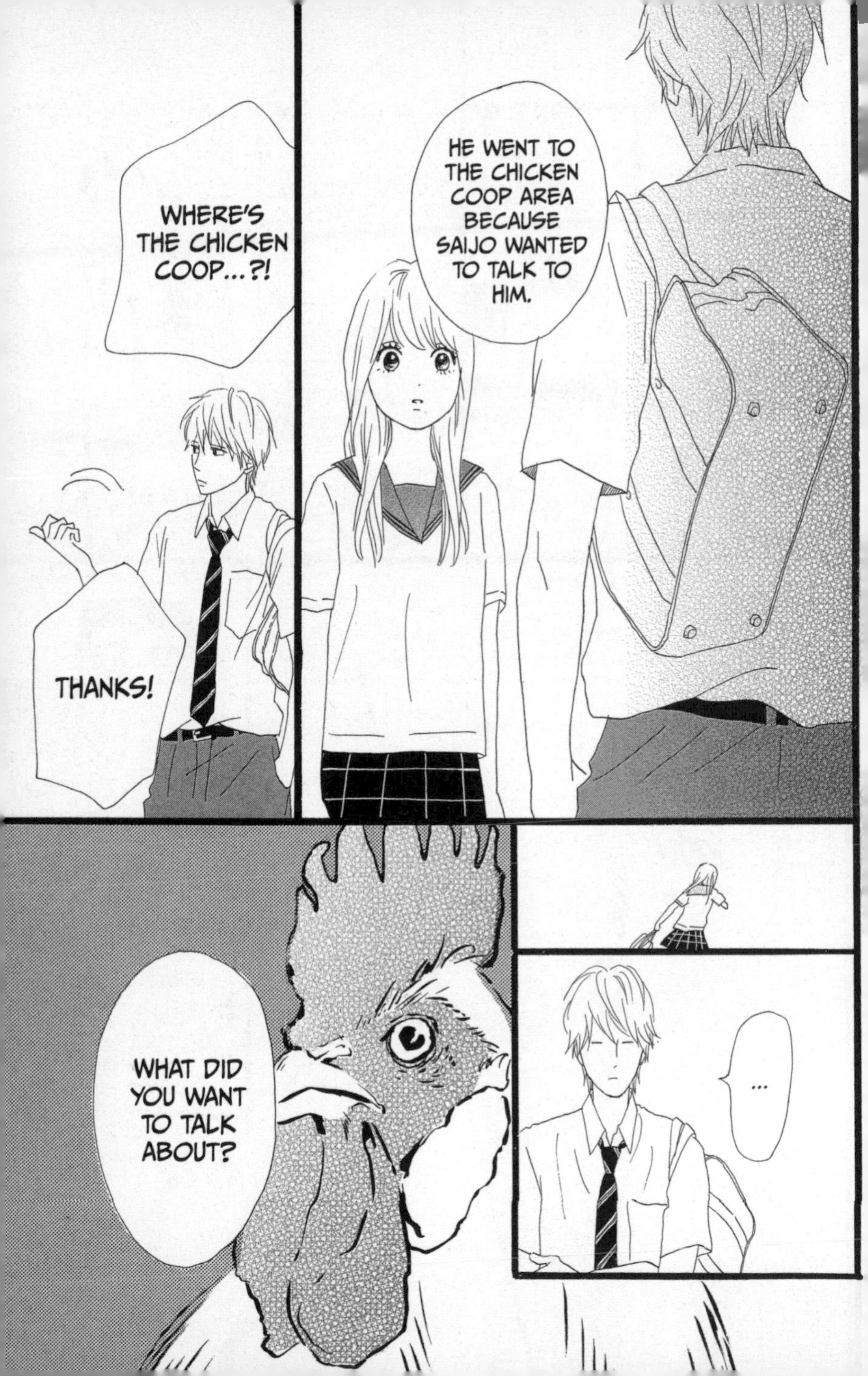
HE WENT TO THE CHICKEN COOP AREA BECAUSE SAIJO WANTED TO TALK TO HIM.
WHERE'S THE CHICKEN COOP...?!
THANKS!
...
WHAT DID YOU WANT TO TALK ABOUT?

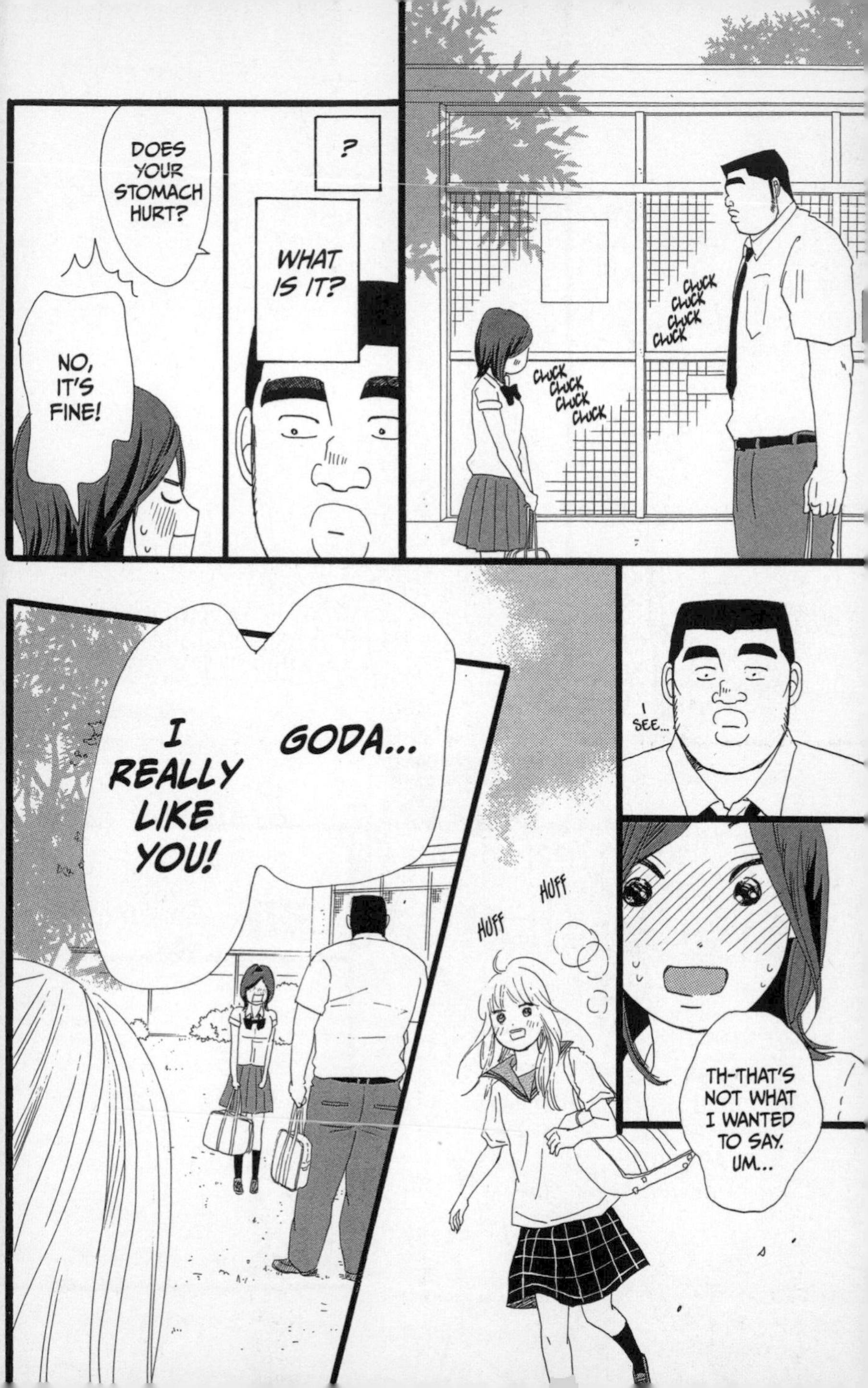
CLUCK CLUCK CLUCK CLUCK
CLUCK CLUCK CLUCK CLUCK
?
WHAT IS IT?
DOES YOUR STOMACH HURT?
NO, IT'S FINE!
I SEE...
TH-THAT'S NOT WHAT I WANTED TO SAY. UM...
HUFF
HUFF
GODA...
I REALLY LIKE YOU!

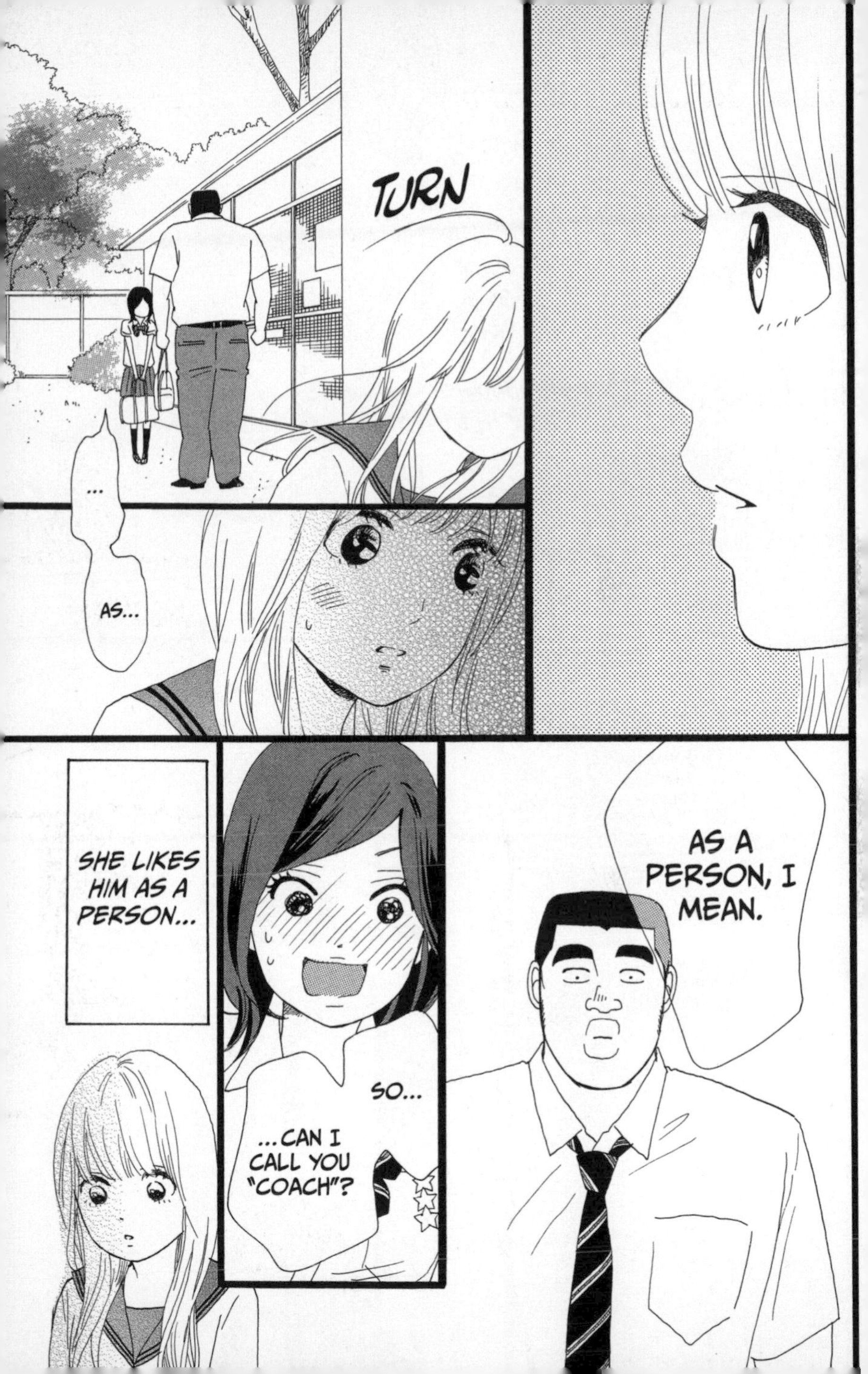
TURN
...
AS...
AS A PERSON, I MEAN.
SO...
...CAN I CALL YOU "COACH"?
SHE LIKES HIM AS A PERSON...

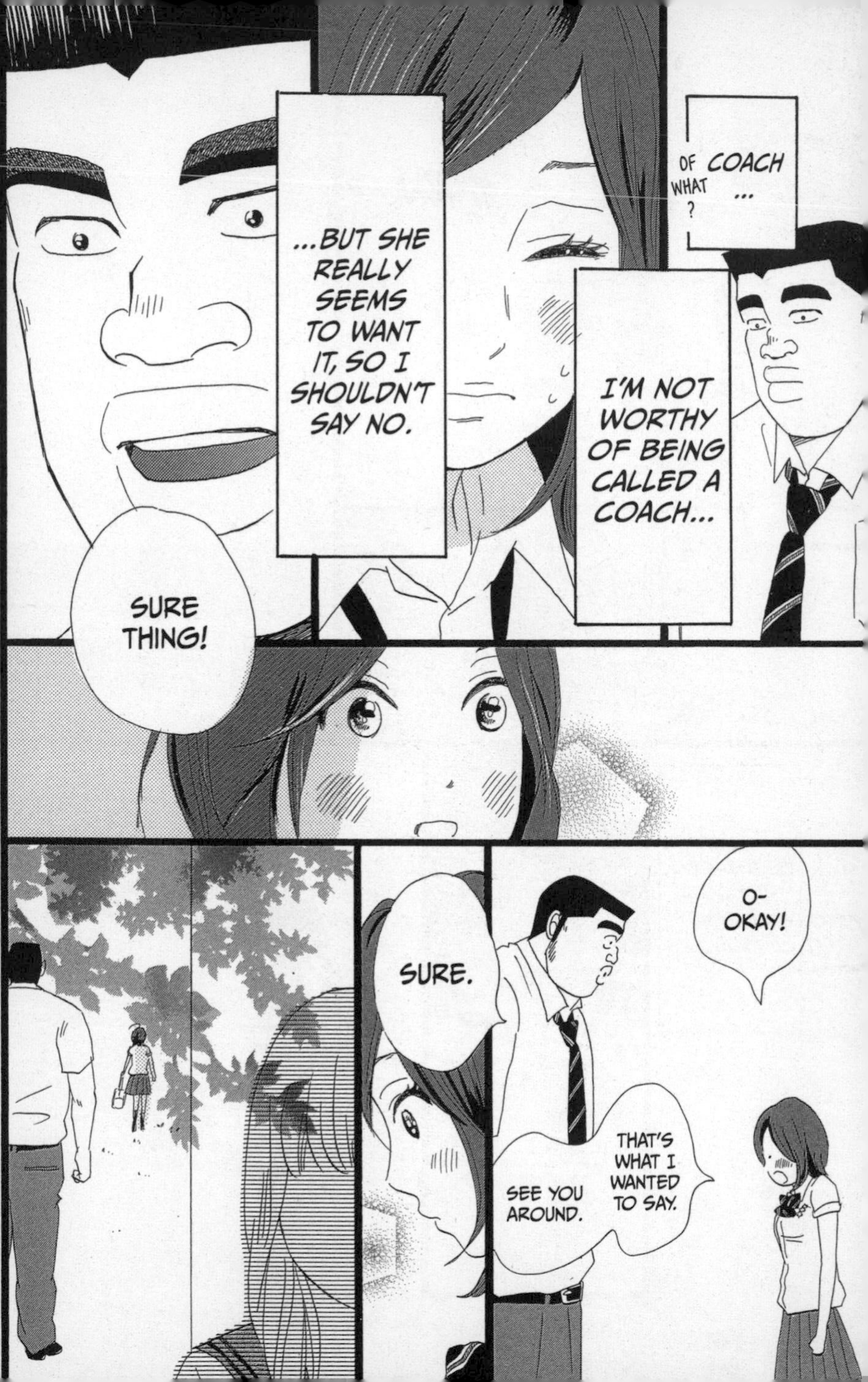
COACH... OF WHAT?
I'M NOT WORTHY OF BEING CALLED A COACH...
...BUT SHE REALLY SEEMS TO WANT IT, SO I SHOULDN'T SAY NO.
SURE THING!
O-OKAY!
THAT'S WHAT I WANTED TO SAY.
SEE YOU AROUND.
SURE.

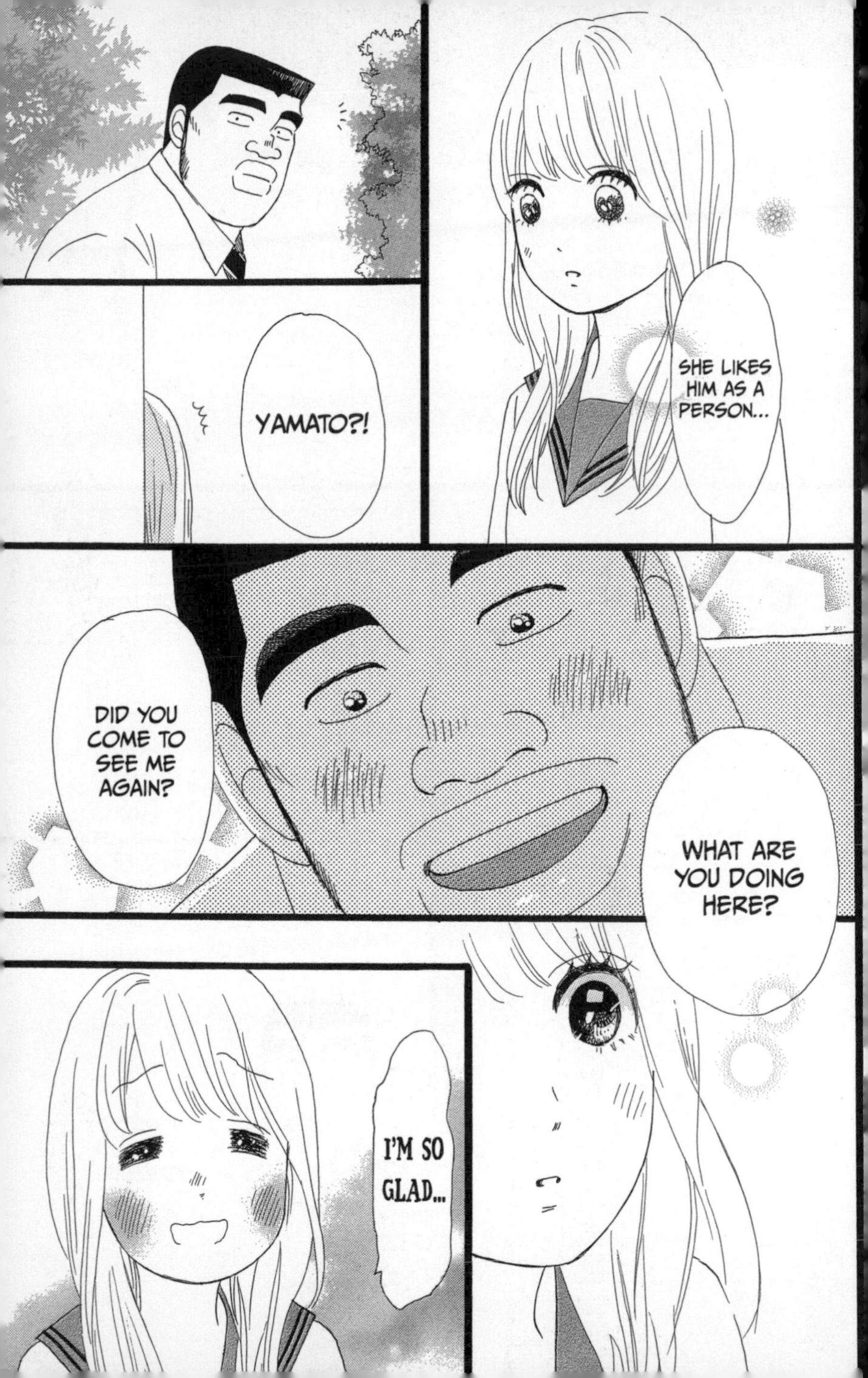
SHE LIKES HIM AS A PERSON...
YAMATO?!
WHAT ARE YOU DOING HERE?
DID YOU COME TO SEE ME AGAIN?
I'M SO GLAD...

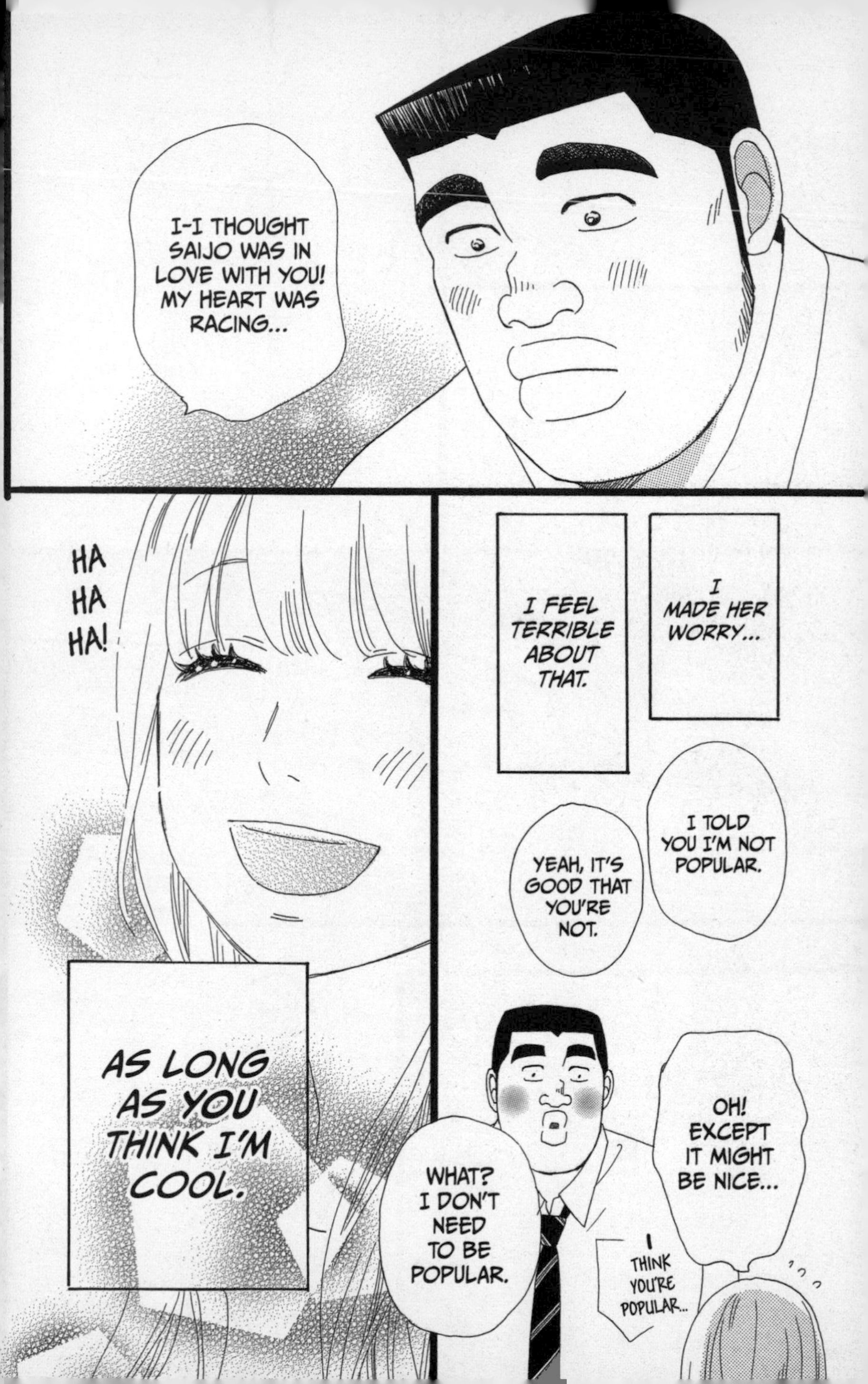

I-I THOUGHT SAIJO WAS IN LOVE WITH YOU! MY HEART WAS RACING...
I MADE HER WORRY...
I FEEL TERRIBLE ABOUT THAT.
I TOLD YOU I'M NOT POPULAR.
YEAH, IT'S GOOD THAT YOU'RE NOT.
OH! EXCEPT IT MIGHT BE NICE...
I THINK YOU'RE POPULAR...
WHAT? I DON'T NEED TO BE POPULAR.
HA HA HA!
AS LONG AS YOU THINK I'M COOL.

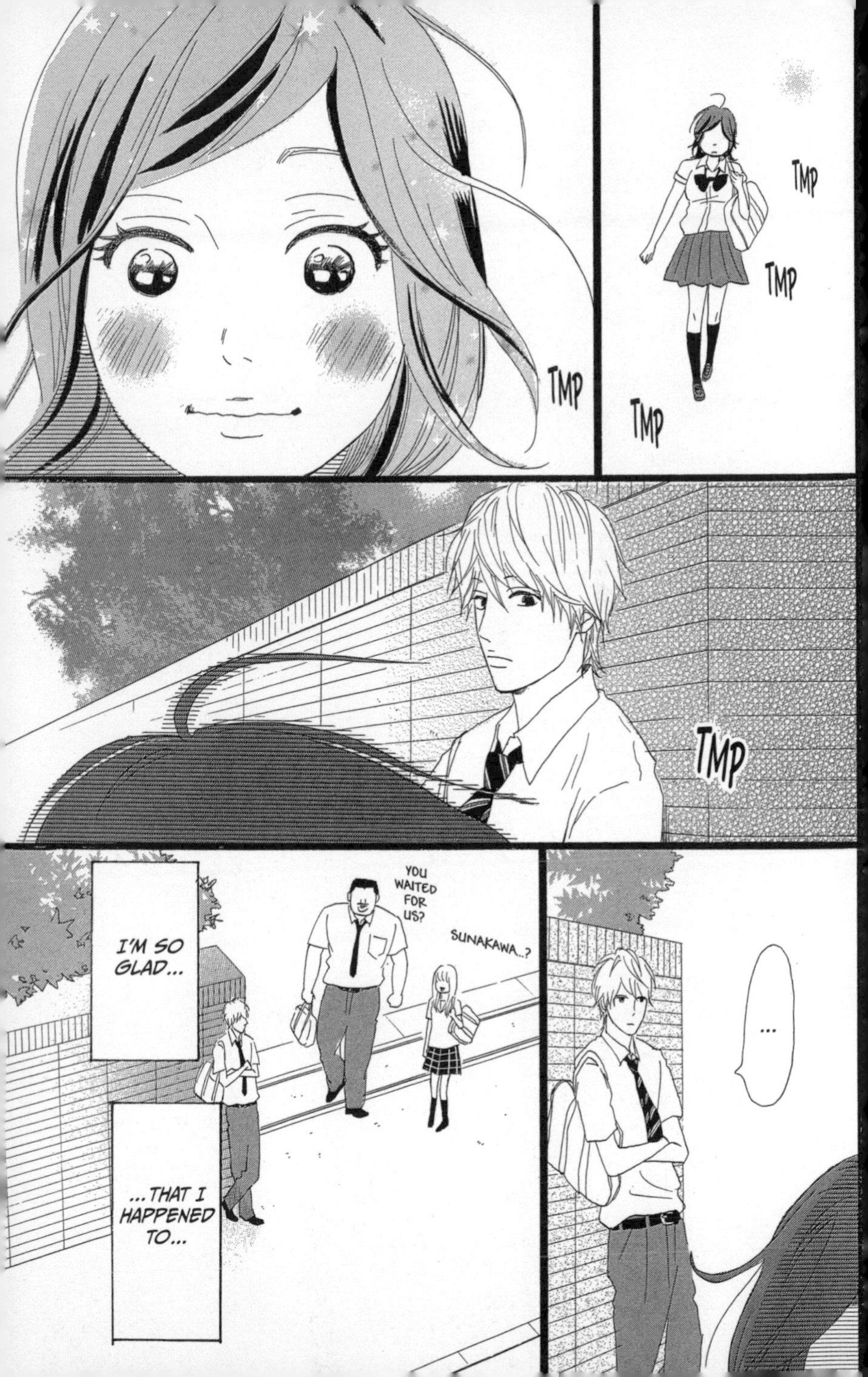
TMP
TMP
TMP
TMP
TMP
...
YOU WAITED FOR US?
SUNAKAWA...?
I'M SO GLAD...
...THAT I HAPPENED TO...

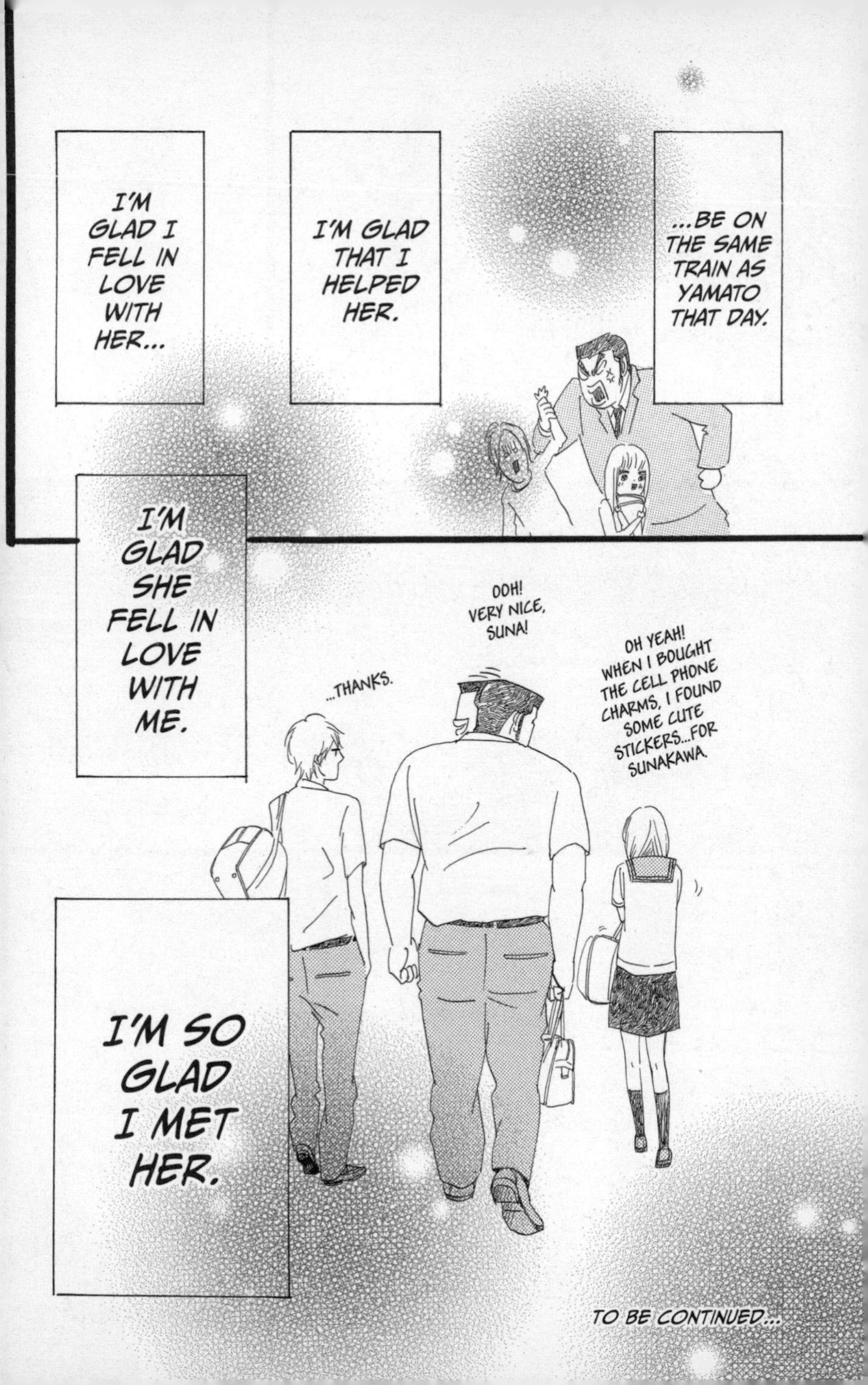
...BE ON THE SAME TRAIN AS YAMATO THAT DAY.
I'M GLAD THAT I HELPED HER.
I'M GLAD I FELL IN LOVE WITH HER...
I'M GLAD SHE FELL IN LOVE WITH ME.
OH YEAH! WHEN I BOUGHT THE CELL PHONE CHARMS, I FOUND SOME CUTE STICKERS...FOR SUNAKAWA.
OOH! VERY NICE, SUNA!
...THANKS.
I'M SO GLAD I MET HER.
TO BE CONTINUED...

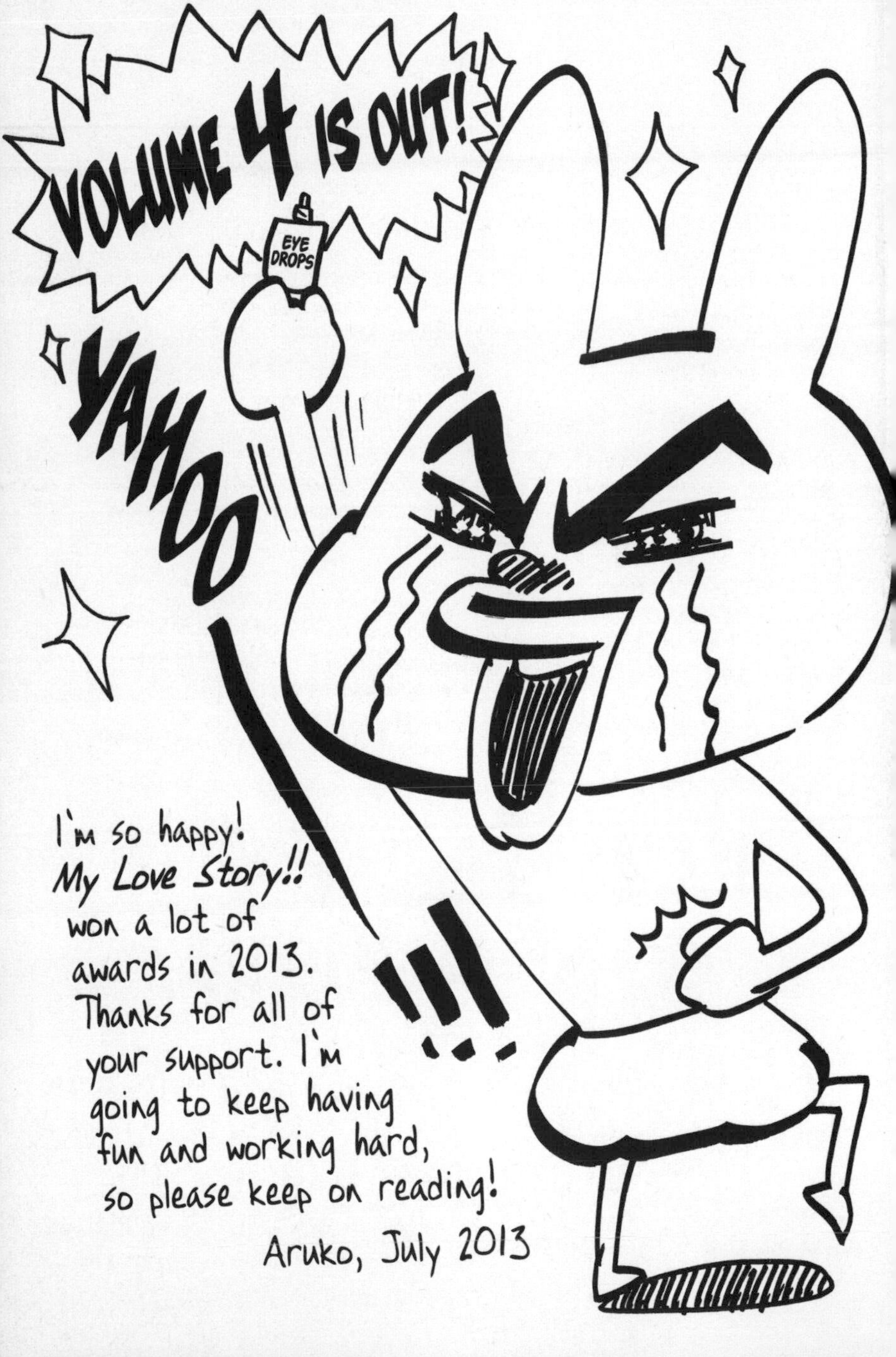
VOLUME 4 IS OUT!
EYE DROPS
YAHOO
!!!

I'm so happy!
My Love Story!! won a lot of awards in 2013. Thanks for all of your support. I'm going to keep having fun and working hard, so please keep on reading!

Aruko, July 2013

Hello! This is Kazune Kawahara, the writer of this manga.
I'm so glad volume 4 is out! \(^o^)/

Ever since I began writing this series, so many fun, joyful and just plain happy things have happened. And every time I think there won't be any more, I'm proved wrong.
Thank you so much!

Sorry if my Japanese is funny.
I'm a native Japanese, too...

Changing the subject...

In *Bessatsu Margaret*, Aruko and Io Sakisaka are doing a crossover between *Ao Haru Ride* and *My Love Story!!*. Sakisaka and Aruko came up with the story, so I had nothing to do with it, but my name is on the front page anyway. I'm very sorry.

(Make sure to check out the crossover!)

So I got to see one of Aruko's storyboards for the first time!
And I got to see Sakisaka's storyboards for the first time! And they made notes giving each other suggestions! (Sorry this is so vague.)
I was so impressed. I know it's a bit rude and obvious to say this, but I was amazed at how professional they were.
I knew that they're pros, but it all made me feel a bit inferior. Wow!
I've got to step up my game.

Sorry. My writing's really crooked, isn't it?

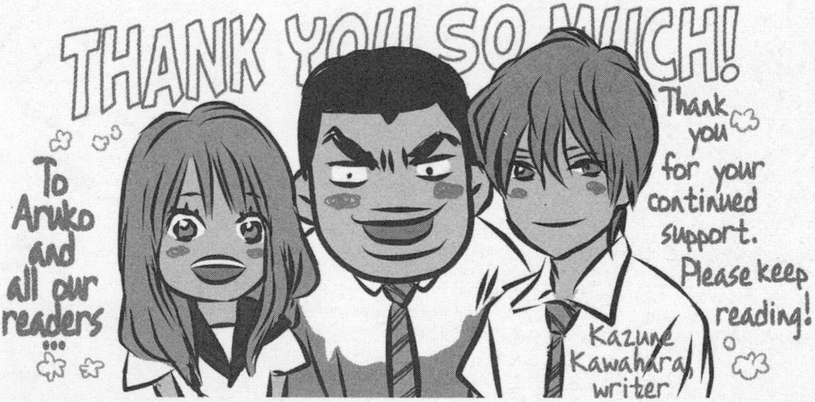
THANK YOU SO MUCH!
To Aruko and all our readers...
Thank you for your continued support. Please keep reading!
Kazune Kawahara, writer

It would be great if you checked out the next volume. I think Aruko would like that too!

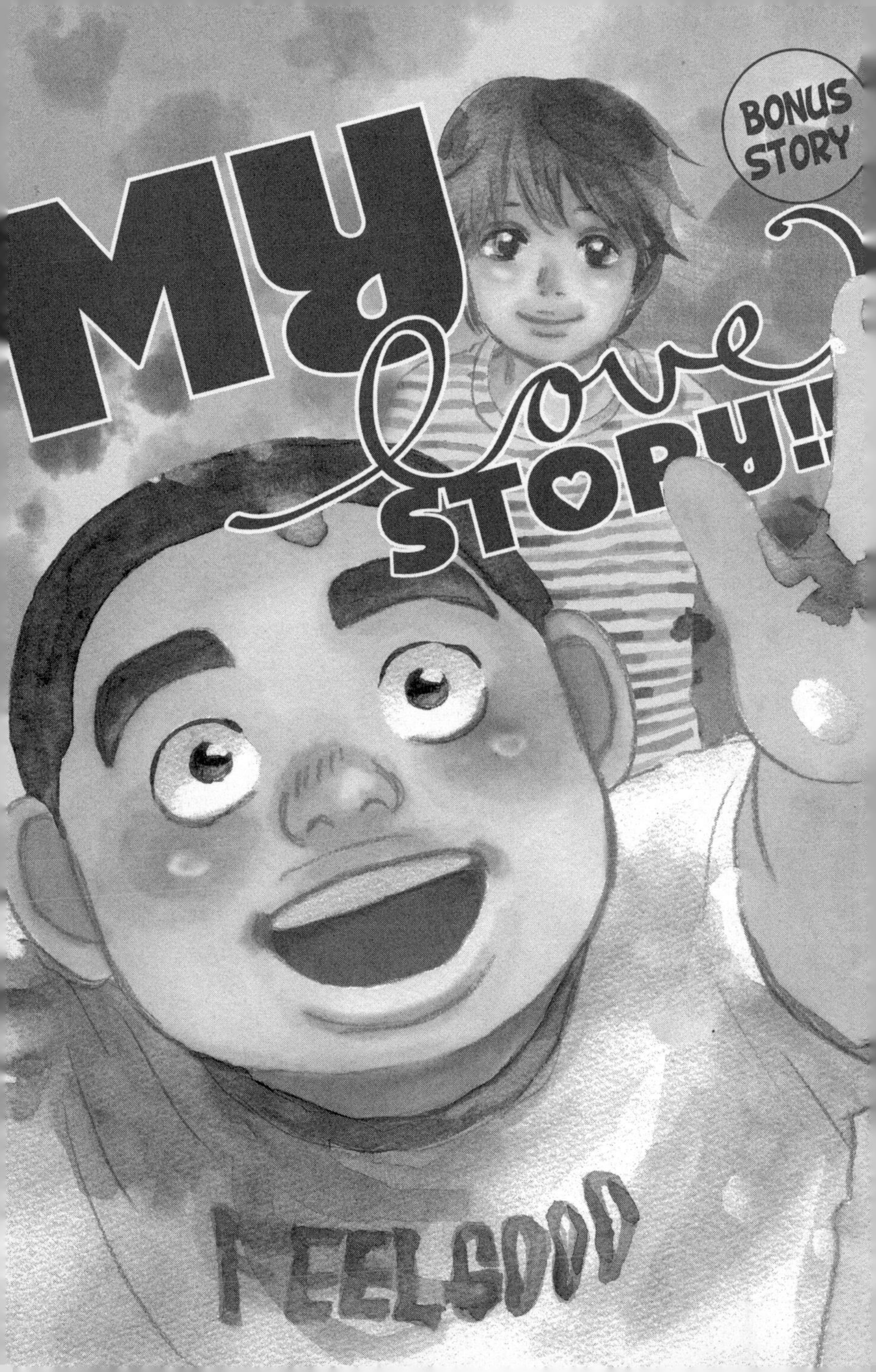
BONUS STORY
My Love STORY!!
FEELGOOD

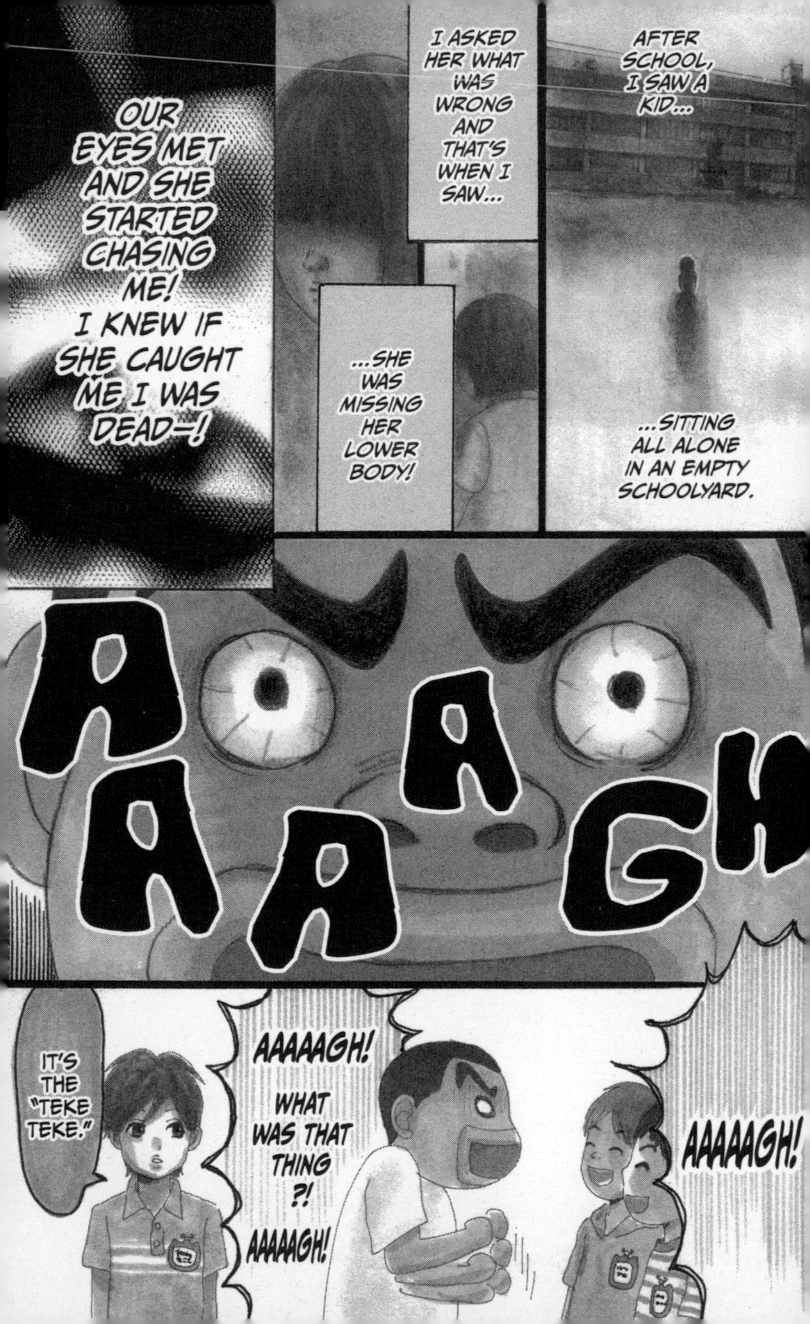
AFTER SCHOOL, I SAW A KID...
...SITTING ALL ALONE IN AN EMPTY SCHOOLYARD.
I ASKED HER WHAT WAS WRONG AND THAT'S WHEN I SAW...
...SHE WAS MISSING HER LOWER BODY!
OUR EYES MET AND SHE STARTED CHASING ME! I KNEW IF SHE CAUGHT ME I WAS DEAD—!
AAAAGH
AAAAAGH!
AAAAAGH!
WHAT WAS THAT THING?!
AAAAAGH!
IT'S THE "TEKE TEKE."

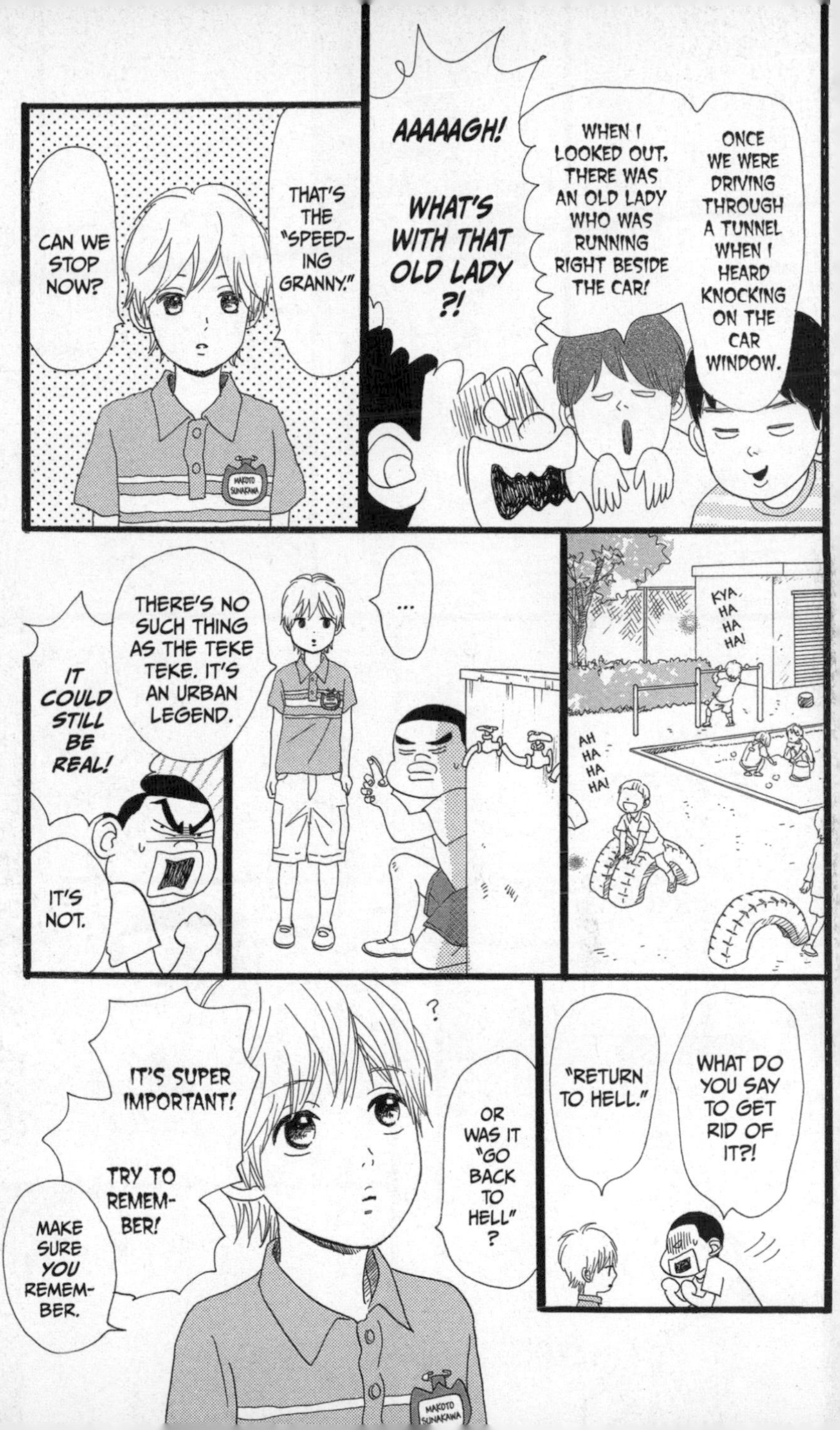
ONCE WE WERE DRIVING THROUGH A TUNNEL WHEN I HEARD KNOCKING ON THE CAR WINDOW.
WHEN I LOOKED OUT, THERE WAS AN OLD LADY WHO WAS RUNNING RIGHT BESIDE THE CAR!
AAAAAGH!
WHAT'S WITH THAT OLD LADY ?!
THAT'S THE "SPEEDING GRANNY."
CAN WE STOP NOW?
KYA, HA HA HA!
AH HA HA HA!
...
THERE'S NO SUCH THING AS THE TEKE TEKE. IT'S AN URBAN LEGEND.
IT COULD STILL BE REAL!
IT'S NOT.
WHAT DO YOU SAY TO GET RID OF IT?!
"RETURN TO HELL."
?
OR WAS IT "GO BACK TO HELL" ?
IT'S SUPER IMPORTANT!
TRY TO REMEMBER!
MAKE SURE YOU REMEMBER.

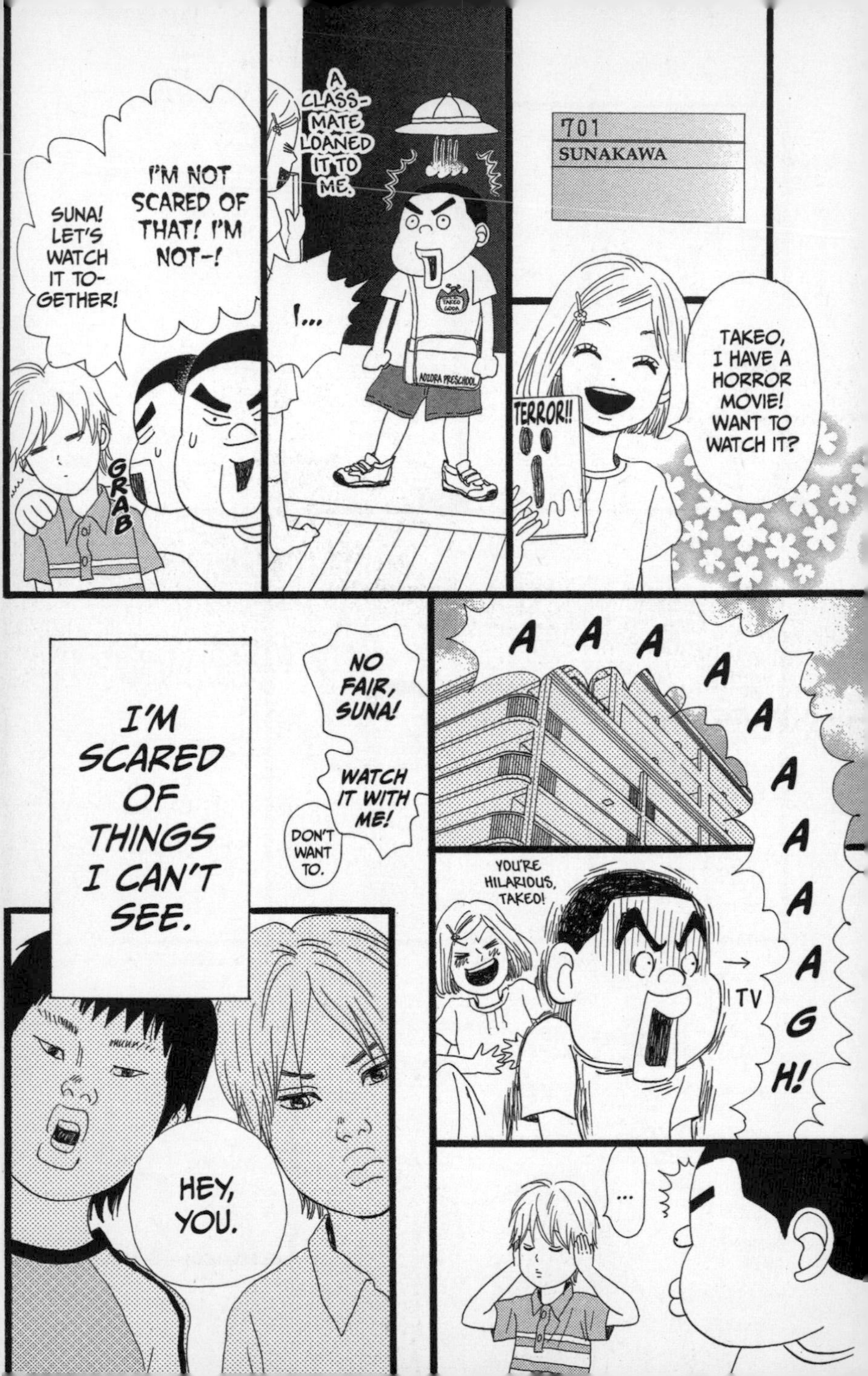
701
SUNAKAWA
TAKEO, I HAVE A HORROR MOVIE! WANT TO WATCH IT?
TERROR!!
A CLASS-MATE LOANED IT TO ME.
TAKEO GODA
AOZORA PRESCHOOL
I...
I'M NOT SCARED OF THAT! I'M NOT-!
SUNA! LET'S WATCH IT TO-GETHER!
GRAB
AAAAAAAAAAAGH!
YOU'RE HILARIOUS, TAKEO!
→ TV
...
NO FAIR, SUNA!
WATCH IT WITH ME!
DON'T WANT TO.
I'M SCARED OF THINGS I CAN'T SEE.
HEY, YOU.

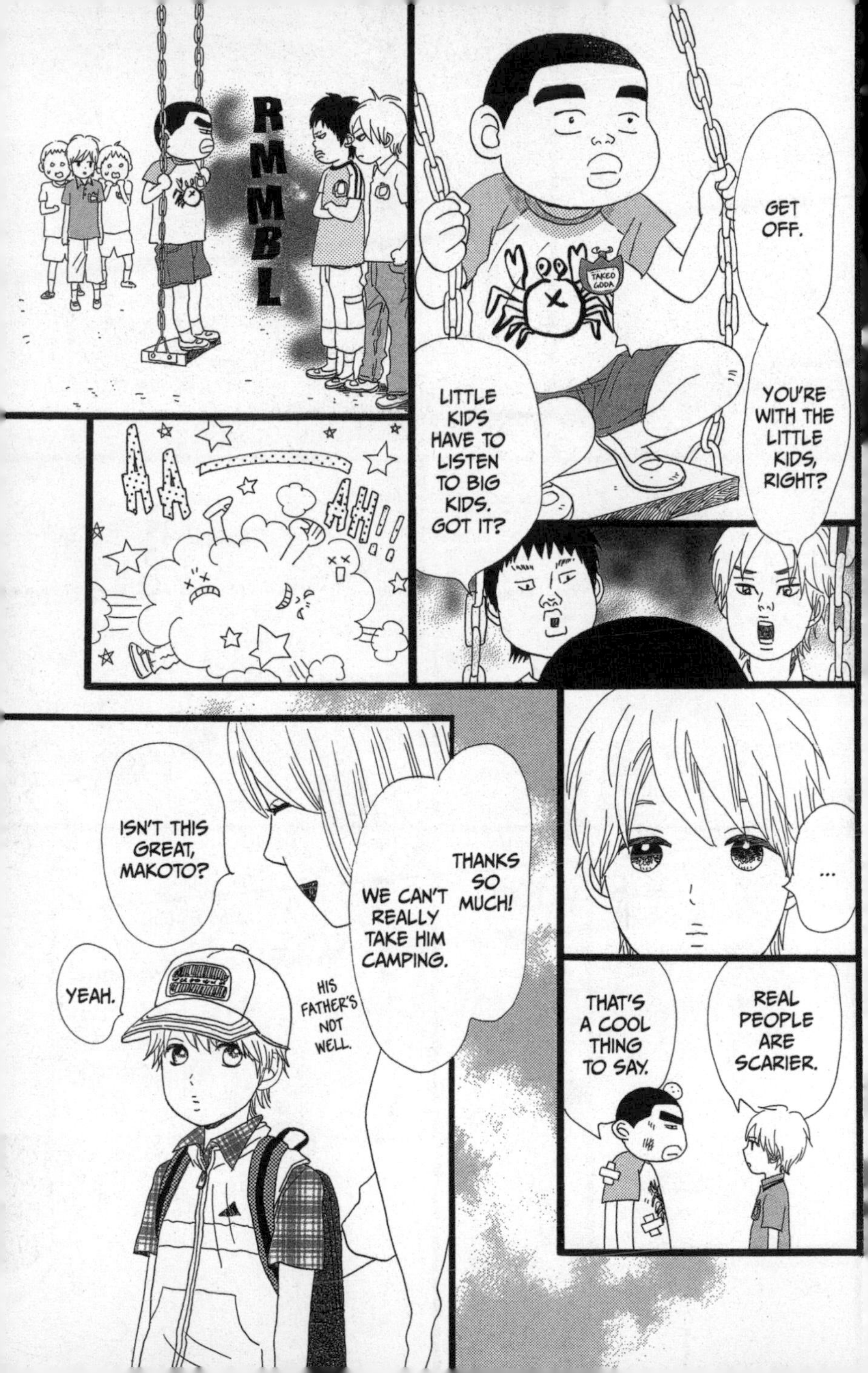
GET OFF.
YOU'RE WITH THE LITTLE KIDS, RIGHT?
TAKEO GODA
LITTLE KIDS HAVE TO LISTEN TO BIG KIDS. GOT IT?
RMMBL
AAAAH!!
...
REAL PEOPLE ARE SCARIER.
THAT'S A COOL THING TO SAY.
THANKS SO MUCH!
WE CAN'T REALLY TAKE HIM CAMPING.
HIS FATHER'S NOT WELL.
ISN'T THIS GREAT, MAKOTO?
YEAH.

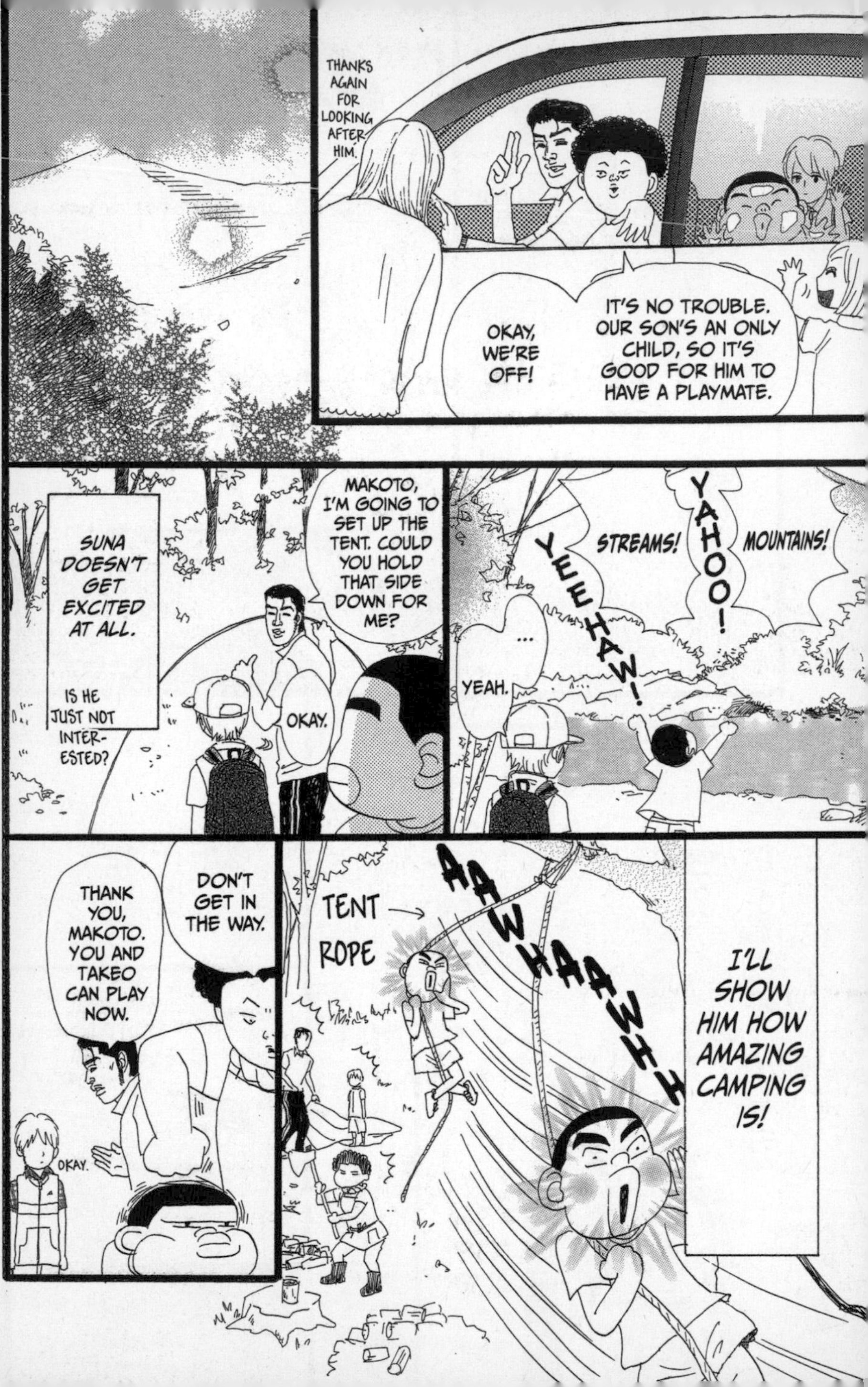
THANKS AGAIN FOR LOOKING AFTER HIM.
IT'S NO TROUBLE. OUR SON'S AN ONLY CHILD, SO IT'S GOOD FOR HIM TO HAVE A PLAYMATE.
OKAY, WE'RE OFF!
YAHOO!
MOUNTAINS!
STREAMS!
YEEHAW!
...
YEAH.
MAKOTO, I'M GOING TO SET UP THE TENT. COULD YOU HOLD THAT SIDE DOWN FOR ME?
OKAY.
SUNA DOESN'T GET EXCITED AT ALL.
IS HE JUST NOT INTER-ESTED?
I'LL SHOW HIM HOW AMAZING CAMPING IS!
AAWHAAAWHH
TENT ROPE
DON'T GET IN THE WAY.
THANK YOU, MAKOTO. YOU AND TAKEO CAN PLAY NOW.
OKAY.

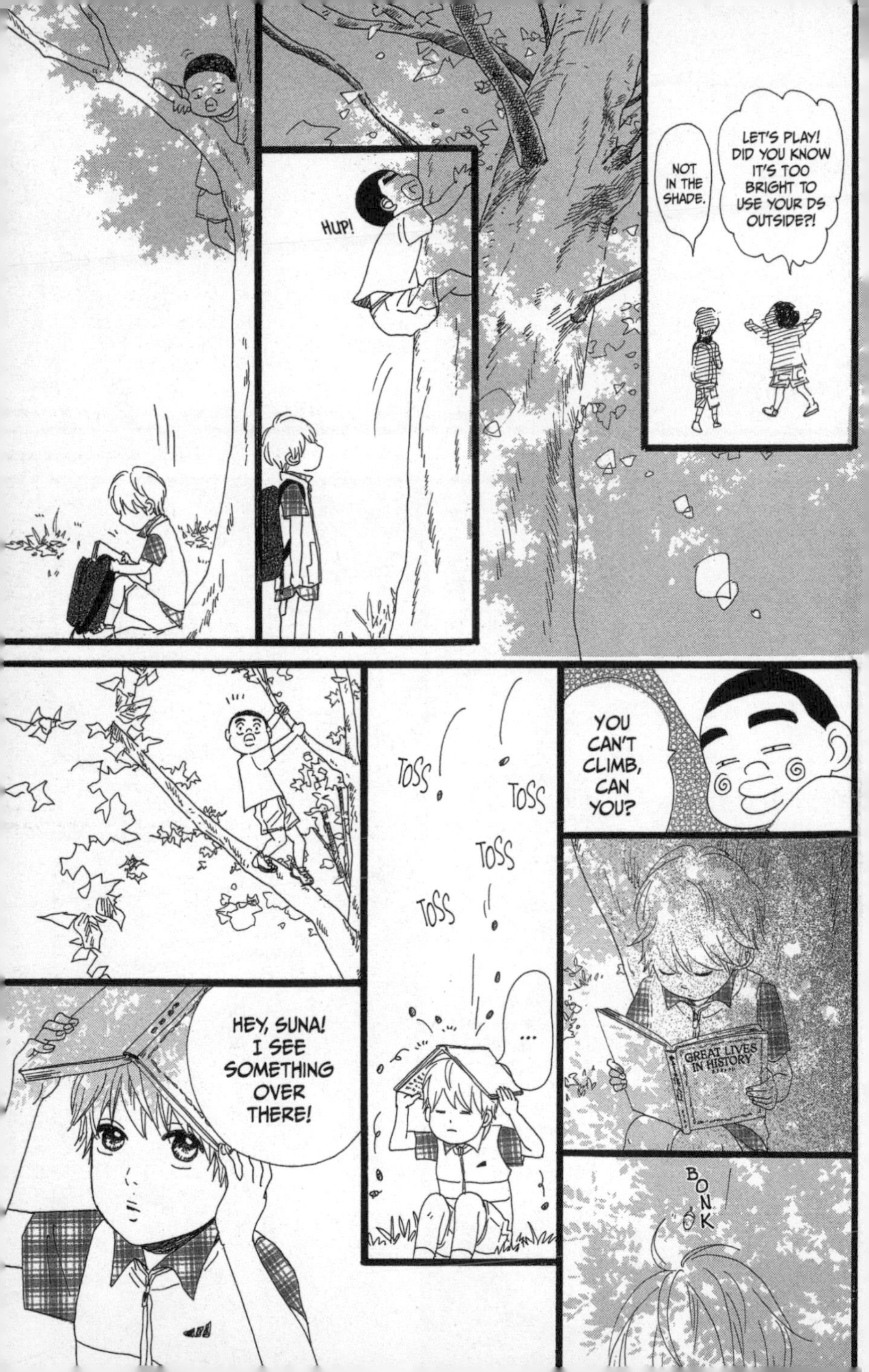
LET'S PLAY! DID YOU KNOW IT'S TOO BRIGHT TO USE YOUR DS OUTSIDE?!
NOT IN THE SHADE.
HUP!
YOU CAN'T CLIMB, CAN YOU?
GREAT LIVES IN HISTORY
BONK
TOSS
TOSS
TOSS
TOSS
...
HEY, SUNA! I SEE SOMETHING OVER THERE!

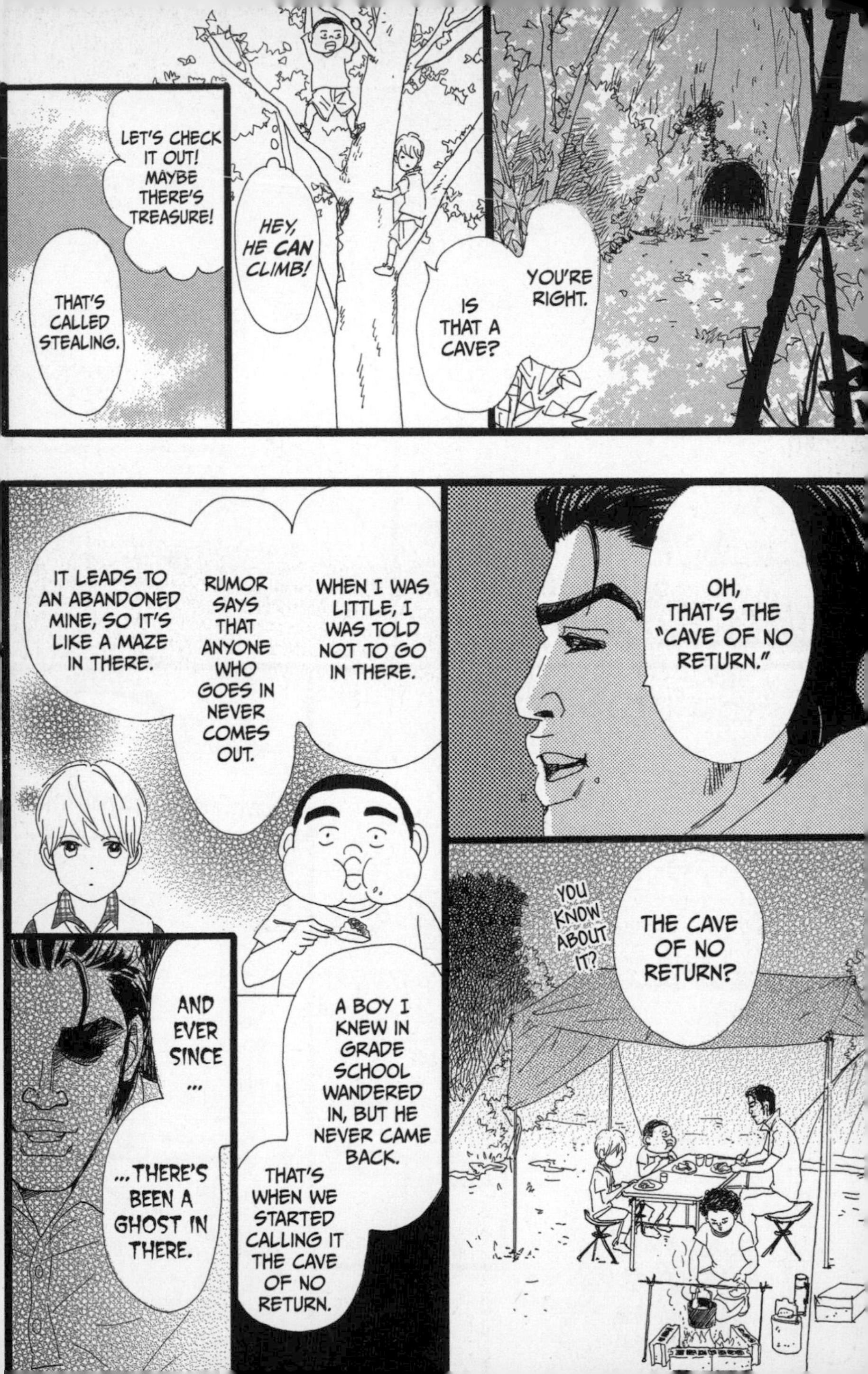
YOU'RE RIGHT.
IS THAT A CAVE?
HEY, HE CAN CLIMB!
LET'S CHECK IT OUT! MAYBE THERE'S TREASURE!
THAT'S CALLED STEALING.
OH, THAT'S THE "CAVE OF NO RETURN."
THE CAVE OF NO RETURN?
YOU KNOW ABOUT IT?
WHEN I WAS LITTLE, I WAS TOLD NOT TO GO IN THERE.
RUMOR SAYS THAT ANYONE WHO GOES IN NEVER COMES OUT.
IT LEADS TO AN ABANDONED MINE, SO IT'S LIKE A MAZE IN THERE.
A BOY I KNEW IN GRADE SCHOOL WANDERED IN, BUT HE NEVER CAME BACK.
THAT'S WHEN WE STARTED CALLING IT THE CAVE OF NO RETURN.
AND EVER SINCE...
...THERE'S BEEN A GHOST IN THERE.

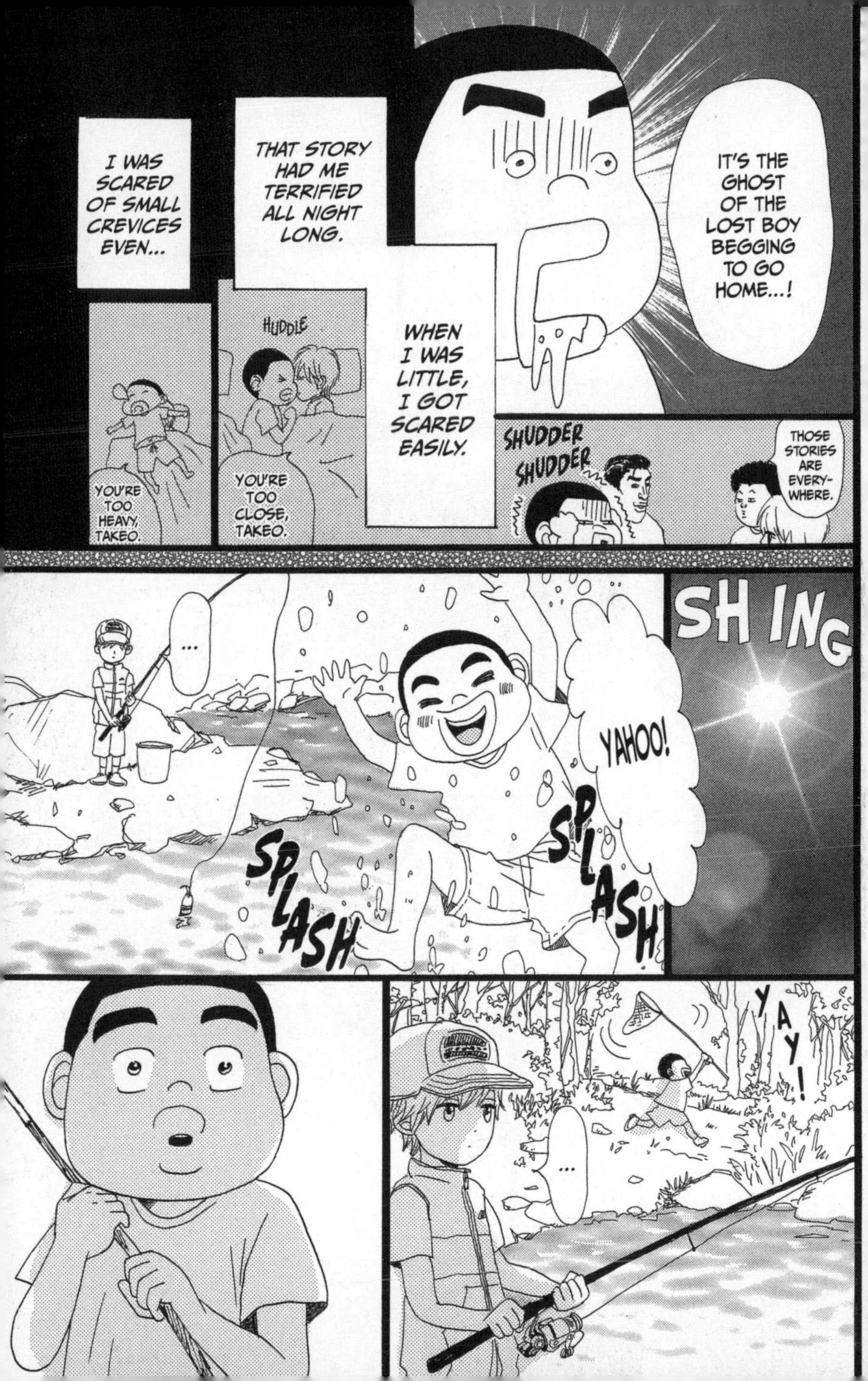
IT'S THE GHOST OF THE LOST BOY BEGGING TO GO HOME...!
THAT STORY HAD ME TERRIFIED ALL NIGHT LONG.
I WAS SCARED OF SMALL CREVICES EVEN...
THOSE STORIES ARE EVERY-WHERE.
SHUDDER SHUDDER
WHEN I WAS LITTLE, I GOT SCARED EASILY.
HUDDLE
YOU'RE TOO CLOSE, TAKEO.
YOU'RE TOO HEAVY, TAKEO.
SHING
YAHOO!
SPLASH
SPLASH
...
YAY!
...

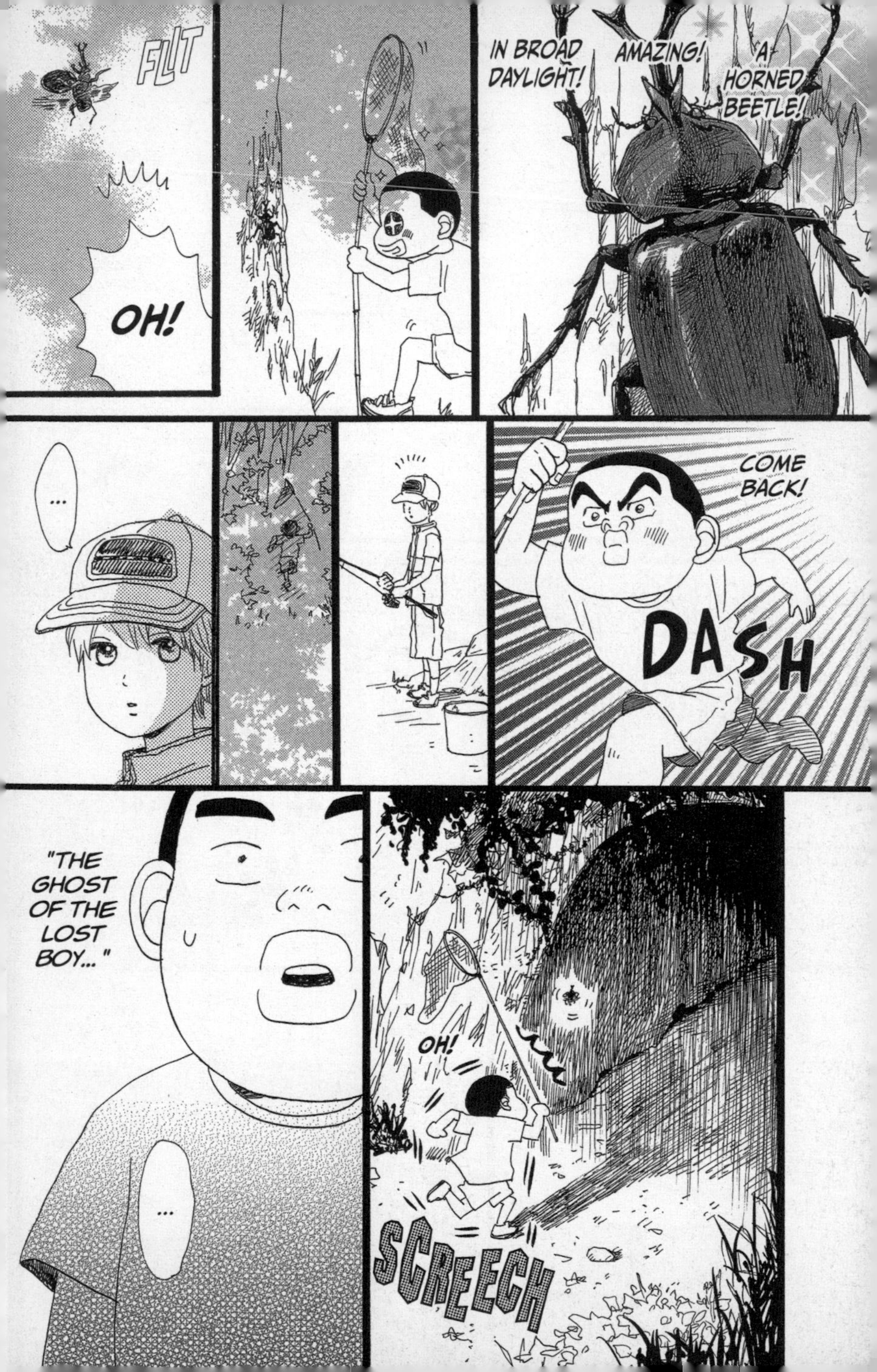
A HORNED BEETLE!
AMAZING!
IN BROAD DAYLIGHT!
FLIT
OH!
COME BACK!
DASH
...
OH!
SCREECH
"THE GHOST OF THE LOST BOY..."
...

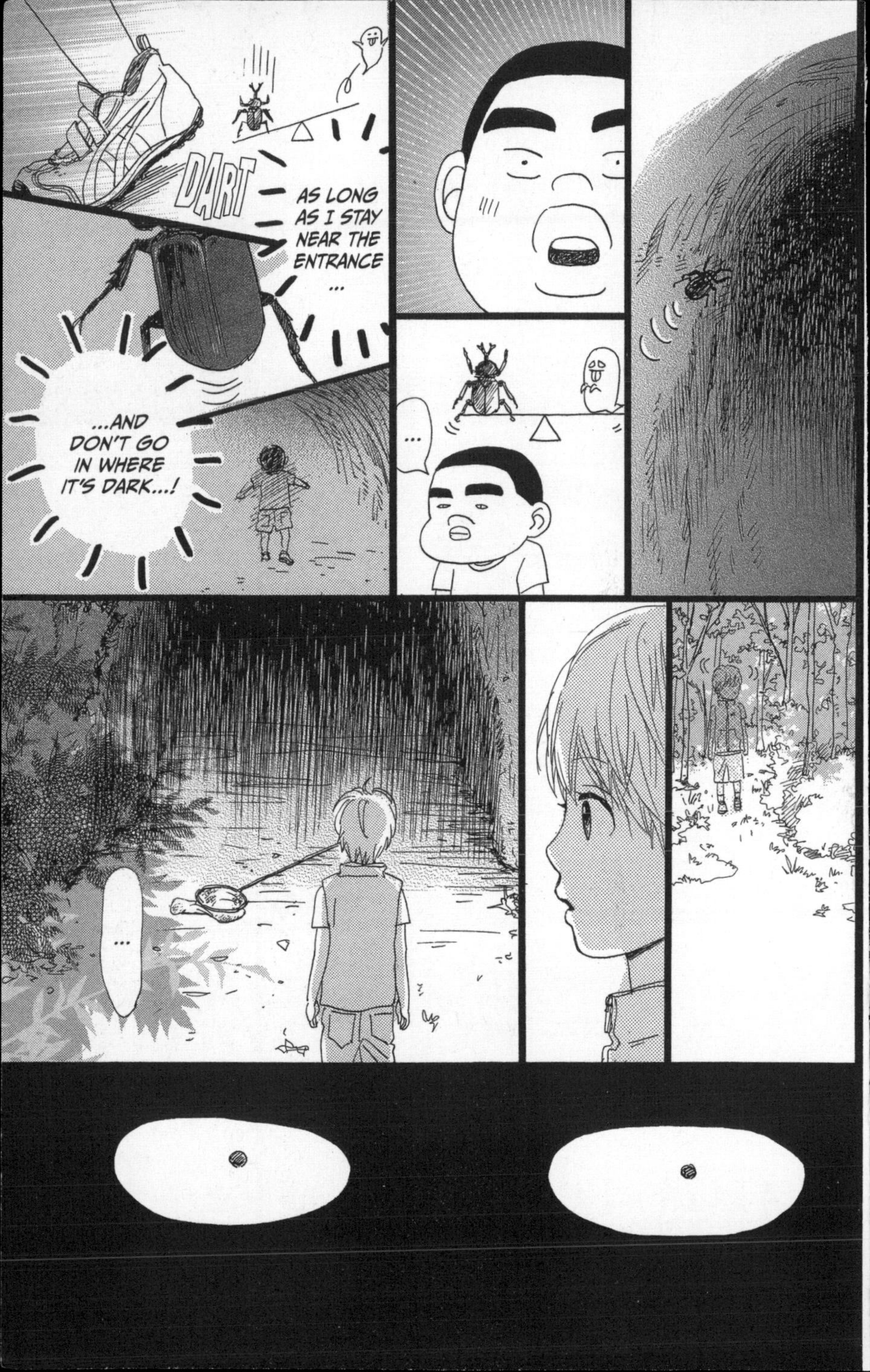
...
DART
AS LONG AS I STAY NEAR THE ENTRANCE ...
...AND DON'T GO IN WHERE IT'S DARK...!
...

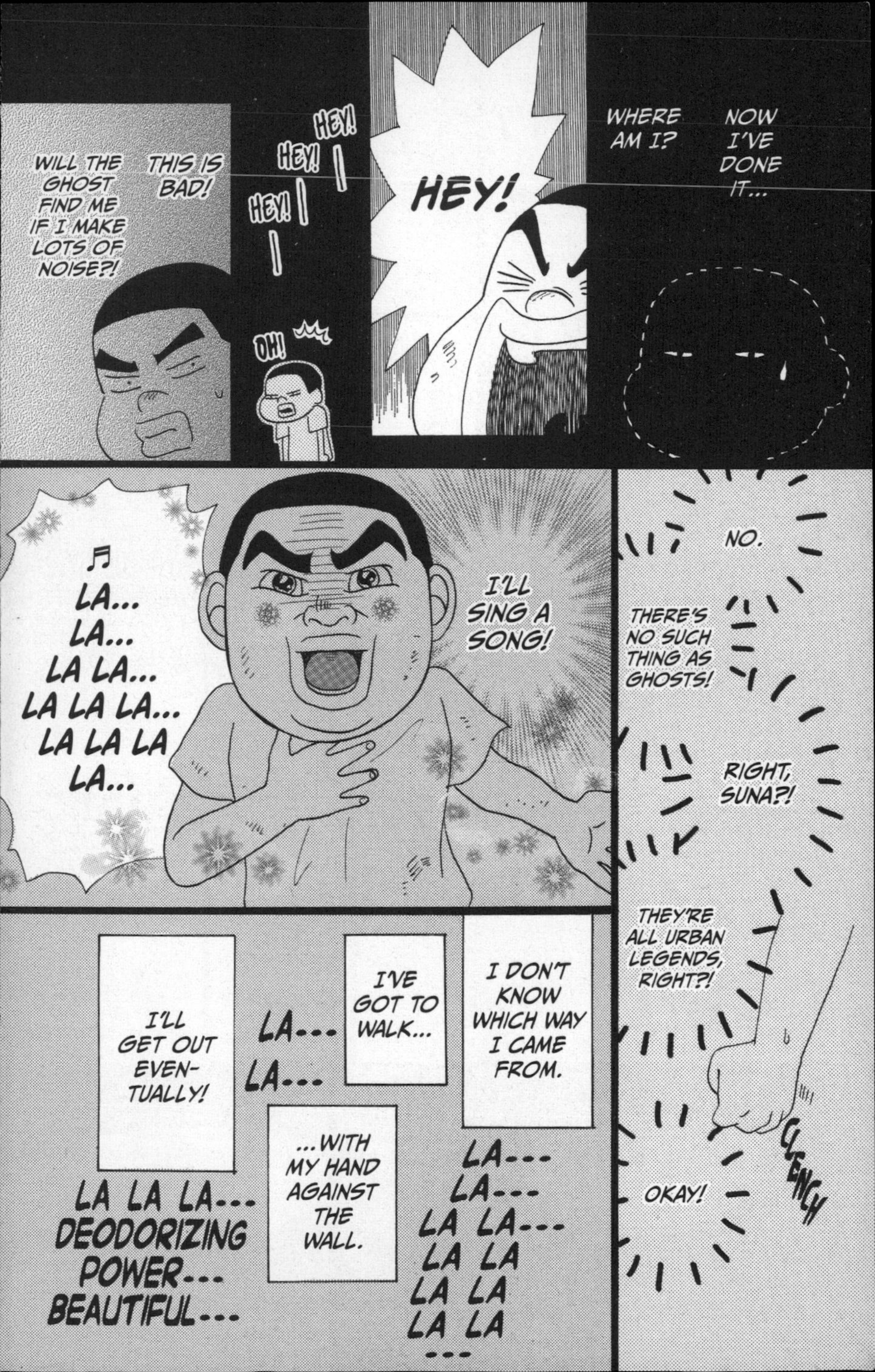
NOW I'VE DONE IT...
WHERE AM I?
HEY!
HEY!
HEY!
HEY!
OH!
THIS IS BAD!
WILL THE GHOST FIND ME IF I MAKE LOTS OF NOISE?!
NO.
THERE'S NO SUCH THING AS GHOSTS!
RIGHT, SUNA?!
THEY'RE ALL URBAN LEGENDS, RIGHT?!
CLENCH
OKAY!
I'LL SING A SONG!
♬ LA... LA... LA LA... LA LA LA... LA LA LA LA...
I DON'T KNOW WHICH WAY I CAME FROM.
LA--- LA--- LA LA--- LA LA LA LA LA LA ---
I'VE GOT TO WALK...
...WITH MY HAND AGAINST THE WALL.
LA--- LA---
I'LL GET OUT EVENTUALLY!
LA LA LA--- DEODORIZING POWER--- BEAUTIFUL---

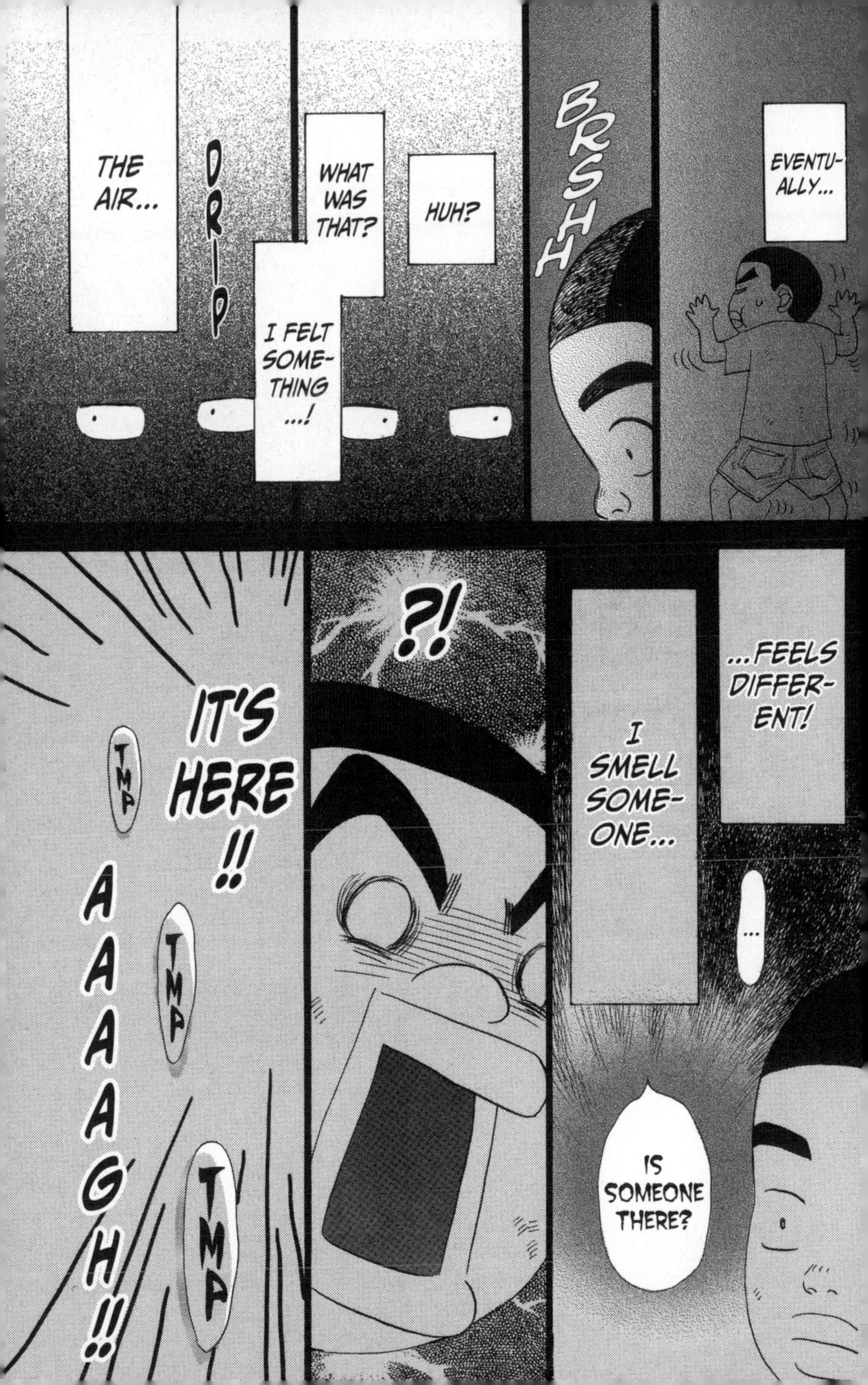
EVENTU-ALLY...
BRSHH
HUH?
WHAT WAS THAT?
I FELT SOME-THING ...!
DRIP
THE AIR...
...FEELS DIFFER-ENT!
I SMELL SOME-ONE...
...
IS SOMEONE THERE?
?!
IT'S HERE!!
TMP
TMP
TMP
AAAAAGH!!

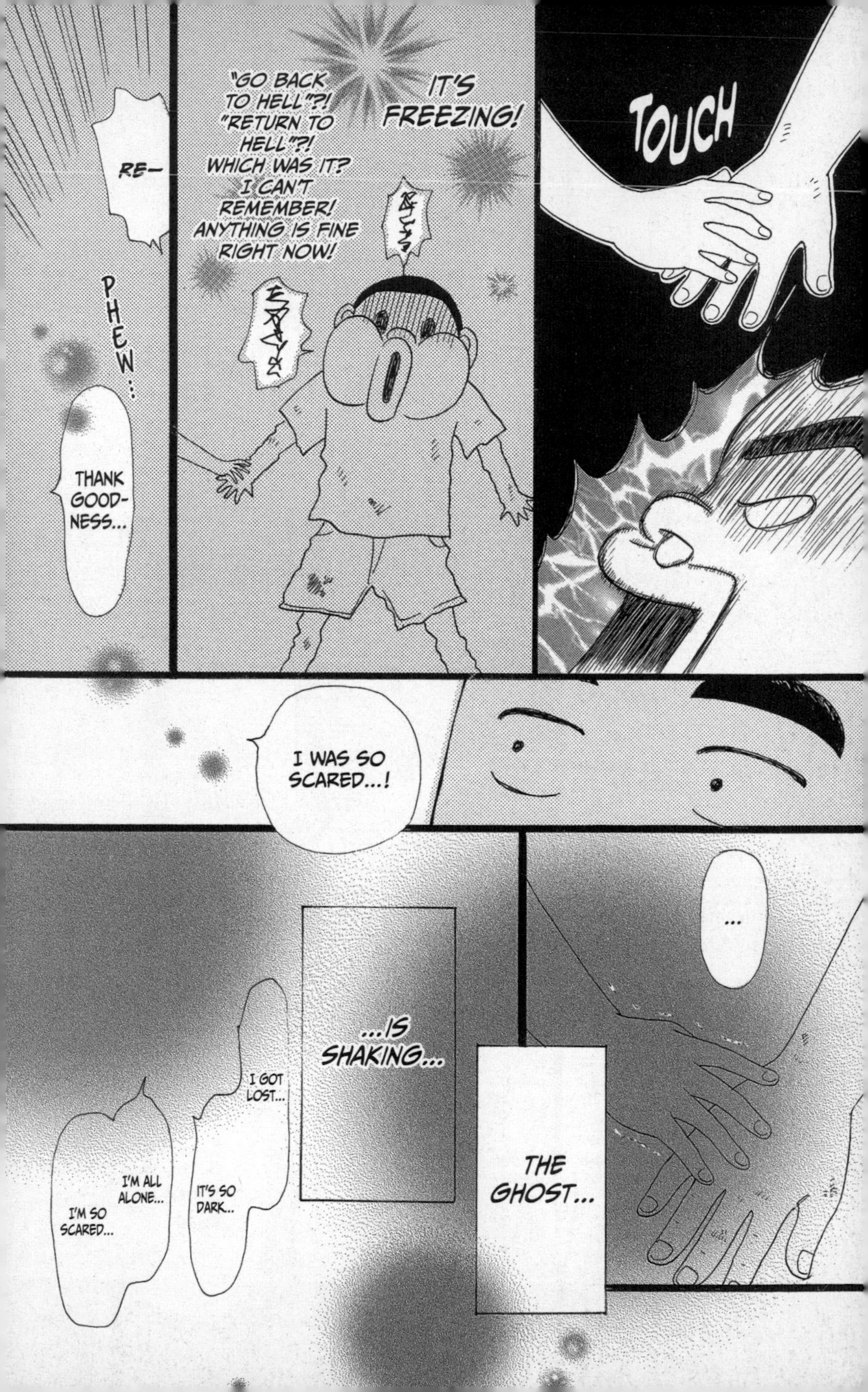
TOUCH
IT'S FREEZING!
"GO BACK TO HELL"?! "RETURN TO HELL"?! WHICH WAS IT? I CAN'T REMEMBER! ANYTHING IS FINE RIGHT NOW!
RE—
PHEW...
THANK GOODNESS...
I WAS SO SCARED...!
...
THE GHOST...
...IS SHAKING...
I GOT LOST...
IT'S SO DARK...
I'M ALL ALONE...
I'M SO SCARED...

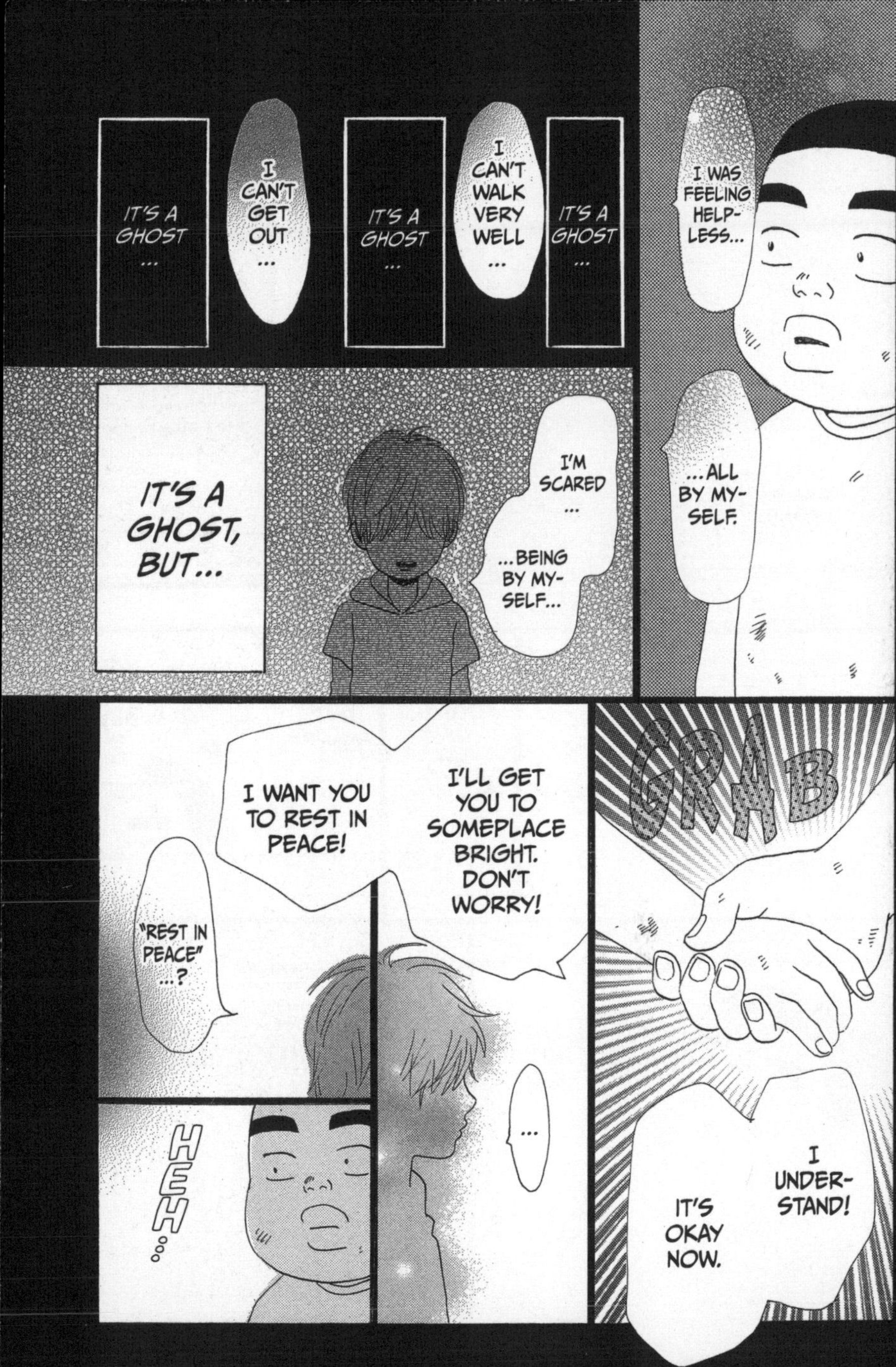
I WAS FEELING HELP-LESS...
...ALL BY MY-SELF.
IT'S A GHOST...
I CAN'T WALK VERY WELL...
IT'S A GHOST...
I CAN'T GET OUT...
IT'S A GHOST...
I'M SCARED...
...BEING BY MY-SELF...
IT'S A GHOST, BUT...
GRAB
I UNDER-STAND!
IT'S OKAY NOW.
I'LL GET YOU TO SOMEPLACE BRIGHT. DON'T WORRY!
I WANT YOU TO REST IN PEACE!
"REST IN PEACE"...?
...
HEH...

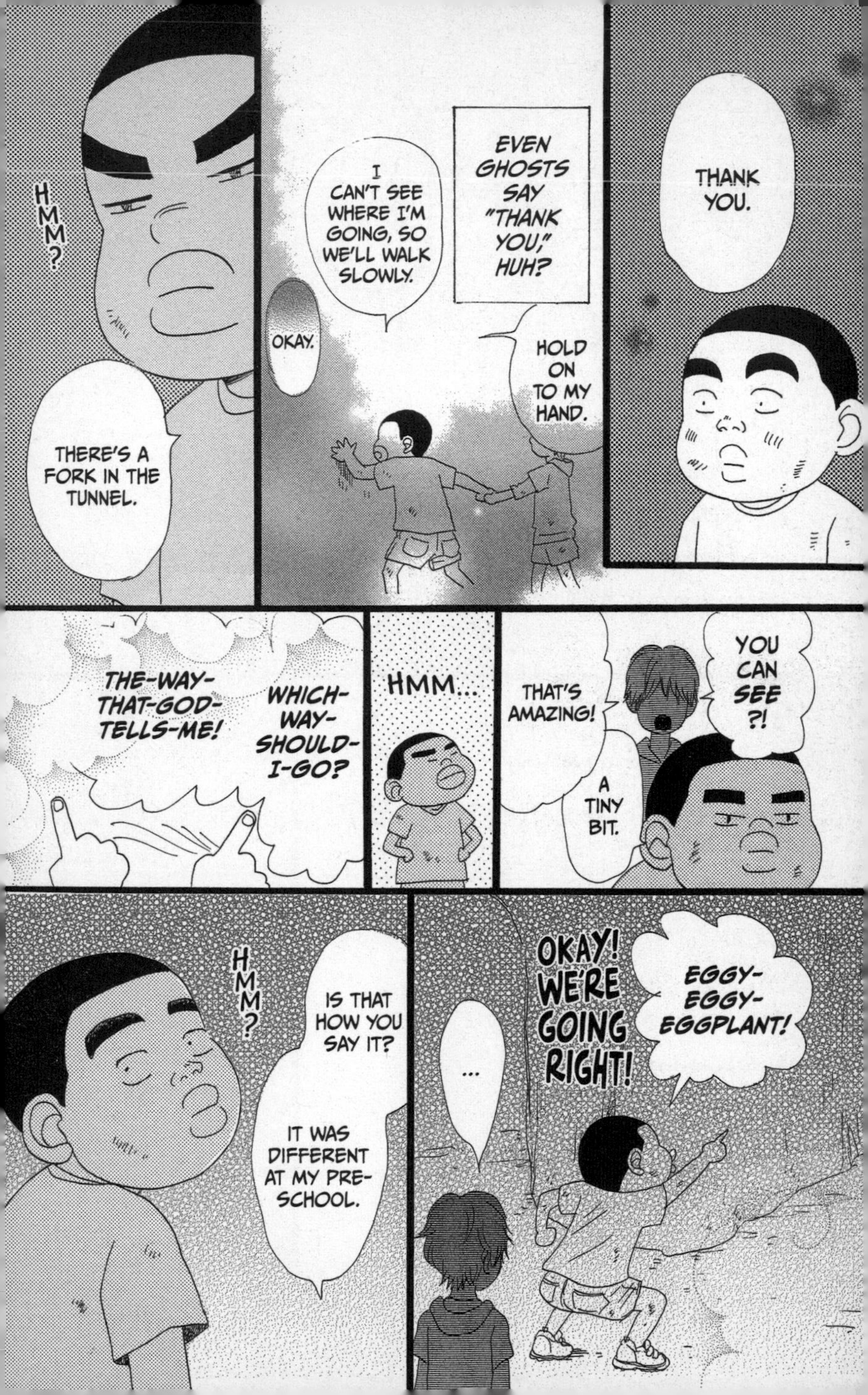
THANK YOU.
EVEN GHOSTS SAY "THANK YOU," HUH?
HOLD ON TO MY HAND.
I CAN'T SEE WHERE I'M GOING, SO WE'LL WALK SLOWLY.
OKAY.
HMM?
THERE'S A FORK IN THE TUNNEL.
YOU CAN SEE?!
THAT'S AMAZING!
A TINY BIT.
HMM...
WHICH-WAY-SHOULD-I-GO?
THE-WAY-THAT-GOD-TELLS-ME!
EGGY-EGGY-EGGPLANT!
OKAY! WE'RE GOING RIGHT!
...
HMM?
IS THAT HOW YOU SAY IT?
IT WAS DIFFERENT AT MY PRE-SCHOOL.

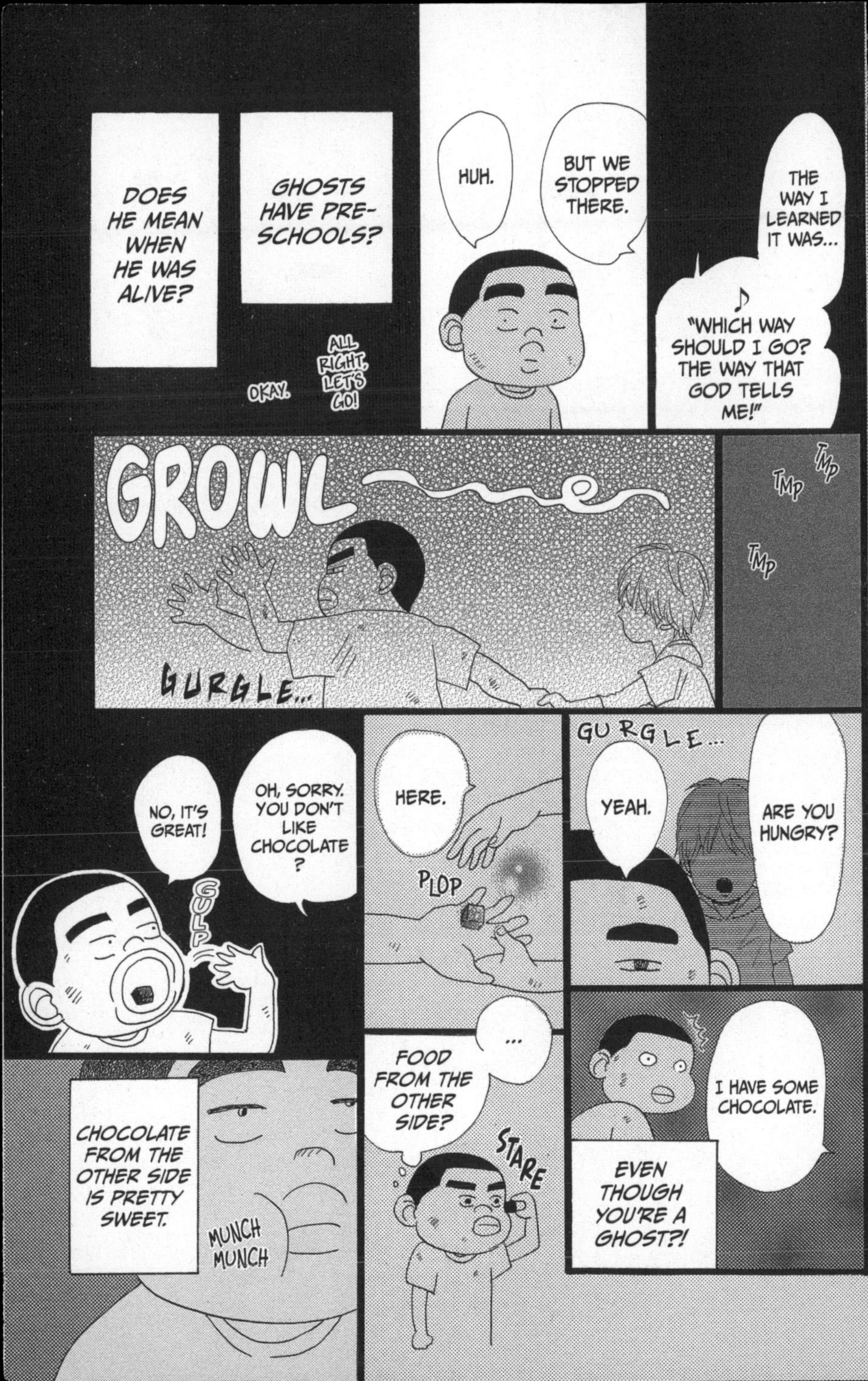
THE WAY I LEARNED IT WAS...
"WHICH WAY SHOULD I GO? THE WAY THAT GOD TELLS ME!"
BUT WE STOPPED THERE.
HUH.
GHOSTS HAVE PRE-SCHOOLS?
DOES HE MEAN WHEN HE WAS ALIVE?
ALL RIGHT, LET'S GO!
OKAY.
TMP
TMP
TMP
GROWL
GURGLE...
GURGLE...
ARE YOU HUNGRY?
YEAH.
I HAVE SOME CHOCOLATE.
EVEN THOUGH YOU'RE A GHOST?!
HERE.
PLOP
...
FOOD FROM THE OTHER SIDE?
STARE
OH, SORRY. YOU DON'T LIKE CHOCOLATE?
NO, IT'S GREAT!
GULP
CHOCOLATE FROM THE OTHER SIDE IS PRETTY SWEET.
MUNCH MUNCH

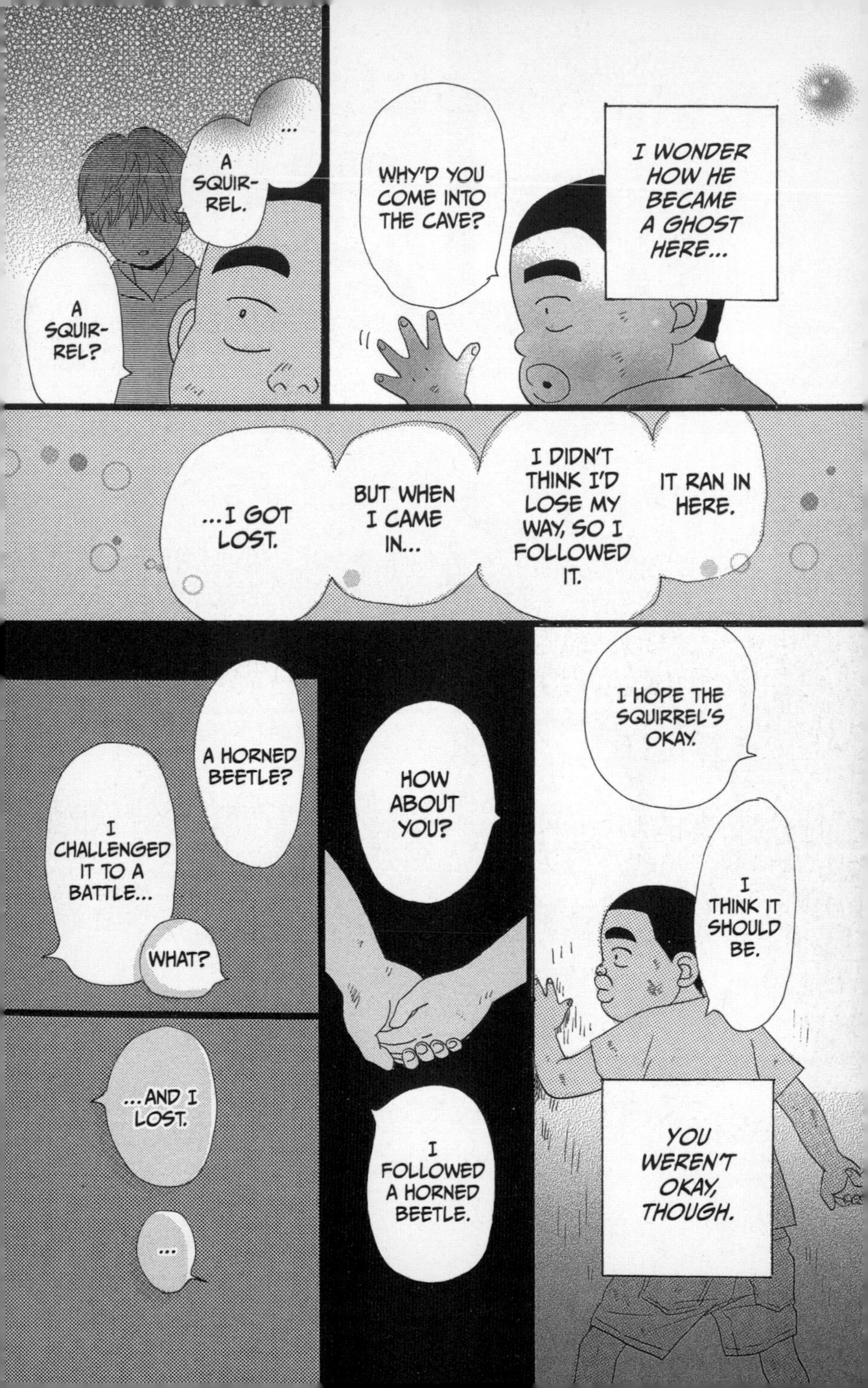
I WONDER HOW HE BECAME A GHOST HERE...
WHY'D YOU COME INTO THE CAVE?
...
A SQUIR-REL.
A SQUIR-REL?
IT RAN IN HERE.
I DIDN'T THINK I'D LOSE MY WAY, SO I FOLLOWED IT.
BUT WHEN I CAME IN...
...I GOT LOST.
I HOPE THE SQUIRREL'S OKAY.
I THINK IT SHOULD BE.
YOU WEREN'T OKAY, THOUGH.
HOW ABOUT YOU?
I FOLLOWED A HORNED BEETLE.
A HORNED BEETLE?
I CHALLENGED IT TO A BATTLE...
WHAT?
...AND I LOST.
...

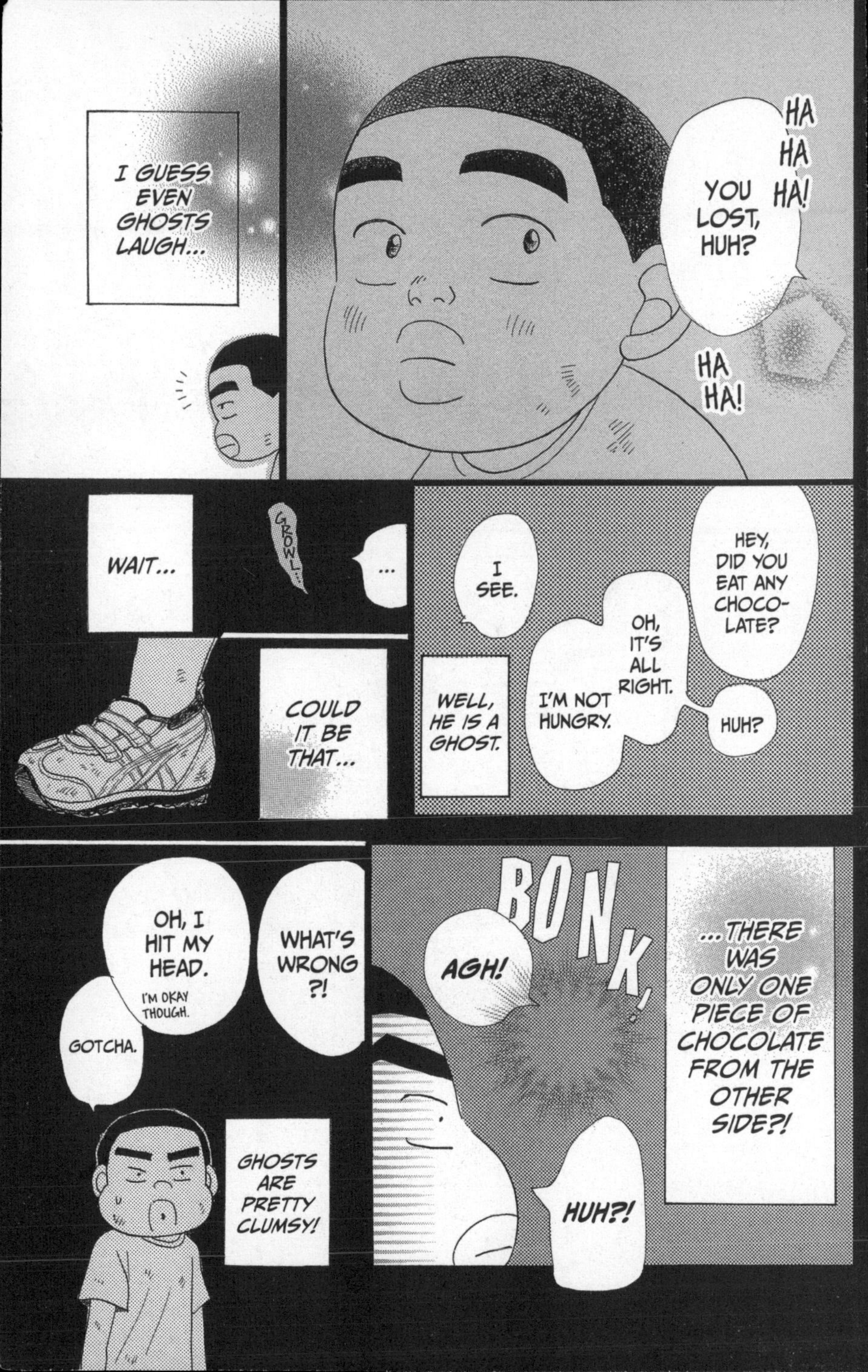
HA HA HA!
YOU LOST, HUH?
HA HA!
I GUESS EVEN GHOSTS LAUGH...
HEY, DID YOU EAT ANY CHOCOLATE?
HUH?
OH, IT'S ALL RIGHT.
I'M NOT HUNGRY.
I SEE.
WELL, HE IS A GHOST.
...
GROWL...
WAIT...
COULD IT BE THAT...
...THERE WAS ONLY ONE PIECE OF CHOCOLATE FROM THE OTHER SIDE?!
BONK,
AGH!
HUH?!
WHAT'S WRONG?!
OH, I HIT MY HEAD.
I'M OKAY THOUGH.
GOTCHA.
GHOSTS ARE PRETTY CLUMSY!

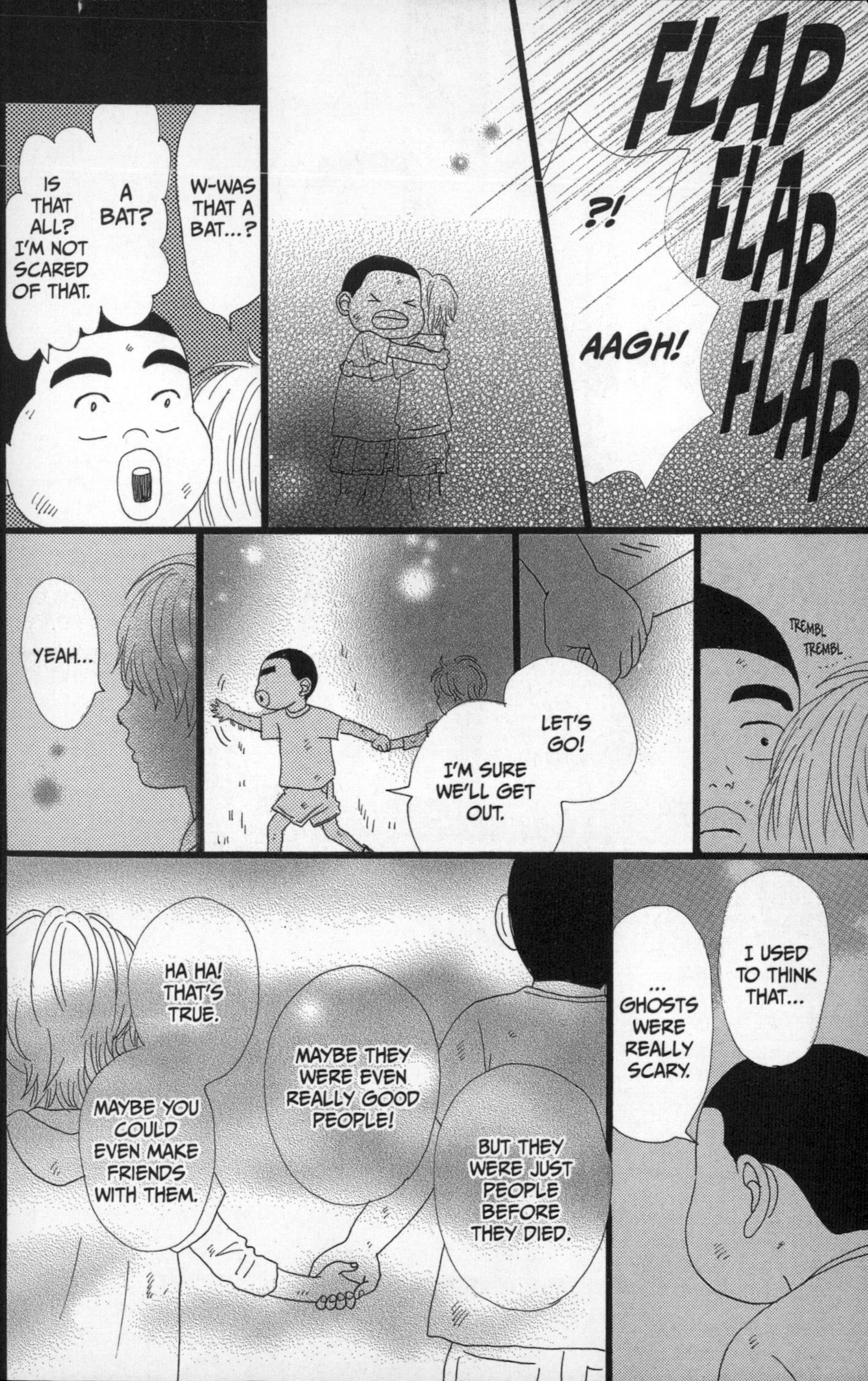
FLAP FLAP FLAP FLAP
?!
AAGH!
W-WAS THAT A BAT...?
A BAT?
IS THAT ALL? I'M NOT SCARED OF THAT.
TREMBL TREMBL
LET'S GO!
I'M SURE WE'LL GET OUT.
YEAH...
I USED TO THINK THAT...
...GHOSTS WERE REALLY SCARY.
BUT THEY WERE JUST PEOPLE BEFORE THEY DIED.
MAYBE THEY WERE EVEN REALLY GOOD PEOPLE!
HA HA! THAT'S TRUE.
MAYBE YOU COULD EVEN MAKE FRIENDS WITH THEM.

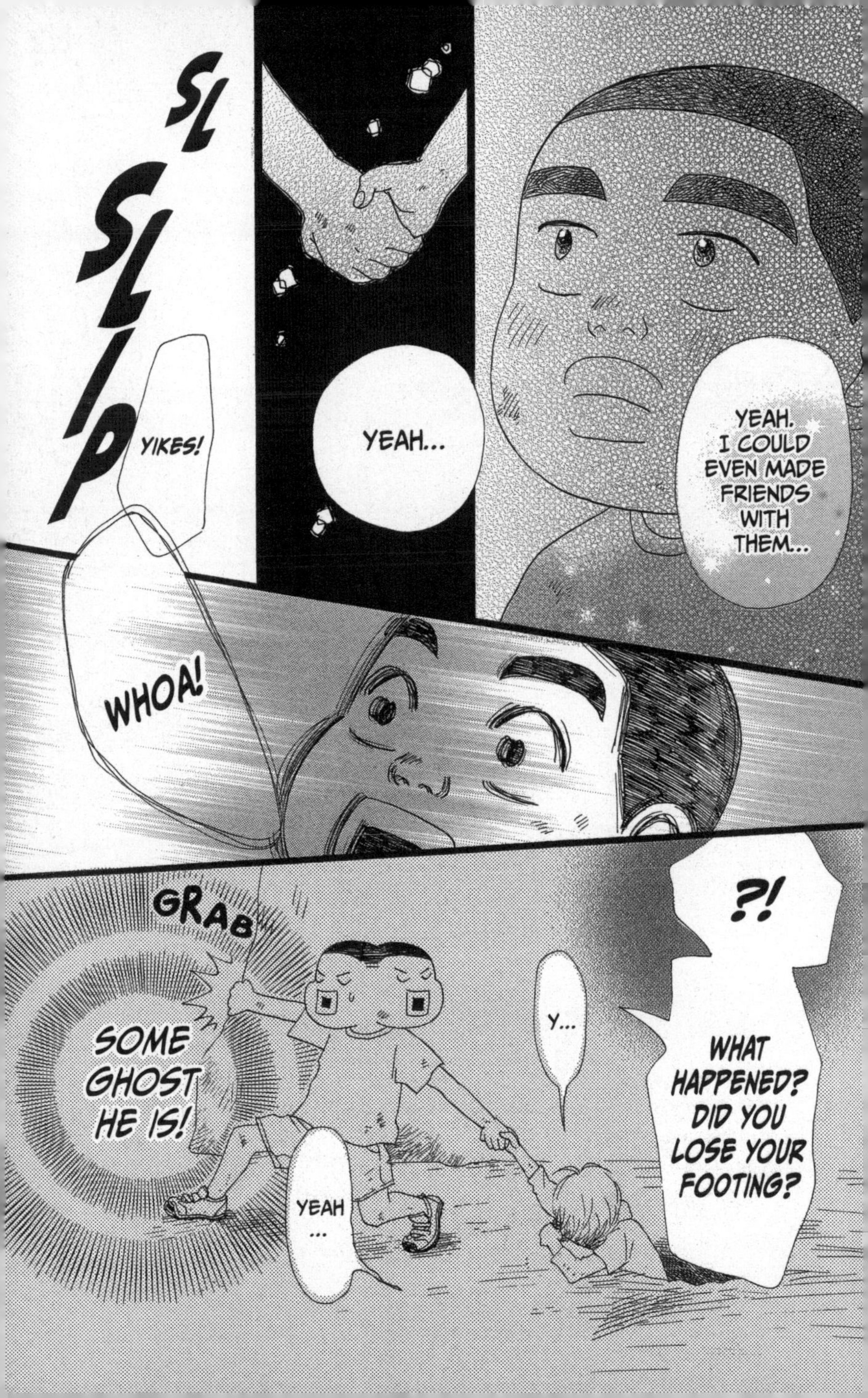
YEAH. I COULD EVEN MADE FRIENDS WITH THEM...
YEAH...
SL SLIP
YIKES!
WHOA!
?!
WHAT HAPPENED? DID YOU LOSE YOUR FOOTING?
Y...
YEAH ...
GRAB
SOME GHOST HE IS!

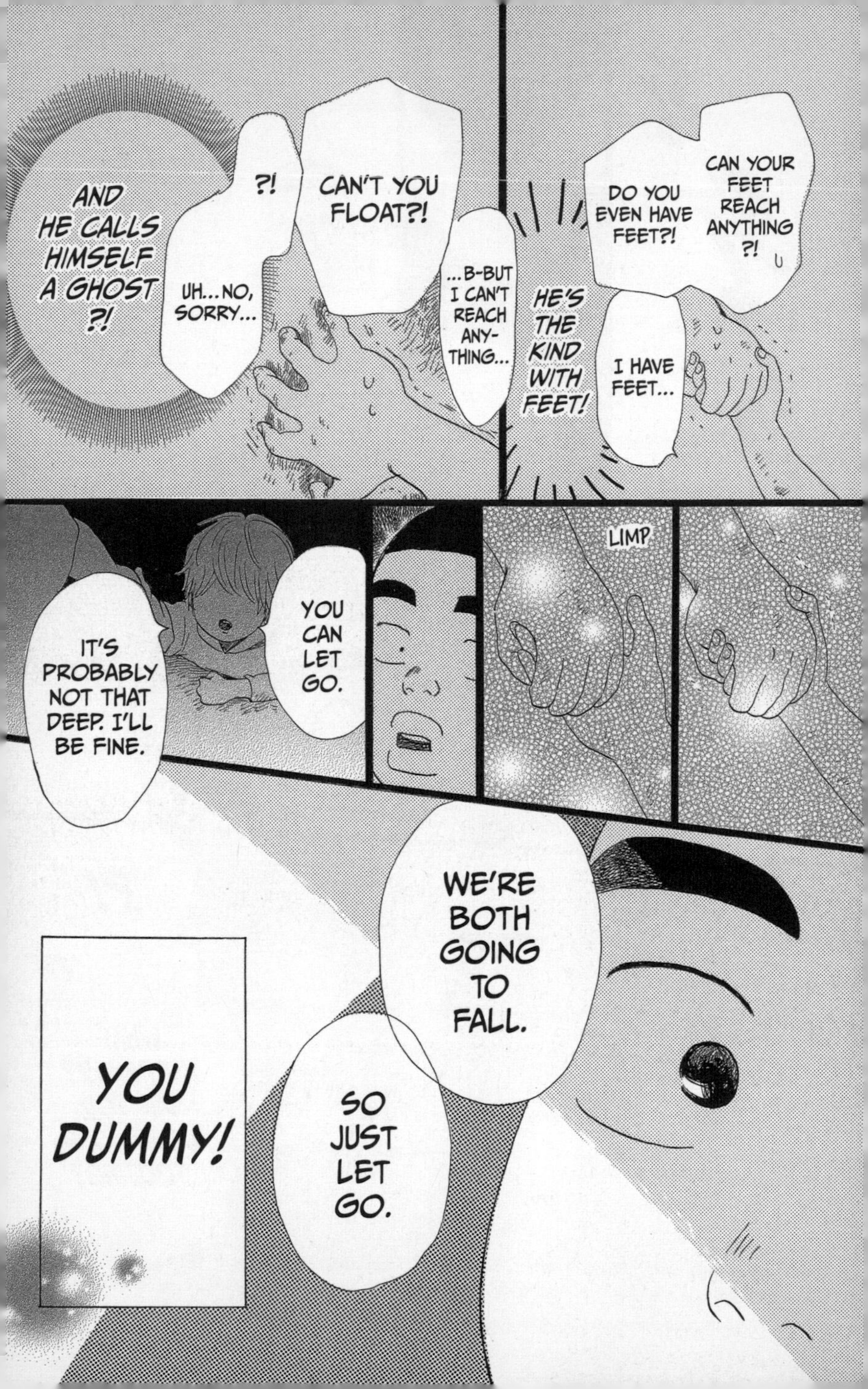
CAN YOUR FEET REACH ANYTHING?!
DO YOU EVEN HAVE FEET?!
I HAVE FEET...
HE'S THE KIND WITH FEET!
...B-BUT I CAN'T REACH ANY-THING...
CAN'T YOU FLOAT?!
?!
UH...NO, SORRY...
AND HE CALLS HIMSELF A GHOST?!
LIMP
YOU CAN LET GO.
IT'S PROBABLY NOT THAT DEEP. I'LL BE FINE.
WE'RE BOTH GOING TO FALL.
SO JUST LET GO.
YOU DUMMY!

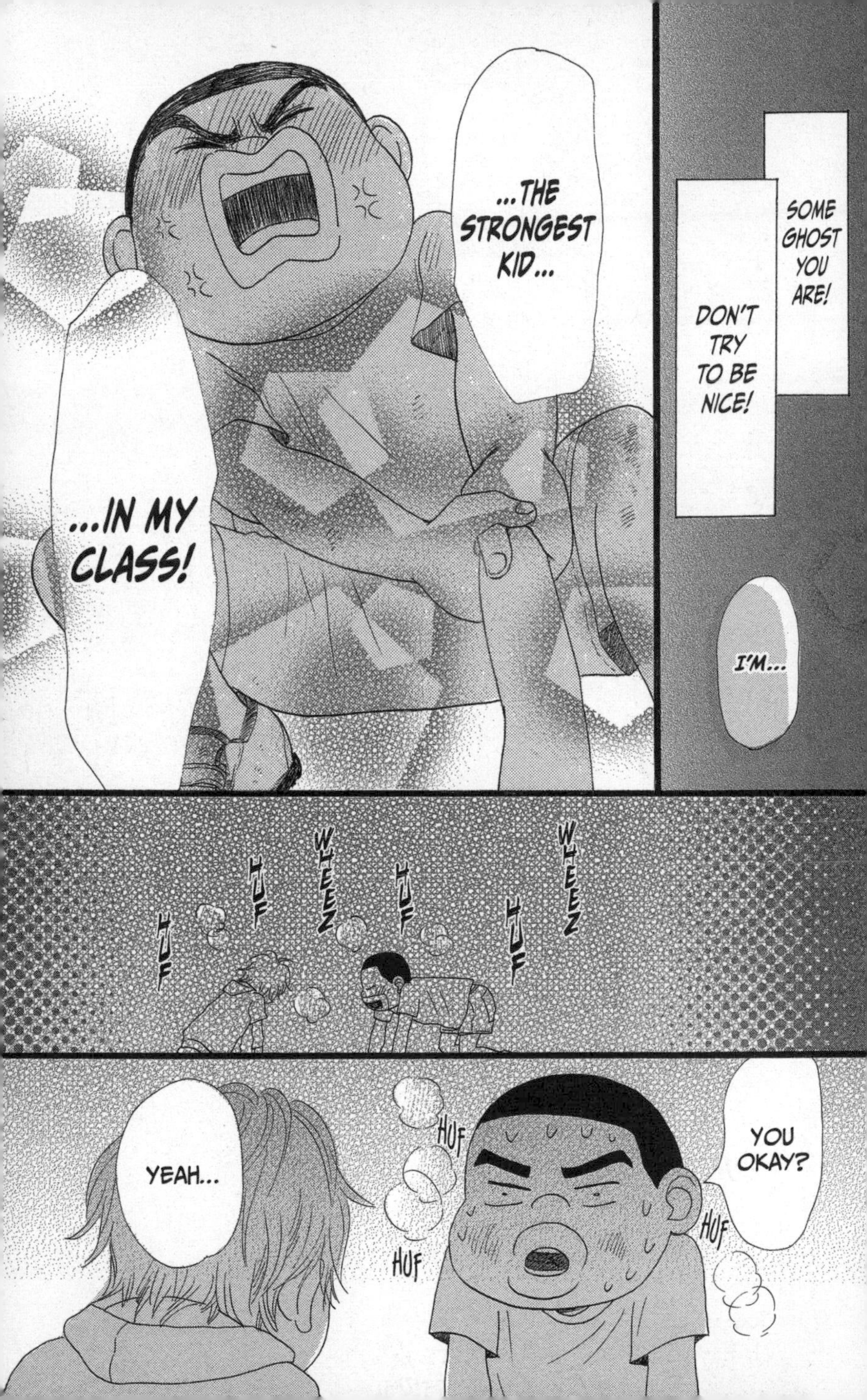
SOME GHOST YOU ARE!
DON'T TRY TO BE NICE!
I'M...
...THE STRONGEST KID...
...IN MY CLASS!
WHEEZ
HUF
HUF
WHEEZ
HUF
HUF
YOU OKAY?
HUF
HUF
HUF
YEAH...

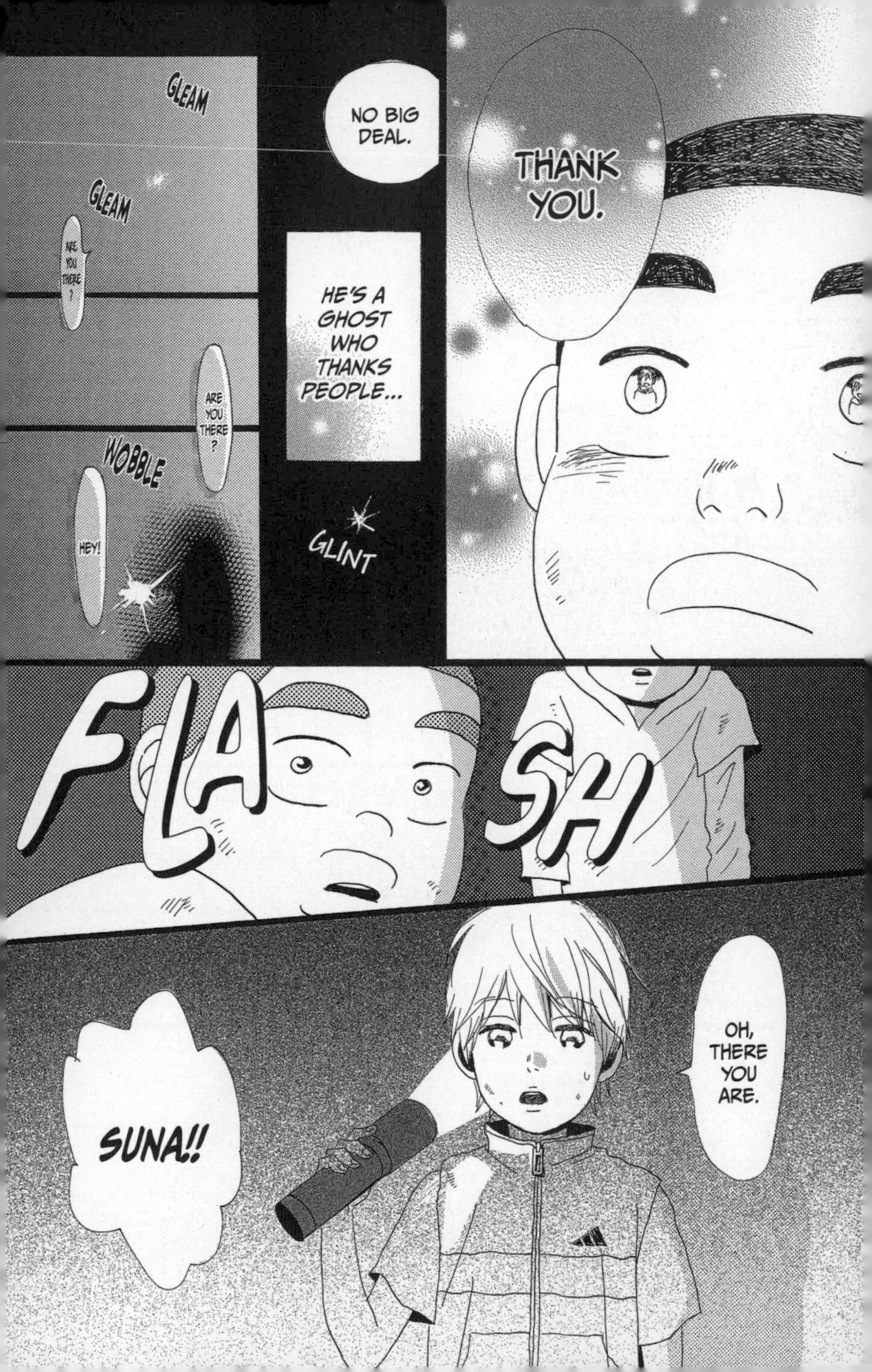
THANK YOU.
NO BIG DEAL.
HE'S A GHOST WHO THANKS PEOPLE...
GLINT
GLEAM
GLEAM
ARE YOU THERE?
ARE YOU THERE?
WOBBLE
HEY!
FLASH
OH, THERE YOU ARE.
SUNA!!

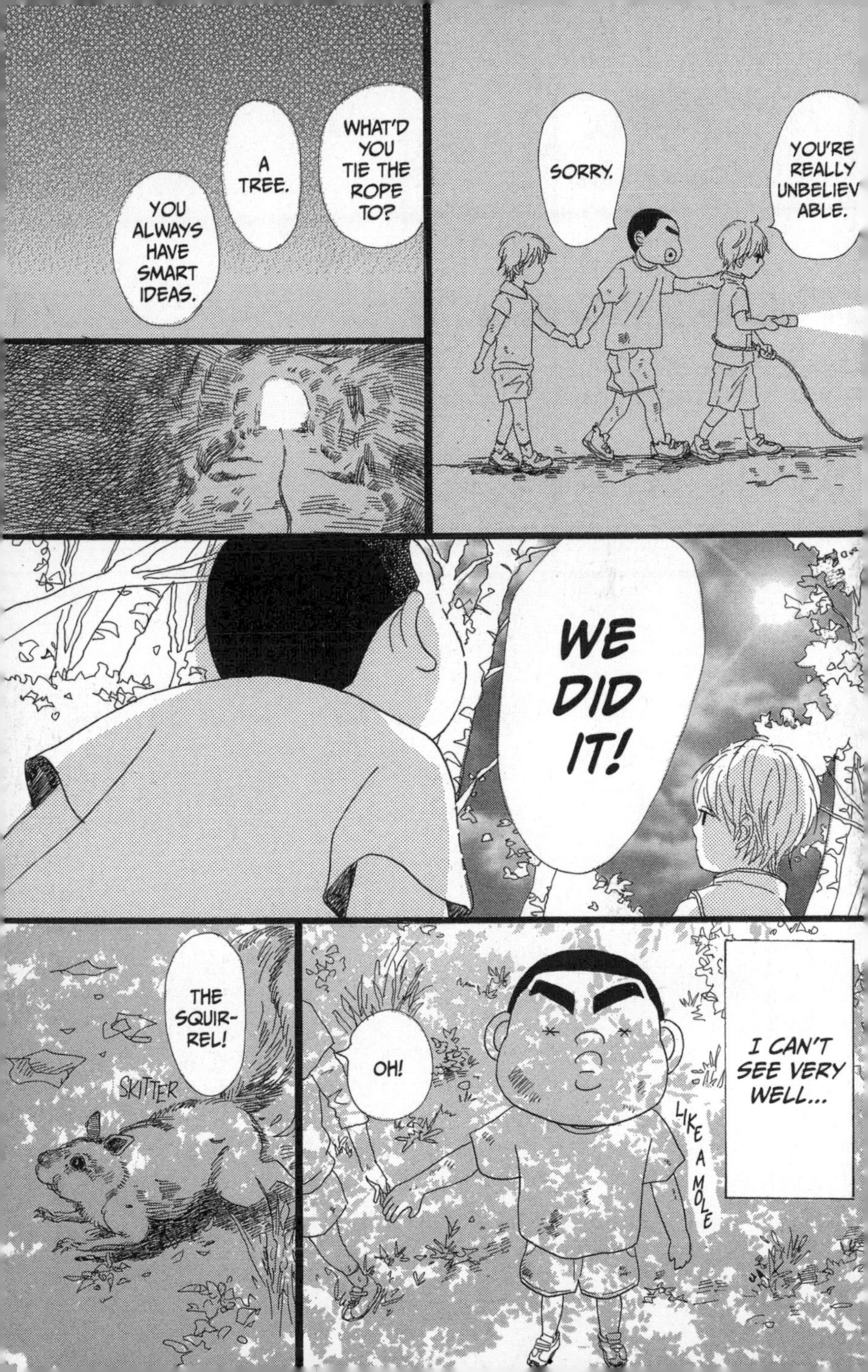
YOU'RE REALLY UNBELIEVABLE.
SORRY.
WHAT'D YOU TIE THE ROPE TO?
A TREE.
YOU ALWAYS HAVE SMART IDEAS.
WE DID IT!
I CAN'T SEE VERY WELL...
LIKE A MOLE
OH!
THE SQUIR-REL!
SKITTER

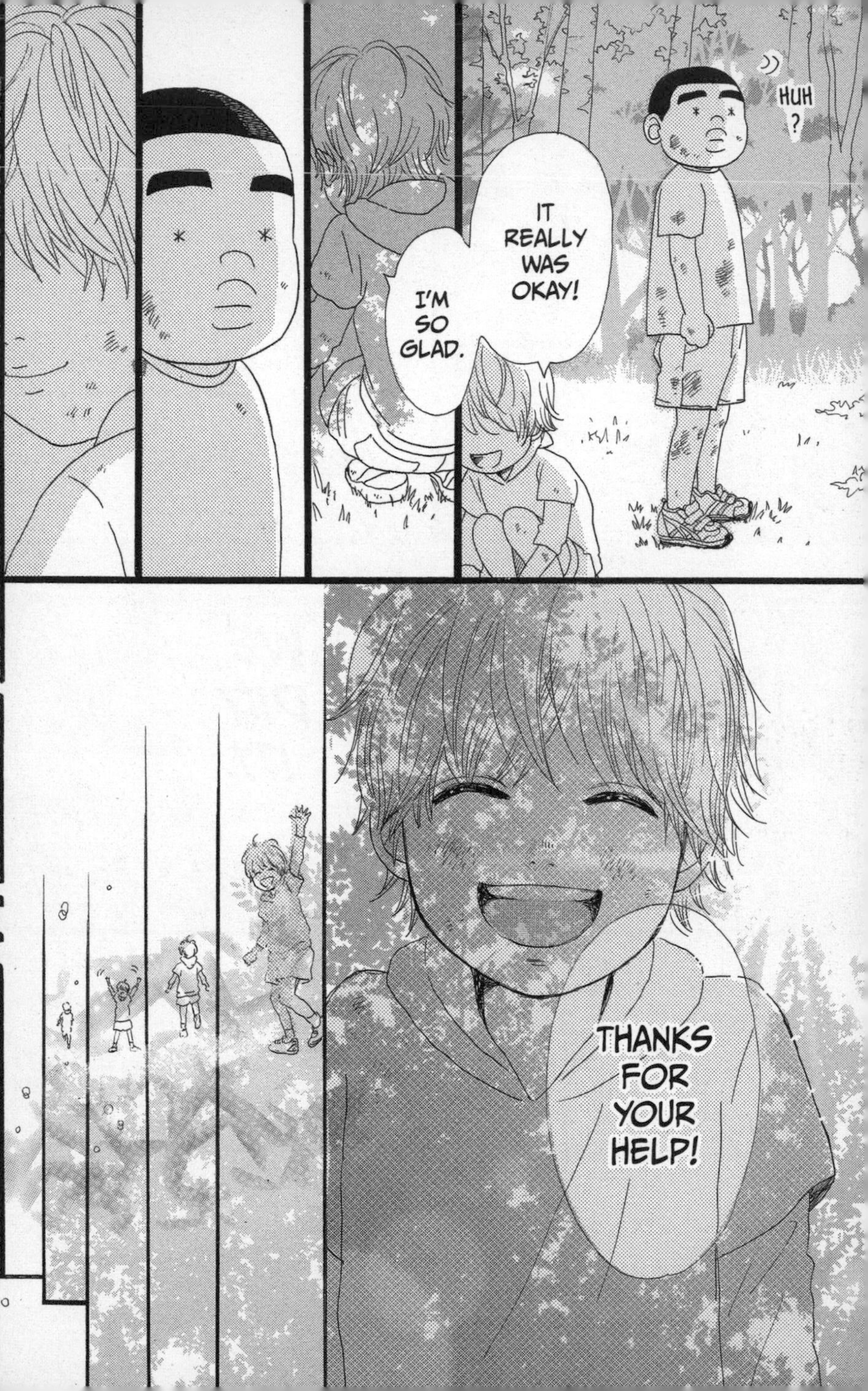
HUH ?
IT REALLY WAS OKAY!
I'M SO GLAD.
THANKS FOR YOUR HELP!

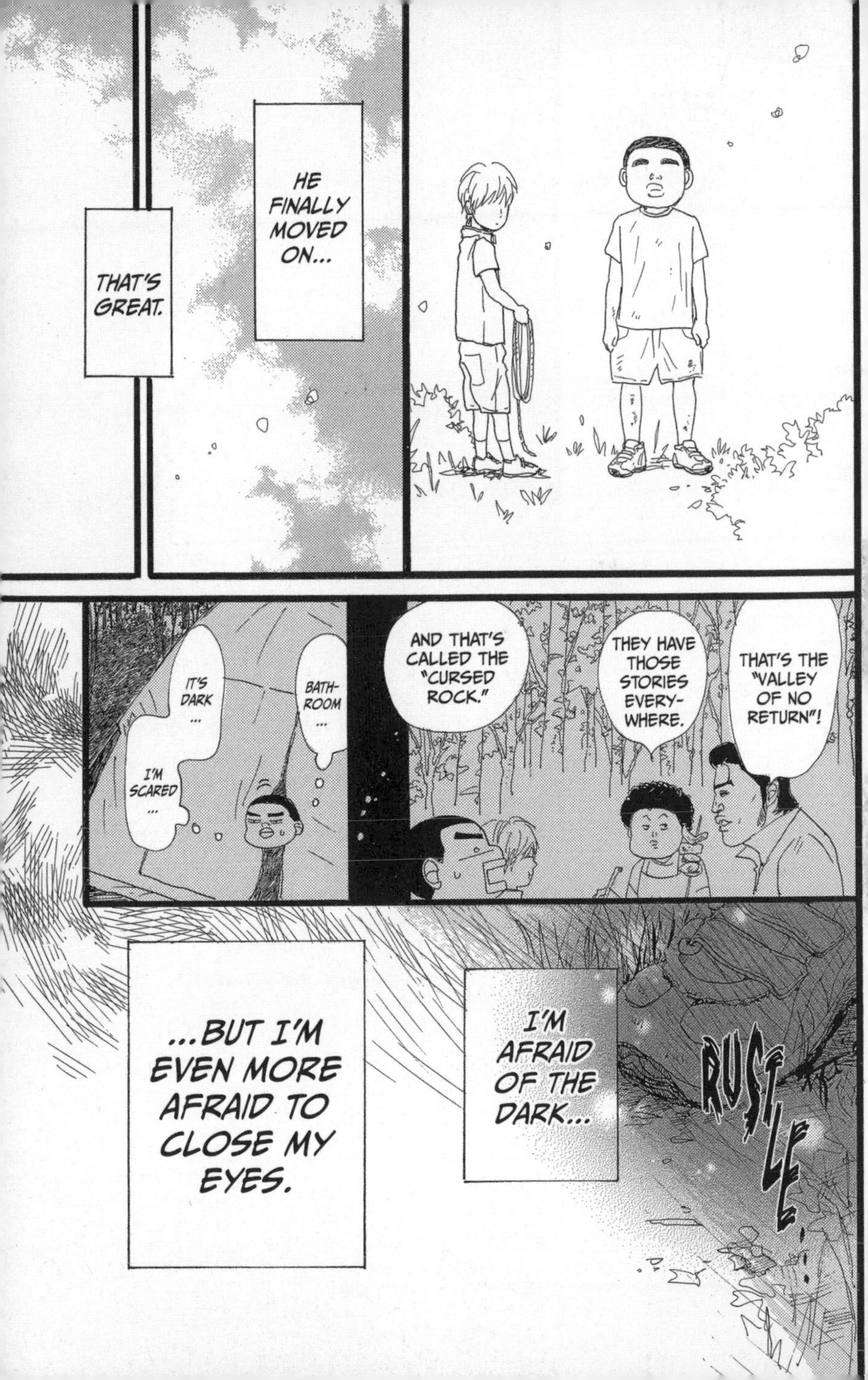
HE FINALLY MOVED ON...
THAT'S GREAT.
THAT'S THE "VALLEY OF NO RETURN"!
THEY HAVE THOSE STORIES EVERY-WHERE.
AND THAT'S CALLED THE "CURSED ROCK."
BATH-ROOM...
IT'S DARK...
I'M SCARED...
RUSTLE
I'M AFRAID OF THE DARK...
...BUT I'M EVEN MORE AFRAID TO CLOSE MY EYES.

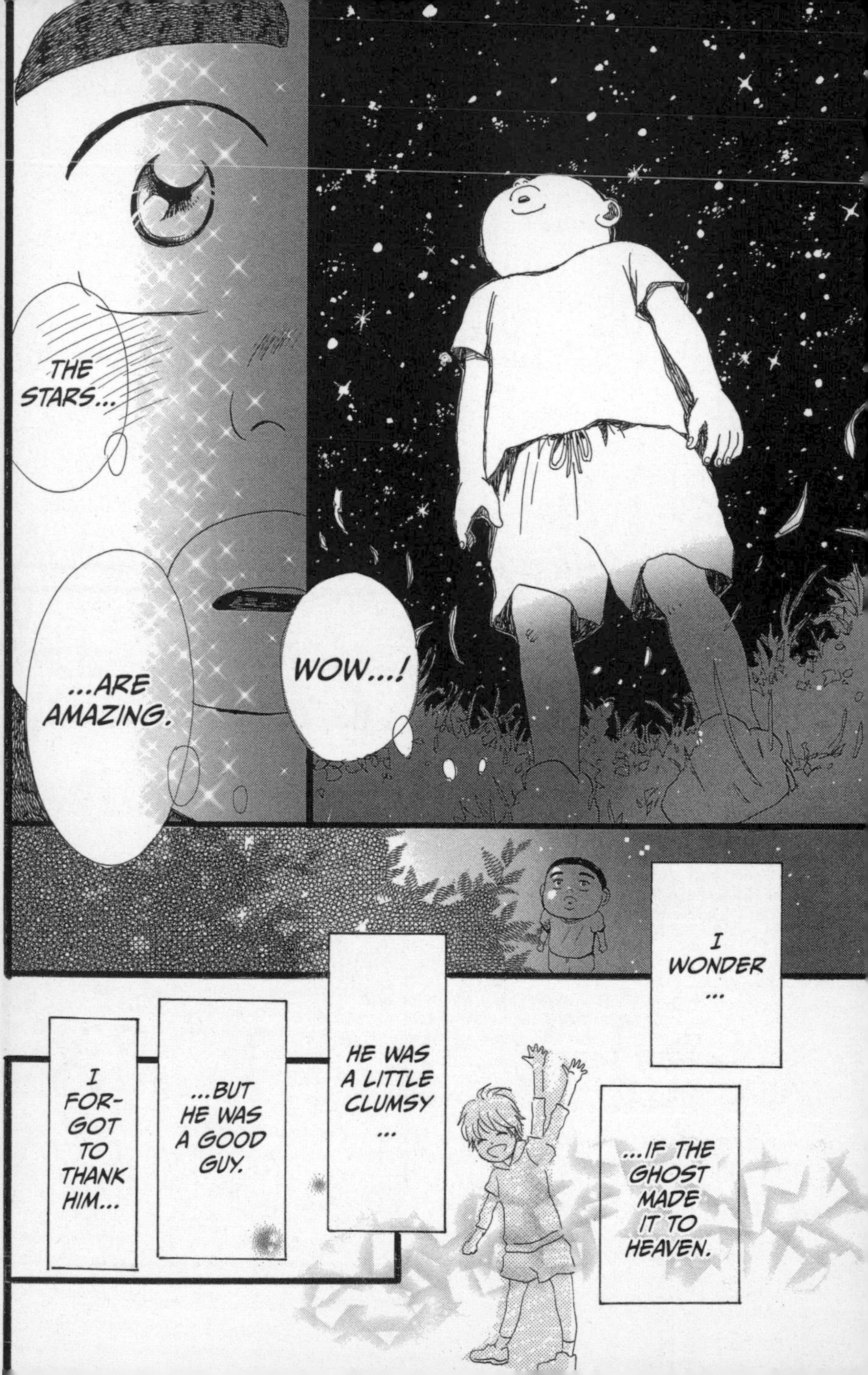
WOW...!
THE STARS...
...ARE AMAZING.
I WONDER...
...IF THE GHOST MADE IT TO HEAVEN.
HE WAS A LITTLE CLUMSY...
...BUT HE WAS A GOOD GUY.
I FORGOT TO THANK HIM...

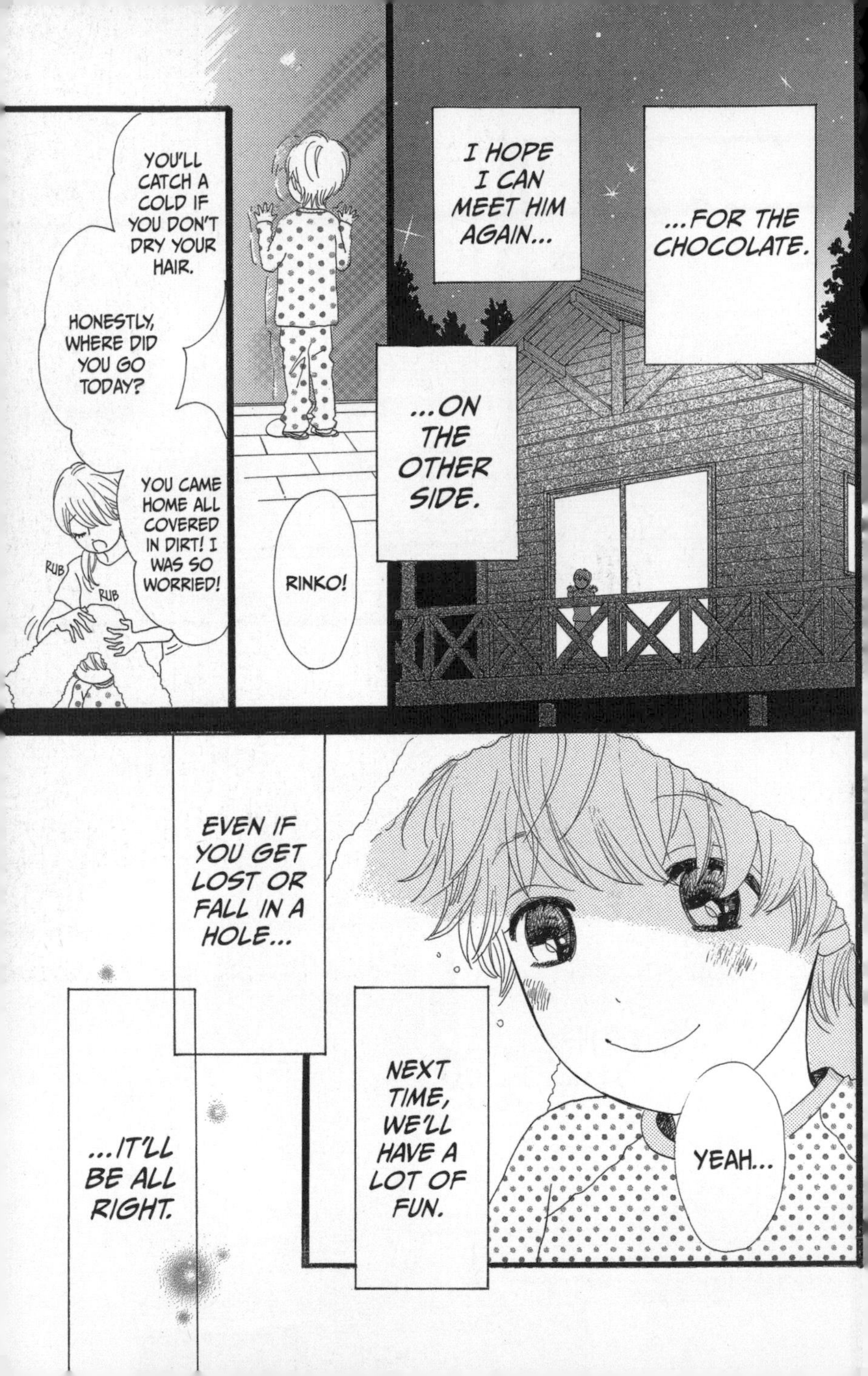
...FOR THE CHOCOLATE.
I HOPE I CAN MEET HIM AGAIN...
...ON THE OTHER SIDE.
RINKO!
YOU'LL CATCH A COLD IF YOU DON'T DRY YOUR HAIR.
HONESTLY, WHERE DID YOU GO TODAY?
YOU CAME HOME ALL COVERED IN DIRT! I WAS SO WORRIED!
RUB
RUB
YEAH...
EVEN IF YOU GET LOST OR FALL IN A HOLE...
NEXT TIME, WE'LL HAVE A LOT OF FUN.
...IT'LL BE ALL RIGHT.

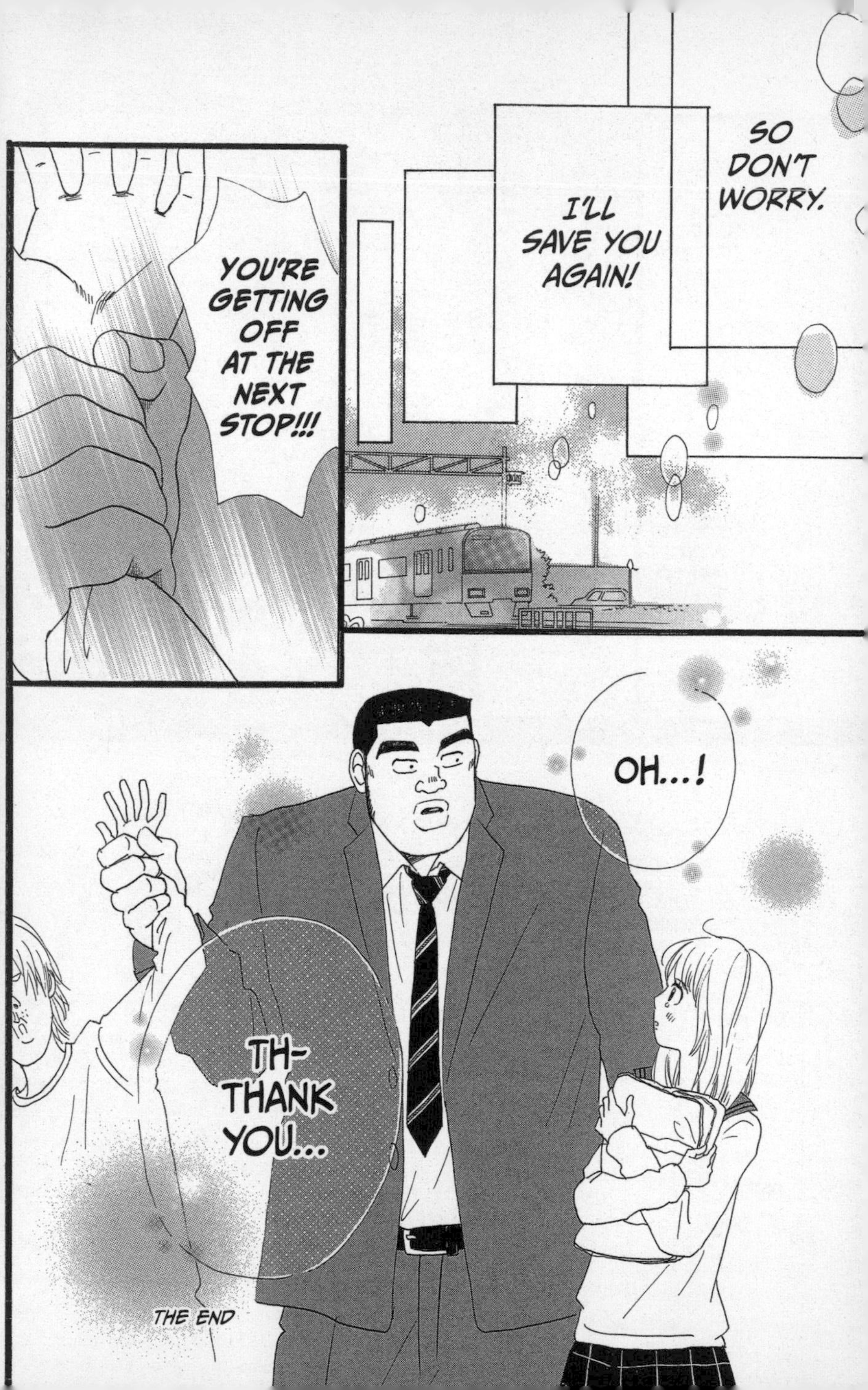
SO DON'T WORRY.
I'LL SAVE YOU AGAIN!
YOU'RE GETTING OFF AT THE NEXT STOP!!!
OH...!
TH-THANK YOU...
THE END

I'm so happy we're on volume 4! \(^-^)/ I feel really lucky that this manga has given me so many fun memories. I feel the happiest when people tell me they enjoy this series. I'm really glad and thankful that Aruko is able to draw it and that I get to be with my family. (^^^)
– Kazune Kawahara

(K)

ARUKO is from Ishikawa Prefecture in Japan and was born on July 26 (a Leo!). She made her manga debut with *Ame Nochi Hare* (Clear After the Rain). Her other works include *Yasuko to Kenji*, and her hobbies include laughing and getting lost.

KAZUNE KAWAHARA is from Hokkaido Prefecture in Japan and was born on March 11 (a Pisces!). She made her manga debut at age 18 with *Kare no Ichiban Sukina Hito* (His Most Favorite Person). Her best-selling shojo manga series *High School Debut* is available in North America from VIZ Media. Her hobby is interior redecorating.

I've never had much interest before, but I've been watching a lot of pro wrestling and baseball lately. My reason for doing this is to look at the athletes' muscles (especially their butts). I think they're gorgeous.
– Aruko

(A)

MY LOVE STORY!!

Volume 4
Shojo Beat Edition

Story **KAZUNE KAWAHARA**
Art by **ARUKO**

English Adaptation ♡ **Ysabet Reinhardt MacFarlane**
Translation ♡ **JN Productions**
Touch-up Art & Lettering ♡ **Mark McMurray**
Design ♡ **Fawn Lau**
Editor ♡ **Amy Yu**

ORE MONOGATARI!!
© 2011 by Kazune Kawahara, Aruko
All rights reserved.
First published in Japan in 2011 by SHUEISHA Inc., Tokyo
English translation rights arranged by SHUEISHA Inc.

Printed in the U.S.A.

Published by VIZ Media, LLC
P.O. Box 77010
San Francisco, CA 94107

10 9 8 7 6 5 4 3 2 1
First printing, April 2015

www.viz.com

www.shojobeat.com